COMPETITION DAMAGES ACTIONS IN THE EU

ELGAR COMPETITION LAW AND PRACTICE

Series Editors: David Vaughan CBE QC, *Brick Court Chambers, London, UK* and Elizabeth Morony, *Partner, Clifford Chance LLP, London, UK*

The *Elgar Competition Law and Practice* series, is a library of works by leading practitioners, competition officials and scholars covering discrete areas of substantive law and procedure in the field of competition and antitrust. Each title is both analytical and descriptive in approach, highlighting and unpicking the legal (and economic) issues that are most critical and relevant to practice. Designed to be detailed, focused reference works, the books in this series offer an in-depth treatment and an authoritative statement on the law, economics and practice in key topics within the field, from *Vertical Agreements* to *Antitrust Damages*, from *Competition and IP* to *Competition in Energy Markets*, and from *Leniency and Fines* to *Article 101* and *Article 102.*

Presented in a format that allows for ease of navigation to a particular point of law, each title in the series is written by specialists in their respective fields, often with insight either from private practice or from an enforcement perspective.

Under the direction and series editorship of two leading figures in competition law practice, the *Elgar Competition Law and Practice* series will be a forum for the highest quality work in competition law, and will form an important reference library for all practicing in the field.

COMPETITION DAMAGES ACTIONS IN THE EU

LAW AND PRACTICE

DAVID ASHTON
European Parliament, Brussels

DAVID HENRY
McDermott Will & Emery, Brussels

Economics contribution from Frank Maier-Rigaud and Ulrich Schwalbe

ELGAR COMPETITION LAW AND PRACTICE

Edward Elgar
Cheltenham, UK • Northampton, MA, USA

Published by
Edward Elgar Publishing Limited
The Lypiatts
15 Lansdown Road
Cheltenham
Glos GL50 2JA
UK

Edward Elgar Publishing, Inc.
William Pratt House
9 Dewey Court
Northampton
Massachusetts 01060
USA

A catalogue record for this book
is available from the British Library

Library of Congress Control Number: 2013944956

This book is available electronically in the ElgarOnline.com Law Subject Collection,
E-ISBN 978 1 78254 076 2

MIX
Paper from
responsible sources
FSC
www.fsc.org
FSC® C013056

ISBN 978 1 78254 075 5

Typeset by Columns Design XML Ltd, Reading
Printed and bound in Great Britain by T.J. International Ltd, Padstow

CONTENTS

Foreword Emil Paulis xi
Acknowledgements xii
Table of Cases xiii
Table of Legislation and Policy Documents xxiii

Introduction 1
1. The Legal Framework 8
2. The Underlying Right to Damages 16
3. Indirect Purchaser Standing and Passing-on 36
4. Proving the Infringement 69
5. Further Substantive and Procedural Issues 102
6. Collective Action 126
7. Private International Law Aspects 171
8. Quantification of Antitrust Damages 210
   By Frank Maier-Rigaud and Ulrich Schwalbe

Index 263

EXTENDED TABLE OF CONTENTS

Foreword Emil Paulis xi
Acknowledgements xii
Table of Cases xiii
    European Court of Human Rights xiii
    European Union xiii
    Member States xv
    United States xix

Table of Legislation and Policy Documents xxiii
    International Treaties xxiii
    Council of Europe xxiii
    European Union xxiii
    Member States xxix
    United States xxxii

INTRODUCTION
I COMPETITION ENFORCEMENT IN THE EU 0.07
II THE COMMISSION'S PRIVATE ENFORCEMENT INITIATIVE 0.08

1. THE LEGAL FRAMEWORK
I THE CASE LAW OF THE ECJ ON REMEDIES 1.01
II THE MOVE FROM RIGHTS TO REMEDIES 1.07
    A Fixing the boundaries between remedial rules and procedural rules *sensu stricto* 1.15
III APPLICATION TO DAMAGES ACTIONS FOR BREACH OF EU COMPETITION LAW 1.17

2. THE UNDERLYING RIGHT TO DAMAGES
I THE ESTABLISHMENT OF THE RIGHT TO DAMAGES AS A MATTER OF EU LAW: *COURAGE V CREHAN* 2.03
    A The proceedings in the English courts 2.03
    B The reference to the ECJ 2.12
    C Further developments: the *Manfredi* judgment 2.16
II NATIONAL LAW: LEGAL BASES FOR DAMAGES ACTIONS FOR BREACH OF EU COMPETITION LAW 2.18
    A Common law 2.19
        1 England and Wales 2.19
        2 Ireland 2.22
    B Civil law 2.24
        1 Germanic systems of law 2.24
            a Denmark 2.24
            b Germany 2.26
            c Greece 2.33
            d Latvia 2.36
            e Lithuania 2.39
            f The Netherlands 2.44
        2 Romanistic systems of law 2.47
            a Belgium 2.47
            b France 2.50

c Italy 2.55
d Spain 2.60
C The tortious nature of litigation for breach of EU competition law 2.62
D The national law analysis: the fault requirement 2.68

3. INDIRECT PURCHASER STANDING AND PASSING-ON

I THE THEORETICAL UNDERPINNINGS OF INDIRECT PURCHASER STANDING AND PASSING-ON 3.001
A Indirect purchaser standing 3.012
B The passing-on defence 3.022
II EU LAW 3.028
A Indirect purchaser standing 3.029
1 The Commission's position on indirect purchaser standing 3.032
B The passing-on defence 3.037
1 The passing-on defence and unjust enrichment 3.044
2 The burden of proof to establish passing-on 3.053
3 Partial passing-on 3.061
4 The Commission's position on the passing-on defence 3.064
III NATIONAL LAW 3.067
A England and Wales 3.069
B Germany 3.074
C France 3.081
D Italy 3.084
IV INDIRECT PURCHASER STANDING AND PASSING-ON IN THE US 3.089
A Antitrust injury 3.090
B The passing-on defence under US law 3.092
C Indirect purchaser standing: the rule in *Illinois Brick* 3.099
1 Exceptions to the rule in *Illinois Brick* 3.105
2 The efficiency of the rule in *Illinois Brick* 3.110

4. PROVING THE INFRINGEMENT

I PRIVATE LITIGANTS' ACCESS TO PROBATIVE DOCUMENTS IN EU CARTEL DAMAGES ACTIONS 4.004
A Access to documents held by the Commission 4.006
B Access to documents held by a national competition authority 4.021
C Access to documents held by the defendant: the *National Grid* proceedings before the English courts 4.036
1 Legitimate expectations 4.044
2 Proportionality 4.045
3 Documents ordered to be disclosed to National Grid 4.046
4 Further developments: the French blocking statute 4.049
D Access to documents held by a third party 4.057
E The Commission's proposals on evidence 4.059
F The Commission's attempts to limit discoverability in US courts 4.061
II THE EVIDENTIAL VALUE OF PRIOR ADMINISTRATIVE DECISIONS 4.071
A Commission decisions: Article 16 of Regulation 1/2003 4.072
1 The judgment of the English Court of Appeal in *Crehan* 4.082
B Commission decisions: Article 9 of Regulation 1/2003 4.086
C NCA decisions 4.088
1 United Kingdom 4.090
2 Germany 4.104
3 Romanistic jurisdictions 4.109

5. FURTHER SUBSTANTIVE AND PROCEDURAL ISSUES

I CAUSATION 5.03
II MEASURE OF DAMAGES 5.07
A Types of damage recoverable 5.08
B Presumption of harm 5.13

1 EU law 5.17
2 National law 5.18
C Exemplary damages 5.21
1 EU law 5.22
2 English law 5.24
III LIMITATION PERIODS 5.47
A EU law 5.47
B National law 5.54
1 United Kingdom 5.55
2 Germany 5.62
IV PROCEDURES FOR RECOURSE TO THE EXPERTISE OF PUBLIC AUTHORITIES BY THE NATIONAL COURTS 5.64
A EU law: consultation of the Commission 5.65
B National law: consultation of the NCA 5.66
1 United Kingdom 5.67
2 Germany 5.68
3 France 5.69
4 Other jurisdictions 5.72
V JOINT AND SEVERAL LIABILITY 5.75

6. COLLECTIVE ACTION

I INTRODUCTION 6.001
A The rationale for collective action 6.008
B Terminology 6.014
C Opt-in and opt-out collective action 6.015
D Assignment of claims 6.033
II COLLECTIVE ACTION AT EU LEVEL 6.034
A Collective action as a matter of EU law 6.034
B EU policy developments 6.041
1 The Green Paper 6.044
2 The White Paper 6.047
3 The draft Directive 6.051
4 The Commission's joint information note 6.055
5 The Commission's 2011 consultation paper 6.057
6 The Commission's proposal and 2013 collective redress initiative 6.061
III COLLECTIVE ACTION IN THE MEMBER STATES 6.072
A United Kingdom 6.073
1 Representative actions 6.076
2 GLOs 6.081
3 s47B of the Competition Act 6.084
4 Further policy developments 6.092
a 2006 DTI consultation 6.093
b 2007 OFT recommendations 6.096
c 2012 BIS consultation 6.098
d 2013 BIS response 6.106
B The Netherlands 6.110
1 Article 3:305a Burgerlijk Wetboek 6.111
2 Bundled claims 6.113
3 Wet Collectieve Afhandeling Massaschade, 2005 6.117
C Denmark 6.127
D Sweden 6.135
E France 6.142
F Italy 6.148
G Assignment of claims 6.150
IV CLASS ACTIONS IN THE UNITED STATES 6.157
A Rule 23 of the Federal Rules of Civil Procedure 6.158
B The Class Action Fairness Act of 2005 6.169

7. PRIVATE INTERNATIONAL LAW ASPECTS

I CHOICE OF COURT 7.005
- A The governing law: Regulation 44/2001 7.006
- B Variety of choices of court 7.010
- C The application of Regulation 44/2001 to parties domiciled outside the EU 7.013
- D General jurisdiction: Article 2(1) 7.016
- E Special jurisdiction: Article 5(3) and Article 6(1) 7.018
- F Founding jurisdiction in tortious actions: Article 5(3) 7.023
  - 1 The application of the *Bier/Shevill* jurisprudence to competition-based litigation 7.026
  - 2 Article 5(3) as a basis for torpedo litigation 7.037
- G Consolidation of claims: Article 6(1) 7.042
  - 1 The English authorities on Article 6(1) 7.043
    - a Interpretation of the EU law concept of 'undertaking' 7.045
    - b Causation 7.050
  - 2 The application of Article 6(1) by the Dutch courts 7.052
- H *Lis pendens* 7.053
  - 1 *Lis pendens* I: Article 27 7.055
  - 2 *Lis pendens* II: Article 28 7.063
    - a Irreconcilability for the purposes of Article 28(3) 7.066
    - b Connected but not identical actions 7.068
    - c The English authorities on Article 28 7.072
    - d Article 28 and the Commission proposal 7.077
  - 3 The application of *lis pendens* to parties domiciled outside the EU 7.081
- I The review of Regulation 44/2001 7.083
  - 1 *Lis pendens* 7.083
  - 2 Litigation involving parties domiciled outside the EU 7.086

II APPLICABLE LAW 7.092
- A The Rome II Regulation and the *lex fori* approach 7.094
  - 1 The general rule: Article 4 7.097
  - 2 Competition-based litigation: Article 6(3) 7.099
    - a Functioning of Article 6(3)(b) 7.102
    - b US law 7.112
  - 3 The desirability of the *lex fori* approach 7.114
- B Alternative solutions: the effects-based approach 7.119
  - 1 Article 6(3)(a) of the Rome II Regulation 7.122
  - 2 Problems with the effects-based approach: *Mosaikbetrachtung* 7.124
  - 3 *Mosaikbetrachtung* as a concurrent matter of jurisdiction and applicable law 7.128

8. QUANTIFICATION OF ANTITRUST DAMAGES

By Frank Maier-Rigaud and Ulrich Schwalbe

I INTRODUCTION 8.001

II DAMAGE CAUSED BY CARTELS AND ABUSIVE CONDUCT 8.005
- A Damage caused by cartels 8.010
  - 1 Types of damage caused by cartels 8.010
  - 2 Economic actors damaged by cartels 8.020
    - a Upstream effects 8.024
    - b Downstream effects 8.029
    - c Effects on producers of complements 8.032
    - d Summary of effects analysis 8.033
  - 3 Illustration 8.036
- B Damage caused by abusive conduct 8.044
  - 1 Types of damage caused by exploitative and exclusionary conduct 8.045
  - 2 Economic actors damaged by exploitative and exclusionary conduct 8.049

III QUANTIFICATION OF DAMAGES 8.052
- A Quantification of damages in cartel cases 8.053
  - 1 Time series analysis 8.055
  - 2 Cross-sectional analysis 8.061
  - 3 Difference-in-differences method 8.065
  - 4 Simulated comparator markets 8.067

		5	Cost-based and profitability-based approaches	8.069
	B		Damage quantification in abusive conduct cases	8.074
		1	Damage caused by abusive behaviour and the counterfactual scenario	8.074
			a Exploitative abuse	8.075
			b Exclusionary abuse	8.078
		2	Illustration: quantification of damages in case of an exclusionary abuse	8.084
			a Phase one	8.086
			b Phase two	8.088
			c Phase three	8.090
	C		Further aspects of damages quantification	8.095
		1	Compounding and discounting damages	8.095
		2	Estimation of after-effects	8.099
		3	Accuracy of statistical methods	8.101
		4	Remoteness and causality	8.104
IV			CONCLUSIONS	8.109
BIBLIOGRAPHY				259

Index 263

FOREWORD

This book is timely in more ways than one. It comes after almost ten years' work on the European Commission's private enforcement initiative, stretching back to the adoption of the Green Paper on damages actions in 2005 and, before that, to the Ashurst study, commissioned in 2003.

From a private practitioner's perspective, the book is timely in that it complements the fast pace of on-going development in the field in terms of litigation before the courts of the Member States. In this regard, it is noticeable that the Competition Appeal Tribunal in London has, over recent years as the provisions of the Enterprise Act 2002 have kicked in, developed a coherent body of jurisprudence in the area. As this book highlights, developments in Germany have also been significant. Indeed, the book brings together some of the most salient developments from the Member State jurisdictions.

The private enforcement initiative is one that in some ways goes beyond the legal field it incarnates. It is symbolic of a closer integration in the style of, most obviously, the United States (US), both in substantive but also theoretical terms, and in terms of what might be called 'legal architecture'. As the introductory chapter brings out, developments in the field at European Union (EU) level mark an important development in terms of the creation of a coherent set of rights enforceable between private parties. It can safely be said that there is no other field of EU law with such a well-developed and practical application in this sense. In difficult times for the Union, such a development in terms of democratisation and the connection between its law and its citizens is only to be welcomed.

Emil Paulis
Director, financial markets, DG Internal Market, European Commission
Former director, policy directorate, DG Competition, European Commission

ACKNOWLEDGEMENTS

The authors would like to thank the following for their comments on, and assistance with, various parts of the text: Louise-Astrid Aberg, Vladimir Bastidas, Jeremy Bentley, Philip Bentley QC, Samuel Buyoya, Alvaro García-Delgado García, Andrea Hamilton, Tanel Kalaus, Michal Kocon, Joey Mathis, Gerard McElwee, Paulius Mencas, Francesco Salerno, Alice Setari, Aiste Slezeviciute, Annika Suominen, Bastian Voell and Christian Vollrath.

David Ashton would like to emphasise that the views expressed in this book constitute his personal opinion and do not reflect the position of the European Parliament.

The law as stated is up-to-date to 11 June 2013.

TABLE OF CASES

EUROPEAN COURT OF HUMAN RIGHTS

Lithgow and others v United Kingdom (9006/80, 9262/81, 9263/81, 9265/81 9266/81, 9313/81, 9405/81) 6.036

Gorraiz Lizarraga and others v Spain (62543/00) 6.036

EUROPEAN UNION

Court of Justice

Case 26/62 Van Gend en Loos [1963] ECR 1 ....1.12, 1.13, 1.14

Cases 48, 49 and 50–57/69 ICI and others v Commission [1972] ECR 619 ....7.109

Case 127/73 BRT v SABAM [1974] ECR 51 ....1.06

Case 43/75 Defrenne v Sabena [1976] ECR 455 ....1.08

Case 21/76 Bier v Mines de Potasse d'Alsace [1976] ECR 1735 ....7.023, 7.026, 7.027, 7.031, 7.032, 7.033, 7.036, 7.129

Case 33/76 Rewe-Zentralfinanz and Rewe-Zentral v Landwirtschaftskammer für das Saarland [1976] ECR 1989 ....1.01

Joined Cases 64 and 113/76, 167 and 239/78, 27, 28 and 45/79 Dumortier Frères [1979] ECR 3091 ....3.039

Case 238/78 Ireks-Arkady v Council and Commission [1979] ECR 2955 ....3.038, 3.039, 3.043, 3.059

Case 68/79 Hans Just v Danish Ministry for Fiscal Affairs [1980] ECR 501 ....1.05, 3.038, 3.041, 3.042, 3.043, 3.045, 3.046, 3.047, 3.059

Case 814/79 Netherlands v Ruffer [1980] ECR 3807 ....7.024

Case C-107/82 AEG Telefunken AG v Commission [1983] ECR 3151 ....7.047

Case 199/82 Amministrazione delle Finanze dello Stato v SpA San Giorgio [1983] ECR 3595 ....1.05, 3.038, 3.052, 3.055, 3.058, 3.059, 3.062

Case 14/83 Von Colson [1984] ECR 1891 ....1.01

Joined Cases C-89/85, C-104/85, C-114/85, C-116/85, C-117/85 and C-125-129/85 A Ahlström Osakeyhtiö and others v Commission (Wood Pulp I) [1988] ECR 5193 ....7.026, 7.092, 7.109, 7.110

Joined Cases 331/85, 376/85 and 378/85 SA Les Fils de Jules Bianco and J Girard Fils SA v Directeur Général des douanes et droits indirects [1988] ECR 1099 ....3.038, 3.044, 3.047, 3.056

Case 144/86 Gubisch Maschinenfabrik v Palumbo [1987] ECR 4861 ....7.070

Case 145/86 Hoffmann v Krieg [1987] ECR 645 ....7.066, 7.074

Case 189/87 Athanasios Kalfelis v Bankhaus Schröder, Münchmeyer, Hengst and Co and others [1988] ECR 5565 ....7.042
Case C-220/88 Dumez France v Hessische Landesbank [1990] ECR I-49 ....7.024
Case C-213/89 R v Secretary of State for Transport, ex parte Factortame (Factortame I) [1990] ECR I-2433 ....1.05
Case C-234/89 Delimitis v Henninger Bräu AG [1991] ECR I-935 ....2.04
Case C-351/89 Overseas Union Insurance Ltd v New Hampshire Insurance Co [1991] ECR I-3317 ....7.081, 7.086
Joined Cases C-6/90 and C-9/90 Francovich v Italian Republic [1991] ECR I-5357 ...1.05, 1.10, 1.11, 1.12, 1.13, 2.14
Case C-271/91 Marshall II [1993] ECR I-4367 ....1.01
Case C-338/91 Steenhorst-Neerings [1993] ECR I-5475 ....1.01
Case C-128/92 Banks [1994] ECR I-1209 ....3.038, 3.061
Case C-129/92 Owens Bank v Bracco [1994] ECR I-117 ....7.074, 7.076
Case C-406/92 The Tatry [1994] ECR I-5439 ....7.041, 7.055, 7.056, 7.057, 7.059, 7.061, 7.064, 7.066, 7.069, 7.071, 7.074
Joined Cases C-46/93 and C-49/93 Brasserie du Pêcheur and Factortame III [1996] ECR I-1029 ....1.05, 1.06, 1.10, 1.11
Case C-68/93 Fiona Shevill and others v Press Alliance SA [1995] ECR I-415 ....7.023, 7.024, 7.025, 7.026, 7.027, 7.031, 7.032, 7.033, 7.034, 7.035, 7.036, 7.128, 7.129, 7.130
Case C-364/93 Marinari v Lloyds Bank [1995] ECR I-2719 ....7.024, 7.129
Case C-66/95 Sutton [1997] ECR I-2163 ....1.01
Case C-188/95 Fantask v Industriministeriet [1997] ECR I-6783 ....1.05
Joined Cases C-192/95 to C-218/95 Société Comateb and others v Directeur Général des Douanes et Droits Indirects [1997] ECR I-165 ....1.05, 3.038, 3.046, 3.047, 3.048, 3.061
Case C-351/96 Drouot Assurances SA v Consolidated Metallurgical Industries [1998] ECR I-3075 ....7.057, 7.059, 7.060, 7.061
Case C-195/98 Österreichischer Gewerkschaftsbund v Austria [2000] ECR I-10497 ....6.034
Case C-344/98 Masterfoods Ltd v HB Ice Cream Ltd [2000] ECR I-11369 ....4.073, 4.082, 4.083, 4.084, 4.088
Case C-412/98 UGIC v Group Josi [2000] ECR I-5925 ....7.015
Joined Cases C-441/98 and C-442/98 Michailidis [2000] ECR I-7145 ....3.038, 3.046, 3.061
Case C-453/99 Courage Ltd v Bernard Crehan [2001] ECR I-6297 ....0.08, 1.02, 1.05, 1.14, 2.02, 2.08, 2.11, 2.12, 2.13, 2.16, 2.17, 2.19, 2.20, 2.32, 2.64, 2.66, 3.001, 3.029, 3.032, 3.037, 3.038, 3.044, 3.068, 3.069, 3.075, 3.085, 4.082, 4.083, 7.042
Joined cases C-204/00 P, C-205/00 P, C-211/00 P, C-213/00 P, C-217/00 P and C-219/00 P Aalborg Portland and others v Commission [2004] ECR I-123 ....5.30
Case C-147/01 Weber's Wine World Handels-GmbH and others v Abgabenberufungskommission Wien [2003] ECR I-11365 ....3.048, 3.049, 3.050, 3.057, 3.059
Case C-281/02 Owusu v Jackson et al [2005] ECR I-1383 ....7.008, 7.009
Joined Cases C-295/04 to C-298/04 Manfredi v Lloyd Adriatico Assicurazioni SpA [2006] ECR I-6619 .1.03, 2.02, 2.09, 2.14, 2.15, 2.16, 2.17, 3.001, 3.029, 3.037, 3.069, 3.075, 5.12, 5.22, 5.34, 5.47, 5.48, 5.54
Case C-413/06P Bertelsmann AG and Sony Corporation of America v Independent Music Publishers and Labels Association (Impala) [2008] ECR I-4951 ....8.014
Case C-199/08 Erhard Eschig v Uniqa Sachversicherung AG [2009] ECR I-8295 ....6.035

Case 360/09 Pfleiderer AG v Bundeskartellamt, judgment of 14 June 2011 (not yet reported) 0.08, 3.029, 4.021, 4.022, 4.023, 4.024, 4.025, 4.026, 4.027, 4.028, 4.029, 4.032, 4.034, 4.035, 4.036, 4.041, 4.042, 4.043, 4.068, 4.65
Case C-17/10 Toshiba Corporation and others v Úřad pro ochranu hospodářské soutěže (not yet reported) 5.31
Case C-404/10 P Commission v Éditions Odile Jacob SAS and Lagardère SCA (not yet reported) 4.008, 4.016
Case C-412/10 Homawoo v GMF Assurances (not yet reported) 7.002
Case C-477/10 P Commission v Agrofert Holding a.s, and others (not yet reported) 4.008, 4.016
Case C-133/11 Folien Fischer AG and Fofitec AG v Ritrama SpA (not yet reported) 7.037, 7.038, 7.039, 7.040, 7.041
Case C-199/11 Europese Gemeenschap v Otis NV and others (not yet reported) 0.08, 3.029, 4.076, 4.077
Case C-332/11 ProRail BV v Xpedys NV (not yet reported) 4.046
Case C-536/11 Bundeswettbewerbsbehörde v Donau Chemie AG and others (not yet reported) 4.028–4.030, 4.032, 4.034

General Court

Case T-102/96 Gencor Ltd v Commission [1999] ECR II-753 ....7.106, 7.107, 7.109, 7.110
Case T-342/99 Airtours plc v Commission [2002] ECR II-2585 ....8.014
Joined Cases T-3/00 and T-337/04 Pitsiorlas v Council [2007] ECR II-4779 ....3.030
Case T-329/01 Archer Daniels Midland Co v Commission [2006] ECR II-3255 ....5.30
Case T-344/08 EnBW Energie Baden-Württemberg AG v Commission, judgment of 22 May 2012 (not yet reported) 4.008, 4.014, 4.015, 4.016, 4.018, 4.019, 4.020
Case T-437/08 CDC Hydrogene Peroxide v Commission, judgment of 15 December 2011 (not yet reported) 4.008, 4.009, 4.010
Case T-330/11 MasterCard Inc and MasterCard Europe v Commission (not yet reported) 4.007
Case T-341/12 R Evonik Degussa GmbH v Commission (not yet reported) 4.013
Case T-345/12 R Akzo Nobel and others v Commission (not yet reported) 4.013

MEMBER STATES

Belgium

Cour de cassation, 24 September 1976, AC 1977, 98 ....2.49
Cour de cassation, 5 September 1996, AC 1996, 708 ....2.49

Denmark

Ekko A/S/Elektrolux Home Products Denmark A/S, Miele A/S and BSH Hvidedvarer A/S Home Appliance Group, judgment of the Sø- og Handelsretten of 15 October 2004 ....2.25

France

Conseil constitutionnel, decision No 89–257, 25 July 1989 ....6.026
Cour de cassation, Com 1 March 1982, No 80–15.834, Bull. civ. IV, No 76 ....2.50
Doux Aliments/Ajinomoto Eurolysine (No. 09–15.816), Cour de cassation, chambre commerciale, judgment of 15 June 2010 ....3.045, 3.081, 3.082, 3.083
UFC Que Choisir, Cour de cassation, première chambre civile, judgment no 531 of 26 May 2011 (10-15.676) 6.144, 6.145
Les Sociétés Coopérative Le Gouessant et Sofral, Cour de cassation, chambre commerciale (11-18.495) 3.036, 3.083
UGAP/CAMIF, Paris Cour d'appel, JCP G 1998, II-10217, judgment of 13 January 1998 ...5.69
UGAP/CAMIF, Paris Cour d'appel, Jurisdata n° 2001–157128, judgment of 22 October 2001 ....5.69
SARL Philippe Streiff Motorsport/SAS Speedy, Paris Cour d'appel, 25ème chambre A, judgment of 28 June 2002, JCP E 2003, JP n° II 1018, p. 2091 ....2.52
Doux Aliments/Ajinomoto Eurolysine, Paris Cour d'appel, judgment of 10 June 2009 ....3.083
Eco System/Peugeot, Paris Tribunal de commerce, judgment of 22 October 1996 ....2.52
SAS Ma Liste de Courses/Société HighCo 3.0, Société HighCo Data, Société Sogec Gestion, Société Sogec Marketing, Paris Tribunal de commerce, 15ème chambre, RG 2011014911, judgment of 24 August 2011 ....4.031
Outremer Télécom/Orange Caraïbes et France Télécom, Paris Tribunal de commerce, 1ère chambre, RG 2010073867, judgment of 8 November 2011 ....4.031
Paris Tribunal de commerce, 1ère chambre, RG 2011030421, judgment of 31 January 2012 ....6.156
SAS Ma Liste de Courses/Société HighCo 3.0, Société HighCo Data, Société Sogec Gestion, Société Sogec Marketing, Paris Tribunal de commerce, 15ème chambre, RG 2011014911, judgment of 16 March 2012 ....4.031
DKT International/Eco-emballages et Valorplast, Paris Tribunal de commerce, 15ème chambre, RG 2012000109, judgment of 16 March 2012 ....4.031

Germany

Bundesgerichtshof, Berliner Transportbeton I, KRB 2/05 (WuW 2005, 1257) 5.18
Bundesgerichtshof, CDC/Dyckerhoff AG, KZR 42/08, 7 April 2009 ....6.154
Bundesgerichtshof, KZR 75/10 (WuW 2012, 57; NJW 2012, 928) 3.054, 3.056, 3.075, 3.076, 3.077, 3.078
Oberlandesgericht Düsseldorf, VI-U (Kart) 14/07 (WuW 2008, 845) 6.153
Oberlandesgericht Düsseldorf, V-4 Kart 5 + 6/11 (OWi) (WuW 2012, 962) 4.027
Oberlandesgericht Karlsruhe, Az. 6 U 118/05 (Kart) 3.076
Landgericht Dortmund, 0 55/02 Kart Vitaminkartell III (WuW 2004, 1182) 5.18
CDC Hydrogen Peroxide/Akzo, Landgericht Dortmund 0.13
Landgericht Düsseldorf, 34-O (Kart) 147/05 (WuW 2007, 519) 6.153
HUK Coberg/AGC and others, Landgericht Düsseldorf 0.13
Landgericht Mannheim, 22 O 74/04 ....3.076
Amtsgericht Bonn, Case 51, Gs 53/09 (WuW 2012, 275) 4.026

Italy

Corte de cassazione, judgment no 2207/2005 .... 2.59, 3.087
Corte de cassazione, judgment no 2305/2007 .... 2.59, 3.087
Naples Corte d'appello, judgment of 26 October 2007 .... 2.58
Naples Corte d'appello, judgment of 9 November 2007 .... 2.58
Naples Corte d'appello, judgment of 18 February 2008 .... 2.59
Naples Corte d'appello, judgment of 19 May 2008 .... 2.59
Albacom SpA c. Telecom Italia SpA, Rome Corte d'appello, judgment no 261/2003 of 20 January 2003 .... 4.108
International Broker/Refining Companies, Rome Corte d'appello, judgment no 1337/2008 .... 3.087
Indaba Incentive co/Società Juventus FC SpA, Turin Corte d'appello, judgment of 6 July 2000 .... 3.084, 3.085
Vincenzo Manfredi/Lloyd Adriatico Assicurazioni SpA, Bitonto Giudice di pace, judgment of 21 May 2007 .... 5.19
Lecce Giudice di pace, judgment of 30 January 2003 .... 3.088

Lithuania

Case No 3K-3-207/2010 UAB Klevo Lapas v AB Orlen Lietuva, judgment of 17 May 2010 .... 2.40

The Netherlands

Gerechtshof Amsterdam

LJN AZ7033 .... 6.117
LJN BO3908 .... 6.124
LJN BV1026 .... 6.124

Rechtbank Arnhem

LJN BZ0403 .... 0.13

Rechtbank The Hague

LJN CA1870, judgment of 1 May 2013, C/09/414499/HA ZA 12-293 .... 4.079, 4.080, 4.081, 7.052

United Kingdom

Competition Appeal Tribunal

Case No 1078/7/9/07 Consumers Association v JJB Sports plc 0.11, 6.085, 6.145
Case No 1147/5/7/09 .... 4.100
Case No 1153/5/7/10 .... 4.100
JJB Sports plc and Allsports Limited v Office of Fair Trading [2004] CAT 17 .... 6.087
BCL Old Co Ltd and others v Aventis SA and others [2005] CAT 2 .... 3.072

Umbro Holdings Ltd, Manchester United plc, Allsports Limited, JJB Sports plc v Office of Fair Trading [2005] CAT 22 ....6.087
Healthcare at Home v Genzyme [2006] CAT 30 ....0.11, 5.04
Albion Water Limited v Water Services Regulatory Authority [2006] CAT 36 ....5.42
Emerson Electric Co and others v Morgan Crucible Company plc and others [2007] CAT 28 (Emerson I) 5.56, 5.57
Emerson Electric Co and others v Morgan Crucible Company plc and others [2007] CAT 30 (Emerson II) 5.56, 5.57
Emerson Electric Co and others v Morgan Crucible Company plc and others [2008] CAT 8 (Emerson III) 5.56, 5.57
BCL Old Co Limited and others v BASF plc and others [2008] CAT 24 (BCL/BASF I) 5.59
Albion Water Limited and Albion Water Group Limited v Water Services Regulatory Authority [2008] CAT 31 ....5.42
Enron v EWS [2009] CAT 7 (Enron I) 4.078, 4.092, 4.093, 4.095
BCL Old Co Limited and others v BASF plc and others [2009] CAT 29 (BCL/BASF II) 5.59
Enron v EWS [2009] CAT 36 (Enron II) 4.090, 5.04, 5.05
Emerson Electric Co and others v Morgan Crucible Company plc and others [2011] CAT 4 ....4.097, 4.100, 4.101
Deutsche Bahn AG and others v Morgan Crucible Company plc and others [2011] CAT 16 ....5.57
2 Travel Group Plc v Cardiff City Transport Services Limited [2012] CAT 19 ....5.03, 5.04, 5.35, 5.36, 5.37, 5.38, 5.39, 5.40, 5.41, 5.45
Albion Water Limited v Dŵr Cymru Cyfyngedig [2013] CAT 6 ....5.42, 5.43, 5.44, 5.45

England and Wales

Supreme Court

Rookes v Barnard [1964] 1 AC 1129 ....5.25, 5.38, 5.41, 5.43
Garden Cottage Foods Limited v Milk Marketing Board [1984] AC 130 ....2.20
Kuddus v Chief Constable of Leicestershire [2002] 2 AC 122 ....5.21
Dubai Aluminium Co Ltd v Salaam and others [2002] UKHL 48 ....5.77
Inntrepreneur and others v Crehan [2006] UKHL 38 ....2.05, 2.10, 4.085
BCL Old Co Limited and others v BASF plc and others [2012] UKSC 45 ....0.13, 5.59
Deutsche Bahn AG and others v Morgan Crucible Company plc and others, UKSC 2012/0209 ....0.13

Court of Appeal

Davies v Swan Motor Co [1949] 2 KB 291 ....5.77
Pan Atlantic Insurance Company Limited and another v Pine Top Insurance Company Limited [1989] 1 Lloyd's Law Reports 568 ....6.079
Gibbs Mew plc v Gemmell [1998] EuLR 588 ....2.05, 2.12
Crehan v Inntrepreneur and others [2004] EWCA 637 ....2.05, 2.08, 2.09, 4.083, 4.084, 4.085
JJB Sports plc v Office of Fair Trading [2006] EWCA Civ 1318 ....6.087
Kolden Holdings Limited v Rodette Commerce Limited [2008] EWCA Civ 10 ....7.059, 7.060, 7.061
Devenish Nutrition and others v Sanofi-Aventis SA and others [2008] EWCA Civ 1086 ....5.34

BCL Old Co Limited and others v BASF plc and others [2009] EWCA Civ 434 (BCL/BASF I) 5.59
Enron v EWS [2009] EWCA Civ 647 (Enron I) 4.092, 4.093, 4.096, 4.097
Cooper Tire & Rubber Company and others v Dow Deutschland and others [2010] EWCA Civ 864 ....7.047, 7.049, 7.074, 7.075
BCL Old Co Limited and others v BASF plc and others [2010] EWCA Civ 1258 (BCL/BASF II) 5.59
Emerald Supplies Limited v British Airways plc [2010] EWCA Civ 1284 ....6.079, 6.080
Enron v EWS [2011] EWCA Civ 2 (Enron II) 5.04, 5.05
Deutsche Bahn AG and others v Morgan Crucible Company plc and others [2012] EWCA Civ 1055 ....5.57
Toshiba Carrier UK Ltd and others v KME Yorkshire Limited and others [2012] EWCA Civ 1190 ....7.049
Emerson Electric Co and others v Mersen UK Portslade Ltd [2012] EWCA Civ 1559 ....4.100

High Court

2001 Folio 398 Prentice Ltd v DaimlerChrysler UK 6.083
Courage Ltd v Crehan [1998] EWHC 281 (Ch) 2.05
Provimi Limited v Aventis Animal Nutrition SA [2003] EWHC 961 (Comm) 2.64, 7.010, 7.030, 7.043, 7.044, 7.046, 7.048, 7.050, 7.051, 7.052, 7.067, 7.072, 7.074, 7.131
Crehan v Inntrepreneur and others [2003] EWHC 1510 (Ch) 2.05, 2.06, 2.08, 2.09
Devenish Nutrition and others v Sanofi-Aventis SA and others [2007] EWHC 2394 ....3.073, 5.26, 5.27, 5.28, 5.29, 5.30, 5.31, 5.32, 5.33, 5.34, 5.39
Emerald Supplies Limited v British Airways plc [2009] EWHC 741 (Ch) 6.077, 6.078, 6.079, 6.080
Cooper Tire & Rubber Company and others v Shell Chemicals UK Limited and others [2009] EWHC 2609 (Comm) 7.032, 7.035, 7.037, 7.046, 7.051, 7.052, 7.059, 7.060, 7.061, 7.074, 7.075, 7.084, 7.085, 7.106, 7.131
Purple Parking Limited and Meteor Parking Limited v Heathrow Airport Limited [2011] EWHC 987 (Ch) 3.026
National Grid Electricity Transmission Plc v ABB Ltd and others [2012] EWHC 869 (Ch) 4.040, 4.041, 4.042, 4.043, 4.044, 4.045, 4.046, 4.047, 4.048, 4.049, 5.65
Secretary of State for Health and others v Servier Laboratories Limited, Servier Research and Development Limited, Les Laboratoires Servier SAS and Servier SAS [2012] EWHC 2761 (Ch) 4.055
Bord Na Mona Horticulture Limited and Board Na Mona plc v BPI and others [2012] EWHC 3346 (Comm) 4.078, 4.100, 7.024, 7.027, 7.029
National Grid Electricity Transmission Plc v ABB Limited and others [2013] EWHC 822 (Ch) 4.049, 4.050, 4.053, 4.054, 4.056

UNITED STATES

US Supreme Court

Hanover Shoe v United Shoe Machinery Corp. 392 US 481 (1968) 3.045, 3.092, 3.093, 3.094, 3.095, 3.096, 3.098, 3.100, 3.102

Hawaii v Standard Oil Co. of California 405 US 251 (1972) 3.091
Brunswick Corporation v Pueblo Bowl-O-Mat, Inc. 97 US 690 (1977) 2.08, 3.091
Illinois Brick Co v Illinois 431 US 720 (1977) 3.015, 3.099, 3.101, 3.102, 3.104, 3.107, 3.109, 3.111
Texas Industries, Inc. v Radcliff Materials, Inc. et al. 451 US 630 (1981) 5.77
Blue Shield of Virginia et al. v McCready 457 US 465 (1982) 3.101
Associated General Contractors of California, Inc. v California State Council of Carpenters 459 US 519 (1983) 3.091, 3.110
Cargill, Inc. et al. v Monfort of Colorado, Inc. 479 US 104 (1986) 3.091
Atlantic Richfield Co. v USA Petroleum Co. 495 US 328 (1990) 3.091
Kansas et al. v Utilicorp United Inc. 497 US 199 (1990) 3.107
F Hoffmann-LaRoche Ltd. v Empagran SA 124 US 2359 (2004) 4.061
Morrison v National Australia Bank Ltd. 130 US 2869 (2010) 6.122

US Court of Appeal

United States v Aluminium Co of America 148 F. 2d 416 (2nd Cir 1945) 7.113
Jewish Hosp. Ass'n v Stewart Mech. Enters. 628 F. 2d 971 (6th Cir 1980) 3.106
County of Suffolk v Long Island Lighting Co. 907 F. 2d 1295 (2nd Cir 1990) 6.165
In re Rhone-Poulenc Rorer Inc. 51 F. 3d 1293 (7th Cir 1995) 6.028
Campos v Ticketmaster Corp. 140 F. 3d 1166 (8th Cir 1998) 3.104
Paper Systems Incorporated v Nippon Paper Industries Co. Ltd. 281 F. 3d 629 (7th Cir 2002) 3.108
Empagran SA v F Hoffmann-LaRoche Ltd. 315 F. 3d 338 (DC Cir 2003) 7.113
Howard Hess Dental Labs. v Dentsply International Inc. 424 F. 3d 363 (3rd Cir 2005) 3.104
Empagran SA v F Hoffmann-LaRoche Ltd. 417 F. 3d 1267 (DC Cir 2005) ...7.003, 7.050, 7.113
Paycom Billing Services v MasterCard International 467 F. 3d 283 (2nd Cir 2006) 3.104
Warren General Hospital v Amgen 643 F. 3d 77 (3rd Cir 2011) 3.008, 3.103, 3.104

US District Court

Atlantic City Electric Company v General Electric Company 226 F. Supp. 59 (SDNY 1964) 6.156
Reilly v Hearst Corp. 107 F. Supp. 2d 1192 (ND Cal 2000) 3.091
In Re: Methionine Antitrust Litigation No 00–1311, 2003 WL 22048232 (ND Cal, 2003) 4.061
In Re: Vitamins Antitrust Litigation 398 F. Supp. 2d 209 (DDC, 2005) 4.061, 4.063, 6.154, 8.058
In Re: Rubber Chemicals Antitrust Litigation 486 F. Supp. 2d 1078 (ND Cal 2007) 4.061
In Re: OSB Antitrust Litigation 2007 WL 2253425 (ED Pa, 3 August 2007) 3.107
In Re: Dynamic Random Access Memory (DRAM) Antitrust Litigation 536 F. Supp. 2d 1129 (ND Cal 2008) 3.091
In Re: TFT-LCD (Flat Panel) Antitrust Litigation 586 F. Supp. 2d 1109 (ND Cal 2008) ...3.091
In Re: Flat Glass Antitrust Litigation II Civ No 08-mc-180 (WD Pa, 2009) 4.061
In Re: Air Cargo Shipping Services Antitrust Litigation No 06-MD-1775, 2009 WL 3077396 (EDNY, 25 September 2009) 4.061, 4.069
In Re: TFT-LCD (Flat Panel) Antitrust Litigation No M 07-1827 SI, 2011 WL 723571 (ND Cal, 2011) 4.061

In Re: Wellbutrin XL Antitrust Litigation Nos 08-cv-2431 and 08-cv-2433, 2012 WL 1657734 (ED Pa, 11 May 2011) 3.104
In Re: Air Cargo Shipping Services Antitrust Litigation No 06-MD-1775, 2011 WL 2909162 (EDNY, 15 July 2011) 4.061
In Re: Air Cargo Shipping Services Antitrust Litigation No 06-MD-1775 (EDNY, 19 December 2011) 4.069
In Re: Automotive Wire Harness Systems Antitrust Litigation MDL No 2311 (ED Mich, 7 February 2012) 3.111
In Re: Automotive Parts Antitrust Litigation, In Re: Wire Harness Cases 2:12-cv-00103-MOB-MKM (ED Mich, 6 June 2013) 3.110

California Supreme Court

Clayworth v Pfizer Inc 233 P 3d 1066 (Cal. 2010) 3.097

TABLE OF LEGISLATION AND POLICY DOCUMENTS

INTERNATIONAL TREATIES

1968 Brussels Convention on jurisdiction and the enforcement of judgments in civil and commercial matters (consolidated version, OJ L 299, 31.12.1972, p 32) 7.006, 7.007
Article 6(1) 7.130
Article 21 .... 7.054
Article 22 .... 7.054, 7.074
Convention on jurisdiction and the enforcement of judgments in civil and commercial matters done at Lugano on 16 September 1988 (OJ L 319, 25.11.1988, p 9) 7.006
Convention on jurisdiction and the recognition and enforcement of judgments in civil and commercial matters done at Lugano on 30 October 2007 (OJ L 339, 21.12.2007, p 3) 7.006
Article 69(4) 7.006
Article 69(5) 7.006

COUNCIL OF EUROPE

European Convention on Human Rights
Article 6 .... 1.10, 6.030, 6.124
Article 13 .... 1.10

EUROPEAN UNION

Consolidated version of the Treaty establishing the European Community
Article 3 .... 2.07
Article 293 .... 7.006
Consolidated version of the Treaty on European Union (OJ C 115, 9.5.2008, p 13)
Article 4(3) 1.01, 1.10, 2.06
Article 19(1) 0.08
Consolidated version of the Treaty on the Functioning of the European Union (OJ C 115, 9.5.2008, p 47)
Article 34 .... 1.06, 1.08, 1.11, 1.14
Article 45 .... 1.08
Article 45(3) 1.08, 1.11
Article 49 .... 1.06
Article 56 .... 1.08, 1.11
Article 101 .... 0.01, 0.07, 1.04, 1.05, 1.06, 1.08, 1.09, 1.11, 1.16, 1.18, 2.05, 2.08, 2.10, 2.12, 2.14, 2.17, 2.27, 2.50, 2.60, 3.026, 3.029, 3.035, 4.029, 4.087, 4.088, 4.107, 5.26, 5.34, 5.57, 5.65, 5.74, 6.052, 6.053, 7.101, 7.026, 7.045, 7.100, 7.109, 7.124
Article 101(1) 1.08, 2.04, 2.06, 2.52, 3.029, 4.083, 4.084, 4.085, 4.101, 6.085
Article 101(2) 0.07, 2.14, 2.64, 2.66
Article 101(3) 0.08, 1.18, 2.04, 3.054
Article 102 .... 0.01, 0.07, 1.04, 1.05, 1.06, 1.08, 1.09, 1.11, 1.16, 1.18, 2.27, 2.50, 2.60, 3.026, 3.029, 3.035, 4.087, 4.088, 5.35, 5.65, 5.74, 6.052, 6.053, 7.011, 7.026, 7.100, 7.109, 7.124
Article 157 .... 1.08
Article 267 .... 5.65
Article 339 .... 4.012

Article 340(2) 3.038, 3.039
Council Regulation No 17 of 6 February 1962, First Regulation implementing Articles 85 and 86 of the Treaty (OJ 13, 21.2.1962, p 204)
Article 9(1) 0.08
Article 19(3) 4.084
Council Directive 76/207/EEC of 9 February 1976 on the implementation of the principle of equal treatment for men and women as regards access to employment, vocational training and promotion, and working conditions (OJ L 39, 14.2.1976, p 40)
Article 6 ....1.01
Council Directive 79/7/EEC of 19 December 1978 on the progressive implementation of the principle of equal treatment for men and women in matters of social security (OJ L 6, 10.1.1979, p 24)
Article 6 ....1.01
Council Regulation (EEC) No 4064/89 of 21 December 1989 on the control of concentrations between undertakings (OJ L 395, 30.12.1989, p 1) 7.106
Council Directive 93/13/EEC of 5 April 1993 on unfair terms in consumer contracts (OJ L 95, 21.4.1993, p 29)
Article 7 ....6.037
Directive 98/27/EC of the European Parliament and of the Council of 19 May 1998 on injunctions for the protection of consumers' interests (OJ L 166, 11.6.1998, p 51) 6.038, 6.049
Council Regulation (EC) No 44/2001 of 22 December 2000 on jurisdiction and the recognition and enforcement of judgments in civil and commercial matters (OJ L 12, 16.1.2001, p 1) 7.002, 7.004, 7.006, 7.007, 7.008, 7.013, 7.014, 7.015, 7.016, 7.053, 7.080, 7.081, 7.082, 7.091, 7.130
Recital 19 ....7.006, 7.054
Article 1(1) 7.008
Article 1(2) 7.008
Article 1(3) 7.007
Article 2 ....7.007, 7.015, 7.020, 7.021, 7.024, 7.045, 7.050, 7.104, 7.119
Article 2(1) 7.016–7.017
Article 4(1) 7.013, 7.081
Article 5(3) 7.007, 7.018, 7.019, 7.023, 7.026, 7.029, 7.032, 7.036, 7.037, 7.039, 7.040, 7.104, 7.119, 7.128, 7.129, 7.130
Article 5(4) 7.019
Article 5(5) 7.019
Article 6 ....7.018
Article 6(1) 6.072, 7.007, 7.012, 7.018, 7.021, 7.027, 7.042, 7.043, 7.044, 7.046, 7.051, 7.052, 7.054, 7.065, 7.066, 7.072, 7.079, 7.104, 7.105, 7.130
Article 6(3) 7.042
Article 22 ....7.013, 7.042
Article 23 ....7.013
Article 27 ....7.012, 7.038, 7.041, 7.054, 7.055, 7.056, 7.057, 7.058, 7.060, 7.062, 7.063, 7.064, 7.068, 7.070, 7.071, 7.081, 7.082, 7.085, 7.086, 7.087, 7.088
Article 27(1) 7.054
Article 27(2) 7.054
Article 28 ....7.012, 7.037, 7.053, 7.054, 7.055, 7.062, 7.063, 7.064, 7.069, 7.071, 7.072, 7.074, 7.076, 7.078, 7.079, 7.080, 7.081, 7.086, 7.087, 7.090
Article 28(1) 7.067, 7.068
Article 28(2) 7.065
Article 28(3) 7.042, 7.054, 7.066, 7.072, 7.073, 7.105
Article 29 ....7.054
Article 34(3) 7.066
Article 59(1) 7.016
Article 60(1) 7.014, 7.017
Regulation (EC) No 1049/2001 of the European Parliament and of the Council of 30 May 2001 regarding public access to European Parliament, Council and Commission documents (OJ L 145, 31.5.2001, p 43) 4.007, 4.013, 4.015, 4.064

Article 4 ....4.007, 4.008
Article 4(2) 4.007
Article 4(2), first indent 4.012
Article 4(2), third indent 4.015
Article 4(3), first subparagraph 4.007
Article 4(3), second subparagraph ...4.007, 4.015, 4.020
Article 7 ....4.007

Council Regulation (EC) No 1206/2001 of 28 May 2001 on cooperation between the courts of the Member States in the taking of evidence in civil or commercial matters (OJ L 174, 27.6.2001, p 1) 4.050, 4.051, 4.056
Article 1(1)(a) 4.051
Article 1(1)(b) 4.051

Council Regulation (EC) No 1/2003 of 16 December 2002 on the implementation of the rules on competition laid down in Articles 81 and 82 of the Treaty (OJ L 1, 4.1.2003, p 1) 0.08, 4.023
Article 2 ....3.035, 3.054
Article 3(2) 7.092, 7.115
Article 6 ....0.08
Article 7 ....4.087, 4.088
Article 9 ....4.086, 4.087
Article 9(1) 4.086
Article 15 ....5.66
Article 15(1) 5.65
Article 15(3) 5.65, 5.71
Article 15(4) 5.66
Article 16 ....4.075, 4.076, 4.078, 4.079, 4.082, 4.088, 4.100, 5.33
Article 16(1) 4.072, 4.073, 4.074, 4.088

Directive 2004/48/EC of the European Parliament and of the Council on the enforcement of intellectual property rights (OJ L 157, 30.4.2004, p 45)
Recital 18 ....6.039
Article 4(1)(c) 6.039
Article 4(1)(d) 6.039

Regulation (EC) No 864/2007 of the European Parliament and of the Council of 11 July 2007 on the law applicable to non-contractual obligations (Rome II) (OJ L 199, 31.7.2007, p 40) 7.002, 7.004, 7.096, 7.120
Recital 6 ....7.116
Recital 21 ....7.123
Article 4 ....7.097, 7.098, 7.123
Article 4(1) 7.098
Article 4(2) 7.098
Article 4(3) 7.098
Article 5 ....7.097
Article 6 ....7.097, 7.123
Article 6(3) 7.099, 7.102, 7.131
Article 6(3)(a) 7.039, 7.100, 7.104, 7.106, 7.119, 7.122, 7.128, 7.129
Article 6(3)(b) 7.100, 7.102, 7.103, 7.104, 7.105, 7.106, 7.107, 7.108, 7.109, 7.110, 7.111, 7.112, 7.119, 7.122, 7.123
Article 6(4) 7.101
Article 7 ....7.097
Article 8 ....7.097
Article 9 ....7.097
Article 32 ....7.002

Regulation (EC) No 593/2008 of the European Parliament and of the Council of 17 June 2008 on the law applicable to contractual obligations (Rome I) (OJ L 177, 4.7.2008, p 6) 7.004

Directive 2009/22/EC of the European Parliament and of the Council of 23 April 2009 on injunctions for the protection of consumers' interests (OJ L 110, 1.5.2009, p 30) 6.038

Regulation (EU) No 1215/2012 of the European Parliament and of the Council of 12 December 2012 on jurisdiction and the recognition and enforcement of judgments in civil and commercial matters (recast) (OJ L 351, 20.12.2012, p 1) 7.002
Article 29 ....7.088, 7.090
Article 30 ....7.090
Article 33 ....7.088, 7.089, 7.090
Article 33(3) 7.090
Article 34 ....7.090
Article 34(1)(a) 7.090
Article 34(3) 7.090
Article 81 ....7.002

Agreement between the Government of the United States of America and the Commission of the European Communities regarding the application of their competition laws (OJ L 95, 27.4.1995, p 47) 4.066
Agreement between the European Communities and the Government of the United States of America on the application of positive comity principles in the enforcement of their competition laws (OJ L 173, 18.6.1998, p 28) ...4.066, 4.067

European Parliament

Report of the Committee on Legal Affairs on the proposal for a regulation of the European Parliament and of the Council on the law applicable to non-contractual obligations ('Rome II') (A6–211/2005)
Amendment 29 ....7.100
Report of the Committee on Legal Affairs on the joint text approved by the Conciliation Committee (A6–257/2007) 7.106
Resolution of 26 March 2009 on the White Paper (P6_TA(2009)187) 6.050
Resolution of 2 February 2012 on 'Towards a coherent European approach to collective redress' (P7_TA(2012)21) 6.003, 6.060

Council

Common Position (EC) No 22/2006 of 25 September 2006 adopted by the Council with a view to the adoption of a Regulation of the European Parliament and of the Council on the law applicable to non-contractual obligations ('Rome II')
Recital 20 ....7.100
Article 6(3) 7.100, 7.129

European Parliament and Council

Joint text approved by the Conciliation Committee on 25 June 2007 for a Regulation of the European Parliament and of the Council on the law applicable to non-contractual obligations ('Rome II') 262

European Commission

Commission Regulation (EC) No 773/2004 of 7 April 2004 relating to the conduct of proceedings by the Commission pursuant to Articles 81 and 82 of the EC Treaty (OJ L 123, 27.4.2004, p 18) 4.003, 4.064
Commission Regulation (EC) No 622/2008 of 30 June 2008 amending Regulation (EC) No 773/2004, as regards the conduct of settlement procedures in cartel cases (OJ L 171, 1.7.2008, p 3) 4.003
Commission Decision 2001/418/EC of 7 June 2000, case COMP/36.545/F3, amino acids (OJ L 152, 7.6.2001, p 24) 3.081
Commission Decision 2003/2/EC of 21 November 2001, case COMP/E-1/37.512, vitamins (OJ L 6, 10.1.2003, p 1) 4.106, 5.26
Commission Decision 2004/337/EC of 20 December 2001, case COMP/E-1/36.212, carbonless paper (OJ L 115, 21.4.2004, p 1) 3.076
Commission Decision 2004/420/EC of 3 December 2003, Case No C.38.359, electrical and mechanical carbon and graphite products (OJ L 125, 28.4.2004, p 45) 4.100
Commission Decision 2005/396/EC of 19 January 2005, case COMP/C.2/37.214, joint selling of the media rights to the German Bundesliga (OJ L 134, 27.5.2005, p 46) 4.087

Commission Decision 2006/903/EC of 3 May 2006, case COMP/F/C.38.620, hydrogen peroxide and perborate (OJ L 353, 13.12.2006, p 54) 4.009
Commission Decision of 24 January 2007, case COMP/38.899, gas insulated switchgear (OJ C 5, 10.1.2008, p 7) 4.014
Commission Decision of 21 February 2007, case COMP/E-1/38.823, elevators and escalators (OJ C 75, 26.3.2008, p 19) 6.116
Commission Decision of 1 October 2008, case COMP/C.39181, candle waxes (not yet published) 4.079, 5.75
Commission Decision of 9 November 2010, case COMP/39258, airfreight (not yet published) 6.156
Commission notice on cooperation between national courts and the Commission in applying Articles 85 and 86 of the Treaty (OJ C 39, 13.2.1993, p. 6) 7.008
Point 44 ....7.008
Commission notice on the co-operation between the Commission and the courts of the EU Member States in the application of Articles 81 and 82 EC (OJ C 101, 27.4.2004, p 54) 2.07
Footnote 4 ....7.008
Commission notice on the rules for access to the Commission file in cases pursuant to Articles 81 and 82 of the EC Treaty, Articles 53, 54 and 57 of the EEA Agreement and Council Regulation (EC) No 139/2004 (OJ C 325, 22.12.2005, p 7) 4.064
Commission notice on immunity from fines and reduction of fines in cartel cases (OJ C 298, 8.12.2006, p 17) 4.011
Point 40 ....4.064
Commission notice on the conduct of settlement procedures in view of the adoption of Decisions pursuant to Article 7 and Article 23 of Council Regulation (EC) No 1/2003 in cartel cases (OJ C 167, 2.7.2008, p 1) 4.003
Commission guidelines on the method of setting fines imposed pursuant to Article 23(2)(a) of Regulation No 1/2003 (OJ C 210, 1.9.2006, p 2) 4.064
Proposal for a directive of the European Parliament and of the Council on measures and procedures to ensure the enforcement of intellectual property rights (COM(2003)46)
Article 5(2), third subparagraph 6.039
Proposal for a regulation of the European Parliament and the Council on the law applicable to non-contractual obligations ('Rome II') (COM(2003)427) 7.094, 7.095
Article 3 ....7.123
Article 5 ....7.123
Amended proposal for a European Parliament and Council regulation on the law applicable to non-contractual obligations ('Rome II') (COM(2006)83) 7.100
Proposal for a regulation of the European Parliament and the Council on the law applicable to contractual obligations (Rome I) (COM(2005)650) 7.094
Proposal for a regulation of the European Parliament and of the Council on jurisdiction and the recognition and enforcement of judgments in civil and commercial matters (recast) (COM(2010)748) 7.085
Article 29(2) 7.085
Article 34 ....7.086
White Paper on modernisation of the rules implementing Articles 85 and 86 of the EC Treaty (COM(1999)101) 0.08
Green Paper on the conversion of the Rome Convention of 1980 on the law applicable to contractual obligations into a Community instrument and its modernisation (COM(2002)654) 7.094, 7.117

Green Paper on the review of Council Regulation (EC) No 44/2001 on jurisdiction and the recognition and enforcement of judgments in civil and commercial matters (COM(2009)175) ...7.054, 7.083, 7.095, 7.100, 7.126
Communication on improving alternative dispute resolution (ADR) in relation to consumer-to-business disputes in the EU (COM(2011)791) 6.090
Communication on a comprehensive approach on personal data protection in the European Union (COM(2012)609) 6.040
Report concerning the application of Directive 2009/22/EC (COM(2012)635) 6.038

Private enforcement initiative

Green Paper on damages actions for breach of the EC antitrust rules (COM(2005)672) 0.01, 0.09, 2.63, 3.044, 5.16, 5.23, 5.81, 5.82, 6.044–6.046
Staff Working Paper: Annex to the Green Paper (SEC(2005)1732) 0.01, 2.63, 3.044, 7.095
White Paper on damages actions for breach of the EC antitrust rules (COM(2008)165) 0.01, 0.09, 2.63, 3.012, 3.032, 3.033, 3.054, 3.064, 4.088, 5.15, 6.047–6.050
Staff Working Paper accompanying the White Paper (SEC(2008)404) 0.01, 2.63, 3.054, 5.15, 6.049
Staff Working Document accompanying the White Paper: Impact Assessment (SEC(2008)405) 0.01, 6.010, 6.027
Proposal for a Council directive on rules governing damages actions for infringements of Articles 81 and 82 of the Treaty, 2009 ....0.09, 3.054, 5.49, 6.069
Recital 6 ....3.033
Recital 17 ....3.065
Recital 18 ....3.034
Article 4 ....6.049, 6.051
Article 5 ....6.053
Article 6(1) 6.053
Article 10(1) 3.065
Article 10(2) 3.034
Article 13 ....2.71
Article 14(1) 5.48
Article 14(2) 4.57
Article 14(3) 5.48
Proposal for a directive of the European Parliament and of the Council on certain rules governing actions for damages under national law for infringements of the competition law provisions of the Member States and of the European Union (COM(2013)404) 0.10, 6.061
Recital 10 ....5.06
Recital 11 ....5.12
Recital 30 ....6.070, 6.071
Recital 35 ....5.17
Article 5 ....4.059
Article 5(1) 4.060
Article 5(2)(a) 4.060
Article 5(2)(b) 4.060
Article 5(3)(b) 4.060
Article 5(3)(c) 4.060
Article 6(1)(a) 4.032, 4.069
Article 6(1)(b) 4.032
Article 6(2) 4.032
Article 6(3) 4.033
Article 7(1) 4.032
Article 7(2) 4.032
Article 8(1)(a) 4.060
Article 8(1)(b) 4.060
Article 9 ....4.088
Article 10(2) 5.51
Article 10(2)(iv) 5.51
Article 10(4) 5.50
Article 10(5) 5.52
Article 11(1) 5.83
Article 11(2) 5.85
Article 11(3) 5.78, 5.86
Article 11(4) 5.86
Article 12(1) 3.066, 6.069
Article 12(2) 6.070
Article 13(1) 3.035
Article 13(2) 3.035, 7.077
Article 13(2)(b) 3.035

Article 13(2), second subparagraph .3.063, 5.07
Article 14(1) 5.12
Article 14(2) 3.001
Article 15(1) 7.077
Article 15(1)(a) 7.079
Article 16(1) 3.035, 4.104, 5.17
Article 16(2) 5.07
Article 17(1) 5.53
Article 18(1) 5.80
Article 18(2) 5.80
Communication on quantifying harm in actions for damages based on breaches of Article 101 or 102 of the Treaty on the Functioning of the European Union (C(2013)3440) 0.10
Staff Working Document (Practical Guide) on quantifying harm in actions for damages based on breaches of Article 101 or 102 of the Treaty on the Functioning of the European Union (SWD(2013)205) 0.10

Collective redress initiative

'Renforcer la cohérence de l'approche européenne en matière de recours collectif: prochaines étapes', information note by Mme Reding, M. Almunia and M. Dalli (SEC(2010)1192) 6.055
Staff Working Document, 'Public Consultation: Towards a Coherent European Approach to Collective Redress' (SEC(2011)173) 6.002, 6.003
Recommendation on common principles for injunctive and compensatory collective redress mechanisms in the member States concerning violations of rights granted under Union law (C(2013)3539) 0.10, 6.003, 6.026, 6.043, 6.062–6.069
Communication on 'towards a European horizontal framework for collective redress' (COM(2013)401) 0.10, 6.003, 6.013, 6.062

MEMBER STATES

Austria

Bundesgesetz gegen Kartelle und andere Wettbewerbsbeschränkungen
§37a 0.13, 4.105
§39(2) 4.028

Belgium

Code civil
Article 1133 ....2.48
Article 1382 ....2.47
Code judicaire
Article 30 ....6.072
Loi sur la protection de la concurrence
Art 42bis§1 ....5.72
Loi sur la protection de la concurrence économique coordonnée le 15 septembre 2006
Article 73§1 ....5.72
Article 73§4 ....5.72

Denmark

Lov om rettens pleje (retsplejeloven) 6.127
Section 254(a) 6.129
Section 254(b) 6.130
Section 254(c) 6.132
Lov om ændring af retsplejeloven og forskellige andre love (Gruppesøgsmål m.v.) 6.127
Bekendtgørelse af konkurrenceloven (LBK No 23, 17 January 2013) 2.24, 2.25
§25 ....2.24

Estonia

Tsiviilkohtumenetluse seadustik
Article 198(2) 5.74
Konkurentsiseadus
Article 56(3) 5.74

Finland

Kilpailulaki (No 948/2011)
Section 20(1) 2.29
Section 49(2) 4.73

France

Code civil
Article 1382 ....1.13, 2.50, 2.51, 2.52, 2.70
Code de commerce
Article L. 420–1 ....2.50, 2.52, 2.53
Article L. 420–2 ....2.50, 2.52, 2.53
Article L. 420–3 ....2.53
Article L. 462–3 ....5.69
Article L. 462–3(1) 5.69
Article L. 470–5 ....5.70
Article R. 462–3 ....5.69
Code de la consommation
Article L. 422–1 ....6.142, 6.144
Article L. 422–1(2) 6.144
Loi n° 68–678 relative à la communication de documents et renseignements d'ordre économique, commercial, industriel, financier ou technique à des personnes physiques ou morales étrangères, 26 July 1968 ....4.049, 4.050, 4.053, 4.054, 4.055

Germany

Bürgerliches Gesetzbuch
§134 ....2.31
§195 ....5.62, 5.63
§199(1) 5.63
§204(2) 5.62
§254 ....2.32
§823 ....2.26, 2.28, 2.71
§823(1) 2.28
§823(2) 2.28, 2.68, 3.077
Zivilprozessordnung
§142(1) 4.036
§253 ....6.154
§287 ....4.108, 6.154
Strafprozessordnung
§406e(2) 4.026
Gesetz gegen Wettbewerbsbeschränkungen 2.26
§1 ....2.27, 2.31
§19 ....2.27
§20 ....2.27
§33 ....2.26
§33(1) 2.30, 3.074
§33(3) 2.29, 3.074
Second sentence 3.074
§33(4) 2.27, 4.104, 5.63
§33(5) 5.62, 5.63
§90(2) 5.68
7th amendment to the GWB 2.26, 2.68, 4.104
8th amendment to the GWB (draft) 2.26
Bundeskartellamt, Private Kartellrechtsdurchsetzung: Stand, Probleme, Perspektiven (2005) 0.03

Greece

Αστικός Κώδικας
Article 174 ....2.34
Article 180 ....2.34
Article 330 ....2.35
Article 914 ....2.33
Hellenic Competition Commission
Decision No 369/V/2007, *NESTLE ΕΛΛΑΣ A.E.* 2.33

Hungary

törvény a tisztességtelen piaci magatartás és a versenykorlátozás tilalmáról
Section 88/C 5.19

Ireland

Competition Act 2002
s14 ....2.22
s14(5)(b) 5.24
Competition (Amendment) Act 2012 .....2.23

Italy

Codice civile 2.55
Article 2043 ....2.56, 2.57, 2.59
Codice del consumo (decreto legislativo no. 206, 6 September 2005)
Article 2(2)(e) 3.088
Article 140(9) 3.088
Article 140-bis 6.148, 6.149
L. 287/90
Article 2 ....3.085
Article 33 ....2.55, 2.56
L. 244/07
Article 2, comma 446 ....6.148
Decreto legge no. 1, 24 January 2012 ......6.149

Latvia

Civillikums
Article 1642 ....2.38
Konkurences likums
Article 11 ....2.37
Article 21 ....2.36

Lithuania

Civilinis Kodeksas, No VIII-1864
Article 1.80 ....2.41
Article 1.81 ....2.41
Article 6.245 ....2.39
Article 6.246 ....2.39
Article 6.248 ....2.39, 2.42
Article 6.263 ....2.39
Konkurencijos Įstatymas, No VIII-1099, 23 March 1999
Article 46(1) 2.39
Article 50(1) 2.39

The Netherlands

Grondwet
Article 17 ....6.124
Burgerlijk Wetboek 6.113
Article 2:26 ....6.111
Article 2:285 ....6.111
Article 3:305a 6.110, 6.112
Article 3:40 ....2.45
Article 6:101 ....2.46
Article 6:162 ....2.44
Wetboek van Burgerlijke Rechtsvordering
Article 1017(3) 6.124
Wet Collectieve Afhandeling
Massaschade 6.109, 6.110, 6.117, 6.118, 6.119, 6.121, 6.123, 6.125, 6.126

Portugal

Código do processo civil
Article 26A 6.017

Spain

Código civil
Article 1902 ....2.60
Ley de enjuiciamiento civil (1/2000) 2.60
Article 11.2 ....6.017
Article 11.3 ....6.017
Ley de defensa de la competencia (16/1989) 2.60
Article 13(2) 2.60
Ley de defensa de la competencia (15/2007) 2.60
Article 1 ....2.60
Article 2 ....2.60
Disposición adicional segunda 2.60

Sweden

Lag 2002:599 om grupprättegång 6.135, 6.138
§8 ....6.136
Regeringens proposition 2001/02:107 ...6.136
Konkurrenslag (lag 2008:579) 6.141
Chapter 3, §25 ....6.141

United Kingdom

Judicature Act 1873 ....4.038
Judicature Act 1875 ....4.038
European Communities Act 1972
s2(1) 2.19
Civil Liability (Contribution) Act 1978 ...5.77
s1(1) 5.77
s2(1) 5.77
Limitation Act 1980
s2 ....5.61
Competition Act 1998 ....5.48, 5.61, 5.67
s2(1) 6.085
s18(1) 5.35, 5.36
s40 ....5.37
s47A 0.11, 2.21, 4.078, 4.091, 4.092, 4.097, 4.100, 4.104, 5.37
s47A(3) 5.55, 5.61
s47A(6)(d) 5.57
s47A(7) 5.55
s47A(8) 5.48, 5.55, 5.57, 5.59, 5.63
s47A(9) 4.093, 4.097
s47B 6.080, 6.084, 6.085, 6.087, 6.090, 6.097
s58 ....4.091
s60 ....3.069
s60(1) 3.069

s60(2) 3.069
Enterprise Act 2002 ....5.55, 6.083
s16(1) 5.67
s16(4) 5.67
s19 ....6.084
Schedule 4, Part 2, paragraph 11 ....5.55
Specified Body (Consumer Claims) Order 2005 (SI No 2365 of 2005) ..6.084, 6.107

Policy documents

Department of Trade and Industry, 'A World Class Competition Regime', July 2001 ....0.04
Department of Trade and Industry, 'A Fair Deal for All – Extending Competitive Markets: Empowered Consumers, Successful Business', 2005 ....6.093
Department of Trade and Industry, 'Representative Actions in Consumer Protection Legislation: Consultation', 12 July 2006 ....6.093
Department for Business, Enterprise and Regulatory Reform, 'Representative Actions in Consumer Protection Legislation: Responses to the Government consultation', March 2008 ....6.093, 6.094, 6.095
Department for Business, Innovation & Skills, 'Private Actions in Competition Law: A Consultation on Options for Reform', April 2012 ....0.03, 3.070, 3.071, 5.20, 6.098–6.105
Department for Business, Innovation & Skills, 'Private Actions in Competition Law: A Consultation on Options for Reform – Government Response', January 2013 ....0.03, 2.21, 3.022, 3.069, 3.071, 5.20, 5.60, 5.87, 6.106–6.109

Office of Fair Trading

Decision number CA98/6/2003 ....6.085, 6.086, 6.087
Decision number CA98/8/2003 ....6.023
Decision number CA98/5/2006 ....6.090
Decision number CA98/1/2008 ....3.36
'Response to the European Commission's Green Paper, Damages actions for breach of the EC antitrust rules', May 2006 (OFT844) 5.16
'Private Actions in Competition Law: Effective Redress for Consumers and Business', Discussion paper, April 2007 (OFT916) 3.070
'Private Actions in Competition Law: Effective Redress for Consumers and Business', Recommendations, November 2007 ....6.092, 6.096
'Private Actions in Competition Law: a Consultation on Options for Reform – the OFT's Response to the Government's Consultation', July 2012 ....6.105

Competition Appeal Tribunal

Competition Appeal Tribunal Rules 2003 ....5.61
Rule 19(2)(k) 4.039
Rule 31 ....5.55, 5.59, 5.61

England and Wales

Civil Procedure Rules
Part 19-II 6.076
Part 19-III 6.081
Part 31 ....4.039
Rule 19.6 ....6.079, 6.080
Rule 19.6(1) 6.076, 6.078
Rule 19.6(4) 6.076
Rule 19.10 ....6.082
Rule 31.17 ....4.058

UNITED STATES

US Constitution
Article III 3.091
Sherman Act 7.106
§1 ....3.091
§2 ....3.091
§7 ....7.112, 7.113
§7(1) 7.112, 7.113
§7(2) 7.113

Clayton Act
§4 ....3.091, 3.099
§5(a) 4.074
§15 ....3.091
§16 ....3.099
Foreign Trade Antitrust Improvements Act 7.003
§6a 7.112
Class Action Fairness Act 6.168, 6.169
Federal Rules of Civil Procedure
Rule 23 ....3.098, 6.157, 6.169, 6.172
Rule 23(a) 6.158
Rule 23(b) 6.158, 6.160, 6.165
Rule 23(b)(1) 6.160, 6.163, 6.165
Rule 23(b)(1)(a) 6.160
Rule 23(b)(2) 6.161, 6.165
Rule 23(b)(3) 6.162, 6.163, 6.166, 6.167
Rule 26(b)(1) 4.062
Public Law 109–2, §2(b)(1)-(3) 6.169
California
Cartwright Act 3.097

INTRODUCTION

I COMPETITION ENFORCEMENT IN THE EU	0.07	II THE COMMISSION'S PRIVATE ENFORCEMENT INITIATIVE	0.08

This book sets out the current state of the law, both at European Union (EU) and Member State level, in relation to actions for damages for loss caused by infringements of Article 101 and 102 of the Treaty on the Functioning of the European Union (TFEU).[1] This two-tier framework for the bringing of damages actions has given rise to the adoption of several Commission papers on the subject,[2] and the reader is referred to these and other publications[3] for the surrounding policy debate. We will discuss and analyse the relevant policy proposals in the chapters that follow, but our purpose is not to make policy recommendations. **0.01**

In terms of methodology, the approach adopted has been to start from EU law, meaning both positive law available in relation to the issues considered as well as any law that can be referred to by analogy, and also policy developments in the field. We then move on to consider the relevant law of the Member States, either used as a means of comparison to EU law, or, as often, in the absence of such law. Finally, we also examine the US system, which is arguably the most mature regime in this field, as a source of comparison to existing, or missing, EU law. **0.02**

As regards national law, we have not exhaustively examined the law of all 27 Member States in relation to each issue. Instead, we have adopted a comparative approach whereby we have selected representative jurisdictions from the major European legal families.[4] This has involved, in the majority of cases, looking at developments from the UK, Germany and France, but we have **0.03**

---

1 Such actions are referred to throughout, in short hand, as '*damages actions*', or '*damages for breach of EU competition law*', or another similar term.

2 See the Commission's Green Paper (COM(2005)672) and accompanying Staff Working Paper (SEC(2005)1732) of 19 December 2005, and its White Paper (COM(2008)165) and accompanying Staff Working Paper (SEC(2008)404) of 2 April 2008. References to the '*Green Paper*' and '*White Paper*' throughout this book are to these documents.

3 See, for example, Ashurst, *Study on the Conditions of Claims for Damages in Case of Infringement of EC Competition Rules*, 31 August 2004, and CEPS/EUR/LUISS, *Making antitrust damages actions more effective in the EU: welfare impact and potential scenarios*, 21 December 2007, which formed the background to the Commission's Impact Assessment of 2 April 2008 (SEC(2008)405) (the '*Impact Assessment*'), adopted at the same time as the White Paper.

4 See further Chapter 2 for the identification of the major European legal families in this regard.

brought in developments from other jurisdictions as and where relevant when considering any given issue. In the present state of law and policy, the UK and Germany are, in some respects, the most fertile grounds in Europe for bringing antitrust damages actions.[5] Moreover, they are of particular interest, as they are currently undergoing extensive antitrust reform.[6]

0.04 It should be noted at the outset that the situation in the EU stands in marked contrast to that in the US, where the contours and parameters of private antitrust enforcement are deeply ingrained in the legal system. As such, the US is by a significant margin ahead of the EU in terms of developing the intricate legal rules concerning private damages actions, such as indirect purchaser standing and passing-on. This can to a large extent be explained by the fact that the vast majority (approximately 90 per cent) of antitrust proceedings in the US are initiated by private parties,[7] while in the EU, by contrast, antitrust enforcement remains the quasi-exclusive preserve of the public enforcement authority. As such, the weight accorded to the objectives to be attained by a system of private damages actions can be, and likely is, to a certain degree different between the two systems.

0.05 In the chapters that follow, we analyse certain key issues on a selective basis. Those issues are, briefly stated, indirect purchaser standing and passing-on, collective redress, and the relevant private international law, namely choice of court and, in the absence of a fully harmonised set of substantive rules as a matter of EU law, the national law applicable to the claim. We have also made a selection of evidential and procedural issues, one of the most important of which is the currently vexed question of access to the file for the purpose of

5 As a general statement of policy in Germany, see for example *Bundeskartellamt*, 'Private Kartellrechtsdurchsetzung: Stand, Probleme, Perspektiven' (2005), which stated that '*Private Kartellrechtsdurchsetzung spielt in Deutschland eine wichtige und wertvolle Rolle*' (which can be translated as '*private antitrust enforcement plays an important and valuable role in Germany*').

6 In May 2012, the German Federal Government published its draft of the 8th amendment to the *Gesetz gegen Wettbewerbsbeschränkungen* (GWB). In the UK, the outstanding recent development is the consultation by the Department for Business, Innovation & Skills (BIS) (BIS, 'Private Actions in Competition Law: A Consultation on Options for Reform', April 2012, and BIS, 'Private Actions in Competition Law: A Consultation on Options for Reform – Government Response', January 2013). The former is referred to throughout as the '*2012 BIS consultation*', and the latter as the '*2013 BIS response*'.

7 See DTI, 'A World Class Competition Regime' (July 2001), at Chapter 8, para 1. The fact that litigation outweighs public enforcement in the US has, however, attracted criticism from some commentators: '*[t]he privatization of antitrust enforcement has many negative consequences. Private litigants often have interests that conflict with those of the intended beneficiaries of antitrust law-i.e. consumers-and can misuse antitrust to facilitate rather than thwart anticompetitive behavior. Further, judges tend to limit their decisions in private litigation to the facts specific to each case. Thus, the fact that most antitrust liability rules are created in private litigation where courts err on the side of deliberate under-inclusion tends to dilute the strength of antitrust norms in public litigation*' (D.A. Crane, 'Antitrust Antifederalism' (2008) 96(1) California Law Review 1, at 38).

substantiating a damages claim. Finally, we conclude with a chapter on the quantification of damages, authored by specialist economists.

This book is not intended as an exhaustive reference work containing details of all competition-related litigation brought in the Member States. Our intention has rather been to introduce the issues, explaining them to an audience which is not necessarily expert, and placing the whole field of competition law litigation in a theoretical, practical and comparative context. **0.06**

I COMPETITION ENFORCEMENT IN THE EU

The antitrust rules contained in the TFEU are enforced both by way of decision taken by competition authorities and other public authorities,[8] and litigation brought before the courts by private parties in relation to an alleged infringement of the competition rules by another private party.[9] While by 'public enforcement' is intended the application of those rules by public authorities, so-called 'private enforcement' consists in their application in civil disputes between private parties and in civil proceedings. Despite the restricted subject-matter of this book, it should be recalled that private enforcement of antitrust rules can take different forms, notably nullity of contracts if they infringe Article 101 TFEU[10] (see Article 101(2) TFEU) or Article 102 TFEU, injunctive relief and damages actions. **0.07**

II THE COMMISSION'S PRIVATE ENFORCEMENT INITIATIVE

There has been an increased interest in the private enforcement of EU competition law in recent years. This process received a significant boost from **0.08**

8 In certain Member States, as is the case in the US, infringement decisions are taken by courts on the introduction of an action by the competition authority. This is the case in Austria, Finland, Ireland and Sweden (in Sweden this model applies only in those cases in which the imposition of fines is sought by the national competition authority). The use of the term 'competition authority' throughout includes reference to courts acting in such a capacity.

9 In the literature and policy documents, these modes of action are often referred to, respectively, as '*public*' and '*private enforcement*' of competition law. In respect of the latter, this may be a misnomer, as the purpose of the action from the point of view of the claimant is not law enforcement, but the specific remedy sought pursuant to a right, whether that be monetary (damages), or, for example, behavioural, such as an action for injunctive relief. The notion of '*private enforcement*' probably derives ultimately from the vocabulary adopted by the Commission in its policy documents, since from the perspective of this institution, competition-related litigation has the primary function of supplementing or, in the wake of the modernisation reform, even replacing the Commission's enforcement activity, where an absence of adequate resources may so require.

10 The editorial style adopted throughout is to use current Treaty references and terminology, even when the source material predates the Lisbon Treaty.

the modernisation of the enforcement of EU competition law carried out around the turn of the millennium, as well as judicial developments at around the same time. Regulation 1/2003[11] aimed at decentralising the enforcement of the antitrust rules by fostering the involvement of national competition authorities and national courts in the application of these rules. Its Article 6 gave the courts of the Member States the power to apply Article 101(3) TFEU, decisions as to the applicability of which had previously been the exclusive competence of the Commission under Article 9(1) of Regulation 17/62.[12] Around the same time, in the *Crehan* judgment of 2001,[13] the Court of Justice[14] (ECJ) ruled that the full effectiveness of Articles 101 and 102 TFEU demands that *everyone* who has suffered a loss because of an infringement of the rules laid down in these articles be able to recover those losses from the infringer.[15]

0.09 As mentioned above, in order to advance its policy aim of facilitating the bringing of antitrust damages claims, the Commission started looking at the issue in 2003 with the launching of the Ashurst study, which led to the adoption of the Green Paper in 2005. This was followed by the White Paper in 2008, and shortly afterwards the Commission attempted to adopt a legislative proposal in the field as almost the final act of the tenure of Commissioner Kroes at DG Competition.[16] In a notorious series of actions, this initiative was apparently pulled from the agenda of the College meeting at the last moment as the result of political pressure put on the President of the Commission.

---

11 Council Regulation (EC) No 1/2003 of 16 December 2002 on the implementation of the rules on competition laid down in Articles 81 and 82 of the Treaty (OJ L 1, 4.1.2003, p 1).

12 Council Regulation No 17 of 6 February 1962, First Regulation implementing Articles 85 and 86 of the Treaty (OJ 13, 21.2.1962, p 204). The Commission had gone further in its White Paper on modernisation of the rules implementing Articles 85 and 86 of the EC Treaty (COM(1999)101), stating that national courts were the most appropriate forum for the enforcement of EU competition law. This is because they are in a position, in contrast to the Commission, to award damages, para 46 '*The national courts for their part are in a better position than the Commission to accede to certain requests by complainants: they can act rapidly through interlocutory proceedings and, unlike the Commission, can grant damages to those who have been the victims of infringements.*'

13 Case C-453/99 *Courage Ltd* v *Bernard Crehan* [2001] ECR I-6297. This judgment is referred to throughout as '*Crehan*'.

14 The abbreviation 'ECJ' is used throughout to refer specifically to the 'Court of Justice', as defined in Article 19(1) of the Treaty on European Union (TEU). 'General Court' is used as per the same provision.

15 As recently reiterated in Case 360/09 *Pfleiderer AG* v *Bundeskartellamt*, judgment of 14 June 2011 (not yet reported) at para 28. Furthermore, in its judgment of 6 November 2012 in Case C-199/11 *Europese Gemeenschap* v *Otis NV and others* (not yet reported), the ECJ extended this principle to cover competition law damages actions brought before a national court by the Commission itself, holding as follows at para 36: '*... EU law must be interpreted as meaning that ... the Commission is not precluded from representing the EU before a national court hearing a civil action for damages in respect of loss caused to the EU by an agreement or practice prohibited by Articles 81 EC and 101 TFEU which may have affected certain public contracts awarded by various institutions and bodies of the EU, there being no need for the Commission to have authorisation for that purpose from those institutions and bodies*'.

16 Proposal for a Council directive on rules governing damages actions for infringements of Articles 81 and 82 of the Treaty, 2009, referred to throughout as the '*draft Directive*'.

After the withdrawal of the so-called 'draft Directive', DG Competition became embroiled in the morass of the Commission's initiative on collective redress, which stretched over several years during the term of the Barroso II Commission, and is indeed still on-going.[17] However, a long-awaited second shot at a legislative initiative, without a provision on collective redress, has recently been adopted,[18] together with a recommendation and a communication on collective redress.[19] Analysis of these documents at the relevant pages throughout this book rounds the story off, for the time being at least, almost exactly ten years since the tender documentation for the Ashurst study was drawn up. **0.10**

While, at first sight, it may be argued that the bringing of private damages actions has not proven to be the panacea that it was envisaged to be,[20] such an assessment is overly simplistic and fails to take into account a number of issues. For example, a significant number of private damages claims is often settled before a final decision is reached.[21] While settlement is to be encouraged as it will often be in the best interests of the parties concerned, this arguably prematurely curtails the development of case law in the area. **0.11**

---

17 See further Chapter 6.

18 Proposal for a directive of the European Parliament and of the Council on certain rules governing actions for damages under national law for infringements of the competition law provisions of the Member States and of the European Union (COM(2013)404). References to '*the proposal*' or '*the Commission proposal*' throughout should be understood as references to this document, unless otherwise stated. At the same time, the Commission adopted a communication on quantifying harm in actions for damages based on breaches of Article 101 or 102 of the Treaty on the Functioning of the European Union (C(2013)3440), as well as an accompanying Staff Working Document ('*Practical Guide*') on quantifying harm (SWD(2013)205).

19 Commission Recommendation on common principles for injunctive and compensatory collective redress mechanisms in the member States concerning violations of rights granted under Union law (C(2013)3539), and Communication on 'towards a European horizontal framework for collective redress' (COM(2013)401). These are referred to as '*the recommendation on collective redress*' and '*the communication on collective redress*' respectively.

20 See, for example, the speech by then Commissioner Kroes, 'Damages Actions for Breaches of EU Competition Rules: Realities and Potentials', Speech/05/613 of 17 October 2005: '*Let me make it clear from the outset that I am convinced that there is great potential in advancing damages cases for breach of the European Competition Rules. Not because I think any of us want to go down the track of litigation culture for its own sake. But rather I think Europe and its businesses and citizens would profit from a stronger competition culture, and an appropriate degree of private enforcement can promote this. A competition culture helps create a fertile environment for business. It contributes to sustainable growth and economic and social welfare for our citizens. And, in other words, it contributes directly to Europe's top priorities.*'

21 Witness in this respect two such illustrative examples from the UK: *Healthcare at Home* v *Genzyme* [2006] CAT 30, and Case No 1078/7/9/07 *The Consumers' Association* v *JJB Sports Plc*. The former was the first time a private action for damages was brought pursuant to section 47A of the Competition Act 1998 following a decision by the Office of Fair Trading (OFT). It was subsequently settled and an order was granted by the Competition Appeal Tribunal (CAT) on 11 January 2007. An interim award was made, but the issues of quantum and exemplary damages were not decided. The latter was the first collective action for damages brought before the CAT under s47B of the Competition Act 1998. Ultimately the case was settled, and the claim withdrawn (see further Chapter 6 for an extensive discussion). For an in-depth study, see B. Rodger, 'Private Enforcement of Competition Law, The Hidden Story: Competition Litigation Settlements in the UK 2000–2005' [2008] ECLR 96.

0.12 Important yet difficult matters of a procedural nature have also occupied the courts with respect to damages actions. As the number of private actions brought before national courts increases, the courts have been faced with novel procedural points of law that have to be addressed. At times, these issues are often litigated all the way to courts of last instance, further prolonging the commencement of any substantive assessment of a private damages claim.

0.13 Moreover, the paucity of extensive and consistent European-wide empirical evidence on the matter belies the fact that there is a growing trend of private damages claims being brought before national courts.[22] For example, the considerable number of cases concerning procedural issues before national courts attests to this growing trend.[23] Indeed, it is the authors' contention that, as the procedural landscape of private actions becomes clearer, claims will be brought in increasing numbers, despite competition law cases being notoriously complex and difficult to run.[24] In that sense, once the docket of procedural cases is cleared, further claims can be brought with a better view as to the procedural requirements. Furthermore, these developments are being accompanied by legislative reform in a number of Member States, such that in our view it is likely that competition law damages actions in the EU will proliferate.[25]

---

22 There have been some useful empirical studies on particular countries such as the United Kingdom. See B. Rodger, 'Competition Law Litigation in the UK Courts: A Study of All Cases to 2004' – Parts I–III in [2006] ECLR 241–248; 279–292 and 341–350, and B. Rodger, 'Competition Law Litigation in the UK Courts: A Study of all Cases 2005–2008' – Parts I and II in [2009] GCLR 93–114 and 136–147; in relation to Germany (albeit limited to two years), see S. Peyer, 'Private Antitrust Litigation in Germany from 2005 to 2007: Empirical Evidence' [2012] Journal of Competition Law and Economics, 8(2) 331–359.

23 As a snapshot, if we take two jurisdictions commonly considered to be among the most advanced in the field of competition law damages actions (England and Wales and Germany), it is evident from the procedural cases that are currently pending that there is an appetite for private litigation. Two such examples in Germany are *CDC Hydrogen Peroxide* v *Akzo* (pending before the *Landgericht* Dortmund), and *HUK Coberg* v *AGC and others* (pending before the *Landgericht* Düsseldorf). In the UK, the Supreme Court recently heard its first competition case, which concerned a procedural issue (*BCL Old Co Limited and others* v *BASF plc and others* [2012] UKSC 45; see further Chapter 5), and has granted leave in another (*Deutsche Bahn AG and others* v *Morgan Crucible Company plc and others*, UKSC 2012/0209, leave granted on 21 December 2012; again, see further Chapter 5).

24 An illustrative example of this is the fact that only recently a Dutch court gave its first substantive damages judgment for an infringement of competition law (see case LJN BZ0403, *Rechtbank* Arnhem, 208812, *Tennet TSO BV* v *ABB BV*, judgment of 16 January 2013).

25 To take but one example, on 1 March 2013 amendments to the Austrian *Bundesgesetz gegen Kartelle und andere Wettbewerbsbeschränkungen* (Austrian federal law on cartels and other restrictions of competition) came into force, changing the law governing the bringing of damages actions in Austria. §37a now provides that the civil courts are bound by a finding of infringement by the *Kartellgericht* (Austrian Cartel Court), other Member State competition authorities, or the Commission: '*Ein Zivilgericht ist an eine in einer rechtskräftigen Entscheidung des Kartellgerichts, der Kommission der Europäischen Union oder einer Wettbewerbsbehörde im Sinn der Verordnung (EG) Nr. 1/2003 getroffene Feststellung, dass ein Unternehmen die in der Entscheidung angeführte Rechtsverletzung rechtswidrig und schuldhaft begangen hat, gebunden.*'

Ultimately, it remains evident that, notwithstanding the slow start, private enforcement in the EU is a topic of the utmost importance to practitioners and in-house counsel because they will increasingly have to advise on the complex matter of antitrust damages exposure. 0.14

1

THE LEGAL FRAMEWORK

I THE CASE LAW OF THE ECJ ON REMEDIES 1.01

II THE MOVE FROM RIGHTS TO REMEDIES 1.07

A Fixing the boundaries between remedial rules and procedural rules *sensu stricto* 1.15

III APPLICATION TO DAMAGES ACTIONS FOR BREACH OF EU COMPETITION LAW 1.17

I THE CASE LAW OF THE ECJ ON REMEDIES

1.01 It is a fundamental principle that, while it creates substantive rights and obligations, EU law depends upon the Member States' courts to give effect to those rights and obligations. Thus Member States are said to have autonomy in the matter of remedies and procedures, subject to the twin conditions of equivalence (meaning that the conditions for a claim based on an infringement of EU law may not be stricter than those for a claim based on similar national law) and minimum effectiveness (meaning that the conditions may not render the enforcement of rights granted by the Treaty unduly difficult). These conditions are themselves derived from the general obligation on Member States to ensure the effective application of EU law and comply with the obligations imposed by former Article 10 EC, now Article 4(3) TEU.[1] This is the case in the absence of legislation governing the matter.

---

1 See, for example, Case 33/76 *Rewe-Zentralfinanz and Rewe-Zentral* v *Landwirtschaftskammer für das Saarland* [1976] ECR 1989. The tests of equivalence and minimum effectiveness were dropped in some later case law in favour of a higher test of adequacy. This line of case law started with Case 14/83 *Von Colson* [1984] ECR 1891 and runs through to Case C-271/91 *Marshall II* [1993] ECR I-4367. It should be noted however that these cases often deal with the interpretation of EU legislation on equal opportunities, such as Council Directives 76/207/EEC and 79/7/EEC, both of which contain an explicit obligation on Member States to introduce into their legal systems '*such measures as are necessary*' to enable all persons who wish to enforce a right under the Directive to be able to '*pursue their claims by judicial process*' (Article 6 of both Directives). This explicit remedial provision may help to explain the Court's willingness to raise the test for remedial effectiveness in this line of case law. Later case law shifted back towards the lower minimum effectiveness test, starting from Case C-338/91 *Steenhorst-Neerings* [1993] ECR I-5475 and running through such judgments as Case C-66/95 *Sutton* [1997] ECR I-2163. The point remains however that no matter which test is used, they are all ways of respecting the principle of remedial autonomy of the Member States and reconciling it with the principle of the *effet utile* of EU law and protection of EU law rights in national courts.

While EU law therefore provides for common rules of substance, the Union legal order does not provide for substantive or procedural rules for the enforcement of EU competition law in private disputes. Furthermore, the ECJ does not have jurisdiction for actions brought by a private party against another private party for damages suffered because of breach of EU competition law. While the ECJ has ruled that the right to the recovery of damages in cases of breach of the EU antitrust rules must be guaranteed as a matter of EU law, it has said itself that in the absence of EU legislation in the field, it is for the Member States and their substantive law to determine the detailed conditions for such a damages claim.[2] **1.02**

The ECJ could, by ruling on references made by national courts, further flesh out what the principles of equivalency and effectiveness mean for the bringing of damages claims based on an infringement of EU competition law.[3] **1.03**

As in other areas, the Union thus depends on the Member States to provide for effective remedies for, and judicial protection of, rights which are created by EU law.[4] There is tension between, on the one hand, the coherence of substantive competition law as embodied in Articles 101 and 102 TFEU and, on the other, the fact that the Union legal order does not have either the procedural or the substantive requirements for granting effective civil redress. **1.04**

So far the creation of remedies in EU law has been for the most part confined to ensuring the effective protection of individuals' rights against Member States. There is case law to this effect in the area of the granting of interim relief while an EU law right is under judicial examination[5]; restitution for charges levied contrary to a provision of EU law by a Member State[6]; and, most importantly in the context of litigation for breach of Articles 101 and 102 TFEU, damages for **1.05**

---

2 *Crehan*, at para 29.

3 See, for example, Joined Cases C-295/04 to C-298/04 *Manfredi* v *Lloyd Adriatico Assicurazioni SpA* [2006] ECR I-6619.

4 See, generally, Van Gerven, Walter, 'Of Rights, Remedies and Procedures' (2000) CMLR 501.

5 Case C-213/89 *R* v *Secretary of State for Transport, ex parte Factortame (Factortame I)* [1990] ECR I-2433.

6 For example Case 68/79 *Hans Just* v *Danish Ministry for Fiscal Affairs* [1980] ECR 501, Case 199/82 *Amministrazione delle Finanze dello Stato* v *SpA San Giorgio* [1983] ECR 3595 and Joined Cases C-192/95 to C-218/95 *Société Comateb and others* v *Directeur Général des Douanes et Droits Indirects* [1997] ECR I-165 (cases concerned with the so-called 'defence' of passing on in this context; briefly, the Court held that the public authority is not required to repay the charges illegally levied if it can show that the trader concerned has passed on the charge to the consumer; in *Société Comateb*, the Court defined the scope of the 'defence' further, holding at para 27 that it applies where '*the charge has been borne in its entirety by another person and the reimbursement of the trader would constitute unjust enrichment*'). See also Case C-188/95 *Fantask* v *Industriministeriet* [1997] ECR I-6783 (no defence of excusable error to restitution of charges levied contrary to EU law). In general, see Van Gerven, *loc. cit.*, 516–521. See also Chapter 3.

breach of EU law by a Member State.[7] The *Crehan* ruling extends this jurisprudence to actions brought by a private party against another private party for breach of EU law, by holding that national courts must under certain circumstances allow individuals to claim damages for breach of EU competition law committed by another individual.

1.06 The idea of EU law remedies in actions against Member States perhaps seems less controversial than that of EU law remedies in actions against private parties. In fact, however, it can be seen that the existence of a remedy in damages against private parties for breach of Articles 101 and 102 TFEU follows from the same principles as give rise to such a remedy against Member States for breaches of other provisions of EU law and is not a revolutionary further step. It is founded on the fact that Articles 101 and 102 TFEU create obligations on and rights for individuals,[8] just as Articles 34 and 49 TFEU,[9] for example, do against Member States.

II THE MOVE FROM RIGHTS TO REMEDIES

1.07 Statements as to the so-called principle of 'procedural autonomy' do not take into account the difficulty in drawing a precise distinction between rights and remedies, and can be seen to have been exposed as over-simple in the case law, which has created, to a limited extent at least, remedies as a matter of EU law.

1.08 Articles 101 and 102 TFEU prohibit certain forms of behaviour, and thus impose obligations on undertakings not to behave in certain ways.[10] Other articles of the Treaty impose obligations on Member States, such as the obligation not to impose quantitative restrictions and measures having equivalent effects (MEQRs) on customs duties on imports contained in Article 34 TFEU, or the obligation not to restrict the freedom to provide services contained in Article 56 TFEU. Certain articles directly give rights to individuals, such as the right to free movement of workers and certain other specific rights flowing from that contained in Article 45 TFEU, especially Article 45(3) TFEU. In fact, Articles 101 and 102 TFEU are almost unique in the Treaty in

7 Joined Cases C-6/90 and C-9/90 *Francovich* v *Italian Republic* [1991] ECR I-5357 and Joined Cases C-46/93 and C-49/93 *Brasserie du Pêcheur* and *Factortame III* [1996] ECR I-1029.

8 Case 127/73 *BRT* v *SABAM* [1974] ECR 51, at para 16.

9 A breach of Article 34 TFEU by Germany was at issue in *Brasserie du Pêcheur*, and a breach of Article 49 TFEU by the UK in *Factortame III*.

10 Article 101(1) TFEU prohibits anti-competitive agreements between undertakings, while Article 102 TFEU prohibits abuses of a dominant position by undertakings.

that they impose obligations not on Member States but on private legal individuals, undertakings.[11]

The question becomes: what further rights flow from the rights and obligations created with respect to undertakings and Member States by the Treaty? The question is of significance because it is not always possible to draw a sharp distinction between rights and remedies. It can be argued that harmonisation of certain conditions relating to remedies in actions for the enforcement of EU law is no more than a necessary consequence of the fact that the Treaty creates in one way or another obligations and rights for individuals and Member States. Harmonisation of remedies in the area of Articles 101 and 102 TFEU therefore, like the harmonisation of remedies in other areas, does not as a general rule offend against the principle of the autonomy of Member States in matters of remedies and procedure.[12] **1.09**

When a right or an obligation is created by law then in order for it to have any effective legal existence the individuals for whose benefit it has been created must be able to enforce it before a court of law.[13] This means not only that such individuals must have access to a court, but also that they must have access to a class of action designed to protect that right.[14] For example, if a legislative measure says that the seller is entitled to recover the price of goods delivered to the buyer but not paid for, then for that right to exist effectively, the seller must be able to take the buyer to court and request that the money be paid to him. Another example might be a law in the field of non-contractual obligations. Such a law might provide, either in legislation or judge-made law, that if A negligently drives his car in such a way as to cause damage to B, then B is entitled to demand from A payment to make up for such damage as he may have suffered. Thus B in this set of circumstances needs to have access to some sort of action for payment in order effectively to enforce A's obligation towards the world to drive carefully. **1.10**

---

11 Cf. also Article 157 TFEU (*'equal pay... for equal work or work of equal value'*; see Case 43/75 *Defrenne* v *Sabena* [1976] ECR 455).

12 There are certain exceptions to this general rule, of course. Exemplary damages are, for example, deemed to run counter to public policy in Germany, while in the same jurisdiction, an opt-out system of collective redress is unconstitutional (see Chapters 5 and 6 respectively).

13 In *Francovich* the court articulates the idea of the effective legal existence of a right or obligation in terms of the obligation on national courts to *'protect the rights which [the provisions of EU law] confer on individuals'* (para 32) and the *'full effectiveness of Community rules'* (para 33) and thus finds it to be *'inherent in the system of the Treaty'* (para 35). It also derives it specifically from Article 4(3) TEU, former Article 10 EC (para 36). This is repeated by the court in *Brasserie du Pêcheur* at para 39. Van Gerven, *loc. cit.* uses *'uniform application'* of EU law as the underpinning principle for his arguments in favour of a certain harmonisation of remedies.

14 Within the scheme of the European Convention on Human Rights (ECHR), the former is guaranteed under Article 6, while the latter is guaranteed under Article 13.

1.11 It should be noted at this point that a law can be enforced in different ways according to whether it confers rights or imposes obligations. In the example of the buyer and the seller, or Article 45(3) TFEU, the legislative measure explicitly confers a right of recovery of the purchase price on the seller (this could be called a 'direct' right). It is a positively expressed, facilitative law which creates by implication a corresponding obligation on the buyer to pay the purchase price. Following from this, it can be said that there exists also a sort of 'secondary' right of the seller to enforce that 'direct' right against the buyer in a court of law when the necessary conditions for the 'direct' right to arise have been shown to have been fulfilled.[15] This secondary right could be called a 'right to enforce'[16] and is closely connected to the seller's remedy. To say that a right has to be enforceable through a legal remedy is very close to saying that the injured party has another 'right' to that remedy; in fact, the confusion in terminology (describing what is essentially a remedy in terms of a right) can be seen to show how closely bound remedies are to pure rights and obligations.

1.12 In the example of the driver, the law does not directly confer any right on B but instead imposes an obligation on A. It is a negatively expressed, prohibitive law, as are most of the articles of the Treaty, including Articles 34, 56, 101 and 102 TFEU. The question then is how to analyse the operation of this obligation in terms of 'direct' rights, 'rights to enforce' and remedies. The jurisprudence of the ECJ as expressed in such judgments as *Van Gend en Loos*[17] and *Francovich* states that rights in EU law can arise expressly under provision of the Treaty, but also as a result of obligations imposed by the Treaty upon individuals, Member States or the EU institutions. Thus rights can arise by implication from the existence of obligations. In the factual scenario of *Van Gend en Loos*, the right flowing from the obligation contained in Article 34 TFEU would be the right to move goods across national borders without having to pay customs duties. This type of right may be classed as a 'direct' right, although it is not directly imposed by the law itself. It is certainly more substantive than a 'right to enforce' and distinguishable from the remedy required to protect it. The 'right to enforce' that right through a legal remedy then arises at a further, though necessarily consequential, stage.

1.13 The example of the driver is somewhat different. It is very difficult to express any 'right' for B which flows from the obligation on A without referring to a

15 Eilmansberger, Thomas, 'The Relationship between Rights and Remedies in EC Law: In Search of the Missing Link' (2004) CMLR 1199, at 1238 ff. uses a similar schema (*'primary obligations/rights'* and *'secondary obligations/rights'*).

16 Thus the court in *Francovich* at para 38 speaks of a *'right to reparation'* and in *Brasserie du Pêcheur* at para 67 of *'the right to reparation which flows directly from Community law'*.

17 Case 26/62 *Van Gend en Loos* [1963] ECR 1.

remedy sought by B. B's 'right' in this situation is to have such damage as is caused to him by A made good by A.[18] In this situation there does not seem to be an intermediate right arising from the obligation imposed in the way identified by the court in *Van Gend en Loos* and *Francovich*. Instead, the only 'right' which exists is B's 'right to enforce' A's obligation against him. In this case the link between rights and remedies is even closer and when a court speaks of protecting the rights of individuals, in such a situation it can only be referring to the protection of a 'right' to a remedy, that is, the remedy itself.

This connection is inherent in the idea of directly effective rights itself. The court in *Van Gend en Loos* spoke of the directly effective rights arising from the obligations on Member States contained in Article 34 TFEU. The Court defines direct effect in the terms of the creation of rights which '*the national court must protect*', meaning rights that the individual can plead before a court of law.[19] This does not define the content of the right in a substantive way. Instead, it shows that the content of the 'right', such as it is, will depend on the way in which it is pleaded by the individual concerned, which in turn will be heavily determined by the remedy that the individual is seeking from that court. **1.14**

A Fixing the boundaries between remedial rules and procedural rules *sensu stricto*

Van Gerven[20] differentiates between, on the one hand, the 'constitutive' conditions of the remedy, which are the same as the 'substantive' conditions for the underlying right to arise, and on the other hand, 'executive' remedial rules, which are required to implement the 'constitutive' elements of the remedy.[21] He therefore distinguishes between two different types of remedial rule, the former which arise as a necessary consequence of the existence of the right in the way outlined above, and the latter which are closer to pure procedural rules. He argues that it is necessary to have complete harmonisation of the former in order to complement the existence of substantive EU law rights which must be the same throughout the Union; while in the case of the latter it is necessary only that they obey the adequate protection principle. He suggests that this **1.15**

18 Cf. Article 1382 of the French *Code civil*: '*Tout fait quelconque de l'homme, qui cause à autrui un dommage, oblige celui par la faute duquel il est arrivé à le réparer.*'

19 See further the discussion at para 2.14 of the Court's answers to the first and second questions in *Crehan*.

20 *Loc. cit.*, especially 524–525.

21 This distinction corresponds to that between the so-called 'remedial' aspects of the civil law governing damages claims for breach of EU competition law, and the purely procedural aspects. The former will be determined by the civil law applicable to the claim, while the latter will be the law of the forum hearing the claim. On these issues, see further Chapter 7.

would strike an appropriate balance between the need for a certain harmonisation of remedies, and respect for the traditional principle of the autonomy of Member States in terms of remedies and procedures.

1.16 The scheme Van Gerven proposes is, however, not always consistent. In his draft proposal for a harmonising regulation,[22] he appears to include in the regulation issues relating to the '*form and extent*' of the remedy, such as the heads of damage which can be recovered, which are described as '*executive*' rules in the earlier paper, which suggests perhaps that he does not wish to insist on this distinction any more. It would seem that such a distinction is not only hard to make, but also might restrict the scope of harmonisation unduly, since it is precisely rules of an '*executive*' character, such as heads of damage rules, standing rules and rules on interest, which also need harmonisation in order to promote as much as possible harmonised private enforcement of the competition rules before national courts. It is not enough simply to assert that an EU law remedy of damages for breach of Articles 101 and 102 TFEU must exist as a matter of principle without also fleshing out that remedy in any harmonising legislation in order to ensure precisely that, as far as possible, such harmonisation of remedies has as much practical impact as possible throughout the Union.

III APPLICATION TO DAMAGES ACTIONS FOR BREACH OF EU COMPETITION LAW

1.17 The conclusion to be drawn is that whenever a legal system creates an obligation or a right, by necessity there must also arise an effective means for the injured party to enforce compliance with the behaviour required ('right to enforce'), whether that is a right to enforce a 'direct' right imposed by a facilitative, positively expressed law, or the right to enforce an obligation imposed by a prohibitive, negatively expressed law against another party. This means could be recovery of compensation (or damages), as in the driver example, or performance of a (contractual) obligation, as in the buyer and seller example. Specific performance and damages are usually classed as 'remedies', and while this classification may have its uses, it can be seen that remedies at least in this sense arise as a necessary consequence of the creation of a legal right or obligation, once the (separate) right of access to a court is added. This must be the case, or else the right would have no effective legal existence. These arguments apply equally to all obligations and rights created by the treaty,

22 Van Gerven, Walter, 'Substantive Remedies For the Private Enforcement of EC Antitrust Rules Before National Courts', in *European Competition Law Annual 2001: Effective Private Enforcement of EC Antitrust Law* (Ehlermann, Claus-Dieter and Atanasiu, Isabela (eds), Hart, Oxford/Portland, 2003), at 53, 90 (Annex 2).

regardless of whether they are obligations imposed on Member States or on private undertakings.

Therefore a single remedy or set of remedies as a matter of EU law for private enforcement actions under Articles 101 and 102 TFEU need not be seen as a major legal revolution. To the extent that the existence and extent of such remedies might be clarified by legislation or by case law of the ECJ, such developments would be doing little more than, in the first instance, making clear and explicit something which must arise from Articles 101 and 102 TFEU of the Treaty. What makes the situation new is firstly the fact that Articles 101 and 102 TFEU are unusual in the Treaty in that they create obligations for private undertakings and not Member States, and secondly that private litigation for breach of Articles 101 and 102 TFEU was until relatively recently hindered by the Commission's monopoly over constitutive decisions on the application or otherwise of Article 101(3) TFEU to agreements and other concerted practices. **1.18**

2

THE UNDERLYING RIGHT TO DAMAGES

I THE ESTABLISHMENT OF THE RIGHT TO DAMAGES AS A MATTER OF EU LAW: *COURAGE V CREHAN* 2.03
- A The proceedings in the English courts 2.03
- B The reference to the ECJ 2.12
- C Further developments: the *Manfredi* judgment 2.16

II NATIONAL LAW: LEGAL BASES FOR DAMAGES ACTIONS FOR BREACH OF EU COMPETITION LAW 2.18
- A Common law 2.19
  - 1 England and Wales 2.19
  - 2 Ireland 2.22
- B Civil law 2.24
  - 1 Germanic systems of law 2.24
    - a Denmark 2.24
    - b Germany 2.26
    - c Greece 2.33
    - d Latvia 2.36
    - e Lithuania 2.39
    - f The Netherlands 2.44
  - 2 Romanistic systems of law 2.47
    - a Belgium 2.47
    - b France 2.50
    - c Italy 2.55
    - d Spain 2.60
- C The tortious nature of litigation for breach of EU competition law 2.62
- D The national law analysis: the fault requirement 2.68

2.01 This chapter gives an outline of the legal basis for claims for damages for breach of EU competition law both as a matter of EU law and as a matter of national law, where relevant. A certain number of Member State jurisdictions have been selected, it being excessively difficult to include all 27 within the scope of this work, but with a view to a classification along comparative lines and to a representation of at least some important legal systems.

2.02 As regards the issue from an EU law perspective, a summary of the seminal case on the issue of the underlying right to damages, the *Crehan* judgment of the ECJ, is given, along with a description of the accompanying national proceedings. We have focussed on the *Crehan* proceedings as it was in this case, as a result of the reference to the ECJ from the English Court of Appeal, that the principle of the availability of a remedy in damages for loss caused by a breach of EU competition law was first established. In addition, we go on to outline the significant developments in this jurisprudence established by the ECJ in *Manfredi*, the other important EU law ruling of general scope in the field to date.

I THE ESTABLISHMENT OF THE RIGHT TO DAMAGES AS A MATTER OF EU LAW: *COURAGE* V *CREHAN*

A The proceedings in the English courts

In the initial proceedings, the defendant was a publican who had entered into a tied house agreement with the claimant under which the defendant was bound to purchase certain quantities of beer from the claimant at fixed prices and the claimant leased the pub to the defendant in return for a rent. The claimant sued for outstanding arrears of rent and the defendant pleaded in his defence that the tying agreement was in breach of EU competition law, and counterclaimed for damages arising as a result of that breach. **2.03**

The Commission had issued decisions in relation to similar tying agreements on the same market, namely the market for the wholesale supply of beer in the UK, and had, in accordance with the substantive tests laid out in *Delimitis II*,[1] found that that market was foreclosed, but nevertheless granted exemptions pursuant to Article 101(3) TFEU. In the present case, which was one of many sets of proceedings brought or threatened by pub tenants against the claimants, the Commission had indicated that it considered that the tying agreement in question was in breach of Article 101(1) TFEU, but that it was considering issuing an exemption under Article 101(3) TFEU, despite the fact that the claimants had withdrawn their notification without any decision having been made in the case. **2.04**

In the initial proceedings in the English courts, the High Court held as a preliminary issue that a party to an unlawful agreement, that is, including an agreement found to be in violation of EU competition law, has no right to sue for damages from another party to the same agreement.[2] Accordingly, it dismissed the proceedings. This point was settled by the reference to the ECJ, which is discussed in more detail below. The proceedings then returned to the English courts, where they were litigated again in the High Court[3] and in the Court of Appeal[4] and House of Lords[5] on issues relating primarily to whether there had in fact been a substantive breach of Article 101 TFEU. **2.05**

1 Case C-234/89 *Delimitis* v *Henninger Bräu AG* [1991] ECR I-935.

2 Judgment of 25 November 1998 in *Courage Ltd* v *Crehan* [1998] EWHC 281 (Ch), applying the decision of the Court of Appeal in *Gibbs Mew plc* v *Gemmell* [1998] EuLR 588.

3 Judgment of 26 June 2003 in *Crehan* v *Inntrepreneur and others* [2003] EWHC 1510 (Ch).

4 Judgment of 21 May 2004 in *Crehan* v *Inntrepreneur and others* [2004] EWCA 637.

5 Judgment of 19 July 2006 in *Inntrepreneur and others* v *Crehan* [2006] UKHL 38.

2.06 In these proceedings, the English High Court found that the agreement between the claimant and the defendant did not infringe Article 101(1) TFEU. The Court of Appeal overturned that finding. It held, referring to former Article 10 EC (now Article 4(3) TEU), as well as policy arguments, that the High Court should have followed Commission authority as evidenced by the decisions taken in related cases dealing with the same market, as well as the position it had taken in discussions with the claimant in relation to the agreement in question.

2.07 The judgment of the English Court of Appeal is notable in particular for the teleological style of argumentation,[6] where the Court reasons for the duty of the national court to follow Commission authority from the principle of loyal cooperation contained in Article 4(3) TEU and develops this through other texts, such as former Article 3 EC, setting out the objectives of the Treaty, and the notice on cooperation with national courts.[7] This is reminiscent of the style of argumentation used by the ECJ itself, and could be seen as a development towards a more 'Europeanised' style of judgment from a national court.

2.08 In its sixth heading of the issues relevant to the appeal, which it describes as whether or not the damages sought by the claimant are in respect of a '*type of loss against which he is protected by Article [101]*', the Court of Appeal appears to be pushing for the introduction of something like the US antitrust principle of antitrust injury.[8] It also recalls the *Schutznorm* concept of German law. Although this is an interesting idea and perhaps desirable as a legal rule in European as well as US private enforcement, this case is perhaps not the best example of how such a rule might function to block undesirable claims. The test is satisfied because the defendant's injury is of such a type as is intended to be protected by antitrust law, even if he did not himself suffer injury directly from the infringement in question in the sense that he was not himself foreclosed from any market.[9] The Court of Appeal may better have explored this point in

---

6 See for example paras 79ff.

7 Commission notice on the co-operation between the Commission and the courts of the EU Member States in the application of Articles 81 and 82 EC (OJ C 101, 27.4.2004, p 54).

8 See para 156 of the judgment of the Court of Appeal, citing the judgment of the US Supreme Court in *Brunswick Corporation* v *Pueblo Bowl-O-Mat, Inc.* (1977) 97 US 690, the leading case on the US federal law theory of antitrust injury (see further Chapter 3).

9 See paras 163–168 of the judgment of the Court of Appeal, where the Court equates this issue with the second question addressed by the ECJ in the *Crehan* reference (see further below). As noted above, the claimant's injury was not suffered as a result of the infringement at stake (foreclosure), as the Court of Appeal notes. It searches hard in the judgment of the ECJ for the notion that the ECJ intended the specific injury suffered by the claimant to have been intended to have been protected, coming to the tentative conclusion that '*the effect of the ECJ decision was to put its imprimatur on the particular claim of Mr. Crehan*' (para 167). It is submitted that this search is essentially fruitless. The simplified questions put by the ECJ at para 17 of its judgment, reformulating the references, simply do not take this issue into account. The ECJ appears to have been more concerned to

terms of a causation issue, possibly as a direct injury requirement. The operability of an antitrust injury test as a matter of EU law would be complicated by the concept of direct effect on which the defendant's claim to damages is built (see further the judgment of the ECJ in these proceedings, below).[10] The English High Court got close to this position without putting it in those terms.[11] The Court of Appeal did deal with causation as the seventh heading of the issues, following the *obiter* conclusion of the trial judge that the claimant would not have suffered damage without the infringing tying agreement, but not that the injury was suffered as a *direct* result of the infringement in question. Such a finding would have played the role of an antitrust injury requirement, as noted above, but may not actually have been possible to arrive at in the proceedings in question. The English courts relied heavily on expert witnesses to try to guess whether the claimant's business would have survived free of the tying agreement, without considering the legal question of whether the loss was actually connected to the type of infringement in question.

Finally, the eighth heading of the issues shows the Court of Appeal grappling with the quantification of the damages themselves. The Court of Appeal went into some detail, reducing the damages considerably from the figure arrived at *obiter* by the High Court of £1,311,500 to £131,336, and postponed a decision on the issue of interest on the damages to a later hearing. As regards the assessment of damages, the Court of Appeal allowed the award of damages for loss of profit as well as actual loss, but dated the assessment of that loss to the time of the loss, that is, the date of surrender of the pub leases, and not to the time of judgment, that is, some ten years later, as the High Court had done, on the grounds that the uncertainties involved in assessing loss in the intervening 2.09

address the question of principle in EU law as to the availability of a remedy in damages for breach of EU law between private parties (see further below). An antitrust injury concept in national or EU law may be desirable, but this is not the place to find it.

10 It could in fact be argued that the entire analytical framework of the judgment of the ECJ in *Crehan* is mistaken. The Court looks at the contractual relationship and then decides that a contracting party can claim relief as long as it does not bear '*significant responsibility*' for that breach. In fact, as noted by the English courts when applying that decision, the contractual issue has nothing to do with the injury suffered. The infringement is a foreclosure, which was not something felt by the claimant. In fact, the ECJ should have framed the issue as one of pure public policy: the infringement of the antitrust rules intervenes from outside the contractual relationship to produce harm, which is suffered by the claimant (that is, a purely tortious claim, classified under English law as breach of statutory duty). Looked at in this way, it becomes clear that in fact some kind of antitrust injury test to link the harm suffered with the infringement in question is necessary (this is the '*breach of statutory duty*' argument referred to by the English Court of Appeal).

11 See para 227 of the judgment of the English High Court: '*The CJEC was specifically considering whether a publican lessee … could have a claim for damages on the ground that his lessor's conduct infringed article [101]. By giving the answer that he could the court must have taken it for granted that this particular defence being put forward by Inntrepreneur could not be maintained. Otherwise the court would have been wasting its time, and would have known it.*'

ten-year period were simply too great.[12] Its award is made up of the actual loss and lost profits up to the date of surrender, plus the value of the leases as at that date had the businesses been successful. The award also bears interest.[13]

2.10 In the event, on appeal the House of Lords held that the trial judge had not been wrong to make his own assessment of the breach of EU competition law. To this extent, the liability of the defendants for damages was overturned, and the findings of the Court of Appeal in this regard became irrelevant. Lord Hoffman specifically notes in his judgment that the issues relating to damages were not argued before the House of Lords, and consequently did not arise for decision.[14]

2.11 Despite this, the reference to the ECJ in the original proceedings produced the finding as to the availability of an EU law remedy in damages for breach of EU competition law,[15] which will be discussed in more detail below.

B The reference to the ECJ

2.12 One of the questions referred to the ECJ by the English Court of Appeal in the initial proceedings was the question of principle as to whether or not an undertaking is entitled to claim damages for loss suffered as a result of a breach of Article 101 TFEU under EU law.[16] The court did not answer that question specifically but merged it with two other questions. Firstly, whether or not a party to a contract which is in breach of Article 101 TFEU may rely upon that article to seek relief from the other contracting party,[17] and secondly, whether a rule of national law that '*parties to an illegal agreement cannot claim damages from*

12 See para 180 of the judgment of the Court of Appeal.

13 A large part of this approach was confirmed by the later judgment of the ECJ in *Manfredi* (see further Chapter 5), where the Court held that, in the case of a claim for damages for breach of EU competition law, under the principle of effectiveness the claimant must be able to claim both actual loss (*damnum emergens*) and loss of profit (*lucrum cessans*), plus interest (paras 95 and 100). The Court did not however consider the issue of the date at which the assessment of damages should be made.

14 The judgment of the House of Lords, at para 73. Specifically, as regards the damages-related aspects of the proceedings, the Court of Appeal had granted leave to appeal to the appellant on the type of loss falling within the scope of Article 101 TFEU, and to the respondent on the quantification of damage. See further Chapter 4 for a discussion of the Court of Appeal judgment in these proceedings.

15 For a discussion of the debate about the nature of the right in damages before the *Crehan* ruling of the ECJ, see A. Komninos, *EC Private Antitrust Enforcement: Decentralised Application of EC Competition Law by National Courts* (Hart, Oxford/Portland, 2008), at 167–169. The analysis which follows concerning the link between the substantive rights laid down in the TFEU regarding competition law and the corresponding private law remedy in damages developed by the ECJ builds on the conceptual discussion in Chapter 1 of the intrinsic link between rights and remedies.

16 Second question, para 16.

17 First question, para 16.

the other party for loss caused to him by being a party to the illegal agreement' is compatible with EU law.[18]

The court answered that third question in the negative, holding that an absolute rule prohibiting a party to an illegal contract from claiming relief in reliance on his own participation in that contract was indeed precluded by EU law.[19] In order to come to that conclusion, the court had to answer the other two connected questions as logically prior steps. The third question only arises if the first question can be answered in the affirmative in principle, though the issue is rather circular in that a rule of the kind at issue in the third question would preclude a positive answer to the first question if it were allowed to stand. Again, the second question has to be answered affirmatively in principle for the third question to arise for consideration. Therefore although the court merges consideration of the three questions, different steps in its reasoning corresponding to the different questions can be identified, which helps in crystallising the reasoning and effects of the judgment.[20] **2.13**

The court based the answer to the first question, that is, the entitlement of individuals who are party to an agreement in breach of Article 101 TFEU to rely on that breach before a national court, on a variety of grounds. Firstly, the general principle that the rights and obligations on individuals created by that Article must be protected by the national courts and therefore there has to be access to a remedy for that enforcement.[21] Secondly, the fact that parties to an agreement in breach of Article 101 TFEU can rely on the nullity sanction of **2.14**

18 Third question, para 16. It can be seen that the first and third questions are indeed very close. The quotation is from the judgment of the English Court of Appeal in *Gibbs Mew*.

19 Para 28.

20 Thus paras 19–24 are addressed to the first question, and paras 25–27 to the second question; since they are both answered in the affirmative, there can be no other possible answer to the third question than a negative one, which the court then states in para 28. Van Gerven, Walter, 'Substantive Remedies For the Private Enforcement of EC Antitrust Rules Before National Courts', *loc cit.* regrets the fact that AG Mischo in his Opinion in the case merged the answers to the second and third questions as this obscured a clear answer on the question of the principle of the existence of a damages remedy in EU law against individuals, but it could be argued that the court, although it also merges the answers to the questions, does deal with them in a logical way so that the answer to the underlying question of principle is clear. It makes sense to merge the questions since they are so closely connected and the answer to the third follows inevitably from affirmative answers to the first two, as the court presents it in its judgment.

21 Paras 19–20 (referring to the general statement of principles at para 31 of *Francovich*) and para 23. This illustrates how the principle of the existence of a remedy as a necessary consequence of the creation of a right or obligation by a law applies equally to the enforcement of obligations against individuals as to that against Member States, though it is worth noting that in this judgment the formulation is not as wide as in *Francovich* in that the court does not talk of liability for breach of EU law by individuals, but liability only for breach of Article 101. However, it is not a difficult progression from there to liability for breach of other provisions of EU law or breach of EU law in general since the same underlying principles can be applied across the board.

Article 101(2) TFEU.[22] It should be noted that this ground relates specifically to the issue of whether a party to the contract can claim damages and the argument about whether or not the illegality of that contract precludes relief, as per the English rule.[23] Thirdly, the fact that Article 101(1) TFEU confers directly effective rights on individuals '*which national courts must safeguard*'.[24]

2.15 As to the second question on principle, the court reverts to the arguments of the *effet utile* of EU law and the need to protect the rights which it confers[25] as the grounds for holding that such protection would be '*put at risk if it were not open to any individual to claim damages for loss caused to him by a contract or by conduct liable to restrict or distort competition*'.

C Further developments: the *Manfredi* judgment

2.16 The Court in *Manfredi* also made a very strong statement of the principle of the availability of damages for breach of EU competition law as a matter of EU law.[26] However, it is worth noting that that statement in this judgment was bound up with a similarly affirmative statement as to a causation requirement (hedged with the usual caveats as to equivalence and effectiveness). However, the causation requirement appears to have been introduced as a result of the way in which the question on principle was framed.[27] In all other respects, the reasoning as to the foundation of the damages action in EU law follows the reasoning set out in *Crehan*.

2.17 The *Manfredi* judgment built on the *Crehan* judgment in specifying certain of the further procedural conditions for damages actions. In relation to causation, as already noted, the Court held that a '*causal relationship between the harm and an agreement or practice prohibited under Article [101 TFEU]*' was required as a condition for an award of damages. In addition, the Court set out conditions

22 Paras 21–22.

23 Thus the discussion of principle is tempered to some extent by the merging of the three questions.

24 Para 23. This point did not perhaps merit inclusion as a separate point as the court presents it since it is rather part of the first grounds that the Treaty creates rights which need protection. Indeed the point at paras 19–20 that the Treaty creates rights and obligations which in this case in particular are vital to the functioning of the common market is incomplete in this context without the addition of the point that such rights require protection by national courts. This part of the Court's reasoning is referred to by the *Manfredi* judgment at para 39 and again at para 58.

25 Para 25; the protection of rights argument is in effect repeated from para 23 (see previous footnote). This part of the Court's reasoning is referred to in the *Manfredi* judgment at para 60.

26 Para 61.

27 See para 20 (Joined Cases C-295/04 to C-297/04), second question, and para 21 (Case C-298/04), third question, which are identical, assuming '*a causal relationship between the agreement or concerted practice and the harm*'.

relating to the court competent to hear such actions,[28] limitation periods[29] and the availability of punitive damages and other aspects of damage quantification.[30]

II NATIONAL LAW: LEGAL BASES FOR DAMAGES ACTIONS FOR BREACH OF EU COMPETITION LAW

In this part we will briefly survey the legal bases for damages actions for breach of EU competition law in the Member States. In doing so, we use a rough division of the legal systems of the Member States into the major families.[31] As this analysis shows, the preponderance of national legal systems, if not all, classifies damages actions for breach of EU competition law as tortious, rather than contractual, in nature. We will also briefly examine certain issues in relation to the tort law regimes which govern damages actions for breach of EU competition law, as they underpin consideration of the substantive issues which follows in the succeeding chapters. **2.18**

A Common law

1 *England and Wales*

The leading case in England and Wales is *Crehan*, discussed above. The case was heard and decided as an action for breach of statutory duty, the statutory duty in question being compliance with the EU competition rules as incorporated into English law by virtue of section 2(1) of the European Communities Act 1972,[32] clearly showing that such actions in English law are classified as tortious. **2.19**

This said, the principle that infringements of competition law can give rise to claims for damages in the English courts had been undisputed since the **2.20**

28 The second question in Case C-298/04, at paras 70–72.

29 See paras 77–82, especially para 78 and the '*practically impossible or excessively difficult*' test set out in para 82.

30 Paras 89 and following.

31 The methodology used for this classification follows the rough division, as far as is relevant for European legal systems, proposed by Zweigert, Konrad and Kötz, Hein, *An Introduction to Comparative Law* (3rd edition, trans. Weir, T., Clarendon Press, Oxford, 1998), at 73.

32 Section 2(1) reads: '*All such rights, powers, liabilities, obligations and restrictions from time to time created or arising by or under the Treaties, and all such remedies and procedures from time to time provided for by or under the Treaties, as in accordance with the Treaties are without further enactment to be given legal effect or used in the United Kingdom shall be recognised and available in law, and be enforced, allowed and followed accordingly; and the expression "enforceable EU right" and similar expressions shall be read as referring to one to which this subsection applies.*'

decision of the House of Lords in *Garden Cottage Foods*, a case pertaining to an abuse of a dominant position.[33]

2.21 Damages actions for breaches of EU competition law may be brought in the Competition Appeal Tribunal under section 47A of the Competition Act 1998 as a follow-on action only, or as either a follow-on or a stand-alone action in the Chancery Division of the High Court.[34]

2 Ireland

2.22 Similar to the competition law framework in its common law neighbour, claims for damages in Irish competition law also find their legal basis in statute. Section 14 of the Competition Act 2002 allows claimants to pursue actions for damages in the appropriate civil court. Such actions are also tortious in nature, being based on the general rules on breach of statutory duty.

2.23 The law governing competition law litigation in Ireland has recently changed as a result of the adoption of the Competition (Amendment) Act 2012, which entered into force on 3 July 2012. Under the provisions of this Act, where the courts, deciding on a proceeding brought by the national competition authority,[35] have made a finding that there was a breach of competition law, claimants in a damages action no longer have to establish the breach, but only have to prove loss and causation, and quantify the damage suffered.

B Civil law

1 Germanic systems of law

a Denmark

2.24 The *Konkurrenceloven* (Competition Act) does not contain any explicit provisions regarding the right to claim damages,[36] although it can be argued that it contains indirect recognition of the right to claim damages under, for example,

33 *Garden Cottage Foods Limited* v *Milk Marketing Board* [1984] AC 130. This established the broad position. The litigation in *Crehan* focussed on the narrower point of the ability of a party to an agreement which violated EU competition law to sue for damages from another party to that agreement.

34 The UK Government has, however, decided to extend the CAT's jurisdiction so as to allow it to hear stand-alone and follow-on cases, and to enable the courts to transfer all types of competition law case to the CAT and *vice versa* (see the 2013 BIS response, at para 4.5).

35 As noted above, the Irish competition enforcement system differs from that in place in many other Member States in that the national competition authority does not have the power to make a finding of infringement of EU or Irish competition law. Only the courts can. The national competition authority can bring cases alone, or in conjunction with the Director of Public Prosecutions.

36 *Bekendtgørelse af konkurrenceloven* (LBK No 23 of 17 January 2013).

§25, which contains specific provisions on the time-barring of claims for damages for breach of competition law.

Claims for damages for competition law infringements are tortious in nature under the general provisions of Danish tort law. According to the preparatory documents accompanying the *Konkurrenceloven*, it follows from general principles of Danish law that when a legal or natural person suffers loss due to an illegal restriction of competition, that loss can form the basis for a civil claim in damages. This was confirmed in the *Ekko/Elektrolux* case,[37] where it was held that a party injured as a result of an infringement of the *Konkurrenceloven* could claim damages, provided that the loss was not passed on. **2.25**

b Germany

German competition law is contained in the *Gesetz gegen Wettbewerbsbeschränkungen* (GWB). Damages claims for infringement of competition law are based on §33 GWB, which constitutes a specific legal basis for tort claims for competition law infringements. Prior to the entry into force of the seventh amendment to the GWB on 1 July 2005, claims for infringement of EU competition law were based on the general tort law provision of §823(2) of the Civil Code (*Bürgerliches Gesetzbuch*, BGB). As a result of the adoption of the seventh amendment, infringements of EU competition law are now included in the scope of §33 GWB, and are therefore based, like claims for infringement of German competition law, on that more specific statutory rule. **2.26**

§33(4) GWB provides that in actions for damages, the claimant may refer to the decision of an antitrust authority or to the infringement of competition law. This means that claims for damages can be brought where Article 101[38] or Article 102[39] TFEU has been breached. **2.27**

It should be noted that, in German law, fault has only a subjective meaning. This can be seen from the text of §823 BGB. In §823(1), fault is defined as either intentional ('*vorsätzlich*') or negligent ('*fahrlässig*') behaviour. The term fault ('*Verschulden*') is not introduced until §823(2), where behaviour without fault is contrasted to behaviour with fault. This makes it clear that illegality *per se* is contrasted with subjective fault, that is, intentional or negligent behaviour as per §823(1). This is further made clear again by §823(1), which contrasts intentional or negligent behaviour with illegality ('*widerrechtlich*'). The upshot **2.28**

---

37 *Ekko A/S/Elektrolux Home Products Denmark A/S, Miele A/S and BSH Hvidedvarer A/S Home Appliance Group*, judgment of the *Sø- og Handelsretten* (Maritime and Commercial Court) of 15 October 2004.

38 See also §1 GWB, the German law equivalent of Article 101 TFEU.

39 See also §§19 and 20 GWB, the German law equivalents of Article 102 TFEU.

of this analysis is that fault in German law has only a subjective sense, and not the objective sense of pure illegality which is possible in French law.

2.29 Exactly this analysis applies in the field of competition, where, under §33(3) GWB, a party is liable in damages for a breach of competition law which is '*vorsätzlich oder fahrlässig*'.[40]

2.30 According to §33(1) GWB, the '*party concerned*' ('*dem Betroffenen*') is entitled to claim damages. The '*party concerned*' may be a competitor or another market participant ('*oder sonstiger Marktktbeteiligter*').[41]

2.31 Claims for damages resulting from an anti-competitive agreement brought by a person who is party to that anti-competitive agreement are also tortious in nature. The invalidity of anti-competitive agreements is established by §134 BGB in conjunction with §1 GWB.

2.32 In addition, the concept of own fault as a grounds for a reduction of awardable damages is also recognised in German law.[42]

c Greece

2.33 The legal basis for claims for damages for breach of EU competition law in Greek law is Article 914 of the Αστικός Κώδικας (Civil Code), which provides that any person who intentionally or negligently causes harm to another person is liable to pay compensation for the damage caused to that person.[43]

2.34 Claims for damages resulting from an anti-competitive agreement by a person who is party to that anti-competitive agreement are also tortious in nature. Under Article 174 of the Αστικός Κώδικας, '*[a]ny contract which contravenes a legal provision that prohibits a particular conduct is rendered, in case no more specific provision is applicable, void*'. In addition, Article 180 of the Αστικός Κώδικας provides that a void contract should be considered to have never existed.

---

40 The same is true of Finnish competition law. Under section 20(1) of the *Kilpailulaki* (Competition Act, No 948/2011), a right in damages lies against a party which has '*intentionally or negligently*' ('*tahallaan tai huolimattomuudesta*') violated national or EU competition law.

41 On the definition of the party with standing to bring competition law damages actions under German law, see further Chapter 3.

42 §254 BGB. Such a rule is found in many European legal systems (see the further analyses below), including the common law legal systems, where it is known as contributory negligence. As a matter of EU law, such a notion could be said to find support in the doctrine of '*significant responsibility*', as laid down by the ECJ in the *Crehan* ruling (see further below).

43 This position was confirmed by Decision No 369/V/2007 of the Hellenic Competition Commission in case *NESTLE ΕΛΛΑΣ Α.Ε.*

Article 330 of the Αστικός Κώδικας also establishes an own fault rule essentially equivalent to the Lithuanian rule referred to below. **2.35**

d Latvia

Claims for damages for a competition law infringement are based on Article 21 of the *Konkurences likums* (Latvian competition act), which explicitly establishes the right to claim damages for breach of competition law. **2.36**

Claims for damages resulting from an anti-competitive agreement by a person who is party to that anti-competitive agreement are also tortious in nature. That is so because Article 11 of the *Konkurences likums* establishes that agreements prohibited under competition law are null and void and thus are considered never to have legally existed. **2.37**

The own fault concept as a grounds for a reduction of awardable damages is also recognised by Latvian law.[44] **2.38**

e Lithuania

The legal basis for claims for damages for breach of national and EU competition law in Lithuanian law is found in Articles 46(1) and 50(1) of the *Konkurencijos Įstatymas* (Lithuanian competition act),[45] and Articles 6.245, 6.246 and 6.263 of the *Civilinis Kodeksas* (Lithuanian Civil Code).[46] Those provisions establish the legal basis for civil law damages claims, which applies also to breaches of Lithuanian and EU competition law. **2.39**

The basic principle in Lithuanian law behind such liability is that every person has the duty to act in such a way as not to cause damage to another person and, accordingly, that any harm caused as a result of illegal action must be compensated by the person responsible upon a claim being made by the injured party (that is, a general tort law doctrine). Broadly, the conditions for tort liability are similar to those found in most European legal systems. The claimant is required to show (i) illegal action; (ii) fault (understood objectively and thus essentially presupposed by illegality); (iii) the presence of damage; and (iv) the existence of a causal link between the illegal conduct and the damage. A recent judgment of the Lithuanian High Court has confirmed that all four aspects need to be proved for a successful claim in damages.[47] **2.40**

---

44 See Article 1642 of the *Civillikums* (Civil Code).

45 No VIII-1099, 23 March 1999 (last amended on 24 September 2009, No XI-434).

46 No VIII-1864, which entered into force on 18 July 2000.

47 Case No 3K-3–207/2010 *UAB Klevo Lapas* v *AB Orlen Lietuva* (17 May 2010).

2.41 Similarly, claims for damages resulting from an anti-competitive agreement by a person who is party to that anti-competitive agreement also give rise to liability and claims for damages. Articles 1.80 and 1.81 of the *Civilinis Kodeksas* establish that contracts contrary to imperative rules of law and to the *ordre public* are null and void and thus are considered to have never legally existed. In this context, competition law rules prohibiting anti-competitive agreements are considered imperative rules forming part of the *ordre public*. Accordingly, if a contract is considered to contravene rules of competition law it would, for the purposes of contract law, be deemed to have never existed. Moreover, on the basis of tortious liability, any person, including a party to the anti-competitive agreement, who suffered damage as a result of the agreement would be able to bring a civil claim for damages against the responsible party.

2.42 Article 6.248 of the Civil Code, however, also provides that where the damages claimed result from fault, including negligence, on the part of the claimant, then any damages awarded shall be decreased proportionately to the degree of fault of the claimant.

2.43 Although the legal basis for antitrust damages claims in Lithuania is well established, in practice to date there have been only a small number of cases seeking damages for breach of competition law. Nonetheless, it is expected that the number of cases will increase, especially owing to expected improvements to the rules on group actions.[48]

f The Netherlands

2.44 The legal basis for claims for damages for infringement of competition law is Article 6:162 of the *Burgerlijk Wetboek* (Civil Code). That provision establishes that any person who commits a tortious act against another, which can be attributed to him, is obliged to compensate any harm caused by that act.

2.45 Claims for damages resulting from an anti-competitive agreement by a person who is party to that anti-competitive agreement are also tortious in nature. That is so because Article 3:40 of the *Burgerlijk Wetboek* establishes that judicial acts contrary to the imperative rules of law and to the public order are null and void. Therefore acts of such a nature are considered to have never legally existed. In this context, competition law rules prohibiting anti-competitive agreements are considered as imperative rules forming part of the public order. Accordingly, if a contract was considered contrary to competition law it would, for the purposes of contract law and civil liability, be deemed to have never existed, and any

48 On 13 July 2011, the Lithuanian Government approved an improved concept of group action, and requested the Ministry of Justice to prepare the legal framework for the legislation.

person, including a party to the anti-competitive agreement, who suffered damage due to that agreement would be able to bring a claim against the responsible party.

The own fault concept as a grounds for a reduction of awardable damages is also recognised by Dutch law.[49] **2.46**

2 Romanistic systems of law

a Belgium

The legal basis for competition law damages claims is Article 1382 of the Belgian *Code civil*. As under French law (below), that provision establishes that every human action, which causes harm to another, obliges the person by whose fault the harm occurred to compensate this harm (a general tort doctrine). The conditions for tort liability are: fault (understood as not acting as a *bonus pater familias* placed in the same circumstances); the presence of damage; and the existence of a causal link between the fault and the damage. **2.47**

Claims for damages resulting from an anti-competitive agreement by a person who is party to that anti-competitive agreement are also tortious in nature. That is so because Article 1133 of the *Code civil* establishes that contracts contrary to the imperative rules of law and to the *ordre public* do not have a justified cause and are null and void. These contracts are considered never to have legally existed. In this context, competition law rules prohibiting anti-competitive agreements are considered as imperative rules forming part of the *ordre public*. Accordingly, if a contract was found to infringe competition law it would, for the purposes of contract law and civil liability, be deemed to have never existed, and any person, including a party to the anti-competitive agreement, who suffered damage due to the agreement would be able to bring a tortious claim. **2.48**

However, as regards a damages claimant who is party to the anti-competitive agreement, the Belgian court may, at its own discretion, deny the damages in whole or in part on the basis of the *in pari causa turpitudinis cessat repetitionem* rule if the damages claimed were the result, either wholly or in part, of fault on the part of the claimant.[50] **2.49**

49 Article 6:101 of the *Burgerlijk Wetboek*.

50 Confirmed by the judgments of the *Cour de cassation* of 24 September 1976, AC 1977, 98 and 5 September 1996, AC 1996, 708.

b France

2.50 Competition law damages actions in France are generally based on the general tort law provision of Article 1382 of the *Code civil*,[51] and the specific competition law provisions of Articles L. 420–1 and L. 420–2 of the *Code de commerce*, as well as Articles 101 and 102 TFEU.[52]

2.51 Article 1382 of the *Code civil* requires the claimant to prove that fault on the part of the defendant caused an alleged damage. Three elements need to be proven for an action to stand, namely fault, the presence of damage and a causal link between the fault and the damage. For antitrust damages actions, the claimant must therefore, in general, allege that the defendant implemented an anti-competitive practice that caused it to suffer harm.

2.52 Under French tort law, the infringement of any legal provision, whether administrative, civil or criminal, constitutes fault for the purposes of Article 1382. Any infringement of French or EU competition law can therefore be considered to satisfy this condition.[53] It should therefore be seen that the concept of fault in French tort law can be either objective or subjective. In its objective sense, it can be satisfied by illegality.[54]

2.53 As regards claims for damages resulting from an anti-competitive agreement by a person who is party to that agreement, such claims are also tortious in nature. Article L. 420–3 of the *Code de commerce* provides that any undertaking, agreement or contractual clause referring to a practice prohibited by Articles L. 420–1 and L. 420–2 shall be void. Competition rules are part of the *ordre public* and any agreement contrary to such shall be null and void retroactively (that is, as if it had never existed). Nullity shall be pronounced by civil or commercial courts upon a claim by the parties to the agreement or by a third party.

---

51 As quoted at para 1.13, note 18. See *Cour de cassation*, Com 1 March 1982, No 80–15.834, *Bull. civ.* IV, No 76. For a discussion of how this provision is to be interpreted in terms of standing to bring damages actions for breach of EU competition law, see Chapter 3.

52 Article L. 420–1 is the substantive equivalent of Article 101 TFEU in French law, and Article L. 420–2 the substantive equivalent of Article 102 TFEU.

53 This principle could be described as a civil law equivalent of the common law cause of action of breach of statutory duty.

54 Several decisions have confirmed this. For instance, in *SARL Philippe Streiff Motorsport/SAS Speedy* (*25ème chambre A*, judgment of 28 June 2002, JCP E. 2003, JP n° II 1018, p 2091), the Paris *Cour d'appel* ruled that a breach of Articles L. 420–1 and L. 420–2 of the *Code de commerce* gives standing for an action on the basis of Article 1382 of the *Code civil*. In the *Eco System/Peugeot* case (judgment of 22 October 1996, not published, but mentioned by D. Fasquelle in 'La réparation des dommages causés par les pratiques anticoncurrentielles', RTD com, n° 4/1998, p 772), the Paris *Tribunal de commerce* found that if the Commission holds that a company has infringed Article 101(1) TFEU, the infringement in itself establishes the fault required under Article 1382 of the *Code civil*.

As regards a rule on own fault, there is no statutory rule in the French codes comparable to the rules of other Member State jurisdictions discussed above. A French judge hearing the case would have to decide the issue. **2.54**

c *Italy*

In Italy, actions for damages caused by a violation of competition law are subject to the rules on non-contractual liability provided for in the *Codice civile*, and Article 33 of L. 287/90 (the Italian national competition law), a provision which gives the courts the power to rule, even in the interim, on violations of that law. **2.55**

Actions for damages under Article 33 of L. 287/90 are considered ordinary civil liability actions, and as such are subject to the provisions of Article 2043 of the *Codice civile*. **2.56**

Pursuant to Article 2043 of the *Codice civile*, anyone who has suffered undue damage caused by a tort is entitled to compensation. This provision covers typical tort liability cases where the damage follows from the violation of a prohibition rule. To assert its right to compensation, the claimant must therefore demonstrate the existence of the constituent elements of a tort claim, that is, an unlawful act by the defendant, unjustly suffered damage and a causal link between the damage suffered and the unlawful act. In addition, the claimant must establish intent or negligence on the part of the defendant. **2.57**

Originally, Italian case law on the point had had some difficulty in terms of classification. A number of cases which the Italian courts were called upon to decide involved agreements in the insurance sector and were characterised by the presence of a contractual relationship between the claimants and the defendant undertakings, leading to judgments declaring the contractual liability of the latter.[55] **2.58**

However, the prevailing position is now to recognise the non-contractual nature of the liability in question. More specifically, in accordance with the instructions given by the *Corte di Cassazione*,[56] the lower courts have held that, when the existence of mechanisms to evade competition rules and distort the normal operation of the market is at stake, protection of a contractual nature cannot be invoked: in fact, the right that needs to be safeguarded does not derive from the contractual tie between the parties, but rather from the rules that are aimed at preventing distortions of competition. Therefore, in these cases, claims for **2.59**

55 See, for example, Naples *Corte d'appello*, judgments of 26 October 2007 and 9 November 2007.

56 *Corte di Cassazione*, judgments no 2207/2005 and 2305/2007.

damages have been linked to non-contractual liability under Article 2043 of the *Codice civile*, and as such are classified as arising in tort.[57]

d Spain

2.60 Under Spanish law, claims for damages find their legal basis in Article 1902 of the *Código civil*. This Article, which regulates liability in tort, establishes that any individual causing damage, either by act of commission or negligence, shall repair the damage caused. This Article is to be read in conjunction with the second additional provision[58] of the national competition law, the *Ley de defensa de la competencia*,[59] which modified the law on civil procedure[60] in order to facilitate the bringing of damages claims for violation of Articles 1 and 2 of the *Ley de defensa de la competencia*, the substantive equivalents of Articles 101 and 102 TFEU.[61]

2.61 In this respect, it is the general regime of tort that applies and, therefore, in addition to the actual loss suffered, the claimant will also be able to claim for lost profits, as well as interest.

C The tortious nature of litigation for breach of EU competition law

2.62 On the basis of the above survey, it is possible to make some remarks about the classification of the civil law aspects of actions for breach of competition law. This classification will, *inter alia*, determine which law applies to the substantive and procedural aspects of the claim over and above the substantive competition law. It will also help to determine the correct forum for the action in question. In the current state of EU law, there are different regimes regulating choice of court and applicable law for contractual and non-contractual actions.[62]

2.63 This issue of the classification of competition law litigation appears not to have received any explicit consideration by either the ECJ or a national court. The

---

57 Naples *Corte d'appello*, judgments of 18 February 2008 and 19 May 2008.

58 *Disposición adicional segunda.*

59 Law 15/2007 of 3 July 2007.

60 *Ley de enjuiciamiento civil*, law 1/2000 of 7 January 2000.

61 It is worth noting that the new regime came into force with the latest version of the *Ley de defensa de la competencia*. Although the previous version (law 16/1989 of 17 July 1989, which expired on 1 September 2007 with the entry into force of law 15/2007), contained a specific provision on claims for damages, this provision (Article 13(2)) was ineffective. Article 13(2) did not facilitate access to damages but, on the contrary, made such access disproportionately difficult and time-consuming by making civil damages claims contingent on the prior exhaustion of all judicial remedies available in relation to administrative acts.

62 On these issues, see Chapter 7.

academic literature is indecisive,[63] though a tendency can perhaps be seen to regard the actions in question as rather tortious than contractual.[64] This view is stated explicitly in the Commission's Green Paper, and is implicit in its White Paper.[65] It is submitted that this is the better view, for the following reasons.

On conceptual grounds, two litigating parties will not contract to break the law. An action for damages supposes a breach of the law by one of the parties only.[66] When this is the case, the breach must intervene from outside the contractual relationship. This must therefore mean that any cause of action arising from that breach is itself non-contractual, even if a contractual relationship may have existed between the parties, and the nullity provision of Article 101(2) TFEU applies. This was exactly the situation in the *Crehan* proceedings, where the cause of action was considered to be breach of statutory duty, a tort in English law, even though the parties had been in a contractual relationship and the nullity provision of Article 101(2) applied to it. The classification of the cause of action does not seem to have been an issue either in the English proceedings, which reached the House of Lords, or in the reference to the ECJ. This is also a distillation of the argumentation used by the English High Court in the *Provimi* proceedings in relation to the validity of the contractual jurisdiction clause heard by the court as a preliminary issue.[67] **2.64**

This line of argument is further supported by the proposition, to be found in several systems of national law, that an agreement in contravention of competition law is considered as a matter of law not only void, but also never to have existed, which rules out *a priori* any contractual claim. **2.65**

This point of view can also be supported by reference to the *Crehan* ruling of the ECJ, where the Court referred to the fact that the nullity provision of Article **2.66**

63 See for example the contributions in Part I.2 (applicable law in the EU – Rome I and II) of Basedow, Jürgen, Francq, Stéphanie and Idot, Laurence (eds), *International Antitrust Litigation: Conflict of Laws and Coordination* (Hart, Oxford/Portland, 2011).

64 Thus '*[t]he characterisation of damage actions brought by one contractual partner against the other is more uncertain*', Fallon, Marc and Francq, Stéphanie, 'Private Enforcement of Antitrust Provisions and the Rome I Regulation', in *ibid.* 63, at 64; '*[i]n brief, neither the Rome II nor the Rome I Regulations seem to provide a clear definition of contractual and non-contractual matters. It is true that the case-law relating to the interpretation of the Brussels I Regulation may be helpful to some extent. However… the difficulties of characterisation will persist in relation to obligations for which neither of the texts provides any specific rule*', Poillot-Peruzzetto, Sylvaine and Lawnicka, Dominika, 'Relevance of the Distinction between the Contractual and Non-Contractual Spheres (Jurisdiction and Applicable Law)', in *ibid.* 131, at 151.

65 See the Green Paper, at section 2.8, and the Staff Working Paper annexed thereto, at para 242, and the Staff Working Paper accompanying the White Paper, at paras 8–9.

66 Cf. the notion of '*significant responsibility*' in the judgment of the ECJ in *Crehan*, at para 34. The whole notion of '*significant responsibility*' could be said to be superfluous if one looks away from the contractual relationship to found liability on purely tortious, public policy grounds.

67 *Provimi Limited* v *Aventis Animal Nutrition SA* [2003] EWHC 961 (Comm).

101(2) TFEU applies to agreements which are in breach of EU competition law.[68] Therefore, any subsequent damages claim cannot have a contractual basis.

2.67 If this argument is accepted, it could even be said that the point is settled as a matter of EU law, with any national provision purporting to take a different approach conflicting with the case law of the ECJ.

D The national law analysis: the fault requirement

2.68 The comparative analysis above supports the proposition that claims for damages for breach of EU competition law are tortious in nature. In English law, they are classified under the heading of claims for breach of statutory duty, and this is supported by the fact that, in German law, such claims were, prior to the entry into force of the seventh amendment to the GWB, based on the general tort provision of §823(2) BGB. Again, the same principle applies in French law, where competition law claims can be seen to be based on general tort law.

2.69 Furthermore, it can be seen that the fault doctrine is central to civil law approaches to non-contractual liability. English law avoids this problem, at least as far as competition law claims are concerned, by means of the concept of the tort of breach of statutory duty, which is strict (that is, the claimant is not required to show fault on the part of the defendant).

2.70 As described above, under French law the fault requirement for a non-contractual claim is satisfied by illegality (the objective sense of '*faute*' for the purposes of Article 1382 *Code civile*). A finding of a breach of competition law constitutes such an illegality. This amounts to the same position as under English law in terms of practical effect. The two systems reach the same result by different means, French law interposing the concept of fault, which is satisfied and therefore, in this type of litigation, redundant.

2.71 Under German law, fault is not automatically established as a result of illegality, but has to be established by proving intentional or negligent behaviour (that is, the subjective meaning of fault), as is clear from §823 BGB, as described above.

---

68 See paras 21 and 22 of the judgment.

This discrepancy can be seen as a major distortion in the landscape of competition law damages claims across Europe.[69]

69 The Commission sought to address this issue in the draft Directive, Article 13 of which reads as follows: '*To the extent that Member States require, in addition to proof of an infringement of Article 81 or 82 of the Treaty, fault to be proven in actions for damages, they shall ensure that, once an injured party has established such an infringement, the infringer is liable for damages unless he shows that he could not reasonably have been aware that his conduct distorted competition*' (emphasis added). Thus the Commission sought to harmonise the issue by proposing a condition of reasonable awareness, which would have cut across national systems.

3

INDIRECT PURCHASER STANDING AND PASSING-ON

I THE THEORETICAL UNDERPINNINGS OF INDIRECT PURCHASER STANDING AND PASSING-ON 3.001
- A Indirect purchaser standing 3.012
- B The passing-on defence 3.022

II EU LAW 3.028
- A Indirect purchaser standing 3.029
  - 1 The Commission's position on indirect purchaser standing 3.032
- B The passing-on defence 3.037
  - 1 The passing-on defence and unjust enrichment 3.044
  - 2 The burden of proof to establish passing-on 3.053
  - 3 Partial passing-on 3.061
  - 4 The Commission's position on the passing-on defence 3.064

III NATIONAL LAW 3.067
- A England and Wales 3.069
- B Germany 3.074
- C France 3.081
- D Italy 3.084

IV INDIRECT PURCHASER STANDING AND PASSING-ON IN THE US 3.089
- A Antitrust injury 3.090
- B The passing-on defence under US law 3.092
- C Indirect purchaser standing: the rule in *Illinois Brick* 3.099
  - 1 Exceptions to the rule in *Illinois Brick* 3.105
  - 2 The efficiency of the rule in *Illinois Brick* 3.110

I THE THEORETICAL UNDERPINNINGS OF INDIRECT PURCHASER STANDING AND PASSING-ON[1]

3.001 Despite the *prima facie* simplicity of the principle of the right to damages for breach of EU competition law as laid down in *Crehan* and *Manfredi*, more complex are a further two particular yet important matters that have to be addressed when reviewing the operation of damages actions in practice. These are the two linked issues of who is entitled to claim, and, provided the right extends to both direct and indirect purchasers, how damages should be awarded in light of the loss sustained by claimants operating at different levels of a supply chain.[2] These two vexing issues are intrinsically complicated matters which lead

1 It is noted that the majority of the literature on passing-on and indirect purchaser standing emanates from the US. Such literature necessarily reflects the idiosyncrasies of the private enforcement system in that jurisdiction.

2 It is understood that antitrust damage may impact upon other parties, for example, upstream input suppliers and producers of complementary goods. This chapter, however, focuses on damage that is passed on down the supply chain, and as such reference is made to direct and indirect purchasers as the harmed parties. See Chapter 8 for a wider discussion of losses incurred by different economic actors outside this factual matrix. Note also that the

to a considerable degree of legal uncertainty.[3] Furthermore, they are two issues where the intersection of antitrust law, policy and economics is particularly acute.

3.002 To illustrate these two linked concepts,[4] let us assume that a cartel participant or a dominant company abusing its market power (for example, a manufacturer) sells its goods at supra-competitive prices to a direct purchaser (for example, a wholesaler). At this juncture of the supply chain, the wholesaler has two options. It can simply absorb the supra-competitive price and continue its commercial activities, thereby suffering a loss in consequence of paying a price that is in excess of the competitive price (often referred to as an 'overcharge').[5] Alternatively, and the more likely course of events, it can pass on this overcharge to an indirect purchaser (for example, the end-consumer), either in whole or in part. In the latter scenario, an indirect purchaser further down the supply chain incurs a loss in the form of higher prices charged and/or reduced quantity supplied by the wholesaler which he, in turn, may or may not be able to pass on. As such, indirect purchasers arguably should be entitled to claim damages on the same premise of injury as direct purchasers, subject to being able to prove that their claim is causally linked and not too remote.

3.003 However, a simplistic supply chain model (even leaving out upstream input suppliers of the infringer) of only three operators does not lend itself to real-world supply chains, where one product often constitutes a component of another (for example, as part of a 'complex product') as the links in the supply chain progress.[6] In addition, the end-consumer is usually the furthest removed from the initial overcharge, thereby potentially occupying the most vulnerable position within the chain, as a result of his inability to pass-on the overcharge. In view of this complexity, there is a very real risk of duplicative recovery if both direct and indirect purchasers can seek damages, raising the question of whether

---

Commission proposal contains a rule in its Article 14(2) for damages actions to be brought in the case of an infringement which relates to supply to the infringers, that is, an infringement which has effects *up* the supply chain.

3 As noted by Denis Waelbroeck and Donald Slater, 'The Commission's Green Paper on Private Enforcement: "Americanization" of EC Competition Law Enforcement?' in *European Competition Law Annual 2006: Enforcement of Prohibition of Cartels* (Ehlermann, Claus-Dieter and Atanasiu, Isabela (eds), Hart, Oxford/Portland, 2007).

4 This illustration finds its basis in the basic example provided in the Roundtable Discussion on Private Remedies: Pass-on Defense; Indirect Purchaser Standing; Definition of Damages, DAF/COMP/WP3/WD(2006)9, 31 January 2006.

5 See Chapter 8, section II.1.2.

6 See Firat Cengiz, 'Passing on Defense and Indirect Purchaser Standing in Actions for Damages Against the Violations of Competition Law: What Can the EC Learn from the US?', CCP Working Paper No. 07–21 (November 2007), at 9; the paper is available at: http://papers.ssrn.com/sol3/papers.cfm?abstract_id=1038521.

the defendant should be able to run the argument that loss has been passed on and that therefore the claim against it should be dismissed in whole or in part.

3.004 The confluence of these issues raises serious policy and practical questions. Fundamentally, the complexity which obtains with respect to the recognition of passing-on and indirect purchaser standing arises from a mix of policy objectives which are not necessarily always compatible with one another and which underpin the rationale for, and practicalities of, antitrust damages actions. Broadly, the antitrust literature identifies three such objectives, namely compensation, deterrence and economical litigation.[7]

3.005 The notion of *compensation* (or fairness) dictates that all injured parties should be able to claim damages for losses sustained. Direct purchasers, while they may be able to establish a causal link to their loss, are often able to pass the overcharge on to indirect purchasers, meaning that the ultimate harm falls on entities situated at the end of the supply chain, who often have no recourse to legal redress. Therefore, within a system where only direct purchasers have standing, compensation is often awarded to a party that has in effect suffered little, if any, harm. In consequence, this would result in the incorrect group of purchasers being compensated, '*such that even when antitrust violators are appropriately punished, damages are allocated contrary to what the social optimum would dictate*'.[8]

3.006 On the other hand, arguments pertaining to effectiveness are built around the idea that it is *deterrence* of anti-competitive violations that should be the primary aim of private antitrust enforcement, and that, as a result, preference should be accorded to only giving standing to direct purchasers. This is because direct purchasers are arguably in the privileged position of having better access to information on price and loss-related issues, and given their often superior resources and greater incentives to bring a claim (indirect purchasers often only incurring marginal damage and therefore arguably displaying 'rational apathy' towards bringing a claim), they are both more likely and better equipped to bring damages claims against companies in violation of the antitrust rules.[9] Moreover, to the extent that indirect purchasers suffered injury arising from

7 See, for example, Barak D. Richman and Christopher R. Murray, 'Rebuilding *Illinois Brick*: A Functionalist Approach to the Indirect Purchaser Rule' (2007) 81 Southern California Law Review 69. See also Cengiz, *loc. cit.*, at 4.

8 Richman and Murray, *loc. cit.*, at 91.

9 *Ibid.*, at 92–96. It has also been noted that '*direct purchasers are currently the key players in civil suits and that a focus needs to be placed on incentivising such potential plaintiffs by putting them in a strong position procedurally*' (David Anderson and Rachel Cuff, 'Cartels in the European Union: Procedural Fairness for Defendants and Claimants' (2011) 34(3) Fordham International Law Journal 385).

alleged passing-on by direct purchasers, they can arguably seek recovery from the direct purchasers.

Achieving procedural efficiency places the focus on the issue of *economical litigation* and the complexity of the quantification of passed-on charges and the subsequent allocation of damages among injured parties. In particular, not only may it prove inefficient in terms of judicial economy to try accurately to calculate overcharges, but the inherent complexity of the exercise may lead to multiple (and duplicative) recovery arising from a confusing set of proceedings.[10] As a result, it could be argued that interests of procedural economy militate in favour of granting standing to bring a claim only to direct purchasers. **3.007**

Difficulties arise in simultaneously achieving the above objectives, as they do not necessarily go hand-in-hand with one another. For example, the objective of compensation conflicts with those of deterrence and economical litigation. Compensation as an objective requires that standing be accorded to both direct and indirect purchasers, as well as recognition of passing on, in order to allow for each claimant, or group of claimants, to be properly and adequately compensated. However, as highlighted above, the computation of the amounts of damages that each claimant (or group of claimants) should be entitled to claim can involve complex and time-consuming analyses of pricing mechanisms, as well as of the micro-economic conditions of the infringing behaviour. Furthermore, in the assessment of complex market structures and sophisticated interconnected supply chains, for example, it can also prove challenging for judges to establish who the direct and indirect purchasers in fact are in a particular case.[11] An apposite example of the courts seeking to establish the identity of the (in)direct purchaser is provided by the US case *Warren General Hospital* v *Amgen*.[12] **3.008**

In a seminal work on the issues of indirect purchaser standing and passing-on, Landes and Posner recognised this clash of objectives, arguing that antitrust policy should accommodate only one of the aforementioned objectives, namely deterrence.[13] To this end, Lander and Posner explain that the goal of deterrence necessarily involves the granting of standing to direct purchasers *only*. This is **3.009**

10 Richman and Murray, *loc. cit.*, at 97.

11 Cengiz, *loc. cit.*, at 9.

12 643 F. 3d 77 (3rd Cir 2011), discussed in more detail below.

13 William M. Landes and Richard A. Posner, 'Should Indirect Purchasers Have Standing To Sue Under the Antitrust Laws? An Economic Analysis of the Rule of *Illinois Brick*' (1979) 46 The University of Chicago Law Review 602, at 605: '*... we believe that achievement of the goals of the antitrust laws requires that deterrence be preferred*'.

because of the array of advantages (for example, of an informational nature) that are at a direct purchaser's disposal.[14] Conversely, owing to the complexities surrounding the issue of indirect purchaser standing, by recognising direct purchasers *and* indirect purchasers as eligible claimants, it is argued that cases would inevitably become inefficient, unwieldy and ineffective.[15]

3.010 Werden and Schwartz also argue that only one customer group in the supply chain should be granted standing, namely the direct purchaser.[16] However, unlike Landes and Posner, they focused on an incentive-based model to analyse the economics of passing-on, arriving at the conclusion that if direct and indirect purchasers could both bring damages claims, then each would in effect have lesser incentive to engage and invest in proceedings, thus undermining deterrence.[17] As also noted by Landes and Posner, this is primarily because both have opposing interests in litigation, and both are expected to attempt to free-ride on each other's attempts to bring a damages claim.[18]

3.011 Two important issues therefore arise: first, should indirect purchasers be entitled to bring actions for compensation in respect of their loss, and what should the outer bounds to such standing be? Second, where the indirect purchaser is afforded standing and brings a damages claim, should it be possible for the antitrust infringer to argue that loss has been passed on?

---

14 *Ibid.*, at 609.

15 *Ibid.*, at 615.

16 Gregory J. Werden, and Marius Schwartz, '*Illinois Brick* and the Deterrence of Antitrust Violations – An Economic Analysis' (1984) 35 The Hastings Law Journal 629, at 667: '*assigning the exclusive recovery right to direct purchasers probably is appropriate*'.

17 See Werden and Schwartz, *loc. cit.*, at 663, noting that '*[t]he critical issue with respect to the numbers of potential plaintiffs, however, is not whether increasing the number of potential plaintiffs will lessen the incentive of each individual plaintiff to invest in detection, but whether the group of all potential plaintiffs will invest less in detection and whether the overall probability that collusion will be detected will fall. With many potential plaintiffs, there is an important interdependence effect; the efforts of each to detect collusion affect the incentives of all others to do so. The precise nature of this interdependence effect depends, in general, on the specific probability-of-detection function that exists. In particular, it depends on whether and to what extent each individual plaintiff's ability to increase the probability that collusion will be detected is affected by the detection efforts of others. If as seems reasonably likely, various potential plaintiffs would examine much the same information in much the same order, then it is likely that this interdependence would cause increased numbers of potential plaintiffs to lower the aggregate level of investment in detecting collusion and thereby reduce the probability that collusion will be detected.*'

18 Landes and Posner, *loc. cit.*, at 625. See also Jacob Rüggeberg and Maarten Pieter Schinkel, 'Consolidating Antitrust Damages in Europe: A Proposal for Standing in Line with Efficient Private Enforcement' (2006) 29(3) World Competition 395, at 402, stating, however, that '*there is a concern that direct purchasers may have a decreased incentive to sue when they are able to pass-on a large part or all of their damages*'.

A Indirect purchaser standing*

The identity of who is the direct purchaser in an antitrust damages claim is generally undisputed. On the other hand, the identity of the indirect purchaser is not as clear-cut. Generally speaking, an indirect purchaser is an entity '*who had no direct dealings with the infringer, but who nonetheless may have suffered considerable harm because an illegal overcharge was passed on to [it] along the distribution chain*'.[19] **3.012**

Once an indirect purchaser has been identified, the issue of whether (and the extent to which) indirect purchasers should be able to bring a claim is crucial as far as litigation is concerned. This is because it raises questions about the appropriate levels of compensation, and the point at which a claim is so remote that it can no longer be connected to the alleged antitrust infringement, thereby making compensation inappropriate and risking over-deterrence. **3.013**

The issue of indirect purchaser standing remains one of considerable judicial and academic controversy. No uniform acceptance of indirect purchaser standing emerges either in the US, where the law differs between the individual States and between the State and federal levels, or in the EU, where the rules are equally distinct among the Member States. In the EU, political, judicial and arguably also academic persuasion lies in favour of giving indirect purchasers standing, assuming that such claimants can be identified. **3.014**

The US Supreme Court effectively prohibited indirect purchaser actions in the seminal case of *Illinois Brick*.[20] In observing the role of indirect purchaser actions and the tension between deterrence and compensation, Hovenkamp stated that **3.015**

> [t]hose who believe that antitrust enforcement should be concerned exclusively with efficiency generally support Illinois Brick. Those who believe that antitrust should be concerned with full compensation to victims generally disapprove. Both positions are ideologically consistent. Permitting indirect purchaser actions would increase the costs of litigation and may result in over-deterrence. However, the *Illinois Brick* rule clearly deprives injured parties of their claim to damages ... In the great majority of situations

* Parts of this section were first published by Sweet & Maxwell in GCLR 2012 5(3), at 111, and are reproduced by agreement with the publishers.

19 White Paper, section 2.1.

20 *Illinois Brick Co* v *Illinois* 431 US 720 (1977). For a recent discussion of *Illinois Brick* and indirect purchaser standing, see Richman and Murray, *loc. cit.*, and Andrew I. Gavil, 'Antitrust Remedy Wars Episode I: *Illinois Brick* from Inside the Supreme Court' (2005) 79 St John's Law Review 553, at 576–605.

the indirect purchaser rule gives the entire damage action to the person who suffered the smaller injury – or in some cases, no injury at all.[21]

3.016 Landes and Posner furthermore advance the argument that even if end-consumers are those who are injured, their purchases may be small, and their incentives and resources to claim for damages limited when compared to those of direct purchasers.[22] As noted above, Landes and Posner placed particular emphasis on deterrence, stating that: '*[t]he most important consideration from the standpoint of deterrence is not who receives the proceeds of any judgment levied against the antitrust violator, but that there be adequate incentives to bring suit and prosecute it to judgment*'.[23]

3.017 Other legal commentators are of the persuasion that denying indirect purchaser standing would not be fair, owing to the fact that to a large extent the damage would not be compensated, and that a direct purchaser would therefore unduly receive a windfall.[24] Such an argument may have merit, yet where damage does lie with purchasers further down the supply chain, it is likely that it is dispersed amongst many purchasers who may only have incurred minimal damage. The question therefore is – even if one were to permit purchasers further down the supply chain to bring a claim – what incentive do those purchasers have to bring a claim where the cost of doing so can significantly outweigh any potential award?

3.018 Of course, one method would be to allow representative or class actions to be brought, thereby bringing together these individual claims and hence ensuring fairness and taking advantage of the efficiencies flowing therefrom. Though such a method of recourse is integral to the US antitrust regime,[25] in the EU, despite recent Commission work on the matter, the debate remains open as to how to design an effective system of collective redress in antitrust, how it should operate and what its parameters should be.[26]

---

21 Herbert Hovenkamp, *Federal Antitrust Policy: The Law of Competition and its Practice* (2nd edition, West Group, St. Paul, Minnesota, 1999), at 621.

22 Landes and Posner, *loc. cit.*, at 609: '*even if direct and indirect purchasers were equally efficient antitrust enforcers, and even if allocation problems could be solved without seriously depleting the recovery pool, deterrence would be weakened if the right to sue were divided among more parties so that each claim was relatively small*'.

23 *Ibid.*, at 608.

24 Rüggeberg, and Schinkel, *loc. cit.*: '*Denying affected parties the right to recover their damages, the rule is deemed unfair by many.*' See also Kent Roach and Michael J. Trebilcock, 'Private Enforcement of Competition Laws' (1996) 34(3) Osgoode Hall Law Journal 461.

25 Note, however, that the rules regarding indirect purchaser standing differ across the US, and that it is not necessarily permitted in all US states. This is discussed in more detail below.

26 See further Chapter 6.

Evidentiary obstacles obtain with respect to actions brought by indirect purchasers, as they might be unable to prove the extent of the harm they have incurred and the causal link between that harm and the infringement, including the issue of remoteness of damage.[27] **3.019**

In practice, such evidential hurdles may be tempered by using 'sound imagination' or a 'broad axe' approach, or by means of legal presumptions, which may not, however, necessarily represent an optimal solution. Furthermore, the adoption of such presumptions may represent an overly controversial shift from current practice in many Member States.[28] **3.020**

In practice, however, what really matters is that claimants weighing up their strategic options, and defendants considering antitrust risk, must know who has standing to bring a claim, what defences are available and in which jurisdiction the claim can be brought. This last problem represents an additional dimension (and complication) in the EU (as discussed in Chapter 7). **3.021**

B The passing-on defence

In the event of passing-on, purchasers who are only indirectly linked to the seller, that is, the cartelist or dominant firm engaged in anti-competitive conduct, suffer a loss by paying the supra-competitive price which has been passed on to them. If there has been such passing-on, the question arises as to whether the original seller and infringer should be permitted to argue that the direct purchaser has not suffered loss because that loss has been passed on to an indirect purchaser. In competition law parlance, the successful invocation of such an argument operates as a defence, though whether it is a defence properly so called is a matter of debate.[29] Be that as it may, the term 'passing-on defence' is an established one in terms of competition law taxonomy, and for ease of reference passing-on will be referred to as a defence for the purposes of this book. **3.022**

27 See Roundtable Discussion on Private Remedies: Pass-on Defense; Indirect Purchaser Standing; Definition of Damages, *loc. cit.*, at 2.

28 See Becket McGrath and Trupti Reddy, 'Proposals for Reform to Private Competition Law Claims under UK Law: All Change Please?' (2012) 4 Global Competition Litigation Review 138, at 140: '*[t]he introduction of a presumption of loss would represent a major departure from current practice, where the interests of justice require that a claimant bears the burden of proving its losses before it can recover … it represents a fundamental interference in the defendant's ability to defend itself against a claim …* '.

29 For example, the UK Competition Law Association has expressed the opinion that the passing-on defence is not a defence as such, arguing that '*it is simply a reflection of the principle that a claimant must prove that he has suffered loss as a result of a tort*', and that passing-on should be taken account of when quantifying harm (see the 2013 BIS response, at para 4.34).

3.023 Passing-on occurs when a direct customer of a supplier who engaged in anti-competitive practices mitigates its own economic loss by passing on an overcharge to its own customers further down the supply chain. The damage incurred by the direct customer can be partially, or wholly, passed on down the supply chain to another entity, including end-consumers. The end-consumer, for example, takes on the mantle of the indirect purchaser, who may or may not have standing to bring a claim against the defendant responsible for the violation of the antitrust rules.

3.024 Against the above observation, by invoking the passing-on defence, the infringer seeks to assert that the overcharge in question has not led to a loss for the claimant (direct purchaser), because that direct purchaser has in turn passed the loss on to its own customers (indirect purchasers). As such, if the upstream defendant succeeds in escaping liability vis-à-vis the direct purchaser – in other words, once it has been established that the direct purchaser has in fact passed the overcharge on to the downstream indirect purchaser – the question whether indirect purchasers, such as end-consumers, should be given standing to claim damages for the loss incurred as a result of an antitrust violation still remains. In other words, if a direct purchaser is successful in its claim, and invocation of the passing-on defence is prohibited, the direct purchaser may be awarded damages for loss which was in fact incurred by another entity.

3.025 If passing-on is not recognised as a possible defence, it could result in the 'unjust enrichment' of the direct purchaser, who, by passing-on the overcharge, could enjoy a level of compensation that is higher than the loss incurred in fact.[30] Furthermore, were a defendant, for example, not able to avail itself of the so-called passing-on defence in the event that indirect purchaser standing is accorded, it may end up having to satisfy multiple damages claims in relation to the same overcharge, thus leading to a situation of over-compensation and over-deterrence (for example, through double or even greater liability). On the other hand, however, if a defendant is able to avail itself of the passing-on defence, this could require a court to systematically engage in protracted, speculative and complex economic analyses.

---

30 We use the term 'unjust enrichment' loosely, that is, as a synonym for an unfair windfall, for example. The EU courts also use this term in a loose manner. It is recognised, however, that, as a matter of English and US law, unjust enrichment is an equitable doctrine that seeks to repay a private claimant for the amount of money by which the *defendant* was unjustly enriched. In English law, the passing-on defence does not operate as part of the remedy of unjust enrichment. See *Chitty on Contracts* (29th edition, Sweet & Maxwell, London, 2004), Vol 1, section 29–026, which reads as follows: '*In some cases the claimant is able to obtain restitution even though he has been able to pass on the loss, in the form of increased charges, to his customers. In such cases a defence of "passing on" is not recognised, because the law is concerned with the enrichment of the defendant at the expense of the claimant and not with what happened to the claimant following the defendant's enrichment.*'

As has been extensively observed, the passing-on defence can substantially increase the complexity of damages claims,[31] as the exact extent of the damage suffered at various points along the supply chain can be very difficult to prove.[32] Often, it may be extremely difficult to calculate or show how (and to whom) damages should be allocated. Permitting the passing-on defence may in practice excessively burden the courts, as they may be required to consider many complex factors, such as the impact of different prices on actual sales.[33] **3.026**

The quantification and allocation of damage can thus become a very complicated exercise. It is, however, an important one, not only for the claimant, who bears the evidentiary burden of proving damage, but also for a cartelist, for example, in order to benefit from the passing-on defence.[34] **3.027**

II EU LAW

There is a clear tendency in EU law, to the extent that it can be said to exist, to allow both the passing-on defence and indirect purchaser standing. Such an approach would significantly distinguish the European position from that in the US at federal level, at least as far as these two important and interconnected issues are concerned. The details of this position will be explored below. **3.028**

A Indirect purchaser standing

In *Crehan*, the ECJ stated that *anyone* who has been harmed by an infringement of antitrust rules must be able to claim compensation for that harm. The Court positively affirmed that Articles 101 and 102 TFEU '*produce direct effects in relations between individuals and create rights for the individuals concerned which* **3.029**

31 Furthermore, a distinction can be drawn between Articles 101 and 102 TFEU, whereby the harm caused by abusive practices is often much more difficult to establish (see further Chapter 8).

32 Roundtable Discussion on Private Remedies: Pass-on Defense; Indirect Purchaser Standing; Definition of Damages, *loc. cit.*

33 That is not to say that judges would not be able to deal with complex economic concepts; see in this respect the judgment of the English High Court in *Purple Parking Limited and Meteor Parking Limited* v *Heathrow Airport Limited* [2011] EWHC 987 (Ch) involving an alleged abuse of a dominant position by preventing access to London Heathrow Terminal forecourts for the performance of certain services. In this case Mann J performed the hypothetical monopolist test for market definition purposes. Moreover, judges are arguably accustomed to overcoming such difficulties in practice by taking an approach which is deemed equitable and not necessarily accurate to the penny when deciding on the award of damages.

34 See Süleyman Parlak, 'Passing-on Defence and Indirect Purchaser Standing: Should the Passing-on Defence Be Rejected Now the Indirect Purchaser Has Standing after *Manfredi* and the White Paper of the European Commission?' (2010) 33(1) World Competition 31, who notes that '*measuring the pass through is therefore desirable, since it enables the judges to discover who has effectively borne the loss as a result of illegal behaviour. The passing-on defence can therefore be seen as a means to accomplish the compensatory justice objective.*'

the national courts must safeguard … It follows from the foregoing considerations that any individual can rely on a breach of Article [101(1)] of the Treaty before a national court …' (emphasis added).[35]

3.030 Subject to the caveat pertaining to causation, it can be said that the ECJ has recognised that indirect purchasers must have standing to bring a private damages claim. Whilst it is a welcome acknowledgment of the entitlement to damages by any individual who suffered loss, in practice establishing the causal relationship between the loss suffered and the anti-competitive behaviour by the defendant can be very difficult. In showing the causal link, '*it is necessary to examine the existence of damage and the assessment of that damage in the light of the normal course of events and real probabilities, not theoretical ones*'.[36] For an indirect purchaser, such causal relationship may be difficult to show, especially in cases where claimants are not privy to sufficient evidence to prove the damage in question.

3.031 In sum, it can be said that indirect purchaser standing is a firmly embedded concept of EU law.

1 The Commission's position on indirect purchaser standing

3.032 The affirmation of the right to damages in *Crehan* was reflected in the White Paper, where the Commission focused on the obstacles that indirect purchasers face in bringing claims against antitrust infringers.[37] Such difficulties find their embodiment in the fact that, according to the White Paper, purchasers at or near the end of the supply chain often find it difficult to adduce enough proof of the existence and extent of the passing-on. As a result, the White Paper suggested that indirect purchasers should be able to rely on the *rebuttable presumption* that the illegal overcharge had been passed on to them in its entirety.

3.033 More light was shed on the position of the Commission by the draft Directive, which encapsulated most of the assessments made in the White Paper. In terms of the issue of indirect purchaser standing, recital 6 to the draft Directive stated that '*[a]ny individual that has suffered harm can claim compensation for the actual loss (damnum emergens) and loss of profit (lucrum cessans), as well as payment of*

35 Paras 23 and 24, repeated in *Manfredi* at para 59. The Court went on to state at para 26 of *Crehan* as follows: '*The full effectiveness of Article 85 of the Treaty and, in particular, the practical effect of the prohibition laid down in Article 85(1) would be put at risk if it were not open to any individual to claim damages for loss caused to him by a contract or by conduct liable to restrict or distort competition*' (emphasis added). This was repeated in the *Manfredi* judgment at para 60, in the *Pfleiderer* judgment at para 28, and, most recently, in the *Otis* judgment at para 41.

36 Joined Cases T-3/00 and T-337/04 *Pitsiorlas* v *Council* [2007] ECR II-4779, at para 300.

37 Section 2.6.

interest accruing from the time the harm occurred until it has actually been compensated. This right is recognised for consumers and undertakings alike, irrespective of the existence of a direct contractual relationship with the infringing undertaking, and regardless of whether or not there has been a prior finding of an infringement by a competition authority' (emphasis added).

In other words, the Commission not only sought to confer upon indirect purchasers the necessary standing to sue, but also to allow stand-alone, and follow-on, actions. The draft Directive also sought to facilitate the bringing of actions by indirect purchasers by allowing for a presumption of passing-on of the overcharge to them.[38] **3.034**

The proposal goes in the same direction. Again, there is a rebuttable presumption of passing-on to the indirect purchaser when certain conditions are met.[39] Furthermore, the proposal clarifies that the indirect purchaser bears the burden of proving passing-on where this is necessary in order to establish its case.[40] Read consecutively with Article 12(1) of the proposal, which states that the burden of proving passing-on as a *defence* rests with the defendant,[41] this might appear contradictory, but it should be borne in mind that both provisions are in accordance with existing jurisprudence. In particular, the rule contained in Article 13(1) of the proposal is in line with Article 2 of Regulation 1/2003, which provides that the burden of proving an infringement of Article 101 or Article 102 TFEU rests with the party alleging the infringement. As recalled by the Commission in the explanatory memorandum to its proposal, this rule applies both to proceedings brought by public authorities, and to litigation brought by private parties before the courts.[42] **3.035**

A rebuttable presumption of passing-on could be said to give rise to problems, however, in terms of the classification of the claimant. Often an indirect purchaser will itself be able to pass on loss to the next purchaser in the chain. In such a situation, there is no reason why a presumption of passing-on should not operate both ways, that is, in favour of, and against, such a claimant.[43] To this extent, the classification of claimants as 'direct' and 'indirect' purchasers, which **3.036**

38 Recital 18 and Article 10(2).

39 Article 13(2). An interesting issue is how this interacts with the presumption of harm proposed at Article 16(1). Could it be argued, for example, that the second condition required for the presumption of passing-on to operate (Article 13(2)(b)) is automatically satisfied by means of the presumption of harm? On presumptions of harm, as distinct from presumptions of passing-on, see paras 5.13–5.20.

40 Article 13(1).

41 See further below.

42 Explanatory memorandum, section 1.3.

43 Exactly this problem is exposed by the judgment of the French *Cour de cassation* in *Les Sociétés Coopérative Le Gouessant et Sofral* (see para 3.083).

derives from US jurisprudence and which has infected, in particular, the work of the Commission in the field, is unfortunate, as the only distinction which matters in a system based on compensation of loss is that between those purchasers who can, and those who cannot, pass on overcharge.

B The passing-on defence

3.037 At paragraph 30 of its judgment in *Crehan*, as repeated in *Manfredi*,[44] the ECJ held that '*Community law does not prevent national courts from taking steps to ensure that the protection of the rights guaranteed by Community law does not entail the unjust enrichment of those who enjoy them.*'

3.038 The passage from *Crehan* set out above draws on previous case law of the ECJ. The possibility of the passing-on defence has been acknowledged by the Court in actions for the extra-contractual liability of the Union under Article 340(2) TFEU,[45] and actions for the recovery of illegally levied duties brought by undertakings against Member States.[46]

3.039 In relation to the recognition of the possibility of the passing-on defence in the context of Article 340(2) TFEU actions, the Court observed in *Ireks-Arkady*, a case concerning a wrongful abolition of production refunds for quellmehl, that '*[t]he Council and the Commission objected to that method [simple quantification consisting of the contested refunds whose elimination was the basis of the action] of calculating the damage on the ground that the quellmehl producers eliminated the damage, or could have done so, by passing on the loss resulting from the abolition of the refunds in their selling prices*'. Furthermore, the Court held that '*in the context of an action for damages, such an objection may not be dismissed as unfounded. In fact, it must be admitted that if the loss from the abolition of the refunds has actually been passed on, or could have been passed on, in the prices the damage may not be measured by reference to the refunds not paid. In that case the price increase would take the place of the refunds, thus compensating the producer.*'[47]

---

44 Para 94.

45 See for example Case 238/78 *Ireks-Arkady* v *Council and Commission* [1979] ECR 2955, referred to at para 30 of *Crehan*.

46 See for example *Hans Just* and Joined Cases C-441/98 and C-442/98 *Michailidis* [2000] ECR I-7145, also both referred to at para 30 of *Crehan*. See also *San Giorgio*, Joined Cases 331/85, 376/85 and 378/85 *SA Les Fils de Jules Bianco and J Girard Fils SA* v *Directeur Général des douanes et droits indirects* [1988] ECR 1099 and *Société Comateb*. See further the Opinion of Advocate-General Van Gerven in Case C-128/92 *Banks* [1994] ECR I-1209, as follows: '*Community law does not prevent the national court from ensuring, in accordance with national law, that the protection of rights guaranteed by the Community legal order does not result in the unjust enrichment of those entitled*' (para 48). See also para 51, which refers to '*the extent to which the damage has been passed on*'.

47 Para 14. See also Joined Cases 64 and 113/76, 167 and 239/78, 27, 28 and 45/79 *Dumortier Frères* [1979] ECR 3091.

In cases regarding the extra-contractual liability of the Union, the passing-on defence has been recognised implicitly, and the Court has analysed statistical price data and the extent to which the damage was passed on. **3.040**

Similarly, in the *Just* case, the ECJ stressed that it should be specified **3.041**

> that the protection of rights guaranteed … by Community law does not require an order for the recovery of charges improperly made to be granted in conditions which would involve the unjust enrichment of those entitled. There is nothing therefore … to prevent national courts from taking account… of the fact that it has been possible for charges unduly levied to be incorporated in the prices of the undertaking liable for the charge and passed on to the purchasers. It is equally compatible with the principles of Community law for courts… to take into consideration… the damage which an importer may have suffered because the effect of the discriminatory or protective tax provisions was to restrict the volume of imports from other Member States.[48]

In *Just*, Denmark had unlawfully charged excessive import taxes on spirits, which the claimant had passed on to his customers by adding the additional tax charge to his usual profit margin. The increased prices resulted in lower sales, lower imports and redundancies among the claimant's staff. **3.042**

The position taken by the ECJ in *Just* is more nuanced than that taken in *Ireks-Arkady*, in that the Court also takes into consideration the issue of reduced sales arising from the unlawful tax levied, which complicates the question of whether or not there was actual unjust enrichment of the party in question (see further below). **3.043**

1 *The passing-on defence and unjust enrichment*[49]

It should be recalled as a fundamental point that the existing case law of the ECJ is limited to stating that EU law does not preclude a rule of national law which seeks to prevent unjust enrichment.[50] It does not explicitly establish the existence of the passing-on defence as a matter of EU law.[51] This is an important difference in approach between US and EU law on the point, even if **3.044**

---

48 Para 26.

49 The reader is referred to footnote 30 for the use of the term 'unjust enrichment' in an EU law context.

50 As stated at para 30 of *Crehan*, above.

51 It could be argued that the very notion of 'unjust enrichment' in this context is superfluous if the correct methodology for the calculation of the amount of damage suffered by all parties affected by the infringement in question is used from the outset.

the latter can only be said to be in an embryonic state of development as far as antitrust damages claims are concerned.[52] As AG Slynn stated in his Opinion in *Bianco*[53]:

> The Court [in Just] did not, however, hold that the fact that charges had been passed on must as a matter of Community law, e.g. pursuant to a general principle forbidding unjust enrichment, mean that any charges wrongly demanded and paid could never be recovered.

3.045 Passing-on does not necessarily result in the unjust enrichment of the claimant because it can equally result in a reduced volume of sales as the trader raises prices.[54] Thus in *Just*, the Court held that passing-on can be taken into account as a defence against the refunding of the illegally levied charge to the claimant, but that equally on the other hand the fact that the claimant may have suffered damage in the form of reduced sales as a result of that charge should also be taken into account in assessing the actual loss.[55]

3.046 The distinction between the extent, if any, of passing-on, and damage suffered in terms of reduced sales is made by the Court in its later case law, such that it could be claimed that it is settled law. The Court held as follows in *Société Comateb*[56]:

> It should be borne in mind, however, that even where it is established that the burden of the charge has been passed on in whole or in part to the purchaser, repayment to the trader of the amount thus passed on does not necessarily entail his unjust enrichment.
>
> In Just ... , the Court stated at paragraph 26 that it would be compatible with the principles of Community law for courts before which claims for repayment were brought to take into consideration the damage which an importer might have suffered because the discriminatory or protective tax provisions had the effect of restricting the volume of imports from other Member States.
>
> As the Advocate General pointed out in paragraph 23 of his Opinion, the trader may have suffered damage as a result of the very fact that he has passed on the charge levied

52 This was also the position taken by the Commission in the Staff Working Paper annexed to its Green Paper, which stated as follows at para 173: '*there is no passing-on defence in Community law; rather there is an unjust enrichment defence which requires (1) proof of passing-on and (2) proof of the lack of reduction in sales or other reductions in income*'.

53 Opinion of Advocate-General Sir Gordon Slynn delivered on 29 September 1987.

54 The consideration as to a reduction in sales in cases where an overcharge is passed on also is suggested by the reasoning of the US Supreme Court in *Hanover Shoe* (below). It is also recalled by the judgment of the French *Cour de cassation* in *Ajinomoto* (see further below), where the court distinguishes between a claim for a loss of an opportunity ('*perte d'une chance*') and a straight overcharge claim (based on an '*excès de facturation*').

55 Paras 19 and 26.

56 Paras 29–32. See also paras 34 and 35 of the *Michailidis* judgment and para 99 of the Court's judgment in Case C-147/01 *Weber's Wine World Handels-GmbH and others* v *Abgabenberufungskommission Wien* [2003] ECR I-11365, as well as paras 45–52 of the Opinion of AG Jacobs in that case.

> by the administration in breach of Community law, because the increase in the price of the product brought about by passing on the charge has led to a decrease in sales…
>
> In such circumstances, the trader may justly claim that, although the charge has been passed on to the purchaser, the inclusion of that charge in the cost price has, by increasing the price of the goods and reducing sales, caused him damage which excludes, in whole or in part, any unjust enrichment which would otherwise be caused by reimbursement.

Quite apart from the desirability of splitting the issue between passing-on and unjust enrichment in any form of action from the point of view of economy of proceedings (*Société Comateb* even foresaw the possibility of two separate actions when this would be the appropriate route under national law),[57] it is questionable to what extent such a distinction could, in any case, be made in a pure damages claim. **3.047**

Indeed, in the later case law of the Court, passing-on and unjust enrichment are expressed as cumulative conditions to be fulfilled for the reduction of the charge on the basis of passing-on. As the Court held in *Société Comateb* at paragraph 27[58]: **3.048**

> Accordingly, a Member State may resist repayment to the trader of a charge levied in breach of Community law only where it is established that the charge has been borne in its entirety by someone other than the trader *and* that reimbursement of the latter would constitute unjust enrichment (emphasis added).

Furthermore, the Court held as follows at paragraph 102 of its judgment in *Weber's Wine World*, a case involving a claim for repayment of an illegally levied duty on alcoholic beverages: **3.049**

> It must therefore be concluded on this point that the rules of Community law on the recovery of sums levied but not due are to be interpreted as meaning that they preclude national rules which refuse – a point which falls to be determined by the national court – repayment of a charge incompatible with Community law on the sole ground that the charge was passed on to third parties, *without requiring that the degree of unjust enrichment that repayment of the charge would entail for the trader be established* (emphasis added).

And further at paragraph 117, as follows: **3.050**

> It follows from the foregoing that the principle of effectiveness referred to at paragraph 103 of this judgment precludes national legislation or a national administrative practice

57 This point is made by AG Slynn in his discussion of the *Just* judgment in his Opinion in *Bianco*, at p 5.

58 Repeated in the judgment of the ECJ in *Weber's Wine World*, at para 94.

which makes the exercise of the rights conferred by the Community legal order impossible in practice or excessively difficult by establishing a presumption of unjust enrichment on the sole ground that the duty was passed on to third parties.

3.051 The disconnection between pure passing-on and the unjust enrichment of the claimant has evolved in the case law of the Court to the point where a presumption that passing-on leads to unjust enrichment is so unfounded as to offend against the EU law principle of effectiveness.

3.052 It is worth noting that Advocate-General Mancini in his Opinion in *San Giorgio* was highly critical of the very possibility of raising passing-on. He made the point that in a competitive market, the price charged by the seller is subject to numerous market forces, and that to try to tie a change in price to the passing-on of a particular tax is a virtually impossible task.[59] He acknowledges two exceptions: where demand is static and supply elastic (a 'text book example' devoid of practical application), and the situation where prices, as well as the tax, are fixed by the State.[60] In such a situation, a passing-on defence should not to be available, since no overcharge could be transferred to the end-consumer. Arguably, this example is particularly appealing in a scenario in which the upstream seller enjoys dominance, or participates in a cartel, and sells the product to downstream retailers who function in a competitive market. More specifically, being susceptible to competitive forces, it would be virtually impossible for such retailers to pass on the overcharge to end purchasers.

2 The burden of proof to establish passing-on

3.053 Although the authorities on the point are weak, in these authors' view, it can nevertheless be said that as a matter of EU law, the burden of proving passing-on lies with the defendant. It is a question of fact for the *defendant* to establish.

3.054 This is the position taken, *inter alia*, by the Commission in its White Paper, draft Directive and proposal (see further below).[61] It can also be argued that some support for this view can be found, by way of analogy, in Article 2 of Regulation 1/2003, which provides that the burden of proving the fulfilment of the conditions set out in Article 101(3), which also operates as a *defence*, falls on the defendant undertaking.

59 See para 6 of the Opinion.

60 Para 8.

61 It was also the position taken by the *Bundesgerichtshof* in its definitive ruling on the issue (see further below).

As regards the important issue of where the burden of proof lies to establish passing-on, in *San Giorgio*, the Court held that a provision of national law which placed the burden of proof on the party claiming repayment to show that it had not passed on the charges to the end-consumer was incompatible with EU law on the grounds that it made it virtually impossible or excessively difficult to secure repayment of the charge wrongly levied and paid. **3.055**

The burden of proof can shift at various stages in the proceedings, as the parties seek to establish – as a question of fact – the existence or otherwise of passing-on to the requisite legal standard (let us assume, for the sake of argument, that this is a balance of probabilities test). Thus once the defendant presents some evidence which would in the absence of any further evidence on the point satisfy the balance of probabilities test, the burden naturally shifts back to the claimant to present contradictory evidence. In his Opinion in *Bianco*, Advocate-General Slynn summed up the matter as fundamentally a question of fact. He stated as follows[62]: **3.056**

> [The administration] may, however, produce evidence which points to there being passing-on or unjust enrichment sufficient to call for rebuttal by the claimant. The evidentiary burden may thus, as is commonplace, shift during the case. The question at the end of the day is whether on the evidence as a whole the charge has been passed on …

This is the case as long as no additional evidentiary presumptions operate in this field (see further below the comments of Advocate-General Jacobs in *Weber's Wine World*). **3.057**

If it does become a question of fact to show passing-on in the individual case, the defendant's burden will often be practically impossible to discharge.[63] It is possible to see the provision as to burden of proof made in *San Giorgio* as rendering the passing-on defence as effectively nugatory in practice.[64] **3.058**

---

62 At page 5. See also para 96 of the Court's judgment in *Weber's Wine World*.

63 See for example Mark Brealey, 'Adopt Perma Life, but follow Hanover Shoe to Illinois? – Who Can Sue for Damages for Breach of EC Competition Law?' (2002) 1 Competition Law Journal 127, at para 19: '*the ECJ has recognised the defence of unjust enrichment in the knowledge that the defence is complicated, difficult to prove and rarely succeeds*'.

64 It is interesting to note the retreat in the case law from the *Ireks-Arkady* judgment, where the test (not satisfied) is whether or not passing-on happened or '*could have*' happened (paras 14 and 16) and the *Just* case (presumption of passing-on foreseen, para 19) to the *San Giorgio* case.

3.059 It is worth noting that Advocate-General Jacobs argued in his Opinion in *Weber's Wine World* that the shifting of the burden of proof onto the defendant could and should be rebalanced in favour of the defendant by allowing for the court to draw inferences from such evidence as is available. He suggested as follows[65]:

> In that context, it is in my view desirable to clarify the case-law by pointing out that, whilst Community law precludes any presumption of unjust enrichment to be refuted by the claimant, it does not preclude the possibility of drawing reasonable inferences from existing evidence. Without such a possibility, the balance might be tilted so far in favour of the claimant as to render the justified aim of preventing unjust enrichment in practice impossible to achieve. It must be possible for the deciding body to take all available relevant evidence into consideration and reach a fair decision taking full account of whatever likelihood there may be that the claimant bore any part of the burden of the tax or suffered any economic loss as a result of its imposition.

3.060 The Court did not, however, take up this suggestion in the judgment in the case.[66]

3 Partial passing-on

3.061 In its judgments in *Société Comateb* and *Michailidis*, the Court also recognised the possibility of partial passing-on.[67] This principle applied to antitrust actions raises the consequential problem of apportionment of damage between different claimants at different levels of the production/distribution chain. This is correct, as a matter of principle, if one wishes to try to estimate as precisely as possible the extent of any unjust enrichment. Nonetheless, it does not give rise to the same complexities as in the field of antitrust when applied in the field of recovery of charges.

3.062 A competition law infringement, such as a cartel, is likely to have wider effects globally in terms of the number of parties affected, either directly or indirectly. A tax case, on the other hand, is likely to be limited to the effects of the passing-on of the one trader subject to the tax. In cases where the claimant is recovering unlawfully paid taxes, recovery is the only purpose of the action. On the other hand, competition law is part of the *ordre public* and closer to the interface between public and private law, meaning that such cases involve not

---

65 At para 60.

66 See paras 109–117 of the judgment.

67 *Comateb* at paras 27 and 28, and *Michailidis* at para 33. See also para 51 of the Advocate-General's Opinion in *Banks*.

just consideration of the compensation of the claimant, but also wider public policy implications in terms of the effectiveness and efficiency of the system as a whole. Finally, the possibility of consumer actions in tax or subsidy cases does not appear to be of any practical relevance.[68] This cannot be said of the field of antitrust (see further Chapter 6).

For all these reasons, the ECJ, which has not yet examined the issue of apportionment in-depth in competition litigation, may wish to distinguish the preceding case law on these grounds. This said, the Commission proposal does contain a rule that national courts shall have the power to '*estimate which share of the overcharge was passed on*'.[69] **3.063**

4 The Commission's position on the passing-on defence

The White Paper suggested that measures should be introduced so as to allow defendants to invoke the passing-on defence in relation to claims for compensation.[70] Furthermore, the Commission clarified that the standard of proof for proving passing-on should not be lower than the standard imposed on the claimant to prove the damage. **3.064**

Recital 17 to the draft Directive recognised that '*when an injured party has reduced its actual loss by passing it on, entirely or in part, to its own purchasers … the loss thus passed on no longer constitutes harm for which the party that passed it on has to be compensated. It is therefore appropriate to allow an infringing undertaking to invoke the passing-on of actual loss as a defence against a claim for damages.*' The draft Directive proposed to recognise passing-on as a defence to be asserted by the defendant.[71] **3.065**

Article 12(1) of the Commission proposal contains a clear rule allowing the passing-on defence. In addition, the proposal indicates that the burden of proving such a defence rests on the defendant, which is in line with existing EU jurisprudence on the point, as described above. **3.066**

68 See para 7 of the Opinion of AG Mancini in *San Giorgio*: '*[i]t is absurd to think of a mass of consumers who, in a system in which the class action is unknown, would bring an action against the State in order to recover minimal amounts*'.

69 Article 13(2), second subparagraph.

70 Section 2.6.

71 See also Article 10(1).

III NATIONAL LAW

3.067 There is little precedent throughout Member State jurisdictions on the issues of indirect purchaser standing and passing-on. That being said, a tendency can be seen, to the extent that there is a clear legal position at all, to allow both the passing-on defence and indirect purchaser standing in the various national laws, though this is not a unanimous position across all national laws as things currently stand.

3.068 It can thus also be argued that, although the EU has not yet adopted a legislative measure resolving the issues of passing-on and indirect purchaser standing, the drive towards an increased level of private damages actions for breach of EU competition law via the judicial route of the *Crehan* line of case law and the political route of the Commission's on-going policy initiative has borne fruit, in that an increased convergence at national level towards a coherent European position on the issues can be seen.

A England and Wales

3.069 The issues of indirect purchaser and passing-on remain open in English law. In general, it is commonly understood that the defence of passing-on can be relied upon, provided that it has been sufficiently proven in fact.[72] However, no definitive stance has yet been taken by the courts, although arguably the *Crehan/Manfredi* jurisprudence of the ECJ leads to the conclusion that the passing-on defence should also be permitted. This jurisprudence should be read together with section 60 of the Competition Act 1998, which requires that the provisions of that Act be applied in a manner that is consistent with EU law.[73]

3.070 The OFT has expressed the view that it is likely to be inappropriate to deny consumers and other end-users the right to claim for damages stemming from infringements of the antitrust rules as they are often the ones who bear the

---

72 This is also the position taken by the UK Government at para 4.38 of the 2013 BIS response, where it states that it '*considers that, under general principles of English tort law, there is no reason why the passing on-defence should not be allowed* ...'.

73 Section 60(1) of the Competition Act 1998 sets out the principle that, so far as is possible and having regard to any relevant differences between the provisions concerned, questions arising in relation to competition within the UK are to be dealt with in a manner which is consistent with the treatment of corresponding questions arising in EU law. In particular, under section 60(2), the courts must act, so far as it is compatible with the provisions of the Competition Act 1998, with a view to ensuring that there is no inconsistency between its decision and the principles laid down by EU law and the European Courts and any relevant decision of the European Courts.

brunt of competition law infringements.[74] In that respect, the Minister of State has said that one of the policy objectives of the Department for Business, Innovation & Skills (BIS) is to '*promote fairness by enabling consumers and businesses who have suffered loss due to anti-competitive behaviour to obtain redress*'.[75] However, to ensure that passing-on does not become a shield for defendants to escape liability, the OFT suggested that the burden of proof of passing-on should always lie with the defendant.[76]

In this context, on 24 April 2012, BIS took a significant step towards encouraging private antitrust actions by publishing its consultation on how best to foster private sector challenges to anti-competitive behaviour. Proposals were made as to how the passing-on defence could be addressed in the UK.[77] The position of the UK Government, as outlined at paragraph 4.49 of the consultation document, was that explicit provision as to the availability or otherwise of the passing-on defence as a matter of national law was not appropriate, and that the issue would be better addressed at EU level. More recent developments confirm that the UK Government will likely not legislate on the matter.[78] The UK Government has also noted that this issue is closely bound up with the matter of the treatment of collective actions, in that it might in such a context be necessary to devise mechanisms for apportionment of loss among the injured parties.[79] **3.071**

It can at the least be said that the concept of passing-on is not alien to English law. The issue was raised before the Competition Appeal Tribunal in *BCL Old Co*, where it was observed that '*the questions of whether the defendants are entitled to raise the "passing on defence" (either upstream or downstream), what is the effect of any such defence, and who bears the burden of proof, are novel and important issues both in this case and for future cases*'.[80] Standing of the indirect purchaser claimants was not disputed, but the case reached settlement before the substantive hearing. There was therefore no definitive ruling on the matter. **3.072**

74 OFT, 'Private Actions in Competition Law: Effective Redress for Consumers and Business', Discussion paper, April 2007, at para 6.18.

75 Foreword to the 2012 BIS consultation.

76 OFT, *loc. cit.*, at para 6.22.

77 Paras 4.44–4.49.

78 See the 2013 BIS response, at para 4.38.

79 As an addendum, it is interesting to note that, in the view of the UK Government, the policy choice of forbidding the passing-on defence while also denying indirect purchaser standing would be contrary to EU law (see the 2012 BIS consultation, at para 4.47, second bullet point).

80 *BCL Old Co Ltd and others* v *Aventis SA and others* [2005] CAT 2, at para 33.

3.073 Arguably, however, it can be said that the passing-on defence, should one decide to use such label, does exist in view of the fact that damages have a compensatory function,[81] and quantification thereof would therefore take passing-on into account.

B Germany

3.074 Under German law, it has never been an issue of contention that the '*party concerned*' ('*dem Betroffenen*') for the purposes of §33(1) GWB included any person or company *directly* affected by the illegal behaviour.[82] Whether indirect purchasers should be accorded standing has been a somewhat divisive issue among academic circles, however. In addition, the text of §33(3) GWB has caused some confusion as to whether or not it allows the passing-on defence.[83] The issues of indirect purchaser standing and passing-on have, however, recently been definitively resolved by the German courts.

3.075 By judgment given on 28 June 2011, the *Bundesgerichtshof* confirmed that indirect purchaser standing and the passing-on defence are both available.[84]

3.076 The original claim was brought by a printer business which had procured paper from a wholesaler which was a 100 per cent subsidiary of one of the parties involved in the carbonless paper cartel previously sanctioned by the Commission.[85] With respect to indirect purchaser standing, the *Bundesgerichtshof* noted that the German legal literature on the ability of indirect purchasers to bring a claim was divided, with some commentators arguing that the possibility of

---

81 See *Devenish Nutrition and others* v *Sanofi-Aventis SA and others* [2007] EWHC 2394.

82 For a discussion of the legal basis for damages actions for breach of competition law in Germany, see Chapter 2.

83 The second sentence of §33(3) GWB reads as follows: '*Wird eine Ware oder Dienstleistung zu einem überteuerten Preis bezogen, so ist der Schaden nicht deshalb ausgeschlossen, weil die Ware oder Dienstleistung weiterveräußert wurde*', which can be translated as follows: '*If a good or service is purchased at an excessive price, a damage shall not be excluded on account of the resale of the good or service.*'

84 Judgment of the *Bundesgerichtshof*, KZR 75/10, 28 June 2011 (WuW 2012, 57; NJW 2012, 928). The *ratio decidendi* of the case reads as follows: (a) '*Einem indirekten Abnehmer der Kartellteilnehmer steht ein Schadensersatzanspruch nach § 823 Abs. 2 BGB in Verbindung mit Art. 101 AEUV zu, wenn er durch das kartellrechtswidrige Verhalten einen Schaden erlitten hat. Die Darlegungs- und Beweislast dafür trägt der indirekte Abnehmer*', and (b) '*Der Vorteil, der dem Geschädigten aus einer Abwälzung des kartellbedingten Preisaufschlags auf seine Abnehmer erwächst, kann unter dem Aspekt der Vorteilsausgleichung zu berücksichtigen sein. Die Darlegungs- und Beweislast für die tatsächlichen Voraussetzungen der Vorteilsausgleichung liegt beim Schädiger*'. The German court relied on the *Crehan/Manfredi* jurisprudence of the ECJ in reaching this conclusion.

85 See Commission decision of 20 December 2001, COMP/E1/36.212. The original claim was dismissed by the *Landgericht* Mannheim (case 22 O 74/04, 29 April 2005). Because the wholesaler from whom the claimant purchased the product was a 100 per cent subsidiary of the cartelist, as a result of which the claimant was a *de facto* direct purchaser, the *Oberlandesgericht* Karlsruhe exceptionally permitted the claim (see *Oberlandesgericht* Karlsruhe, Az 6 U 118/05 (Kart), 11 June 2010), awarding damages of €100,000.

indirect purchaser claims would lead to an excessive extension of standing, to the disadvantage of defendants.

Observing, however, that the damaging effects of a cartel do not merely remain with a direct purchaser, the *Bundesgerichtshof* made it explicit that indirect purchasers fall within the scope of protection (*geschützten Personenkreis*) afforded by §823(2) BGB.[86] **3.077**

Not admitting indirect purchaser standing would mean that those entities that often bear the brunt of anti-competitive conduct would not have a remedy. Furthermore, the *Bundesgerichtshof* observed that direct purchasers would be less inclined to bring a claim in those situations where they stand to profit themselves from a cartel.[87] In other words, prohibiting indirect purchaser standing would lead to an enforcement gap. Furthermore, indirect purchaser standing cannot be prohibited *per se* on the basis that the number of claimants would multiply or that there would be evidentiary difficulties in proving where the damage lay.[88] **3.078**

In this regard, the court emphasised the importance of the burden of proof,[89] and stressed that it would be for the indirect purchaser to prove its own damage.[90] In the opinion of the court, this is sufficient to prevent the risk of the infringer being obliged to pay the same damage twice, that is, to direct and indirect purchasers. **3.079**

With respect to the passing-on defence, the court held that this was admissible as long as it would not lead to the unjust enrichment of the claimant.[91] The burden of proof for establishing passing-on lies with the defendant.[92] **3.080**

---

86 Para 24.

87 This would be especially the case with respect to 'cost-plus' contracts between a direct purchaser and its customers, para 33.

88 Para 27.

89 Para 29.

90 Para 44 *et seq*. (see the *ratio decidendi*, referred to above).

91 '*Mit dem unionsrechtlichen Effizienzgebot ist es jedoch vereinbar, den Ersatzanspruch nach nationalem Recht zu versagen, wenn sich sonst eine ungerechtfertigte Bereicherung des Berechtigten ergeben würde.*'

92 Para 64.

C France

3.081 Passing-on and, implicitly, indirect purchaser standing were addressed in the *Ajinomoto Eurolysine* case, a damages action following on from the Commission's lysine cartel decision in 2002, where the undertaking Ajinomoto Eurolysine was considered a driving force in the cartel.[93]

3.082 In this case, Doux Aliments, an indirect purchaser of lysine from Ajinomoto Eurolysine via Ceva Santé Animale (the direct purchaser), brought an action for damages against the cartelist, Ajinomoto Eurolysine. Doux Aliments argued that the cartel had the effect of increasing the price of lysine by 30 per cent and therefore claimed damages and interest thereon corresponding to 30 per cent of its lysine purchases.

3.083 Overruling the Paris *Cour d'appel*,[94] the *Cour de cassation* held that the passing-on defence was admissible, finding that the lower instance court had failed to establish whether the claimant had passed on the price increase.[95] In a more recent follow-on damages action, also resulting from the Commission's lysine decision, the *Cour de cassation* held that it was for the claimant, an indirect purchaser, to show that an overcharge had not been passed on. This point of principle was justified on the grounds that passing-on of an overcharge is the normal and expected course of events.[96] Furthermore, it is implicit in the *Ajinomoto Eurolysine* judgment that indirect purchasers have standing under French law.

93 Commission Decision 2001/418/EC of 7 June 2000, case COMP/36.545/F3, amino acids (OJ L 152, 7.6.2001, p 24).

94 Paris Cour d'appel, judgment of 10 June 2009.

95 *Doux Aliments/Ajinomoto Eurolysine* (No 09–15.816), *Cour de cassation, chambre commerciale*, judgment of 15 June 2010. With respect to the lower court's finding, the *Cour de cassation* held as follows: '*Alors que d'autre part en énonçant que "la circonstance que les sociétés Doux auraient été en mesure de répercuter ce surcoût sur les hausses de prix du produit est sans incidence sur l'étendue du droit des appelantes à réparation", cependant que l'intimée faisait valoir à titre principal que les sociétés Doux, qui ne justifiaient pas l'absence de répercussion de ce surcoût sur les prix, n'établissaient ainsi pas l'existence même du préjudice invoqué, la Cour d'appel a privé sa décision de base légale au regard de l'article 1382 du Code civil*'.

96 *Les Sociétés Coopérative Le Gouessant et Sofral* (11–18.495), *Cour de cassation, chambre commerciale*: '*Mais attendu que... l'arrêt après avoir relevé que la répercussion des coûts est la pratique commerciale habituelle et normale, retient que les sociétés Coopérative Le Gouessant et Sofral ne démontrent pas qu'elles n'avaient pas pu répercuter les effets de la hausse des prix de la lysine sur leurs clients; qu'en l'état de ces constatations et appréciations ..., la cour d'appel qui n'a pas inversé la charge de la preuve, a pu statuer comme elle a fait; que le moyen n'est pas fondé*' (emphasis added). This takes the idea of a presumption of passing-on to its logical conclusion: not only can an indirect purchaser benefit from it, but it can also, as in this case, suffer from it, where it is not the final consumer of the product in question.

D Italy

The *issue* of passing-on was explicitly considered by the Italian courts in the *VIH/Juventus FC* proceedings decided by the Turin *Corte d'appello* (Court of Appeal) in application of national competition law.[97] However, the court analysed the issue of passing-on in terms of contributory negligence. The defendant had contracted to sell two tied products at inflated prices to the claimant on condition *inter alia* that they were tied when sold to end-consumers. **3.084**

The *Corte d'appello* dismissed the claim. Whilst it found that the agreement between VIH and Juventus was restrictive of competition under Article 2 of L. 287/90, as it fixed prices and tied the sale of the tickets for the football match to the sale of other unrelated products, it found that the claimant had agreed to the restrictive agreement with the intent to pass on any overcharge to final purchasers, and had therefore contributed to the damage caused.[98] The court found that the claimant had not itself suffered damage because the persons actually harmed by the unlawful conduct were those who bought the tickets with the tied products. **3.085**

As such, it can be said that the passing-on defence is not specifically recognised in Italy. However, the current position can be summarised by reference to the following two points: (i) claimants can only seek damages for losses *actually* incurred, and (ii) they must not have concurred in causing the losses in question. **3.086**

In relation to indirect purchaser standing, it has been stated by the *Corte de cassazione* that the provisions of competition law inherently protect *all parties* who may be affected by violations of antitrust law.[99] Therefore, relying on the interpretation of the Rome *Corte d'appello* of 31 March 2008,[100] and with reference to Italy's general civil liability principles, claims by indirect purchasers are in theory applicable. **3.087**

Furthermore, if consumers suffer harm as a result of, for example, an anti-competitive agreement between companies, they are also able to rely on consumer protection provisions, such as Articles 2(2)(e) and 140(9) of the *Codice del consumo* (Consumer Code),[101] in order to claim damages.[102] **3.088**

97 Turin *Corte d'appello*, *Indaba Incentive co/Società Juventus F.C. SpA*, judgment of 6 July 2000.

98 This logic recalls the condition of '*significant responsibility*' to be established later by the ECJ in the *Crehan* ruling. Under that framework, it could have been argued that the claimant did not have a claim for damages on the grounds that it bore such responsibility for the distortion of competition.

99 Judgments no 2207/2005 and 2305/2007.

100 *International Broker/Refining Companies*, judgment no 1337/2008.

101 *Decreto legislativo* no 206, 6 September 2005.

102 Lecce *Giudice di pace*, 30 January 2003.

IV INDIRECT PURCHASER STANDING AND PASSING-ON IN THE US*

3.089 It should be noted that, whereas in the EU consideration of these two issues tends to start from the '*any individual*' requirement of the jurisprudence of the ECJ, that is, from the entitlement to standing of the indirect purchaser, in the US, analysis is the other way round, that is, it starts from the availability of the passing-on defence, and from there moves to consideration of indirect purchaser standing. Thus the US Supreme Court settled the former issue some time before it settled the latter (see below). This could be said to reflect the preoccupation of the US system with deterrence, whereas legal policy in the EU to date has been focussed more on compensation.

A Antitrust injury

3.090 As a preliminary issue, it is necessary to give a brief description of the concept of antitrust injury in US antitrust law.

3.091 §4 of the Clayton Act provides a private cause of action for parties injured by violations of §§1 and 2 of the Sherman Act.[103] Moreover, apart from the requirements set out in Article III of the US Constitution, plaintiffs pleading breach of competition law must also show antitrust standing.[104] In particular, all claimants seeking damages under the US antitrust provisions must allege an injury to their business or property that is causally linked to an antitrust violation and is the type of injury the antitrust laws were intended to prevent, that is, antitrust injury.[105] In *Associated General Contractors* v *California State Council of Carpenters* (*AGC*),[106] the US Supreme Court held that a plaintiff's ability to sue under the antitrust laws depends on the balancing of five factors, the most important of which is a demonstrable '*antitrust injury*'. To have such an injury, the plaintiff must participate in the same market that the defendant allegedly harmed through its conduct. In other words, a plaintiff should not be able to bring a claim if its 'injury' is too far removed from the alleged

* Parts of this section were first published by Sweet & Maxwell in GCLR 2012 5(3), at 111, and are reproduced by agreement with the publishers.

103 See 15 USC §15. Section 4 of the Clayton Act permits the recovery of treble damages by '*any person … injured in his business or property by reason of anything forbidden in the antitrust laws*'. (*Ibid.*, at §15(a)). Section 15 of the Clayton Act entitles '*[a]ny person … threatened [with] loss or damage by a violation of the antitrust laws*' to obtain an injunction (*Ibid.*, at §26).

104 See *Reilly* v *Hearst Corp.* 107 F. Supp. 2d 1192 (ND Cal 2000), at 1195 (citing *Cargill Inc.* v *Monfort of Colo, Inc.* 479 US 104 (1986), 109–113).

105 See *Atlantic Richfield Co.* v *USA Petroleum Co.* 495 US 328 (1990), 334; *Brunswick Corporation* v *Pueblo Bowl-O-Mat, Inc.*, at 489; *Cargill*, at 109; see also *Hawaii* v *Standard Oil Co. of Cal.* 405 US 251 (1972), 263.

106 459 US 519 (1983).

infringement.[107] The concept of antitrust standing also requires the plaintiff to show that there are no other parties that have been more directly harmed.

B The passing-on defence under US law

In its judgment in *Hanover Shoe*,[108] the US Supreme Court disallowed the passing-on defence, and ruled that direct purchasers can collect the entire anti-competitive overcharge even though they may have passed on all or part of the overcharge. **3.092**

The case concerned the unlawful refusal by the defendant, who had a monopoly in the shoe machinery market, to sell shoe machines, and instead only provided such machines on the basis of long-term leasing contracts, which resulted in the claimant, a shoe manufacturer, paying higher prices for the machines. The defendant argued that the claimant had not suffered loss since it had passed on the higher prices to its own customers, who bought the shoes. **3.093**

The Supreme Court rejected the passing-on defence primarily for two reasons. Firstly, allowing such a defence would unduly complicate competition law claims for damages, as it would involve attempts to trace the effects of the overcharge on the purchaser's prices, sales costs and profits. The Court held as follows[109]: **3.094**

> We are not impressed with the argument that the sound laws of economics require recognizing this defense. A wide range of factors influence a company's pricing policies. Normally the impact of a single change in the relevant conditions cannot be measured after the fact; indeed a businessman may be unable to state whether, had one fact been different … he would have chosen a different price. Treble damages actions would require long and complicated proceedings involving massive evidence and complicated theories.

The Court acknowledged that much of an overcharge is passed down the distribution chain, but stated that at whatever price the direct purchaser sells, the price he paid the defendant remains illegally high, and his profits would be greater if his costs were lower. **3.095**

---

107 See, for example, *In Re: Dynamic Random Access Memory (DRAM) Antitrust Litigation* 536 F. Supp. 2d 1129 (ND Cal 2008), 1137–1138. On the other hand, a different result obtained in *In re TFT-LCD (Flat Panel) Antitrust Litigation* 586 F. Supp. 2d 1109 (ND Cal 2008), 1123–1124, where the court declined to dismiss consumers' claims in the absence of a clear statement by state legislatures (or state courts) that AGC applies to the antitrust law of that state.

108 *Hanover Shoe* v *United Shoe Machinery Corp.* 392 US 481 (1968).

109 At 492–3.

3.096 Secondly, the Court ruled that permitting the passing-on defence would lessen the effectiveness of the private enforcement remedy. It stated that there would be a risk that antitrust infringers would retain the fruits of their illegality, as incentives to bring actions would be too widely dispersed, meaning that no one would be available to bring an action. Purchasers at each stage of the distribution chain would have to meet the challenge that they passed on the higher price to their customers, and end-consumers would only have a tiny stake in the lawsuit and little interest in attempting a class action. The Court considered that direct purchasers were best positioned to sue, and that if the passing-on defence were allowed, this would increase the risks and reduce the benefits of direct purchaser suits, so that such suits might not be brought, thus weakening antitrust enforcement.

3.097 However, in its decision in *Clayworth*,[110] the California Supreme Court ruled in favour of precluding the passing-on defence under the Cartwright Act, subject to two exceptions, the most important of which obtains to the situation where there is the potential for duplicative recovery by direct and indirect purchasers. It should be noted that under Californian state law, both direct and indirect purchasers have standing to sue.

3.098 The decision in *Hanover Shoe* also needs to be placed in context. At the time of the case, the Electrical Equipment Antitrust Cases were pending before the federal courts.[111] In these cases, the defendants, manufacturers of turbine generators, transformers and switchgear, had overcharged the electricity utility plaintiffs, which had added the overcharge to their rate bases and thus passed it on to consumers in the form of retail electric power rates, which had been approved by state public service commissions. Although the actions of the defendants were very negatively perceived by the public, more so than in the case of *United Shoe*, they had a better passing-on defence, which they were pleading in the various actions. Furthermore, at the time of *Hanover Shoe*, Rule 23 of the Federal Rules of Civil Procedure (FRCP) had not been enacted, and class actions had not been developed, meaning that the risk of ultimate consumers not having a remedy was stronger than it is today.[112]

---

110 *Clayworth* v *Pfizer Inc* 233 P 3d 1066 (Cal. 2010).

111 Between 1961 and 1964, 1,919 separate antitrust actions were filed against manufacturers of electrical equipment in 36 federal judicial districts. See, generally, Phil C. Neal and Perry Goldberg, 'The Electrical Equipment Antitrust Cases: Novel Judicial Administration' (1964) 50 American Bar Association Journal 621.

112 See Chapter 6 for a discussion of the class action regime under US federal law.

C Indirect purchaser standing: the rule in *Illinois Brick*

It has been established by the US Supreme Court that, with some exceptions, the only group entitled to seek damages under federal antitrust law is direct purchasers.[113] **3.099**

The limitations in relation to indirect purchaser actions in US federal court flow from the US Supreme Court's treatment of the passing-on defence in two primary cases. As described above, in 1968, the Court issued its ruling in *Hanover Shoe*, in which it rejected the use of the passing-on defence by the defendants. The Court decided that the passing-on defence can only be used if a defendant meets the '*normally … insurmountable*' burden of establishing evidence to prove the passing-on. This addressed and highlighted the problems of using the passing-on defence by the *defendant.* **3.100**

It was not until *Illinois Brick* that the Court considered the implications of the limits of the passing-on defence on the *plaintiff*. Since defendants were unable to use the passing-on defence, the Court reasoned that the same principles barred indirect purchaser actions, except in three narrow circumstances, described below.[114] **3.101**

The consequence of the combined effect of the decisions in *Hanover Shoe* and *Illinois Brick* is that indirect purchasers are, generally, not allowed to pursue their claims for damages in US federal court. Around half of the US states, as well as the District of Columbia and Puerto Rico have, however, 'repealed' *Illinois Brick* and adopted state-level legislation that allows indirect purchasers to seek damages under state law. In addition, indirect purchasers were also granted recourse to the equitable doctrine of unjust enrichment. As such, indirect purchasers have three options when seeking damages in the United States: firstly, fit within an *Illinois Brick* exception and bring the claim in federal court (with the possibility of treble damages); secondly, bring a claim under State law for damages; or thirdly, bring a claim for unjust enrichment. **3.102**

Given the above, and in view of the attractive incentives available to direct purchasers, there are often questions, especially in complex supply chains, about who the direct purchaser actually is. Emerging case law indicates that direct purchasers are likely to be the entities with which the defendant actually **3.103**

---

113 In particular, in relation to §§4 and 16 of the Clayton Act.

114 See also *Blue Shield of Virginia et al.* v *McCready* 457 US 465 (1982), at 476–477, where the Supreme Court observed that '*antitrust violation[s] may be expected to cause ripples of harm to flow through the Nation's economy*', but also found that there is '*a point beyond which the wrongdoer should not be held liable*'.

engaged in a financial transaction. In one of the most recent cases to consider the issue, *Warren General Hospital* v *Amgen*, the US Court of Appeals for the Third Circuit held that Warren General Hospital was not a direct purchaser because it had purchased Amgen's drugs directly from a wholesaler. Warren argued, however, that its actual relationship vis-à-vis Amgen was that of a direct purchaser, despite the fact that it had obtained the products from the wholesaler.[115] The court rejected this argument, ruling that Warren was an indirect purchaser and, as such, did not have the necessary standing to claim damages from Amgen under federal law.

3.104 The Court noted that the commercial exchange took place between the wholesaler and Warren, which implied that Warren was only a direct purchaser vis-à-vis the wholesaler. Therefore, Warren's purchase from Amgen could only be considered as being indirect.[116] From this it follows that, as a preliminary point, putative plaintiffs need to consider with whom they conducted their transaction, since it is with that party that they will be entitled to be a direct purchaser, and, in effect, entitled to seek compensation. On the other hand, for those claims which are more 'distanced', the plaintiff will have an 'indirect' relationship, and his options will be as set out below.

1 *Exceptions to the rule in* Illinois Brick

3.105 As noted above, three narrow exceptions exist under which indirect purchasers are able to bring actions for damages under federal law. Importantly, the three exceptions apply when there is no other direct purchaser that is likely to be harmed.

3.106 The first exception relates to the idea of 'ownership or control'. Specifically, it allows for the use of the passing-on defence by a claimant in cases where the direct purchaser is owned or controlled by the defendant.[117]

---

115 Amgen had required Warren to negotiate the purchase requirements and prices directly with Amgen, communicate directly with Amgen about net costs and any other issue relating to the drugs, and enter into contracts directly with Amgen, whereby the contract was negotiated at Warren and serviced by Amgen, and costs and rebates were set by Amgen and were irrespective of the wholesaler's purchases. Moreover, when Warren received rebates, it received them directly from Amgen.

116 *Warren*, at 88. See also *Howard Hess Dental Labs* v *Dentsply International Inc.* 424 F. 3d 363 (3rd Cir 2005), at 372–375; *In Re: Wellbutrin XL Antitrust Litigation* Nos 08-cv-2431 and 08-cv-2433, 2012 WL 1657734 (ED Pa, 11 May 2011). See further *Campos* v *Ticketmaster Corp.* 140 F. 3d 1166 (8th Cir 1998), at 1168–1169 and 1171 (finding that individual ticket purchasers' claims were barred by *Illinois Brick*, that the individuals were not purchasers of '*ticket distribution services*' because '*[t]he plaintiffs' inability to obtain ticket delivery services in a competitive market is simply the consequence of the antecedent inability of the venues to do so*'); *Paycom Billing Services* v *MasterCard International* 467 F. 3d 283 (2nd Cir 2006) (ruling that a merchant lacked standing to assert claims against MasterCard because the financial transaction was directly with its bank, not with MasterCard).

117 See, for example, *Jewish Hosp. Ass'n* v *Stewart Mech. Enters.* 628 F. 2d 971 (6th Cir 1980), at 974–975.

The second exception, the 'cost-plus' exception, applies when the customer is committed to purchasing a fixed quantity of a manufacturer's product; regardless of the price.[118] In other words, where the indirect purchaser is committed to purchasing a fixed quantity of product, it insulates the direct purchaser from market responses to the overcharge. As a result, it is not necessary to determine whether and how much of the overcharge is borne by the indirect purchaser. In practice, however, the cost-plus exception is construed very narrowly and applies only where the direct purchaser will suffer no injury.[119] **3.107**

The final exception is the 'co-conspirator' exception, where the direct purchaser is a direct participant in the cartel. In other words, the indirect purchaser has to be able to allege that it will be able to prove a conspiracy, and in so doing will be able to prove that it is not an indirect purchaser, since the direct purchaser participated in the cartel.[120] **3.108**

The exceptions set forth above are very limited. Thus, under federal law, indirect purchasers have almost no recourse to damages, and can only seek injunctive relief. However, as noted above, more than half of the US states have passed state laws that 'repeal' *Illinois Brick*. As a result, indirect purchaser plaintiffs can, and do, bring claims against defendants under state law. In states that permit indirect purchasers to seek damages, the level of damages available is, correspondingly, determined by state law, but is typically not trebled and is in any event limited to damages based upon sales made within the state. **3.109**

2 *The efficiency of the rule in* Illinois Brick

The success of the Supreme Court's attempt to limit indirect purchaser actions and streamline litigation is, however, debatable. Firstly, states must still contend with the issue of causation. Many states, but not all, have resorted to applying federal law on causation, namely the US Supreme Court's decision in *AGC* in relation to antitrust injury. This suggests an effort to limit liability in the context of indirect purchaser cases by many states under their own laws. This issue is, however, still the subject of litigation.[121] **3.110**

---

118 *Illinois Brick*, at 736.

119 *Kansas* v *Utilicorp United* 497 US 199 (1990), at 217; *In Re: OSB Antitrust Litigation* 2007 WL 2253425 (ED Pa, 3 August 2007) ('*Courts have almost never applied this exception*').

120 *Paper Systems Incorporated* v *Nippon Paper Industries Co. Ltd.* 281 F. 3d 629 (7th Cir. 2002), at 632–634.

121 See *In Re: Automotive Parts Antitrust Litigation, In Re: Wire Harness Cases* 2:12-cv-00103-MOB-MKM (ED Mich, 6 June 2013), at 26: '*some states apply the AGC factors, some states have enacted harmonization statutes that require courts to interpret the state antitrust laws in accordance with federal law, some states allow consideration of federal law, and some have declined to adopt the AGC factors*'.

3.111 Second, so many states permit indirect purchaser actions that courts are increasingly filled with 'classes' of plaintiffs under state law which remove their cases to federal court, where pre-trial proceedings take place alongside direct purchaser claims. To the extent that indirect purchasers bring their case in state court, defendants (or plaintiffs) can seek to 'remove' the case to federal court. In complex cases involving a number of separate lawsuits, a party can, and often does, seek for all of the federal cases against it to be consolidated into a single case for pre-trial proceedings. This is done through use of a procedure before the Judicial Panel on Multidistrict Litigation (JPML).[122] This creates some efficiencies, but is nevertheless a complex, expensive and time-consuming process. The result, in the view of some commentators, is a system so complex that it would be better simply to allow indirect purchaser claims to proceed under federal law, that is, to overrule *Illinois Brick*.[123]

122 For instance, on 7 February 2012, the JPML ordered the consolidation of all of the cases against the suppliers of automotive wire harnesses into a single case for pre-trial proceedings. That case will now proceed in the US District Court for the Eastern District of Michigan (see *In Re: Automotive Wire Harness Systems Antitrust Litigation* MDL No 2311 (ED Mich, 7 February 2012)).

123 See Antitrust Modernization Commission, Separate Statement of Commissioners Burchfield, Delrahim, Jacobson, Kempf, Litvack, Valentine and Warden, at 397–398.

4

PROVING THE INFRINGEMENT

I PRIVATE LITIGANTS' ACCESS TO PROBATIVE DOCUMENTS IN EU CARTEL DAMAGES ACTIONS 4.004
- A Access to documents held by the Commission 4.006
- B Access to documents held by a national competition authority 4.021
- C Access to documents held by the defendant: the *National Grid* proceedings before the English courts 4.036
  - 1 Legitimate expectations 4.044
  - 2 Proportionality 4.045
  - 3 Documents ordered to be disclosed to National Grid 4.046
  - 4 Further developments: the French blocking statute 4.049
- D Access to documents held by a third party 4.057
- E The Commission's proposals on evidence 4.059
- F The Commission's attempts to limit discoverability in US courts 4.061

II THE EVIDENTIAL VALUE OF PRIOR ADMINISTRATIVE DECISIONS 4.071
- A Commission decisions: Article 16 of Regulation 1/2003 4.072
  - 1 The judgment of the English Court of Appeal in *Crehan* 4.082
- B Commission decisions: Article 9 of Regulation 1/2003 4.086
- C NCA decisions 4.088
  - 1 United Kingdom 4.090
  - 2 Germany 4.104
  - 3 Romanistic jurisdictions 4.109

The aim of this chapter is to give a brief introduction to certain evidentiary issues which are key to any attempt to bring a damages action for breach of EU competition law. **4.001**

As explained in Chapter 2, damages actions for breach of competition law are tortious in nature. As with all actions for tortious liability, the claimant has to prove the infringement, identify the causal link between the infringement and his loss and quantify that loss. A peculiarity of competition law litigation is that proof of the infringement can often be adduced from a decision by the public authority. **4.002**

In terms of proving the infringement, access to evidence held either by a competition authority or another party, including the defendant, is crucial. Access to documents may prove particularly important in the current enforcement climate. For example, conscious of the extensive resources required to deal with cartel cases, the Commission of late has initiated a drive to settle cartel cases under its settlement programme.[1] A corollary of this is that publicly **4.003**

1 Commission Regulation (EC) No 622/2008 of 30 June 2008 amending Regulation (EC) No 773/2004, as regards the conduct of settlement procedures in cartel cases (OJ L 171, 1.7.2008, p 3), and Commission notice on

available decisions will likely henceforth contain only limited information that can be relied upon in follow-on damages actions, rendering them more difficult to substantiate. Apart from the critical issue of access to documents, the evidential value of public enforcement decisions can circumvent the requirement to prove the infringement in so-called 'follow-on' actions, thus lightening the evidential burden on a claimant.

I PRIVATE LITIGANTS' ACCESS TO PROBATIVE DOCUMENTS IN EU CARTEL DAMAGES ACTIONS

4.004 A private litigant who has suffered loss as the result of an illegal cartel may bring his claim for damages before the competent court of a Member State. He may do this prior to any official decision being taken by the Commission or the national competition authority as to the existence of the cartel, or he may wait for the adoption of such a decision. The advantage of this second possibility – often referred to as a 'follow-on' action – is that the existence of the cartel will have been established by the Commission or the national competition authority, and the private party can concentrate on proving his loss, and the causal link between the cartel and that loss. In preparing his case he will probably want to see the documents in the possession of the Commission or the national competition authority in the hope of finding evidence to support his case. This is one type of 'access' to documents that will be examined in this chapter. In addition to this, the private litigant would be interested in having sight of documents in the defendants' possession or control that would assist his case. This is another type of 'access' to be examined in this chapter. Then, last of all, there is also the possibility that a third party may hold evidence that could be used by the private litigant. This type of access is also examined in this chapter.

4.005 It is not just because a person or public body holds documentary evidence that could assist a private litigant that the latter has a right to inspect that evidence and take copies. The existence of such a right depends on national and EU law.

A Access to documents held by the Commission

4.006 A particularity of the EU legal system is that is has rules on allowing members of the public to obtain documents held by the EU institutions. Public access to documents held by the EU institutions was introduced in 1994, based on

---

the conduct of settlement procedures in view of the adoption of Decisions pursuant to Article 7 and Article 23 of Council Regulation (EC) No 1/2003 in cartel cases (OJ C 167, 2.7.2008, p 1).

practice in the Scandinavian countries.[2] The purpose of the legislation is to create a more transparent public administration, not to facilitate discovery of documents in civil litigation. Notwithstanding this, given the absence of any formal system of discovery in the civil law Member States and in EU law generally, litigants have been experimenting with using the legislation on public access to documents in order to obtain evidence to assist them in private antitrust damages claims.

The rules on public access to documents held by the EU institutions are provided for by Regulation (EC) No 1049/2001 (the 'Access to Documents Regulation').[3] This Regulation institutes a right of access to documents of the institutions, that is to say, all documents held by an institution whether drawn up or received by it, in all activities of the EU. This right of access is available to any EU citizen, any natural person residing in a Member State, and any legal person having its registered office in a Member State.[4] There are some important exceptions in the Access to Documents Regulation. These exceptions to the general right of access should be construed narrowly. In such instances, a delicate balance has to be struck between the competing interests of, on the one hand, preserving an effective system of public enforcement and, on the other hand, facilitating the functioning of a viable system of private enforcement. This conundrum tends to manifest itself in the context of access to leniency documents and, to date, when faced with this dilemma the Commission has exhibited a tendency to err on the side of preventing access to documents in order to safeguard the credibility of its leniency programme. The exceptions which the Commission generally invokes when it seeks to resist applications for access to leniency applications are framed, under Article 4 of the Access to Documents Regulation, in the following terms[5]: **4.007**

> The institutions shall refuse access to a document where disclosure would undermine the protection of:
>
> – commercial interests of a natural or legal person, including intellectual property;

2 For extended analysis of the development of access to documents in the EU, see I. Osterdahl, 'Openness v Secrecy: Public Access to Documents in Sweden and the European Union' (1998) 23(4) ELR 336, and M. A. De Leeuw, 'The Regulation on Public Access to European Parliament, Council and Commission Documents in the European Union: Are Citizens Better Off?' (2003) 28(3) ELR 324.

3 Regulation (EC) No 1049/2001 of the European Parliament and of the Council of 30 May 2001 regarding public access to European Parliament, Council and Commission documents (OJ L 145, 31.5.2001, p 43).

4 According to Article 7 of the Access to Documents Regulation, the institution will, within 15 working days from registration of an application for access to a document, either grant access to the document requested or, in a written reply, state the reasons for the total or partial refusal to do so. However, see para 34 of the judgment of the General Court of 25 January 2012 in case T-330/11 *MasterCard Inc and MasterCard Europe* v *Commission* (not yet reported), where it was held that '*[t]here is no legal principle that deprives the administration of the power to reply to an application, even outside the time-limits laid down for that purpose*'.

5 Article 4(2) and the first and second subparagraphs of Article 4(3) of the Access to Documents Regulation.

- court proceedings and legal advice;
- the purpose of inspections, investigations and audits,

unless there is an overriding public interest in disclosure …

Access to a document, drawn up by an institution for internal use or received by an institution, which relates to a matter where the decision has not been taken by the institution, shall be refused if disclosure of the document would seriously undermine the institution's decision-making process, unless there is an overriding public interest in disclosure.

Access to a document containing opinions for internal use as part of deliberations and preliminary consultations within the institution concerned shall be refused even after the decision has been taken if disclosure of the document would seriously undermine the institution's decision-making process, unless there is an overriding public interest in disclosure.

4.008 In the context of cartel damages actions, in particular,[6] these provisions were put to the test in the important cases of *CDC Hydrogene Peroxide*[7] and *EnBW Energie.*[8]

4.009 The first of these cases to be decided, *CDC Hydrogene Peroxide*, concerned a request for access to no more than the index of the Commission's file relating to its investigation and fining of the participants in a cartel in the hydrogen peroxides sector.[9]

4.010 Cartel Damage Claims (CDC), a Belgian special-purpose company that manages antitrust claims on behalf of alleged cartel victims, brought a damages claim against the defendants before the *Landgericht* Dortmund in March 2009. In order to acquire evidence to support its case, CDC sought access to the index of the Commission's file pursuant to the Access to Documents Regulation so that it could request the disclosure of individual documents before the national court.

4.011 The Commission argued, *inter alia*, that disclosure of the index would undermine the commercial interests of the companies under investigation through the divulgation of business secrets. It would also undermine the purpose of the

6 Article 4 of the Access to Documents Regulation was also put to the test in the context of access to documents relating to merger control proceedings. See, for example, the judgments of the ECJ of 28 June 2012 in Cases C-404/10 P *Commission* v *Éditions Odile Jacob SAS and Lagardère SCA* (not yet reported) and C-477/10 P *Commission* v *Agrofert Holding a.s, and others* (not yet reported).

7 Case T-437/08 *CDC Hydrogene Peroxide* v *Commission*, judgment of 15 December 2011 (not yet reported).

8 Case T-344/08 *EnBW Energie Baden-Württemberg AG* v *Commission*, judgment of 22 May 2012 (not yet reported).

9 Commission Decision of 3 May 2006, case COMP/F/38.620, hydrogen peroxide and perborate (not yet published).

Commission's antitrust investigation and its leniency programme[10] by deterring companies from cooperating with the Commission. CDC challenged the Commission's decision before the General Court.

The Court ruled that the Commission had wrongly refused to disclose the index of its investigation file to CDC. The Commission had not established that access to the index would undermine the protection of business secrets pursuant to the first indent of Article 4(2) of the Access to Documents Regulation. According to the Court, the index did not contain any business secrets, so the refusal of its disclosure could not be justified by the protection of business secrets. **4.012**

The General Court also ruled that the Commission had not established that access to the index would undermine the protection of the purpose of investigations. The Court observed that leniency programmes – the effectiveness of which the Commission sought to protect – were not the only means of ensuring compliance with EU competition law, but that private damages actions are also a means of achieving this objective. Accordingly, the Commission had not met the requisite legal standard.[11] **4.013**

In the second case, *EnBW Energie*, the nature of the requested documents was more complex. It arose out of the Commission's fining decision in the *Gas Insulated Switchgear* cartel.[12] For the purposes of substantiating its claim against the cartel perpetrators, EnBW – a publicly quoted electricity utility company – requested access to several documents held by the Commission. The Commission refused. For the purposes of its assessment, the Commission grouped the requested documents into the following categories: **4.014**

(1) documents provided in connection with an immunity or leniency application, namely statements from the undertakings in question and all

10 Commission notice on immunity from fines and reduction of fines in cartel cases (OJ C 298, 8.12.2006, p 17).

11 Several of the cartel members in this case recently obtained interim relief from the General Court ordering the Commission to refrain from publishing a more complete version of a non-confidential version of the Commission's decision placed on its website in September 2007. The applicants had argued that publication of the disputed information would *inter alia* be an infringement of the obligation of professional secrecy, which is afforded protection under Article 339 TFEU, and represent a clear disregard for the confidentiality of the information which they had submitted to the Commission in order to benefit from the leniency notice. The applicants also argued that the decision to publish a more complete version of the decision amounted to an *implicit* grant of access to information under the Access to Documents Regulation. The latter argument was, however, rejected. Given the complexity of the matter, the President of the General Court held that there was a *prima facie* case, and stopped publication of the additional information pending examination within the main proceedings (see Order of the President of the General Court of 16 November 2012 in case T-345/12 *R Akzo Nobel and others* v *Commission* (not yet reported), and Order of the President of the General Court of 16 November 2012 in Case T-341/12 *R Evonik Degussa GmbH* v *Commission* (not yet reported)).

12 Commission Decision of 24 January 2007, case COMP/38.899, gas insulated switchgear (OJ C 5, 10.1.2008, p 7).

documents submitted by them in connection with the immunity or leniency application;

(2) Commission requests for information and parties' replies to those requests;

(3) documents obtained during Commission inspections, namely documents seized at on-the-spot inspections at the premises of the undertakings concerned;

(4) the confidential version of the statements of objections and the parties' replies thereto;

(5) internal documents of the Commission, divided into the following two subcategories:

  (a) documents relating to the facts, namely background notes on the conclusions to be drawn from evidence gathered, correspondence with other competition authorities, and consultations with other Commission departments;

  (b) procedural documents, namely inspection warrants, inspection reports, lists of documents obtained in the course of inspections, documents concerning the notification of certain documents, and file notes.

4.015 The Commission was of the view that each of the categories of documents requested by EnBW, that is, categories 1–5(b) above, fell within the exception provided for in the third indent of Article 4(2) of the Access to Documents Regulation, and that the documents in category 5(a) also fell within the exception set out in the second subparagraph of Article 4(3) of that Regulation. The Commission stated that it could see nothing that indicated there was an overriding public interest in granting access to the documents requested. It gave as its reason for refusing to grant *partial* access to the case file the fact that all the documents contained in the file were covered in their entirety by the exceptions listed in the Access to Documents Regulation.

4.016 EnBW challenged the Commission's refusal before the General Court. The Court stated, as a general proposition, that the Commission was obliged to review each of the documents requested before deciding whether or not it fell within one of the exceptions to the right of access.[13] The Court nevertheless

13 For a contrasting position in the context of access to documents in a merger control context, see *Éditions Odile Jacob SAS* and *Agrofert Holding a.s.* In these cases, the ECJ held that the Commission is permitted to apply a general presumption that document disclosure in the context of merger control proceedings undermines, in principle, the protection of the commercial interests involved and the protection of the purpose of investigations relating to those proceedings. This therefore obviates the need for the Commission to carry out an individual examination of documents.

recognised that there were exceptions to the obligation to review each document, notably:

- in situations where it is obvious, on the basis of a general presumption, that access must be refused or granted;
- when a single justification may be applied to documents belonging to the same category, if they contain the same type of information; or
- in exceptional cases where the administrative burden entailed by a specific, individual review of the documents would prove particularly heavy, thus exceeding the limits of what may reasonably be required.

The General Court noted that the Commission had not reviewed each document individually, yet no general presumption was applicable in the present case. As far as concerned the Commission's review by category, its reasoning was essentially the same for documents in each of the categories 1, 2, 4 and 5(a): the Commission had adopted the view that disclosure of the documents would make companies less likely to come forward to apply for leniency. This led the Court to conclude that the Commission's division of the documents into categories was artificial: it did not reflect real differences in the content of the documents within the various categories. **4.017**

As far as the documents in category 3 were concerned (documents obtained during on-the-spot inspections), the Court held that the Commission was entitled to carry out a review of these documents *by category*, but solely in relation to the exception concerning the protection of the purpose of investigations. However, the Court noted that in EnBW's case, the Commission had already adopted the fining decision, and so there was no investigation in progress that would have been jeopardised by the disclosure of the requested documents. Furthermore, the General Court observed that the concept of '*purpose of investigations*' does not extend beyond the particular cartel proceedings at hand; it does not cover the whole of the Commission's policy with regard to the punishment and prevention of cartels. Moreover, once again the General Court recalled that leniency programmes are not the only means of ensuring compliance with EU competition law, but that actions for damages can also make a significant contribution in this context. **4.018**

As far as the exception pertaining to an unreasonable amount of work in dealing with the request for access to the relevant documents was concerned, the General Court held, *inter alia*, that the Commission may only dispense with the individual and specific review after it has investigated thoroughly all other options and explained in detail in its decision the reasons why those other options involve an unreasonable amount of work. **4.019**

4.020 With regard to Article 4(3), second subparagraph, of the Access to Documents Regulation, the General Court observed that the Commission had failed to establish to the required legal standard that all the documents within category 5(a) had the status of '*opinions*' within the meaning of that provision. Furthermore, insofar as the documents within category 5(a) were opinions, the Court considered that the Commission had made a manifest error in deciding that their disclosure would seriously undermine its decision-making process.

B Access to documents held by a national competition authority

4.021 The leading case in respect to access to documents held by national competition authorities is *Pfleiderer AG* v *Bundeskartellamt*, although the principle decided in that case is of wider application than to documents held by a national competition authority (NCA).

4.022 Pfleiderer, a firm active in the wood industry, was considering bringing a damages claim against members of a paper cartel. It sought access to the cartel files held by the German competition authority in order to substantiate its claim. A dispute arose subsequently in the German court as to whether disclosure of the documents submitted by companies that had cooperated with the German competition authority would undermine the national leniency programme. The German court referred this question to the ECJ for a preliminary ruling as to whether the provisions of EU competition law are to be interpreted as meaning that cartel victims can be granted access to leniency applications received by a Member State.

4.023 The ECJ ruled as follows[14]:

> The provisions of European Union law on cartels, and in particular Council Regulation (EC) No 1/2003 … must be interpreted as not precluding a person who has been adversely affected by an infringement of European Union competition law and is seeking to obtain damages from being granted access to documents relating to a leniency procedure involving the perpetrator of that infringement. It is, however, for the courts and tribunals of the Member States, on the basis of their national law, to determine the conditions under which such access must be permitted or refused by weighing the interests protected by European Union law.

4.024 In reaching this result, the ECJ did not follow the more nuanced view of Advocate-General Mazák, according to which leniency documents that existed

14 Para 33.

before the cartel was uncovered could be disclosed in follow-on civil proceedings, but that submissions drafted for the purpose of revealing the infringement should be protected from disclosure.[15]

The ECJ did not provide any concrete guidance on factors judges should take into account in assessing whether and which documents should be disclosed to a damages claimant. As a result, the national judge is left with a wide margin of discretion when deciding whether to order disclosure of a particular document in a given case. **4.025**

Just to complete the story, it should be noted that the referring national court refused to give the claimant access to leniency submissions held by the national competition authority.[16] The national court held, on the basis of §406e(2) of the *Strafprozessordnung* (Code of criminal procedure), that access to leniency documents could be refused because the purpose of inspections would be compromised if access were granted.[17] The judgment does not, however, bar all access to potentially useful incriminating documents; the court further ruled that access can be provided to documents that have not been provided voluntarily to the competition authority, that is, documents that were already in the possession of cartelists and therefore ran the danger of being confiscated. **4.026**

In the meantime, and in line with the *Pfleiderer* ruling in relation to proceedings before the *Bundeskartellamt*, the *Oberlandesgericht* Düsseldorf in proceedings against several coffee roasters held that third parties would not be granted access to leniency submissions.[18] It was specifically held that maintaining the confidentiality of leniency applications outweighs any interests of a claimant in gaining access to the file. This can be justified by the need to safeguard the effectiveness of the leniency programme, such that the interest in keeping secret leniency materials outweighs a claimant's interest in gaining sight of them.[19] Access to redacted versions of a fining decision is sufficient to ensure that the legitimate interests of claimants are protected. **4.027**

15 Opinion of Advocate-General Mazák delivered on 16 December 2010.

16 *Amtsgericht* Bonn, Case 51, Gs 53/09, 18 January 2012 (WuW 2012, 275).

17 This position coincides with that jointly taken by all European Competition Network (ECN) authorities on the importance of appropriate protection of leniency material in the context of damages actions (see the Resolution of the Meeting of Heads of the European Competition Authorities of 23 May 2012, 'Protection of Leniency Material in the Context of Civil Damages Actions').

18 *Oberlandesgericht* Düsseldorf, V-4 Kart 5 + 6/11 (OWi) (WuW 2012, 962), judgment of 22 August 2012. As a result of the fact that two of the defendants appealed the decisions of the *Bundeskartellamt* imposing fines, the proceedings were referred by the *Bundeskartellamt* to the *Oberlandesgericht*.

19 '*Das Interesse aller aktueller und ehemaliger Betroffener und Nebenbetroffener an der Geheimhaltung ihres Bonusantrages einschließlich der ihnen beiliegenden Anlagen ist gewichtiger als das Interesse der Antragsteller, den Akteninhalt insoweit einsehen zu können.*'

4.028 Some of the issues raised in *Pfleiderer* were further considered by the ECJ in the *Donau Chemie* proceedings.[20] At issue in this case was a rule of Austrian law forbidding access to the file in a competition proceeding to a third party unless *all* parties had agreed to allow access.[21] The case was therefore the mirror-image of *Pfleiderer*, that is, the point was raised by the NCA in relation to a rule not allowing access to the file.[22]

4.029 Against the principles enunciated in *Pfleiderer*, the ECJ categorically held that national law must not preclude the possibility for the national court to perform a balancing exercise of the interests involved when determining whether to provide access to third-party claimants to documents, including documents received under a leniency programme, which form part of the file in national proceedings under Article 101 TFEU. A rule requiring the consent of the parties to the main proceedings denies the national court the opportunity to carry out such a weighing-up of interests.[23] This is of particular importance when the documents in question might constitute the sole basis for an action for damages brought by parties alleging loss.[24] The ECJ held that such an over-restrictive rule is liable to render the exercise of the right to compensation which a potential claimant derives from EU law excessively difficult.[25] Such a rule therefore runs counter to the principle of effectiveness as enshrined in EU law.

4.030 Again, however, the ECJ did not provide any real guidance as to the factors judges should take into account when assessing whether and which documents should be disclosed to a damages claimant. In relation to leniency documents, the Court held in successive paragraphs that refusal to allow access to such documents would need to be '*based on overriding interests relating to the protection of the interest relied on [that is, the public interest involved in operating a leniency programme]*',[26] and that '*it is only if there is a risk that a given document may*

---

20 Judgment of the ECJ of 6 June 2013 in Case C-536/11 *Bundeswettbewerbsbehörde* v *Donau Chemie AG and others*. At para 65 of his Opinion in the case delivered on 7 February 2013, Advocate-General Jääskinen had argued that '*an absolute ban on access to the court files held by the Cartel Court, absent the consent of the parties, is a disproportionate impediment to the right of access to a court as guaranteed by Article 47 [of the Charter of Fundamental Rights]*'.

21 §39(2) of the *Bundesgesetz gegen Kartelle und andere Wettbewerbsbeschränkungen*.

22 It should be noted that the rule disallowing access except with the consent of all parties was an exception to general Austrian law on access to documents held by public authorities.

23 See para 37 of the Court's judgment.

24 See paras 32 and 39.

25 Para 39.

26 Para 47.

actually undermine the public interest relating to the effectiveness of the leniency programme that non-disclosure of that document may be justified'.[27]

The issue of access to documents in the context of an action for damages is also a live one in France. In two cases, the Paris *Tribunal de commerce* ordered the *Autorité de la concurrence* to disclose documents, such as non-confidential versions of third-party written observations, to damages claimants following the closure of an investigation.[28] In a further case, the Paris *Tribunal de commerce* authorised a party to produce before the court documents from the file of the *Autorité de la concurrence*.[29] **4.031**

Since the judgments of the ECJ in *Pfleiderer* and *Donau Chemie*, the Commission issued its long-awaited proposal, which treats the issue of whether and which documents held in a national competition authority's file can be disclosed to a third-party damages claimant. Specifically, the proposal provides categorically that leniency corporate statements must never be disclosed,[30] and are not admissible as evidence in an action for damages.[31] The Commission deems that disclosure of such documents would have a particularly detrimental impact on leniency programmes.[32] On the other hand, the following categories of evidence can be disclosed (and relied upon as evidence), but only *after* a competition authority has brought antitrust proceedings to a close[33]: **4.032**

(i) information prepared by a natural or legal person specifically for the proceedings of a competition authority (such as replies to a request for information); and

27 Para 48. The original version of this paragraph read as follows: '*[t]he mere risk that a given document may actually undermine the public interest relating to the effectiveness of the leniency programme is liable to justify the non-disclosure of that document*'. This was subsequently replaced by the Court with the version quoted above. The language of the case was German, and the German-language version of para 48 reads as follows: '*Nur wenn Gefahr besteht, dass ein bestimmtes Schriftstück konkret das öffentliche Interesse an der Wirksamkeit des nationalen Kronzeugenprogramms beeinträchtigen könnte, kann die Nichtweitergabe dieses Schriftstücks gerechtfertigt sein.*' Given the change in the English-language version, it could be considered that a qualification such as '*concrete*' should be made to the term '*risk*'.

28 *15ème chambre*, judgment of 24 August 2011 in *SAS Ma Liste de Courses/Société HighCo 3.0, Société HighCo Data, Société Sogec Gestion, Société Sogec Marketing* (RG 2011014911), confirmed by *15ème chambre*, judgment of 16 March 2012; and *15ème chambre*, judgment of 16 March 2012 in *DKT International/Eco-emballages et Valorplast* (RG 2012000109).

29 *1ère chambre*, judgment of 8 November 2011 in *Outremer Télécom/Orange Caraïbes et France Télécom* (RG 2010073867).

30 Article 6(1)(a). The prohibition on a national court to disclose leniency corporate statements also extends to settlement submissions (Article 6(1)(b)).

31 Article 7(1).

32 See the Commission's explanatory memorandum, section 1.2.

33 Article 6(2) and Article 7(2).

(ii) information that was drawn up by a competition authority in the course of its proceedings (such as a statement of objections).

4.033 Disclosure of other types of evidence on the file of a competition authority may be disclosed to a damages claimant at any time.[34]

4.034 The question arises how, in the event that the proposal becomes a legally binding Directive, its provisions can be reconciled with the ECJ's rulings in *Pfleiderer* and *Donau Chemie* which hold that a national court must perform a balancing exercise weighing the respective interests in favour of disclosure of the information and the protection of that information provided voluntarily by an applicant for leniency. Clearly, with respect to leniency corporate statements at least, the ECJ's prescriptions would find no application.

4.035 Although *Pfleiderer* was about access to documents held by the national competition authority, the principle stated by the ECJ in that case is of application also in cases where a claimant relies on national rules of procedure in order to obtain access to documents held by the defendants. These rules will be examined below.

C Access to documents held by the defendant: the *National Grid* proceedings before the English courts

4.036 The European legal landscape in matters of access to documents held by the defendants (often referred to as 'discovery') is characterised by a fundamental divide between the common law legal systems in, for example, England and Wales, the Republic of Ireland and the US, on the one hand, and the civil law systems in the rest of Europe, on the other. In the common law systems there is a standard procedure whereby the parties to civil litigation can and do obtain copies of certain relevant documents in the possession or control of the other parties. Such procedures are generally unknown in the civil law systems.[35] As far as EU law is concerned, there are no rules on 'discovery' of documents held by the opposing parties in civil litigation (although as the *Pfleiderer* case illustrates, there are rules on obtaining documents from the state authorities).

---

34 Article 6(3).

35 In Germany, for example, there are rules pertaining to access to documents held by a defendant. These rules are restrictive in scope, however. For example, §142(1) of the *Zivilprozessordnung* states that a court may direct one of the parties to produce records or documents, as well as any other materials, that are in its possession and to which one of the parties *has made reference* ('*Das Gericht kann anordnen, dass eine Partei oder ein Dritter die in ihrem oder seinem Besitz befindlichen Urkunden und sonstigen Unterlagen, auf die sich eine Partei bezogen hat, vorlegt. Das Gericht kann hierfür eine Frist setzen sowie anordnen, dass die vorgelegten Unterlagen während einer von ihm zu bestimmenden Zeit auf der Geschäftsstelle verbleiben.*').

The following discussion of access to documents held by the defendants will therefore be limited to the common law systems, taking England and Wales as the paradigm.[36] **4.037**

Discovery was originally an equitable remedy developed in England and Wales. When the common law became so formalised and strict that it did not always do justice, claimants would petition the King for justice. The King delegated such petitions to the Lord Chancellor, and the Lord Chancellor's court – the Court of Chancery – became the institution that granted equitable relief – a sort of 'court of conscience'. The practice of the Court of Chancery gradually became formalised in a similar manner. Equity consists in that body of rules that was developed by the Court of Chancery prior to its merger with the common law courts by the Judicature Acts of 1873 and 1875 to form the Supreme Court of Judicature. The procedural remedy of discovery was the result of one of those rules. The original principle behind discovery was that a party should not be able to avoid a personal legal obligation just because he, and nobody else, had the document that established the existence of this obligation. The principle of discovery has developed considerably since those early days in the thirteenth–sixteenth centuries. The modern rationale for discovery is that it helps to clarify the issues being litigated, it enables the parties to see the strengths and weaknesses of their respective cases, and so encourages settlement out of court. In this way it contributes to an efficient administration of justice. **4.038**

The English rules of disclosure are now contained in Part 31 of the Rules of Civil Procedure (CPR).[37] The term 'discovery' has been replaced by the more descriptive term 'disclosure and inspection of documents'. This new term reveals a clear distinction between two phases of the process, a disclosure stage in which the parties to the civil litigation exchange lists of their documents, and an inspection stage during which a party can exercise the right to inspect a document and obtain copies. Issues of whether a particular document should not be open for inspection, for example, because it is covered by legal professional privilege, are dealt with after disclosure of the lists of documents and prior to exercise of the right of inspection. **4.039**

In *National Grid Electricity Transmission Plc* v *ABB Ltd and others*,[38] the question arose whether certain defendants to a follow-on damages claim were entitled to withhold the following documents from inspection by the claimant: **4.040**

36 There is further discussion of the Commission's attempts to intervene in discovery in private litigation before the US courts below.

37 See also Rule 19(2)(k) of the Competition Appeal Tribunal Rules 2003.

38 [2012] EWHC 869 (Ch).

(i) the confidential version of the Commission's decision imposing fines in the *Gas Insulated Switchgear* case;

(ii) the responses (including any accompanying documents) to the Commission's statement of objections by investigated companies in the ABB defendant group;

(iii) the responses by the investigated companies in the ABB defendant group to requests for information made by the Commission that explain the meaning of pre-existing documents relating to the operation and/or effects of the cartel, or otherwise provide information on the operation and/or effects of the cartel.

4.041 Initially the claimant had requested that the High Court order the Commission to produce these documents itself but, in the light of the ECJ's ruling in *Pfleiderer*, the claimant changed its request in favour of an order against the defendants.

4.042 The High Court deemed that the *Pfleiderer* ruling applied to the Commission's leniency programme and to national leniency programmes and, accordingly, applied it to National Grid's request for documents containing leniency materials. The Court endeavoured, however, to move beyond *Pfleiderer's* relatively loose parameters and clarify the boundaries of those documents that contain elements of leniency materials and may be subject to disclosure.

4.043 In line with *Pfleiderer*, the High Court performed the 'balancing exercise' as advocated by the ECJ, focusing on two principles: the principle of legitimate expectations and the principle of proportionality.

1 Legitimate expectations

4.044 The High Court held that the principle of legitimate expectations, as embodied in the expectation that leniency documents would not be disclosed, did not apply in the present case. The High Court did, however, note that one relevant factor related to the principle of legitimate expectations is whether disclosure would increase the leniency applicants' exposure to liability as compared to the liability of parties that did not cooperate. The High Court noted that if only ABB had been sued (for example, on the basis that it was not appealing the decision so there was no reason to delay a trial), that would be a powerful factor against disclosure of leniency materials, even allowing for the fact that ABB might then have been able to make a contribution claim against the other participants in the cartel.

2 *Proportionality*

The High Court proceeded to examine the scope of disclosure in terms of proportionality, a principle that also underpins the English rules on disclosure and inspection. The High Court considered it necessary to apply the principle of proportionality having regard for the questions (i) whether the information was available from other sources, and (ii) whether the leniency materials were relevant to the issues in the case. The Court found that, to the extent that the information sought from the disclosure was of real assistance, there were no other reasonable means available for National Grid to obtain the information. In terms of relevance, it was noted that a blanket objection to disclosure on the grounds that this might prejudice the Commission's leniency programme was not acceptable but, equally, it would be wrong to permit disclosure of the entire leniency materials without closer examination. **4.045**

3 *Documents ordered to be disclosed to National Grid*

As regards the Commission's confidential decision, the High Court considered each document on a paragraph-by-paragraph basis and held that a number, but not all (32 paragraphs in total), of the redacted passages of the decision should be disclosed. **4.046**

As regards the other documents, that is, the responses by Arriva and ABB to the Commission's request for information, the High Court held that only very limited passages from a few of those documents should be disclosed. With regard to ABB's materials, the justification for disclosure appeared to be that the materials disclosed provided mainly explanations concerning documents already in the Commission's possession that may have already been disclosed to National Grid. **4.047**

On the other hand, the High Court ruled that under the two-pronged balancing assessment, certain documents should not be disclosed. These included ABB's responses to the Commission's statement of objections and certain other parts of documents supplied by Arriva. The High Court found that these documents were not of particular relevance to the proceedings at hand and that the interest of protecting information supplied under the leniency programme outweighed the interest of providing disclosure to assist the claim for damages. **4.048**

4 *Further developments: the French blocking statute*

In another ruling arising from the *National Grid* litigation, the English High Court ordered that documents in the hands of the French defendant companies **4.049** to the proceedings be disclosed before it.[39] Such order was made despite a French law prohibiting, on pain of criminal sanctions, the release of information and documents on matters of an economic, industrial, financial or technical nature which might harm the sovereignty, security or economic interests of France to a foreign court, the so-called 'French blocking statute'.[40]

4.050 In order to overcome concerns that disclosure of the relevant documents would be prevented by the French blocking statute, the English High Court initially attempted to make use of Regulation 1206/2001, which deals with the taking of evidence in a cross-border context (the 'Evidence Regulation').[41]

4.051 The Evidence Regulation provides for two alternative methods for the taking of evidence in another Member State, as follows:

(i) a request that evidence be taken by the competent court in the foreign State under Article 1(1)(a) (the court-to-court method);
(ii) a request to the competent authority for the taking of evidence directly in the foreign State under Article 1(1)(b) (the direct method).

4.052 An attempt at obtaining disclosure via the direct method was thwarted both by objections from the French Ministry of Justice, and by the prospect of further delays.

4.053 Following the failure to obtain disclosure under the Evidence Regulation under the direct route, National Grid renewed its application for specific disclosure against the French defendant companies. Again, the French defendants raised the concern that this would expose them to criminal sanctions under the French blocking statute.

4.054 Despite such concerns, and in his discretion, the judge granted National Grid's claim for specific disclosure, notwithstanding the fact that compliance by the French defendants with such an order would in all probability violate the French blocking statute.

4.055 In exercising his discretion to order production of the relevant documents by the French defendants, the judge held that the critical question was the likelihood of any prosecution being brought against the French defendants

39 [2013] EWHC 822 (Ch).

40 *Loi n° 68–678 relative à la communication de documents et renseignements d'ordre économique, commercial, industriel, financier ou technique à des personnes physiques ou morales étrangères*, 26 July 1968, as amended.

41 Council Regulation (EC) No 1206/2001 of 28 May 2001 on cooperation between the courts of the Member States in the taking of evidence in civil or commercial matters (OJ L 174, 27.6.2001, p 1).

under the French blocking statute. In light of the following factors he held that the application for disclosure should be granted:

(i) there had only ever been one instance of a successful prosecution under the blocking statute, which had arisen in very exceptional circumstances;
(ii) the blocking statute was generally regarded as a defence mechanism against abusive US discovery requests against French companies facing litigation in the US. Furthermore, it was observed that even when French companies do comply with regular US disclosure orders, they are not prosecuted under the French blocking statute;
(iii) it was inconceivable that the French authorities would institute criminal proceedings against a French company for that company's compliance with English procedural rules in proceedings where the English court exercised jurisdiction over the French defendants under EU law, and where the proceedings pursued an objective of EU policy as endorsed by the ECJ.[42]

The judge's order for disclosure in this case was not affected by the availability of the court-to-court method under the Evidence Regulation. In his view, the Evidence Regulation is not essentially concerned with the provision of disclosure between parties to litigation at all. Rather, the Evidence Regulation is based on the *taking of evidence* in another Member State. Furthermore, it was considered that enough time had already been spent on the abortive attempt to use the direct route under the Evidence Regulation.[43] **4.056**

D Access to documents held by a third party

In practice, leniency documents will not be held by third parties; they will be held by the leniency applicants themselves, and these persons will be the defendants in the follow-on damages claims. **4.057**

---

42 See also the judgment of the English High Court in *Secretary of State for Health and others* v *Servier Laboratories Limited, Servier Research and Development Limited, Les Laboratoires Servier SAS and Servier SAS* [2012] EWHC 2761 (Ch), at para 55: '*I have carefully considered the potential impact of the French Blocking Statute, but in common with the three English courts which have so far had to consider the issue I am not persuaded that the risk of prosecution to which it might expose the French defendants or their officers is more than theoretical. The absence of any successful prosecution in France for breach of the statute, over a period of more than thirty years, with the single exception of the Christopher X case, in my judgment speaks for itself.*'

43 It should be noted that there is no obligation to make use of the Evidence Regulation: see paras 44 and 45 of the judgment of the ECJ of 21 February 2013 in case C-332/11 *ProRail BV* v *Xpedys NV* (not yet reported), where the Court held that the Evidence Regulation '*does not restrict the options to take evidence situated in other Member States, but aims to increase those options by encouraging cooperation between the courts in that area… [I]n certain circumstances, it may be simpler, more effective and quicker for the court ordering such an investigation, to take such evidence without having recourse to the regulation*'.

4.058 For completeness, however, mention should be made of the rules contained in the England and Wales CPR that provide for access to documents held by third parties.[44] There is no right of access without a prior order from the court. The court may make an order for access to documents held by a third party only when the documents in question are likely to support the applicant's case or adversely affect the case of another party to the proceedings. In addition, it must be established that disclosure is necessary in order to dispose fairly of the claim or to save costs. If the court considers that an order for disclosure and inspection may be made, the scope of that order is not necessarily the same as for 'standard disclosure and inspection' in the case of access to documents held by a party to the proceedings. The court must specify the documents or classes of documents which the respondent must disclose. The court may also require the third party to specify in his disclosure any of those documents which are no longer in his control. Last of all, the court may, and usually will, require the respondent to specify any of those documents in respect of which he claims a right or a duty to withhold inspection, for example, for reasons of legal professional privilege.

E The Commission's proposals on evidence

4.059 In its legislative proposal, the Commission makes some bold suggestions in terms of rules on the disclosure of evidence in competition law damages actions. These proposals apply both to evidence held by the parties to the litigation in question, and to evidence held by third parties. Put briefly, the Commission is seeking to introduce on an EU-wide level a system similar to discovery as known in the common law, as explained above.[45]

4.060 The proposal provides that, in principle, national courts should be able to order the disclosure of evidence, whether evidence is in the hands of the defendant or claimant and whether it is included in the file of a competition authority or not.[46] This general principle is, however, hedged with the types of circumscription that one would expect in a mature system of document disclosure in order to prevent abuse of process. For example, a party must show that the evidence requested is relevant to the claim or defence,[47] and specify in as much detail as possible the item or category of evidence requested.[48] The courts, for their part, are only to order disclosure where it is proportionate to do so, taking into account, for example, the scope and cost of disclosure and whether the evidence

44 CPR, Rule 31.17.

45 The Commission even refers to the proposed system as '*disclosure of evidence*' in the title of Article 5.

46 Article 5(1).

47 Article 5(2)(a).

48 Article 5(2)(b). This provision, in particular, recalls civil law approaches to evidence, and helps to balance the proposal between the common law and the civil law.

requested contains confidential information.[49] Furthermore, failure or refusal to comply with a court's order for disclosure or destruction of relevant evidence in certain circumstances must be met with appropriate sanctions.[50]

F The Commission's attempts to limit discoverability in US courts

Although damages before the US courts are not usually available to the parties in follow-on actions arising from a decision of the Commission or an NCA,[51] the Commission has intervened in several US civil proceedings as *amicus curiae* to stop the discovery of EU documents submitted by leniency applicants.[52] This is notably because of a fear that production of documents would have a chilling effect on the EU's leniency programme.[53] **4.061**

In the context of EU antitrust proceedings, US discovery requests are usually made by EU companies seeking damages in the US for infringements of EU rules in view of the broad access rights granted there. The broad extent to which US courts can order discovery of documents is almost unparalleled in any other jurisdiction. According to Rule 26(b)(1) FRCP, '*parties may obtain discovery regarding any non-privileged matter that is relevant to any party's claim or defence – including the existence, … nature, custody … and location of any documents or other tangible things and the identity and location of persons who know of any discoverable matter*'. **4.062**

There have been between ten and fifteen cases where the Commission has intervened in first instance proceedings in the US to stop the discovery of EU **4.063**

49 Article 5(3)(b) and (c).

50 Article 8(1)(a) and (b).

51 See the decision of the US Supreme Court in *F Hoffmann-La Roche Ltd.* v *Empagran SA* 124 US 2359 (2004).

52 A recent example is the *In Re: Air Cargo Shipping Services* proceedings (in relation to the first round of settlements, *In Re: Air Cargo Shipping Services Antitrust Litigation* No 06-MD-1775, 2009 WL 3077396 (EDNY, 25 September 2009); in relation to the approval of nine further settlements, *In Re: Air Cargo Shipping Services Antitrust Litigation* No 06-MD-1775, 2011 WL 2909162 (EDNY, 15 July 2011)). Previous examples include *In Re: TFT-LCD (Flat Panel) Antitrust Litigation* No M 07–1827 SI, 2011 WL 723571 (ND Cal, 2011); *In Re: Vitamins Antitrust Litigation* 398 F. Supp. 2d 209, 226 (DDC, 2005); and *In Re: Methionine Antitrust Litigation* No 00–1311, 2003 WL 22048232 (ND Cal, 2003).

53 See, for example, *In Re: Rubber Chemicals Antitrust Litigation* 486 F. Supp. 2d 1078 (ND Cal 2007). See also the following declaration of Philip Lowe, then Director-General of DG Competition, in *In Re: Flat Glass Antitrust Litigation II* Civ No 08-mc-180 (WD Pa, 2009): '*[t]he ordered production, or uncertainty in this regard, of submissions that a company has prepared and produced exclusively for the European Commission's antitrust proceedings in civil proceedings for damages could seriously undermine the effectiveness of the Leniency Programme and jeopardize the European Commission's investigation of cartels*'.

documents as either *amicus curiae* or via a letter on behalf of the defendant.[54] As a general rule, the Commission's stance on the discovery of EU documents in the US is that nothing should be disclosed during on-going procedures. After proceedings have come to an end, however, the Commission draws a distinction between pre-existing documents and attachments thereto, which can be disclosed, and documents drawn up for the actual procedure, which should not be disclosed.

4.064 Despite the Commission's objections to the discoverability of EU documents in the US, the legal bases upon which the Commission may rely to stop the discovery of such documents, that is, Regulation 773/2004,[55] the Commission's notice on access to the file,[56] its leniency notice[57] and its fines guidelines,[58] are weak.

4.065 As a result, the Commission has relied on comity to try to stop the discovery of such documents. Comity arguments do not, however, guarantee that documents exchanged in EU antitrust proceedings will not be discoverable by private litigants in the US.

4.066 The concept of comity is an elusive one.[59] It is a principle of private international law which generally describes a policy whereby a country voluntarily

54 See the letter of De Bronett in *In Re. Vitamins Antitrust Litigation*: '*Should all documents and statements provided to the Commission by companies/US defendants as a result of a leniency application, have to be communicated to US plaintiffs in the course of a US civil litigation, the effectiveness of the EU antitrust procedures could indeed be seriously undermined.*'

55 Commission Regulation (EC) No 773/2004 of 7 April 2004 relating to the conduct of proceedings by the Commission pursuant to Articles 81 and 82 of the EC Treaty (OJ L 123, 27.4.2004, p 18).

56 Commission notice on the rules for access to the Commission file in cases pursuant to Articles 81 and 82 of the EC Treaty, Articles 53, 54 and 57 of the EEA Agreement and Council Regulation (EC) No 139/2004 (OJ C 325, 22.12.2005, p 7).

57 See point 40: '*The Commission considers that normally public disclosure of documents and written or recorded statements received in the context of this notice would undermine certain public or private interests, for example the protection of the purpose of inspections and investigations, within the meaning of Article 4 of Regulation (EC) No 1049/2001, even after the decision has been taken.*'

58 Commission guidelines on the method of setting fines imposed pursuant to Article 23(2)(a) of Regulation No 1/2003 (OJ C 210, 1.9.2006, p 2).

59 Primary EU law is silent on the principle of comity. The principles of comity and positive comity do, nonetheless, form an integral part of the EU/US agreements of 1991 and 1998: see the agreement between the Government of the United States of America and the Commission of the European Communities regarding the application of their competition laws (OJ L 95, 27.4.1995, p 47), and the agreement between the European Communities and the Government of the United States of America on the application of positive comity principles in the enforcement of their competition laws (OJ L 173, 18.6.1998, p 28). The latter agreement supplements the former.

takes other countries' interests into account when deciding upon an antitrust law issue, and that any such decision does not negatively impact those interests.[60]

Despite comity's voluntary nature, EU defendants have invariably been successful in defending discovery requests in the US. In this context, the US Department of Justice has recognised the importance of other nations' leniency programmes in safeguarding the integrity of its own system of leniency. With respect to the EU's leniency programme in particular, the Department of Justice has declared that '*the European Commission has been one of the Division's closest partners in the fight against international cartels*', and '*[o]ver ninety percent of the international cartels that have been prosecuted by the Division were active in Europe as well as in the United States … If companies that have dual exposure in the United States and the European Union are dissuaded from applying for leniency with the European Commission, then they may also choose not to apply for leniency in the United States… Due to the critical role of the Division's leniency program in its international anti-cartel enforcement program as described above, harm to the EC leniency program could result in harm to the Division's ability to detect and successfully prosecute international cartels that target U.S. businesses and consumers.*'[61] **4.067**

It has been suggested that the ECJ's judgment in *Pfleiderer* may have the infelicitous consequence of making it more difficult for the Commission to argue persuasively that documents disclosed to it by companies subject to an EU cartel investigation should not be disclosed to private litigants in litigation before the US courts. In particular, it has been argued that the ECJ's stance in *Pfleiderer* could be interpreted by US courts to mean that the confidentiality of leniency statements in the EU is itself not absolute. **4.068**

As things currently stand, this is, however, unlikely. Firstly, the US courts have historically shown deference to the EU's leniency programme. Secondly, US practice following *Pfleiderer* seems to allay fears that this would be the case.[62] Finally, the Commission's recent proposal emphatically states that leniency **4.069**

60 According to the Organisation for Economic Co-operation and Development (OECD), the concept of *positive* comity describes a '*voluntary policy calling for a country to give full and sympathetic consideration to other countries' important interests while it is making decisions concerning the enforcement of its own competition law*', while *negative* comity involves '*a country's consideration of how it may prevent its law enforcement actions from harming another country's important interests*', OECD, Committee on Competition Law and Policy, 'Report on Positive Comity' (1999), para 5.

61 Letter of Scott D. Hammond, Deputy Assistant Attorney General for Criminal Enforcement, Antitrust Division, Department of Justice, in *In Re: Flat Glass Antitrust Litigation II*.

62 See *In Re: Air Cargo Shipping Services Antitrust Litigation* No 06-MD-1775 (EDNY, 19 December 2011).

corporate statements should never be disclosed by a national court to a third-party antitrust damages claimant.[63]

4.070 Unless and until there is a definitive US Supreme Court ruling on whether or not documents exchanged in EU antitrust proceedings are discoverable in the US, there is no guarantee that legal arguments, including comity, in support of stopping the discoverability of EU documents in the US will be taken into account. The Commission has therefore been considering whether to refrain from its usual practice of intervening at first instance in these cases so that the US Supreme Court is given the opportunity to give a definitive ruling on the matter.[64]

II THE EVIDENTIAL VALUE OF PRIOR ADMINISTRATIVE DECISIONS

4.071 The burden of proving the infringement is removed if, in cases where there is a prior administrative infringement decision in relation to the same behaviour, the claimant can rely on that finding before the national court as proof of the infringement.

A Commission decisions: Article 16 of Regulation 1/2003

4.072 The governing law in relation to the evidential value of Commission decisions in competition law damages claims before the national courts is Article 16(1) of Regulation 1/2003, the first sentence of which provides as follows:

> When national courts rule on agreements, decisions or practices under Article 81 or Article 82 of the Treaty which are already the subject of a Commission decision, they cannot take decisions running counter to the decision adopted by the Commission.

4.073 Article 16(1) is in effect a codification of the *Masterfoods* jurisprudence of the Court of Justice,[65] in which the Court had considered the issue of the extent to which a national court is obliged to stay proceedings pending an appeal on the substance of a decision of the Commission relating to the same infringement.

4.074 The effect of Article 16(1) in practice is to render Commission decisions binding on national courts. It is a more far-reaching provision than the

63 Article 6(1)(a), discussed above.

64 For a more complete discussion of the principle of comity, see Damien Geradin, David Henry and Marc Reysen, 'Extraterritoriality, Comity and Co-operation in EC Competition Law', in *Cooperation, Comity, and Competition Policy* (Andrew T. Guzman (ed), Oxford: Oxford University Press, 2010).

65 Case C-344/98 *Masterfoods Ltd* v *HB Ice Cream Ltd* [2000] ECR I-11369.

equivalent provision in US law, §5(a) of the Clayton Act,[66] which provides that decisions in actions brought by the public authorities shall constitute a '*prima facie*' finding in actions before the civil courts '*as to all matters respecting which said judgment or decree would be an estoppel as between the parties thereto*'.

It should be remembered that the scope of the rule contained in Article 16(1) is that the national court is under a duty to abstain from a decision which conflicts with an actual or intended Commission decision (a '*negative duty of abstention*'), rather than that the national court is absolutely bound by a Commission decision ('*positive binding effect*').[67] An important difference between the two is that, in the former case, the national court is free to seize the ECJ in case of doubt. **4.075**

The scope of the rule contained in Article 16 was further elucidated by the ECJ in its recent judgment in the *Otis* case, involving a damages action brought by the Commission itself for loss sustained by the Union as a result of the elevators and escalators cartel. In its judgment, the ECJ specified that the rule set out in Article 16 applies to damages actions brought before the courts of the Member States.[68] Furthermore, it specified that, in the context of such actions, Article 16 renders the decision of the Commission effectively binding on the national court as regards the existence of the substantive infringement, but that the national court remains free to rule on causation and the existence of damage.[69] **4.076**

This division is entirely consistent with the distinction between substantive law and law relating to remedies and legal procedure, as set out in Chapter 1. The *Otis* judgment is thus a logical extension of pre-existing principles and case law of the ECJ to the sphere of damages actions. **4.077**

The scope of the rule contained in Article 16 was also recently considered by the English High Court in *Bord Na Mona Horticulture Limited and Board Na Mona plc* v *BPI and others*.[70] Very simply, the High Court held that the claimants could adduce evidence as to a parallel infringement on a different market, or to the **4.078**

66 15 USC §16.

67 See Komninos, *loc. cit.*, at 115–117.

68 Para 51. See further para 54, where the ECJ described the Article 16 rule as a '*specific expression of the division of powers*' between the national courts and the EU courts, Commission decisions being appealable on substance to the latter.

69 Para 65. This corresponds to a distinction between the public law effects of the Commission decision, however wide they may be, and the private law analysis carried out by the national court. See further para 66, where the ECJ states that '… *even when the Commission has in its decision determined the precise effects of the infringement, it still falls to the national court to determine individually the loss caused to each of the persons to have brought an action for damages. Such an assessment is not contrary to Article 16 of Regulation No 1/2003*' (emphasis added).

70 [2012] EWHC 3346 (Comm).

effect that the infringement found by the Commission had distortive effects on a separate geographic market, without contravening the rule set out in Article 16.[71]

4.079 A further issue in relation to Article 16 is the interconnection between the procedural aspects of damages actions and an appeal of an administrative decision on the substance. This issue was recently considered by the *Rechtbank* (District Court) of The Hague in an action for damages brought by CDC against members of the paraffin wax cartel.[72] The defendants had appealed the Commission decision to the General Court, and argued before the national court that the damages actions pending before it should therefore be stayed, pending the outcome of this appeal.

4.080 The Dutch court held, *inter alia*, that the points that appeared to be at issue in the action before it and those subject to appeal were fundamentally different, and were not of such a nature as to be capable of leading to a conflicting outcome. The court held that, in any event, there were many issues that had to be straightened out in the interim before liability was definitively established by the General Court.

4.081 For example, one important procedural point that remained to be argued before the Dutch court was the question of whether the assignment of the claims to CDC was valid, such that a bundled claim could in fact be brought by CDC.[73] The court held that an inquiry into such procedural points had no bearing on the validity of the Commission decision, but rather dealt with the possibility for CDC to bring a claim, and was not capable of leading to any inconsistency with EU law. Furthermore, staying proceedings would lead to unnecessary delays in the administration of justice, especially given the potential for delay at the General Court, and the possibility of further appeal to the ECJ. The Dutch court further stated that proceedings could in any event be stayed at a later stage if it were felt that there was a real risk of inconsistency with EU law.

---

71 This applies only to actions brought before the ordinary courts in England and Wales, and not to actions brought before the CAT, where the claimant must restrict the pleadings to the findings of infringement made in the regulator's decision. This is not, however, an issue of compliance or otherwise with Article 16 of Regulation 1/2003, but of the interpretation of s47A of the Competition Act 1998. See further the discussion of the *Enron I* proceedings below.

72 Judgment of the *Rechtbank* of The Hague of 1 May 2013, LJN CA1870, C/09/414499/HA ZA 12–293. The paraffin wax cartel had been the subject of a Commission Decision which found the defendants to have engaged in price-fixing practices for paraffin wax (Commission Decision of 1 October 2008, case COMP/C.39181, candle waxes (not yet published)).

73 See Chapter 6 for a discussion of assignment of claims.

1 *The judgment of the English Court of Appeal in* Crehan

Some guidance on the interpretation of Article 16 was given by the English courts in the *Crehan* proceedings.[74] The decision of the Court of Appeal in those proceedings went beyond the *Masterfoods* jurisprudence. The Court based its finding of infringement to a very great extent on '*deference*' to previous decisions of the Commission in relation to agreements on the same market, though not the agreement before the court in the proceedings in question, and to administrative measures taken by the Commission in relation to the agreement before the court. The Court held that it was '*obliged under the duty of sincere cooperation to give to the Commission much greater deference than that which the [first instance] judge … was prepared to give*' (the High Court had found that there was no substantive infringement). **4.082**

The precise scope of this duty of '*deference*' was unclear from the judgment. The Court held that the first instance court should not have heard evidence attacking the Commission decision in the Whitbread proceedings (also relating to the on-sale beer market in the UK), and that in '*second guessing*' the Commission and not following that decision the first instance judge '*erred in law*'.[75] In addition, the Court appears to have found that the first instance court should have deferred to the view expressed by the Commission in its administrative proceedings in relation to the agreement in question even in the absence of a formal decision. In this regard, the Court referred to a comfort letter issued by the Commission in January 2000 in relation to the modified Inntrepreneur agreement from which the Court infers that the Commission's view was that Article 101(1) applied to the original agreement as relevant to the proceedings in hand. In the comfort letter, the Commission stated that leases pre-1998 in its view infringed Article 101(1). **4.083**

Furthermore, the Court of Appeal referred to a letter written by the Commission in November 1997 in response to a complaint made by Inntrepreneur tenants in relation to the original Inntrepreneur agreement. In this letter the Commission referred to an earlier notice issued under Article 19(3) of Regulation 17/62 for third party comment in respect of the Inntrepreneur agreement in anticipation of a prohibition decision. The Court deduced from this letter that the Commission expected the national court to '*take into account*' its '*conclusions*' as expressed at that point in the Inntrepreneur proceedings, as well as in the related proceedings such as the Whitbread proceedings, in which at **4.084**

---

74 See Chapter 2 for a description of these proceedings before the English and EU courts.

75 Para 98 of the judgment of the Court of Appeal.

that point no formal decisions had been issued, to the effect that the agreement infringed Article 101(1).[76]

4.085 However, the judgment of the Court of Appeal was overturned by the House of Lords, which held that the trial judge had not been wrong to make his own assessment of the substantive breach of EU competition law. The principal basis for this decision was that the defendant was not the addressee of the Commission decision in question.[77] In this regard, the House of Lords refers to the Commission's own letter of November 1997 in the proceedings,[78] which indicated that the national court, which had at that point been seized by Mr Crehan and other claimants, was in a position to rule on the substantive infringement of Article 101(1) in the Inntrepreneur proceedings.

B Commission decisions: Article 9 of Regulation 1/2003

4.086 Another issue pertaining to the evidential value of Commission decisions in an antitrust context is the legal status of so-called 'commitment decisions' under Article 9 of Regulation 1/2003. The essence of a commitment decision can be found in Article 9(1), which reads:

> Where the Commission intends to adopt a decision requiring that an infringement be brought to an end and the undertakings concerned offer commitments to meet the concerns expressed to them by the Commission in its preliminary assessment, the Commission may by decision make those commitments binding on the undertakings. *Such a decision may be adopted for a specified period and shall conclude that there are no longer grounds for action by the Commission* (emphasis added).

4.087 Given its nature, a commitment decision is silent as to the existence (past or present) of a violation of Article 101 or 102 TFEU. As opposed to Article 7 of Regulation 1/2003, there is no formal finding of infringement under Article 9 of Regulation 1/2003. In return for abiding by a commitment, the Commission effectively settles the case with the company under investigation. As a result, a claimant cannot rely on a commitment decision as proof of an infringement before a national court for the purposes of bringing a follow-on damages action. That is not to say, however, that commitment decisions have no evidential value. A commitment decision may act as a 'red flag' for further scrutiny of a

---

76 Para 97.

77 See for example para 14 of the judgment, per Lord Hoffmann: '*If an action before a national court raises a question of fact which has already been decided by the Commission in proceedings relating to other participants in the same market, ought the national court to follow the Commission or is it free to reach a different conclusion?*' (emphasis added). See, for the same point, para 6, per Lord Bingham.

78 Para 65 (per Lord Hoffmann).

company's conduct by a potential claimant.[79] Furthermore, certain useful facts may emerge from such commitment decisions which may facilitate the bringing of a stand-alone action.

C NCA decisions

There is no rule as yet as a matter of EU law as to the evidential value of an NCA decision in private litigation.[80] The Commission proposal does however, in its Article 9, set out a rule extending the *Masterfoods* jurisprudence of Article 16 of Regulation 1/2003 to decisions taken by NCAs applying EU competition law or national competition law in parallel to EU law. Under the proposal, national courts could not take a decision '*running counter*' to such a decision by an NCA. This directly echoes the language of Article 16(1) of Regulation 1/2003. **4.088**

Given the absence as yet of a rule at EU level on the binding effect of NCA decisions, it is still useful to look at national law on the point. In certain jurisdictions a decision of the NCA has binding force. In others it does not, but in these jurisdictions it is often the case that it has instead high evidential value. **4.089**

1 *United Kingdom*

In the UK, damages actions following on from a public infringement decision, where only causation and quantum fall to be determined, can be brought in the CAT on the basis of an infringement decision by the OFT or the Commission. All other damages actions are to be brought in the ordinary courts. The provision for the bringing of an action in the CAT is without prejudice to the right to bring any action before the ordinary courts.[81] **4.090**

In damages proceedings before the ordinary courts in the UK, a decision of the OFT that either national competition law or EU competition law has been violated, or a decision of the CAT on appeal from a decision of the OFT to **4.091**

---

79 See, for example, Commission Decision of 19 January 2005, case COMP/C-2/37.214 joint selling of the media rights to the German Bundesliga, where the Commission noted that, according to its preliminary assessment, '*the exclusive selling of the commercial broadcasting rights by the League Association could restrict competition between the clubs and companies in the first and second divisions*' (para 1) (emphasis added).

80 See Komninos, *loc. cit.* at 117–118, for a discussion of the desirability of extending the rule in *Masterfoods* to decisions taken by NCAs. See also the White Paper at section 2.3, which set out proposals with respect to the binding effect of NCA decisions. In particular, the Commission '*sees no reason why a final decision on Article [101] or [102] taken by an NCA in the European Competition Network (ECN), and a final judgment by a review court upholding the NCA decision or itself finding an infringement, should not be accepted in every Member State as irrebuttable proof of the infringement in subsequent civil antitrust damages cases*'.

81 See para 8 of the judgment of the Court of Appeal in *Enron II* [2011] EWCA Civ 2.

either of these two effects, binds the court.[82] Similarly, in damages actions for breach of competition law brought before it, the CAT is bound by a decision of the OFT that either national competition law or EU competition law has been violated, a decision of the CAT on appeal from a decision of the OFT to either of these two effects, or an infringement decision by the Commission.[83]

4.092 In the first *Enron* proceedings, the Court of Appeal,[84] on appeal from the judgment of the CAT,[85] considered the precise scope of a follow-on action under s47A of the Competition Act 1998, and what exactly binds the Tribunal in this context.

4.093 The way in which the CAT is bound by the prior administrative decision is determined specifically by s47A(9), which provides that '… *the Tribunal is bound by any decision … which establishes that the prohibition in question has been infringed*'. In *Enron I*, the Court of Appeal held that the CAT must not go beyond the strict finding of infringement made by the NCA, in such a way for example as to infer from the decision infringements which are not its strict subject-matter.

4.094 In the proceedings, the claimant seeking damages alleged *inter alia* an overcharge in relation to prices paid by it to the defendant for coal haulage services provided pursuant to contract over a given period. In fact, the infringement decision by the public authority (the Office of Rail Regulation, ORR) had found that the defendant had engaged in price discrimination vis-à-vis the claimant, but had not made a finding of overcharge.

4.095 Such a finding was inferred by the CAT on the basis that the price charged by the defendant to the claimant was higher than that charged, or proposed, to other market participants tendering for services in respect to which the defendant and the claimant were in competition. According to the CAT, it was at least arguable that the defendant should to that extent have reduced the prices it was charging to the claimant, thereby generating a claim for an overcharge as a result of the fact that it failed to do so.[86]

---

82 s58 of the Competition Act 1998.

83 s47A of the Competition Act 1998.

84 [2009] EWCA Civ 647.

85 [2009] CAT 7.

86 Para 41 of the judgment of the CAT, referring to para B21(c) of the original decision of the ORR, which had referred to the failure of the defendant to offer the claimant '*price reductions similar to those offered to [its] other customers*'.

The higher prices charged by the defendant to the clamant were, in effect, the substance of the finding by the ORR of price discrimination, but did not constitute a finding of overcharge. The decision of the ORR was clear on the point. In holding that the higher prices were unlikely to constitute the basis for a finding of overcharge, the Court of Appeal pointed out that the price paid by the claimant to the defendant for services provided was fixed by an existing contract which pre-dated the time period in which the defendant engaged in price discrimination activities.[87] To this extent, if there was a claim for an overcharge at all, it could only be for that part of the duration of the contract. In any case, the exercise conducted by the Court of Appeal was to search carefully the decision of the ORR to determine which findings of infringement it in fact made, not those which it could have made, or should have made on a correct interpretation of the facts.[88] **4.096**

The principle established by the judgment of the Court of Appeal is therefore that, in deciding a follow-on claim for damages under s47A of the Competition Act, the CAT is bound to follow the finding of infringement made in the public authority's decision.[89] Conversely, the Tribunal cannot go beyond that finding of infringement in any way, including by inferring a finding of infringement from extraneous matters of fact referred to in the decision in question.[90] **4.097**

There has also been extensive litigation before the CAT and the Court of Appeal of the issue of the precise identity of the parties on whom administrative decisions are binding in subsequent litigation. **4.098**

It can be said that it has been established as a matter of English law that the binding force of prior administrative decisions only applies as against the actual addressee of the decision. This will often be the parent company in a corporate **4.099**

87 See para 33 of the judgment of the Court of Appeal, summarising this part of the claimant's pleadings as being to the effect that '*to continue to charge the prices actually paid under the contract [originally concluded by the parties] constituted an abuse of [the defendant's] dominant position in the market*'. See also para 50 (the prices charged under the original contract did not necessarily amount to a discrimination in themselves).

88 See para 40: '*[b]ut we are not concerned on this application with how the ORR should have approached this issue [that of construing what elements are required to show discriminatory conduct] ... The only question for the Tribunal ... is whether the ORR made a finding of competitive disadvantage in relation to overcharging of the kind alleged ...*'

89 The clearest formulation of this legal principle in the judgment is to be found at para 31, where the Court held that '*[t]he use of the word "decision" [in s47A(9)] makes it clear that s47A is differentiating between findings of fact as to the conduct of the defendant made as part of the overall decision and a determination by the regulator that particular conduct amounts to an infringement .... It is not open to a claimant ... to seek to recover damages through the medium of s47A simply by identifying findings of fact which could arguably amount to such an infringement. No right of action exists unless the regulator has actually decided that such conduct constitutes an infringement ...*'

90 This principle was applied by the CAT in its later judgment in *Emerson* (see, for example, para 59).

structure, it being the Commission's fining practice to impose the fine on the top company in the group in the hope that this will most likely result in payment.[91]

4.100 Thus in *Emerson Electric Co and others* v *Morgan Crucible Company plc and others*,[92] the CAT came to the conclusion that only the formal addressee of the decision in question (in this case, the Commission's carbon and graphite products decision[93]) could be sued for damages on the basis of s47A of the Competition Act 1998.[94] The decision of the Tribunal was upheld by the Court of Appeal.[95]

4.101 Both the CAT and the Court of Appeal rejected the argument that the administrative decision could have binding effect upon the subsidiary on the basis that it is part of the same undertaking as its parent, which was an addressee of the decision.[96] Such an argument would represent a conflation of arguments as to the jurisdiction of the CAT under domestic law with the wider EU competition law principle of undertaking as used by the Commission in its fining practice.[97] This means that bottom-up attribution of liability is permissible as part of the Commission's fining practice, but that top-down attribution in subsequent related litigation is not.

---

91 See further paras 7.047–7.049 for examination of the impact of the Commission's fining practice on damages actions.

92 [2011] CAT 4. It is interesting to note that two other cases before the CAT, which had been stayed pending the outcome of this point in the *Emerson* proceedings, were since dismissed by consent of the parties (Cases No 1147/5/7/09 and 1153/5/7/10, both relating to the methionine cartel).

93 Commission Decision 2004/420/EC of 3 December 2003, Case No C.38.359, electrical and mechanical carbon and graphite products (OJ L 125, 28.4.2004, p 45).

94 As noted at para 39 of the judgment of the English High Court in *Bord Na Mona*, under s47A, the Tribunal is bound by the decision of the public authority, either the Commission or the NCA, in the same way as under Article 16 of Regulation 1/2003.

95 *Emerson Electric Co and others* v *Mersen UK Portslade Ltd* [2012] EWCA Civ 1559. See in particular para 79, and para 81 for the finding that the issue of which companies might make up an undertaking has no bearing on the issue of which companies can be held to be liable for damages pursuant to s47A of the Competition Act 1998. This point is restated, though in perhaps slightly unfortunate language, at para 86(7) in the judge's conclusions.

96 See for example para 51 of the judgment of the CAT: '*The Commission appears simply to be stating that it is sufficient to address, convict and penalise Topco in order to cover the participation in the particular infringement of any and all other members of the group. There is nothing to indicate that the Commission means that although only Topco is named as addressee, the decision is also being directed through that medium to other legal persons who are therefore equally bound by it.*' See similarly para 82 of the judgment of the Court of Appeal: '*[t]he issue of liability has been clearly and unambiguously determined by the Commission in its Decision … if the Commission had intended to impose such liability [on Carbone GB, the UK-domiciled subsidiary] for infringement, it could and should have either named Carbone GB as an addressee in the operative part of the Decision or defined the address undertaking as including not only Carbone SA [the parent] but also all subsidiary entities owned or controlled by it as being liable for infringements of article 101(1) FEU.*'

97 It could further be claimed that what is essentially a dubious practice on the part of the Commission in order to extract the greatest fine possible in relation to any given infringement is being exposed by its interaction with the private law consequences of related damages claims.

The judgment of the CAT is divided into two parts.[98] In the first, the Tribunal addresses the question of the operative part of the Commission decision, allowing itself to arrive at a strict interpretation of its own jurisdiction on the grounds that the addressees can be readily identified from that part. **4.102**

The Tribunal then goes on to address the issue of whether liability can be established on the basis of the recitals to the Commission decision. Here the task is more difficult, as the recitals are open to a wider variety of interpretations than the operative part. The Tribunal holds that there is nothing *as a matter of fact* in the recitals which would enable it to hold that the Commission had found that that subsidiary in question had participated in the infringement. However, it specifically leaves open the question of what the situation would be *as a matter of law* had there been such a finding in the recitals. This could conceivably include a finding by the Commission that the subsidiary had participated in the infringement by virtue of being part of the infringing undertaking in the wider sense.[99] **4.103**

2 Germany

§33(4) GWB provides that in actions for damages for breach of EU or national competition law, the court is bound by a decision of the Commission or a national competition authority, either the *Bundeskartellamt* or the national competition authority of another Member State, applying EU or national competition law, as appropriate.[100] It also provides that the court is similarly bound by a decision of the court of another Member State insofar as that court has the function to issue administrative decisions finding an infringement or to decide on an appeal against an administrative decision.[101] **4.104**

---

98 Paras 18–32 and 36–52 constitute the first part, and paras 33–35 and 52–62 the second.

99 See para 58: '*there may be material in the recitals from which it could be inferred that at the material time Carbone GB was part of the same undertaking as Carbone SA, but no determination to that effect appears in the Decision*'.

100 Insofar as this rule relates to Commission decisions, like s47A of the Competition Act 1998, it restates the rule contained in Article 16(1) of Regulation 1/2003.

101 In its report on the seventh amendment to the GWB, which introduced these rules, the *Monopolkommission* recommended that the binding effects of public decisions apply only as against the actual addressees of the decision and not against all members of the cartel. The *Monopolkommission* argued for this position on the grounds that only the addressees of the decision would have had or would have the right to challenge the decision. The contrast is with the position of a non-addressee, who would be bound by a decision the validity of which it could not challenge and thus would be left without effective protection of its rights of defence. Secondly, the *Monopolkommission* argued that if the decision only binds addressees, this will preserve the incentive for cartel members to go for leniency.

4.105 It should be noted that the German system is, so to speak, more federalist on this point as it recognises the binding force of decisions taken by the competition authorities of other Member States.[102]

4.106 In its judgment in a claim arising out of the vitamins cartel, the *Landgericht* Dortmund relied on the fining decision made by the Commission in relation to the vitamins cartel as to its finding of infringement.[103] The decision had found the defendant to be the instigator and main beneficiary of the collusive price-fixing agreements, including the implementation of market share allocations, minimum prices and target prices, coordinated behaviour towards certain customers, and a monitoring system.

4.107 However, a distinction should be made between the evidential value of the Commission decision concerning the finding of an infringement and the assessment of the concrete damage caused by that infringement. The German court relied exclusively on the Commission decision when it stated that there had been an infringement of Article 101 TFEU.

4.108 Concerning the calculation of the actual damage, two aspects have to be distinguished due to the legal basis. The relevant provision is §287 *Zivilprozessordnung* (Code of Civil Procedure), which allows the judge to carry out an estimation of the damage in question under the following two conditions: firstly, where the exact sum cannot be determined; and, secondly, where there are facts available that lead to the conclusion that damage has been caused at all. The judgment only refers to the Commission decision as an indicator for the existence of damage. The calculation/estimation of the damage which follows, however, is not (at least not explicitly) based on the Commission figures.

3 Romanistic jurisdictions

4.109 In France, decisions of the NCA, the *Autorité de la concurrence*, do not bind the courts. The same is true of the Italian system. However, in both jurisdictions, such decisions do have high evidential value. This is illustrated, in relation to

---

102 Austrian law has moved in the same direction with the adoption of §37a of the *Bundesgesetz gegen Kartelle und andere Wettbewerbsbeschränkungen*, which provides that the civil courts are bound by a finding of infringement by the *Kartellgericht* (Austrian Cartel Court), other Member State competition authorities or the Commission.

103 Commission Decision 2003/2/EC of 21 November 2001, case COMP/E-1/37.512, vitamins (OJ L 6, 10.1.2003, p 1). The decision imposed a total fine of €855.22 million, of which the defendant alone was subject to a fine of €462 million. In evaluating the evidence, the judgment of the *Landgericht* Dortmund stressed that the Commission decision was '*rechtskräftig*', that is, that there were no other legal means available to challenge it in court.

Italy, by the judgment in the *Telecom Italia/Albacom* proceedings, where the Rome *Corte d'appello* relied on the infringement decision of the national competition authority, the AGCM, in finding a substantive infringement.[104]

104 *Albacom SpA. c. Telecom Italia SpA*, judgment no 261/2003 of 20 January 2003.

5

FURTHER SUBSTANTIVE AND PROCEDURAL ISSUES

I CAUSATION 5.03

II MEASURE OF DAMAGES 5.07
- A Types of damage recoverable 5.08
- B Presumption of harm 5.13
  - 1 EU law 5.17
  - 2 National law 5.18
- C Exemplary damages 5.21
  - 1 EU law 5.22
  - 2 English law 5.24

III LIMITATION PERIODS 5.47
- A EU law 5.47
- B National law 5.54
  - 1 United Kingdom 5.55
  - 2 Germany 5.62

IV PROCEDURES FOR RECOURSE TO THE EXPERTISE OF PUBLIC AUTHORITIES BY THE NATIONAL COURTS 5.64
- A EU law: consultation of the Commission 5.65
- B National law: consultation of the NCA 5.66
  - 1 United Kingdom 5.67
  - 2 Germany 5.68
  - 3 France 5.69
  - 4 Other jurisdictions 5.72

V JOINT AND SEVERAL LIABILITY 5.75

5.01 Having proven the infringement, the claimant in an action for damages for breach of EU competition law will then have to identify the causal link between the infringement and his loss, and quantify that loss. This chapter outlines the law as regards these two issues, and then goes on to consider some further issues of a generally procedural nature which are important in bringing a damages action for breach of EU competition law.

5.02 The methodology employed has been, generally speaking, to treat issues insofar as they are specific to competition law actions, rather than attempting to explore in-depth general conditions pertaining to tortious liability, as a matter of either EU or national law.

I CAUSATION

5.03 Causation is a difficult issue, and in the few decided cases available in the field of antitrust, courts tend to use a but-for test. This is by necessity an imprecise science, as the application of the test will depend very heavily on the facts of the case. The English courts, for example, have applied the but-for test.[1] There are,

1 See the judgment of the CAT in *Cardiff Bus*, at paras 77–84, rejecting any alternative approach.

however, very few decided awards of damages from any jurisdiction, England and Wales included.

From a legal perspective, the basic pattern is that, the further a claim is from an infringement, the harder it becomes to establish causation.[2] In England and Wales, the first of only two awards of damages made to date by the CAT, the award made in the *Cardiff Bus* case,[3] was restricted to a claim for lost profits,[4] the court denying the claims for loss of the business as a going concern and loss of a business opportunity on grounds of causation.[5] In *Enron/EWS II*,[6] the first claim to be taken to final decision, that for loss of a business opportunity, was again denied by the CAT for reasons connected to causation. **5.04**

The claim in *Enron II* was for loss of a business opportunity in the form of the opportunity to bid for a separate supply contract. The CAT split the causation issue into two parts, firstly, that the claimant would have sought to bid for the contract in question in the absence of the infringement, and secondly, that the third party in question would have awarded the contract to the claimant in those circumstances. The Tribunal applied a balance of probabilities test to the first part, and a lower test of a '*real or substantial chance*' to the second part in respect of the actions of the third party.[7] It found that in neither case was the requisite standard of proof met by the claimant.[8] **5.05**

The complexity of the causation issue is reflected by the fact that, in its proposal, the Commission has not attempted to regulate it. The Commission, in fact, limits itself to saying that the principles of equivalence and effectiveness apply, as they do to all issues not explicitly covered by the proposal.[9] **5.06**

---

2 See also Chapter 8, section 3.3 for an economic perspective on the issues of causation and remoteness. Legally speaking, even if it may not be more difficult to show causation in a given case of a claim which is far from the underlying infringement, courts may be reluctant to allow more remote claims to succeed as a matter of legal policy.

3 See also *Healthcare at Home* v *Genzyme*, involving an interim award of damages.

4 See paras 339–418.

5 See paras 443–445 in relation to the loss of a business opportunity claim, and paras 419–442 in relation to the claim for the loss of the business as a going concern. See especially paras 430, 431 and 433 for the causation point in relation to the latter claim.

6 [2009] CAT 36.

7 See para 85(a) and (b) of the judgment.

8 Paras 91–154 for the first issue, and paras 155–221 for the second.

9 See recital 10.

II MEASURE OF DAMAGES[10]

5.07 In its proposal, the Commission makes the basic provision that the quantification of damage should not render the exercise of the right to damages '*practically impossible or excessively difficult*', which is little more than a restatement of the EU law principle of effectiveness in this context.[11] Furthermore, it requires Member States to ensure that national courts are able to '*estimate*' the damage suffered.[12]

A Types of damage recoverable

5.08 In terms of competition law damages, it is important to note that there are generally two types of loss that can be distinguished: pecuniary loss resulting from the overcharge, and what is termed the 'lost sales effect'. On the one hand, violations of competition law can evidently result in pure economic loss sustained via the purchase of products at supra-competitive prices. For example, loss can arise from inflated prices that are imposed on downstream traders by cartelists or firms that abuse their dominant position. Artificially inflated prices can in turn cause a decrease in the expected and/or actual profits of those customers. These are losses that are specific to, and directly experienced by, the entity that has purchased the goods at a higher price resulting from an infringement of the competition rules.

5.09 On the other hand, however, violations of competition law likewise lead to social losses. In particular, when, as a result of the infringing behaviour, prices increase and/or output decreases, this leads to the creation of a deadweight (welfare) loss to society, or more descriptively, a 'lost sales effect'.[13]

5.10 In particular, in a situation where a direct purchaser passes on an element of the overcharge, often the average consumer will react by buying less.[14] As a result of lost sales volumes, the direct purchaser can be expected to offer the price/quantity combination that maximises its profits, which in turn implies that less will be purchased at a higher price. Furthermore, the loss of sales volumes in relation to one product in this context may have a spill-over effect on other

10 The economics of the quantification of damage in competition litigation is dealt with in Chapter 8.

11 Article 16(2).

12 *Ibid.* See also para 9 of the communication on the quantification of harm. This recalls the rule proposed in the second subparagraph of Article 13(2) that, in relation to the proposed rebuttable presumption of passing-on in the case of an action brought by an indirect purchaser, the court should be able to estimate how much of the overcharge had been passed on in such a situation (see above, Chapter 3).

13 See further Chapter 8, section 2.1.1 (in relation to cartels), and section 2.2.1 (in relation to abuses).

14 See Theon van Dijk and Frank Verboven, 'The Passing-on Defence and the Full Compensation Principle', Concurrences N° 3–2010, at 9–10.

products of the same brand. This is because consumers may (temporarily or permanently) boycott an entire brand on the basis of the inflated price of one particular branded product. Although they can be very substantial, such 'brand damages' nevertheless constitute one of the most challenging types of loss to quantify and prove.[15]

In most Member States, the guiding principle in terms of the recovery of damages is that of *restitutio in integrum*, which includes both actual loss (*damnum emergens*) and loss of profit (*lucrum cessans*). **5.11**

This approach was confirmed as a matter of the EU by the ECJ in *Manfredi*, where the Court held that, under the principle of effectiveness, the claimant in a damages action for breach of EU competition law must be able to claim both actual loss and loss of profit, plus interest.[16] This is restated by the Commission in its proposal[17] and in the accompanying communication on the quantification of harm.[18] Furthermore, the proposal includes a rule specifically allowing claims for lost profits in the context of indirect purchaser actions.[19] **5.12**

B Presumption of harm

Despite making it easier for purchasers to claim damages by shifting the burden of proof to the defendant, the introduction of a presumption of harm has, however, been strongly debated at both Member State and EU level. **5.13**

Arguably, such a presumption can be efficient in that it shifts the burden of proof to the defendant, which presumably can avail itself of the most useful data for estimating the price and output effect of the cartel. Furthermore, it has been recognised that a presumption in relation to overcharge can have a significant impact on the dynamics of damages actions: defendants cannot limit themselves to addressing the claimant's damage analysis, but instead have to engage in a substantial analysis themselves should they want to rebut the presumption.[20] It has been recognised that a presumption of harm alters the expected costs and rewards of litigation, rendering it more likely that claimants and **5.14**

15 See also Chapter 8. It is useful to note that, in econometric terms, the overcharge is the price increase multiplied by the quantity bought at the higher price. As such, even a slight increase in price is capable of producing a significant total overcharge. For instance, a price increase of as little as €2 for a product that is sold in 500,000 units per year will result in an overcharge of €1 million.

16 See paras 95 and 100.

17 Recital 11.

18 Para 6.

19 Article 14(1).

20 CDC, damages analysis, available at: http://www.carteldamageclaims.com/.

defendants save resources by reaching settlements on terms that are reasonable.[21]

5.15 The acceptance of a presumption of harm could mean, however, that the defendant might be put in a position whereby it would have to at the same time argue for and against passing-on. This is because it would have to show both that the overcharge was passed on (thereby establishing that direct purchasers did not suffer loss), and that it was not, however, passed on to the indirect purchasers, so as to avoid compensating them. Clearly, '*if the defendant in those actions cannot prove the passing-on vis-à-vis those who claim there was no passing-on of overcharge, nor rebut the presumption that is invoked by those who rely on the alleged passing-on, he may face multiple liability for the same overcharge*'.[22]

5.16 In other words, introducing a presumption of harm would not solve the problem of quantifying the passed-on element, even if it may render it easier for direct and indirect purchasers to claim damages, while strengthening the element of deterrence. This point was observed by the OFT, which stated that '*... some multiple liability ... is not objectionable in policy terms – the risk of having to pay damages more than once would increase the deterrent effect of the EC competition rules and reduce the incidence of infringements*'.[23]

1 EU law

5.17 The idea of a presumption of harm features in the Commission's proposal. Article 16(1) provides that, in the case of a cartel, '*it shall be presumed that the infringement caused harm*'.[24] The presumption is rebuttable.

2 National law

5.18 Along the same lines, and in a similar bid to facilitate the bringing of antitrust claims, two cases before the German courts have debated whether an assumption can be made as to whether a cartel overcharge exists or not. In a vitamins cartel case, the *Landgericht* Dortmund held that a market price was generally lower than a cartel price.[25] The judgment seems to establish an unrebuttable presumption that a cartel leads to excessive prices. However, in its later

---

21 *Ibid.*

22 Commission Staff Working Paper accompanying the White Paper, at 67.

23 OFT, 'Response to the European Commission's Green Paper: Damages Actions for Breach of the EC Antitrust Rules', May 2006, at 18.

24 According to recital 35 to the proposal, such a presumption is limited to cartel infringements as such infringements are more secret in nature, meaning that the information asymmetry affecting the claimant is more acute.

25 *Landgericht* Dortmund, 0 55/02 Kart Vitaminkartell III, 1 April 2004 (WuW 2004, 1182), at para 26: '*Nach der Lebenserfahrung ist davon auszugehen, dass ein im Wettbewerbspreis gefundener Preis niedriger ist als ein kartellierter Preis.*'

judgment in the *Berliner Transportbeton* case, the *Bundesgerichtshof* took a more moderate approach.[26] It held that there might be exceptional cases where a cartel does not lead to higher prices, or where at least the causal link cannot be proven. The court then went on to state that the standard of proof required to show that a cartel had not gained any advantage from its activity would be higher the longer the cartel's duration and the greater its geographic coverage.[27] Thus, both courts presume higher prices, but the *Bundesgerichtshof* leaves the door open to a rebuttal.

One Member State has introduced a rebuttable presumption of harm by means of legislation, namely Hungary. The Hungarian Competition Act (*törvény a tisztességtelen piaci magatartás és a versenykorlátozás tilalmáról*, TPVT) provides that injured parties bringing a claim against members of a price-fixing cartel can rely on the rebuttable presumption that '*the infringement affected the price by 10% unless the contrary is evidenced*'.[28] **5.19**

Other Member States have looked at the issue. For example, the UK Government considered the introduction of a rebuttable presumption of loss in cartel cases, to the effect that a cartel affects prices by a fixed amount of 20 per cent.[29] Such a presumption of loss was, however, ultimately shelved.[30] **5.20**

26 *Bundesgerichtshof*, KRB 2/05 (WuW 2005, 1257).

27 '*Je länger und nachhaltiger ein Kartell praktiziert wurde, und je flächendeckender es angelegt ist, um so höhere Anforderungen sind an die Darlegungen des Tatrichters zu stellen, wenn er einen wirtschaftlichen Vorteil aus der Kartellabsprache verneinen will*' (para 22).

28 Section 88/C, applicable to damages arising after September 2008. In the Italian judgment in the *Manfredi* proceedings, the Bitonto *Giudice di pace* (Justice of the Peace) concluded that there was a '*simple presumption*' ('*presonzione semplice*') of an overcharge of 20 per cent, which the defendant had failed to rebut (Bitonto *Giudice di pace*, *Vincenzo Manfredi/Lloyd Adriatico Assicurazioni SpA*, judgment of 21 May 2007).

29 2012 BIS consultation, para 4.40. The economic literature also suggests that cartels can raise prices in respect of the goods or services in question by as much as 20 per cent to 35 per cent or even higher. See, for example, the study prepared for the Commission entitled 'Quantifying Antitrust Damages: Towards Non-binding Guidance for Courts' (Oxera/Komninos, Assimakis, December 2009). See also the report by Connor and Lande, finding that cartels overcharge on average between 18 per cent and 37 per cent in the US, and between 28 per cent and 54 per cent in the EU (John M. Connor and Robert H. Lande, 'The Size of Cartel Overcharges: Implications for US and EU Fining Policies' (2006) 51(4) Antitrust Bulletin 983). For a criticism of the 20 per cent presumption as proposed by the UK Government, see Derek Ridyard, 'BIS Consultation on Private Actions in Competition Law: an Economist's Perspective' (2012) 5(4) GCLR 151. Interestingly, he notes that '*[i]f the 20 per cent impact presumption was soundly based on empirical evidence, this would itself raise much more substantial issues about the adequacy of the public enforcement regime, since it would suggest that basing fines on a figure set at 10 per cent of a company's relevant turnover would systematically fail to allow competition authorities to provide adequate deterrence*'.

30 See the 2013 BIS response, at paras 4.36–4.37.

C Exemplary damages

5.21 A further issue is whether a defendant can be made liable to pay exemplary (or punitive) damages to a claimant in addition to a payment compensating him for loss incurred as a result of a breach of the EU competition rules. In terms of taxonomy, exemplary damages are additional to an award which fully compensates the claimant for his loss, and their purpose is to punish and deter the wrongdoer.[31]

1 EU law

5.22 At EU level, the matter was addressed in the *Manfredi* case, where the ECJ held as follows[32]:

> In accordance with the principle of equivalence, if it is possible to award specific damages, such as exemplary or punitive damages, in domestic actions similar to actions founded on the Community competition rules, it must also be possible to award such damages in actions founded on Community rules. However, Community law does not prevent national courts from taking steps to ensure that the protection of the rights guaranteed by Community law does not entail the unjust enrichment of those who enjoy them.

5.23 It can therefore be said, as a matter of law, that exemplary damages are not anathema to EU law. In terms of policy, the Commission appeared to be much more open to the idea of exemplary damages, at least as regarded competition policy, at the time of the Green Paper.[33] The Commission's thinking on the point has since then, however, been dramatically toned down, such that paragraph 31 of the recommendation on collective redress reads as follows: '*punitive damages, leading to overcompensation in favour of the claimant party of the damage suffered, should be prohibited*'.[34]

2 English law

5.24 At Member State level, exemplary damages are only available in England and Wales, Ireland[35] and Cyprus. As mentioned above, in other Member States, the guiding principle in terms of damage available is that of *restitutio in integrum*. In

31 See *Kuddus* v *Chief Constable of Leicestershire* [2002] 2 AC 122 per Lord Nicholls: '*Exemplary damages or punitive damages, the terms are synonymous, stand apart from awards of compensatory damages. They are additional to an award which is intended to compensate a plaintiff fully for the loss he has suffered, both pecuniary and non-pecuniary. They are intended to punish and deter.*'

32 Para 99.

33 The Green Paper had included the option of double damages for horizontal cartels which could be automatic, conditional or at the discretion of the court (option 16).

34 See further Chapter 6.

35 Section 14(5)(b) of the Competition Act 2002.

Germany, for example, an award of exemplary or punitive damages is regarded as contrary to public policy.[36]

In England and Wales, an award of exemplary damages is only granted in exceptional circumstances. In this respect, it is well-established in English law that exemplary damages *may* be appropriate in the following three situations: (i) oppressive, arbitrary or unconstitutional conduct by '*servants of the government*'; (ii) conduct calculated to make a profit which may well exceed the compensation payable to the claimant; and (iii) cases authorised by statute.[37] **5.25**

The issue of the availability of exemplary damages in the specific context of competition law damages actions before the English courts was first decided before the High Court in *Devenish*. *Devenish* was a follow-on action from the Commission's vitamins cartel decision, in which eight pharmaceutical companies were found to have entered into eight market sharing and price cartels in relation to vitamin products in breach of Article 101 TFEU. The cartel participants were fined €855 million. One company was granted full immunity from fines with regard to its participation in two of the cartels. **5.26**

In *Devenish*, it was accepted that, on the facts, the case fell within the second category of exemplary damages identified above, that is, conduct calculated to make a profit which may well exceed the compensation payable to the claimant. This was because of the Commission's finding that the defendants had taken part in the cartels '*with full knowledge of the illegality of their actions*'. Ultimately, however, exemplary damages were not awarded. **5.27**

The High Court looked at the issue on a number of grounds, some based in EU law, others in English law, all of which led the judge to conclude that an award of exemplary damages was not available. **5.28**

As to the first EU law grounds, the High Court held that the principle of *ne bis in idem* (double jeopardy) precluded the award of exemplary damages in a case in which the defendants had already been fined (or had fines imposed and then reduced or commuted to zero) by the Commission.[38] **5.29**

---

36 See W. Wurmnest, 'Recognition and Enforcement of U.S. Money Judgments in Germany' (2005) 23 Berkeley Journal of International Law 175, at 196.

37 These three categories were laid down by Lord Devlin in the leading English case on exemplary damages, *Rookes* v *Barnard* [1964] 1 AC 1129. In particular, with regard to the second category, it was held that '*[c]ases in the second category are those in which the defendant's conduct has been calculated by him to make a profit for himself which may well exceed the compensation payable to the plaintiff… Where a defendant with a cynical disregard for the plaintiff's rights has calculated that the money to be made out of his wrongdoing will probably exceed the damages at risk, it is necessary for the law to show that it cannot be broken with impunity.*'

38 Para 52. However, when considering the issue of double jeopardy later in the judgment as a matter of English law, the judge held less forcefully that '*[i]n my judgment the fact that a defendant has been fined for his conduct is a*

5.30 As cited by the judge in *Devenish*,[39] the statement of the Court of First Instance (CFI) in *Archer Daniels* provides a useful summary of the principle of *ne bis in idem*.[40] According to the CFI, *ne bis in idem* precludes double punishment when three elements can be shown to be present: identity of facts; identity of offender and identity of the legal interest protected.[41]

5.31 In *Devenish*, the first two tests were held, with some argument, to be satisfied, the facts required to be pleaded for a claim of exemplary damages being held to have already been found by the Commission in its decision, and the parties to the litigation and the addressees of the Commission's decision being held to be the same.[42] Of perhaps the greatest interest is the court's examination of the third test, namely identity of interest. On this point, the High Court held that the Commission's fine and a possible award of exemplary damages served the same interest, namely to punish and deter the wrongdoer.[43]

5.32 The court further held that the fact that the fine of one of the defendants had been reduced to zero as a result of the application of leniency had no impact on the issue of double jeopardy.[44] The judge held that the starting point for the application of leniency was the imposition of a fine, such that possibility of double punishment still existed. The judge then went on to look at the policy considerations behind leniency, holding that, given the importance of leniency programmes from the perspective of uncovering and deterring cartels, the application of the Commission's leniency notice served the important '*policy aim*' of encouraging whistleblowers, which was more important than punishing participants in a cartel. The judge held that the national court should not

---

powerful factor against the award of exemplary damages, although it may not be conclusive in itself' (para 64; emphasis added).

39 Para 41.

40 Judgment of the CFI of 27 September 2006 in Case T-329/01 *Archer Daniels Midland Co* v *Commission* [2006] ECR II-3255.

41 Para 290 of the judgment, which reads as follows: '*the principle of ne bis in idem prohibits the same person from being sanctioned more than once for the same unlawful conduct in order to protect one and the same legal interest. The application of that principle is subject to three cumulative conditions: the identity of the facts, the unity of offender and the unity of legal interest protected.*' See also joined cases C-204/00 P, C-205/00 P, C-211/00 P, C-213/00 P, C-217/00 P and C-219/00 P *Aalborg Portland and others* v *Commission* [2004] ECR I-123, at para 338.

42 By way of comparison, in its judgment of 14 February 2012 in Case C-17/10 *Toshiba Corporation and others* v *Úřad pro ochranu hospodářské soutěže* (not yet reported), the ECJ held that the identity of facts test was not satisfied where the territories to which the different punishments related were not the same, the Commission fine relating to the territory of the EU and the fine imposed by the NCA to the territory of the Czech Republic pre-accession. This case concerned the fines imposed on the same cartel by the Commission and the Czech NCA for the period prior to 1 May 2004.

43 Paras 46 and 48.

44 Para 51.

'*undermine that policy*' by awarding exemplary damages against a company that had benefited from leniency.[45]

As to the second EU law grounds, the High Court held that an award of exemplary damages would '*run counter*' to Article 16 in a case where the Commission had already imposed a fine, insofar as such an award would be taken as meaning that '*the national court had concluded that the fines imposed by the Commission … were insufficient to punish and deter*'.[46] This would also be the case where such a fine had been reduced, either wholly or in part, as a result of the application of leniency. **5.33**

The issue of exemplary damages was not appealed. The discussion on appeal on the availability of restitutionary damages is nonetheless useful for the discussion on exemplary damages.[47] Arden LJ examined two questions of EU law relating to awards of restitutionary damages. The first issue concerned whether EU law prevented the award of restitutionary damages. This was answered in the negative. The second issue was concerned with whether the availability of a restitutionary award was required for the purposes of the principle of the effectiveness of EU law. It was held that it clearly emerged from rulings such as *Manfredi* that purely compensatory damages are sufficient to ensure that the rights of private persons are safeguarded under Article 101 TFEU. In particular, it was held that '*the doctrine of effectiveness is therefore directed to ensuring sufficient remedies rather than the fullest possible remedies. <u>An action for compensatory damages fulfils the requirements of sufficiency</u>*' (emphasis added). **5.34**

In July 2012, the Competition Appeal Tribunal awarded both compensatory and exemplary damages to 2 Travel Group plc as a victim of an abuse of a dominant position by Cardiff City Transport Services.[48] The judgment is only the second competition law follow-on damages claim to have reached trial in England and Wales, and the first pertaining to the Chapter II prohibition contained in s18(1) of the Competition Act 1998 (the UK law equivalent of Article 102 TFEU). **5.35**

On 18 November 2008, the OFT decided that between 2004 and 2005, Cardiff Bus had infringed s18(1) by engaging in predatory conduct amounting to an **5.36**

---

45 If this were the case, '*a more guilty wrongdoer would escape liability for exemplary damages, while a less guilty wrongdoer, whose fines had been commuted would not*'.

46 Para 54.

47 [2008] EWCA Civ 1086. In terms of taxonomy, a restitutionary award is an award of money assessed by reference to the wrongdoer's gain, rather than by reference to the victim's loss.

48 *2 Travel Group Plc* v *Cardiff City Transport Services Limited* [2012] CAT 19.

abuse of a dominant position on the relevant market.[49] In particular, in response to 2 Travel's entry into the market with a new no-frills bus service, Cardiff Bus had introduced its own competing no-frills service. Cardiff Bus' buses had run on the same routes and at similar times of day to those run as part of 2 Travel's no-frills services, and had been run at a loss until shortly after 2 Travel's exit, when Cardiff Bus had withdrawn them. Evidence adduced showed that Cardiff Bus planned to launch its no-frills services not as a true market testing exercise, but in order to divert potential customers away from 2 Travel. Furthermore, the OFT had identified evidence that Cardiff Bus launched its competing no-frills services with exclusionary intent.

5.37 Cardiff Bus had benefited from immunity under s40 of the Competition Act, which provides limited immunity from financial penalties for conduct of minor significance in relation to infringements of the Chapter II prohibition. The OFT had therefore refrained from imposing a fine on Cardiff Bus. 2 Travel subsequently brought a follow-on damages action against Cardiff Bus before the CAT under s47A of the Competition Act 1998.

5.38 In the damages proceedings, 2 Travel contended that it was entitled to exemplary damages under the first two of these three heads as identified in *Rookes* v *Barnard*. While the first head was summarily rejected by the CAT, the second gave rise to some interesting points of principle. The CAT ruled that in any case where exemplary damages are sought, the competition law infringement must have been an intentional breach of the law, or at least reckless, so as to be regarded as sufficiently outrageous to fall within the second category of exemplary damages outlined above. Recklessness is equated with the taking of an unacceptable risk. The CAT considered that it will only be in those cases where an undertaking is aware that its proposed conduct is either probably unlawful or clearly unlawful that a risk can be classed as unacceptable, bearing in mind that it can be extremely difficult to determine which unilateral acts by a dominant undertaking are pro-competitive and which are anti-competitive.[50] Whether the risk is, in fact, unacceptable also depends upon all the facts of the case, including any expected pro-competitive effects of the conduct, the degree and seriousness of any anti-competitive effects, the motive of the undertaking and the practicability of achieving the same commercial or pro-competitive aim by following a different course of action with less serious anti-competitive effects.

---

49 Decision number CA98/1/2008.

50 See Richard Whish and David Bailey, *Competition Law* (7th edition, Oxford: Oxford University Press, 2012), at 192: '*the application of [the Chapter II prohibition] involves a competition authority or a court having to decide whether that behaviour deviates from "normal" or "fair" or "undistorted" competition, or from "competition on the merits", none of which expressions is free from difficulty*'.

Furthermore, against the fact that the object of exemplary damages is to punish and deter, the CAT considered the impact of the OFT's initial decision finding an infringement of the Chapter II prohibition. In this respect, the CAT found no policy reason to stop it from awarding exemplary damages. On the facts of the case, the CAT held that there were no pro-competitive effects emerging from the behaviour in question, but that there were indeed serious anti-competitive effects, and that there was an exclusionary intent. The CAT held that Cardiff Bus' conduct had been outrageous, and absent an award of exemplary damages, a compensatory award would have been insufficient. Furthermore, the CAT held that the questions of policy arising in this case were very different from those arising in *Devenish* – one being that there was no conflict of policy objective between upholding a robust leniency programme and deterring defendants generally or specifically. As a result, the CAT exercised its discretion to award exemplary damages of £60,000. **5.39**

Overall, when awarding exemplary damages, the CAT also laid down the following instructive guiding principles that should be borne in mind: whilst exemplary damages do have to punish and deter, they have to bear some relation to the compensatory damages being awarded; and in assessing the amount of exemplary damages, regard must be had to the economic size of the defendant; and the economic and regulatory context within which the award of exemplary damages is given. In this case, Cardiff Bus was an entity with an association with a local authority, as a result of which it could be considered that it would no doubt take very full account of the judgment and adhere to the law in the future. **5.40**

In light of the fact that the vast majority of private actions brought under English law reach settlement, the CAT's judgment provides valuable guidance for practitioners seeking to bring damages claims in the future. In this respect the findings of the CAT at the end of its judgment are particularly illuminating[51]: **5.41**

> We are under no illusions but that this Judgment is likely to incentivise the bringing of claims for exemplary damages in competition cases. That is a matter for future Tribunals. We would only emphasise that the mere fact that an infringement of the competition rules has been found is insufficient to justify the pleading of such a claim. In any case where exemplary damages are sought, it will be necessary to plead, and to plead with specificity, facts and matters alleging that the competition law infringement in question was executed either intentionally in breach of the law or recklessly so as to be regarded as sufficiently outrageous as to fall within Lord Devlin's second category [in Rookes v Barnard]. Otherwise, we consider, the claim will fall to be struck out.

51 Para 598.

5.42 Exemplary damages and their application to a case of infringement of the Chapter II prohibition were further examined by the CAT in *Albion Water Limited* v *Dŵr Cymru Cyfyngedig*.[52] Albion Water brought a follow-on damages action against Dŵr Cymru Cyfyngedig on the basis of prior administrative decisions that the defendant had abused its dominant position by engaging in an illegal margin squeeze,[53] and by charging excessive and unfair prices.[54]

5.43 In this case the claim was limited to the second category for which English law permits an award of exemplary damages following *Rookes* v *Barnard*, that is, conduct calculated to make a profit which may well exceed the compensation payable to the claimant.

5.44 Despite an award of compensatory damages of £1.85 million to Albion Water, it was held, however, that the conditions for an award of exemplary damages were not met. This was essentially for two reasons.[55]

5.45 Firstly, it was held that the defendant had not acted in cynical disregard of Albion Water's rights. Applying the test laid down in *Cardiff Bus*, discussed above, the CAT held that, on the basis of the evidence before it, it could not be shown that the defendant was aware that the abusive price charged in this case was either clearly or probably unlawful.

5.46 Secondly, there was an absence of evidence showing that the defendant '*deliberately closed its eyes to the excessive nature of the price because it had calculated, in however broad a fashion, that the money it was likely to make from issuing [the abusive price] was likely to exceed any damages that it would be liable to pay to Albion in the event of a successful claim*'.

III LIMITATION PERIODS

A EU law

5.47 In *Manfredi*, the ECJ held that rules on limitation periods were to be determined by national law, in accordance with the principles of equivalence and effectiveness. In particular, the ECJ held that a rule under which the limitation period ran from the time when an infringement began, and not from the time

52 [2013] CAT 6.

53 *Albion Water Limited* v *Water Services Regulatory Authority* [2006] CAT 36.

54 *Albion Water Limited and Albion Water Group Limited* v *Water Services Regulatory Authority* [2008] CAT 31.

55 See para 366 of the judgment.

when it ceased in the case of a continuous infringement, could make it '*practically impossible or excessively difficult*' for the claimant to exercise its right to claim damages.[56] Accordingly, Article 14(2) of the draft Directive provided that '*Member States shall ensure that the limitation period does not begin to run before the day on which a continuous or repeated infringement ceases*'.

It should be borne in mind that the findings of the ECJ in *Manfredi* on limitation periods, as well as the German law discussed below, are broad in scope in that they cover limitation periods in any action for damages for breach of EU competition law, whether this is a follow-on or stand-alone action. The more detailed statutory rules in the UK Competition Act 1998 (see below), and the complex litigation to which they have led, are concerned with the more limited, but in some ways more complex, field of follow-on actions only. Thus the draft Directive contained a more general rule on limitation periods in all types of damages litigation in its Article 14(1), which is correspondingly less precise in what it provides, and a more precise rule on follow-on actions in its Article 14(3). Interestingly, the Commission chose in that provision to follow the rule adopted by the CAT and provide for a limitation period of two years in connection with follow-on actions, providing further that the period runs from the time when '*the infringement decision has become final*'. This corresponds, *grosso modo*, to the rule set out in s47A(8) of the Competition Act 1998, though the litigation that this provision has given rise to, as set out above, shows that even such an apparently simple rule can lead to a great deal of complexity in interpretation in practice. **5.48**

In its proposal, the Commission has chosen a unified approach applying to all types of action. There is no distinction in the rules proposed between follow-on and stand-alone actions. **5.49**

The basic provision is Article 10(4), which provides that the limitation period should be at least five years. This is longer than the two-year period currently provided for in UK law for follow-on actions before the CAT, but more in line with the general tort law rules of the Member States which would govern, in the absence of any more specific rules, stand-alone actions in particular.[57] **5.50**

Article 10(2) of the proposal provides that the limitation period should start to run from the moment of knowledge of the claimant of the behaviour constituting the infringement, the fact that it was an infringement and the fact that the **5.51**

56 *Manfredi*, paras 78 and 82.

57 Note in any case the intention of the UK Government, discussed in more detail below, to align the limitation period in the CAT to the limitation period for ordinary tortious actions before the High Court at six years.

infringement caused harm to him. The first two of these conditions will automatically be met in the case of a follow-on action. Furthermore, the Commission proposes, in Article 10(2)(iv), that the limitation period should only start to run once the claimant is aware of the identity of the infringer. Again, in the case of a follow-on action, this will be clear from the infringement decision of the public authority, though this provision might raise the sort of questions which have given rise to the extensive litigation before the CAT on who exactly is taken as being bound by a public infringement decision in subsequent damages actions.

5.52 One final part of the proposal worth mentioning is that, in the Commission's view, there should be provision for the limitation period to be suspended in the event that a public authority opens an investigation or other proceeding in relation to the infringement alleged by the claimant. In such a case, the limitation period shall start to run again at the earliest one year after the investigation or proceeding shall have been brought to a close.[58]

5.53 As a final point, it should be mentioned that the proposal also contains a rule whereby the limitation period is to be suspended in the case of commencement of a dispute resolution process in relation to the same behaviour. The suspension only has effect as between the parties which are actually involved in the dispute resolution process.[59]

B National law

5.54 As observed above, as held by the ECJ in *Manfredi*, in the absence of specific rules on the issue as a matter of EU law, limitation periods in actions for breach of competition law are, in the present state of the law, a question of national law.

1 United Kingdom

5.55 The statutory basis for limitation periods for actions for breach of EU or national competition law brought before the CAT is complex: the relevant provisions are s47A(3) of the Competition Act 1998, as inserted by the Enterprise Act 2002, and Rule 31 of the Competition Appeal Tribunal Rules 2003, adopted on the basis of paragraph 11 of Schedule 4, Part 2 of the Enterprise Act and to be read together with s47A(7) and (8) of the Competition Act.

58 Article 10(5).
59 Article 17(1).

In *Emerson I*,[60] the CAT decided that where any addressee of a Commission decision had appealed that decision before the General Court, permission was required for a damages claim to be brought against any addressee of the same decision, including an addressee which had not appealed the Commission decision. Applying this judgment, in *Emerson II*[61] the CAT allowed permission for a claim to be brought against an addressee which had not appealed the Commission decision, but in *Emerson III*[62] denied permission for a claim to be brought against addressees which had appealed the Commission's decision. **5.56**

Despite the conclusions of the CAT in the *Emerson* litigation, and reversing the judgment of the Tribunal in the particular case, in its judgment in *Deutsche Bahn*,[63] the Court of Appeal held that, where one of a number of infringers of Article 101 TFEU had not appealed a Commission decision establishing liability for the same infringement against all of them, the time limit for an action under s47A(8) against all infringers, including the infringer which had chosen not to appeal the decision, started to run from the date of delivery of the judgment of the General Court.[64] **5.57**

Despite the justifications put forward by Mummery LJ as to procedural economy,[65] it is, as the reverse side of the same coin, at least arguable that the judgment will open up delays in proceedings which might not in all cases be justified. In addition, the interaction of the findings of this judgment with the position of leniency applicants will be controversial. **5.58**

In *BCL/BASF I*,[66] the Court of Appeal held that the time limit under s47A(8) was not interrupted by an appeal on the fine only. The time limit could only be interrupted by an appeal against the finding of infringement. This meant that the claim in question, which had been brought against a defendant which had appealed the decision against it as to fine only, was time-barred. In *BLC/BASF* **5.59**

---

60 *Emerson Electric Co and others* v *Morgan Crucible Company plc and others* [2007] CAT 28.

61 *Emerson Electric Co and others* v *Morgan Crucible Company plc and others* [2007] CAT 30.

62 *Emerson Electric Co and others* v *Morgan Crucible Company plc and others* [2008] CAT 8.

63 *Deutsche Bahn AG and others* v *Morgan Crucible Company plc and others* [2012] EWCA Civ 1055, on appeal from the CAT ([2011] CAT 16).

64 See in particular para 112 of the judgment of the Court of Appeal, where Mummery LJ bases the decision on the argument that an appeal against a Commission decision is primarily concerned with whether or not the infringement per se existed at all, and only secondarily, if at all, with the identity of the infringing party or parties, which mirrors the passive construction of s47A(6)(d) of the Competition Act 1998 ('*a decision of the European Commission that the prohibition in Article 81(1) or Article 82 of the Treaty has been infringed*'). On 21 December 2012, the Supreme Court granted Morgan Crucible leave to appeal the Court of Appeal judgment.

65 See para 119 of the judgment.

66 *BCL Old Co Limited and others* v *BASF plc and others* [2009] EWCA Civ 434, reversing the judgment of the CAT ([2008] CAT 24).

II,[67] the Court of Appeal held, following from its decision in *BLC/BASF I*, that there was no power contained in the Competition Appeal Tribunal Rules 2003 to extend the time limit of two years set out in Rule 31 thereof so as to overcome the barring of the action. The Supreme Court held that the effect of the decisions of the Court of Appeal in the *BLC/BASF* litigation, which meant that the claim in question was held to have been time-barred almost seven years after it should have been brought and so left the claimant without a remedy, did not offend against the EU law principles of the effective protection of EU law rights, and legal certainty.[68]

5.60 It should be noted that in the 2013 BIS response,[69] the UK Government proposed harmonising the limitation periods in the CAT with the limitation periods for ordinary tortious actions before the High Court. This was as a consequence of the proposed reform of granting the CAT jurisdiction to hear stand-alone as well as follow-on actions, meaning that its jurisdiction becomes co-terminous with that of the ordinary courts.

5.61 The proposal was to align limitation periods in the CAT to those of the ordinary courts, that is, as regards actions brought in England and Wales, the longer six-year period as specified in s2 of the Limitation Act 1980.[70] This 'upwards harmonisation' can be seen as fitting with the over-arching policy goal of facilitating competition law litigation. The Government did not set out how it proposed to achieve this, but it could be done by way of amendment to the Competition Act 1998 and the 2003 Rules.[71] In addition, it can be presumed that the case law of the CAT on the various aspects of limitation periods as set out above remains valid, that is, the basic period changes from two to six years, but that the other rules, such as the commencement of the period from the date of the finding of infringement by the public authority, the suspensory effect of appeals of such a finding, and so on, remain unchanged.

---

67 *BCL Old Co Limited and others* v *BASF plc and others* [2010] EWCA Civ 1258, at para 46, reversing the judgment of the CAT ([2009] CAT 29) as to the question of principle of the power of the Tribunal to extend the time limit.

68 *BCL Old Co Limited and others* v *BASF plc and others* [2012] UKSC 45, paras 29–40 of which deal with the issue decided in *BLC/BASF I*, namely that the limitation period set out in Rule 31 was not delayed by an appeal on the fine (see in particular paras 29 and 39), and paras 41–43 of which deal with the issue decided in *BLC/BASF II*, namely that the Competition Appeal Tribunal Rules did not contain a power to extend the time limit set out in Rule 31.

69 Paras 4.4 and 4.7.

70 The Government notes that a five-year period would apply in Scotland. Northern Ireland is subject to the same rules as England and Wales in this regard.

71 Perhaps the simplest way of all would be by means of deletion of s47A(3) and Rule 31.

2 *Germany*

§33(5) GWB provides that the limitation period for an action for damages for breach of EU competition law shall be suspended where the Commission or an NCA starts proceedings ('*ein Verfahren einleitet*'). The provision refers to §204(2) BGB, which provides that such suspension shall end six months after a decision is reached in the proceedings in question ('*der rechtskräftigen Entscheidung... des eingeleiteten Verfahrens*'). The standard limitation period in German law is three years.[72] **5.62**

German law does not refer explicitly to a suspension of the limitation period in respect of an appeal of a Commission or NCA decision, as s47(8) of the UK Competition Act 1998 does, despite the fact that §33(4) GWB provides for the binding effect of such a decision (see above), but merely to the suspensive effect of the opening of proceedings by the Commission or the national competition authority. However, it can be argued that the three-year period provided for in §195 BGB can be considered to start to run from the moment when the public infringement decision is made.[73] This means that the suspensive effect of §33(5) GWB will, in a large number of cases, be redundant, and avoids problems of coordination between public and private actions to which the general nature of that provision could otherwise have given rise. **5.63**

IV PROCEDURES FOR RECOURSE TO THE EXPERTISE OF PUBLIC AUTHORITIES BY THE NATIONAL COURTS

It should be noted that 'specialist authorities' in this context most often refers to public bodies with responsibility for enforcing competition law, that is, most obviously the Commission or the national competition authority of each Member State, but can also in some circumstances refer also and particularly to a court, for example, in those Member States, such as Austria, Ireland and Sweden where, based on the US model, competition cases are resolved by a judgment of that court on an application, as the case might be, by the NCA, and not by a decision issued by the NCA. **5.64**

---

72 §195 BGB.

73 This argument is based on §199(1) BGB, which provides that '*Die regelmäßige Verjährungsfrist beginnt... mit dem Schluss des Jahres, in dem (1) der Anspruch entstanden ist und (2) der Gläubiger von den den Anspruch begründenden Umstanden und der Person des Schuldners Kenntnis erlangt oder ohne grobe Fahrlässigkeit erlangen müsste.*' Under such a construction, the knowledge requirement contained in the second sentence is assumed to be fulfilled on publication of the decision.

A EU law: consultation of the Commission

5.65 Article 15(1) of Regulation 1/2003 empowers the national court to ask the Commission for its opinion on questions concerning the application of the EU competition rules whenever the court is applying Article 101 or 102 TFEU. Article 15(3) empowers NCAs to make written submissions to the court of their Member State on their own initiative, and to submit oral observations with the permission of the court. Further to the same provision, the Commission is empowered to make written submissions to the court of any Member State on its own initiative and to make oral submissions with the permission of the court '*[w]here the coherent application of Article [101] or [102 TFEU] so requires*'.[74] In addition, national courts can make a reference to the ECJ for a preliminary ruling under Article 267 TFEU.

B National law: consultation of the NCA

5.66 Consultation provisions exist in a number of national laws as to the existence of the infringement.[75] As in the case of the binding effect of NCA decisions on national courts, it is often not clear whether these provisions relate to application of national law only, or also apply to cases involving alleged breach of EU law.

1 United Kingdom

5.67 In the UK, provision exists for secondary legislation to be passed enabling the transfer of proceedings from the ordinary courts to the CAT for the determination of an infringement.[76] The ordinary court will then give effect to any such determination by the CAT. The court can also transfer so much of any proceedings as relate to a damages action which the CAT is empowered to hear under the Competition Act.[77]

---

74 See, for example, the submissions of the Commission in the *National Grid* proceedings before the English High Court, which related to the possible disclosure of material contained in leniency documents in the light of the judgment of the ECJ in *Pfleiderer*, as discussed in Chapter 4.

75 Article 15(4) of Regulation 1/2003 expressly states that the powers conferred on NCAs by Article 15 are '*without prejudice to wider powers to make observations before courts conferred on competition authorities of the Member States under the law of their Member State*'.

76 Enterprise Act 2002 s16(1). In its January 2013 consultation response, the UK Government proposed enabling the courts to transfer all types of competition law proceeding to the CAT, and *vice versa*, either by means of secondary legislation adopted on the basis of s16(1) of the Enterprise Act, or by other means.

77 Enterprise Act 2002 s16(4).

2 Germany

§90(2) GWB allows a representative of the *Bundeskartellamt*, in cases where it is appropriate to protect the public interest, to make written and oral statements to the court, and even to question the parties, witnesses and experts.[78] **5.68**

3 France

Under Article L. 462–3 of the *Code de commerce*, it is possible for the courts to consult the *Autorité de la concurrence* on points relating to competition law. The opinion given by the *Autorité de la concurrence* pursuant to this provision, though generally considered to be important for the outcome of the case, does not bind the requesting court.[79] The *Autorité de la concurrence* can only render an opinion after an adversarial process.[80] In particular, it must draft a report, which is notified to the parties.[81] **5.69**

Furthermore, Article L. 470–5 of the *Code de commerce* provides as follows: **5.70**

> Pour l'application des dispositions du présent livre [Livre IV de la liberté des prix et de la concurrence], le ministre chargé de l'économie ou son représentant peut, devant les juridictions civiles ou pénales, déposer des conclusions et les développer oralement à l'audience. Il peut également produire les procès-verbaux et les rapports d'enquête.

Under this provision, the minister could intervene in the proceedings to assist the claimant in discharging the burden of proof as to a claim. In substance, it recalls the *amicus curiae* provision of Article 15(3) of Regulation 1/2003 as far as regards the Commission's role in the application of EU law (see above). **5.71**

---

78 This provision reads as follows: '*Der Präsident des Bundeskartellamts kann, wenn er es zur Wahrung des öffentlichen Interesses als angemessen erachtet, aus den Mitgliedern des Bundeskartellamts eine Vertretung bestellen, die befugt ist, dem Gericht schriftliche Erklärungen abzugeben, auf Tatsachen und Beweismittel hinzuweisen, den Terminen beizuwohnen, in ihnen Ausführungen zu machen und Fragen an Parteien, Zeugen und Sachverständige zu richten. Schriftliche Erklärungen der vertretenden Person sind den Parteien von dem Gericht mitzuteilen.*'

79 In its judgment in the *UGAP/CAMIF* case, the Paris *Cour d'appel* found an abuse of a dominant position, despite a report submitted by the then *Conseil de la concurrence* to the court which found that an abuse could not be established, though dominance could (Paris *Cour d'appel*, JCP G 1998, II-10217, judgment of 13 January 1998; Paris *Cour d'appel*, Jurisdata n° 2001–157128, judgment of 22 October 2001).

80 See Article L. 462–3(1): '*Elle ne peut donner un avis qu'après une procédure contradictoire.*'

81 See Article R. 462–3 of the *Code de commerce*.

4 Other jurisdictions

5.72 In *Belgium*, when the outcome of a case is dependent on a competition issue, the court before which the case is pending can submit a request for a preliminary ruling to the *Cour de cassation*,[82] which will render a decision which is binding in that case.[83]

5.73 In *Finland*, when adjudicating a damages claim, the civil court can request a statement from the KKV (Finnish Competition Authority)[84] if the assessment of the case requires special competition expertise.

5.74 In *Estonia*, under the *Konkurentsiseadus* (Competition Act),[85] the court is obliged to join the national competition authority to the proceedings in order to give an opinion in all proceedings where Article 101 or Article 102 TFEU is being adjudicated. This is in line with the *Tsiviilkohtumenetluse seadustik* (Code of Civil Procedure),[86] that stipulates that a person or authority entrusted with the task of protecting the public interest is to be party to proceedings where the law so provides. However, in practice the courts have been reluctant to join the NCA in this way, and in any case have indicated that such an opinion would have no binding force.

V JOINT AND SEVERAL LIABILITY

5.75 A further issue of importance in the context of damages actions for breach of EU competition law is that of joint and several liability. This is partly a matter of procedure and partly a matter of substantive law. Put very briefly, it means that, in relation to any given infringement of the law, the parties found to have committed that infringement are all liable to make good the full amount of the loss caused to the injured party. A corollary of this, in a competition context, is that a claimant can seek compensation from *any* of the members of the cartel for the *total* loss suffered as a result of that cartel. Bringing an action against one or

82 Article 73§1 of the *loi sur la protection de la concurrence économique coordonnée le 15 septembre 2006*. Under the predecessor to this Act, the *loi sur la protection de la concurrence* of 1 July 1999, references were to be made to the Brussels *Cour d'appel*. They were obligatory, except in the case of litigation before the *Cour de cassation* (Art 42bis§1).

83 Article 73§4.

84 Section 49(2) of the *Kilpailulaki*. The request can be made on the court's own initiative, or at the request of one of the parties.

85 Article 56(3).

86 Article 198(2).

two defendants for the entirety of the loss incurred is not an unknown phenomenon before the English courts, for example.[87]

A system of joint and several liability is often accompanied by the possibility for the infringers to bring proceedings between themselves for recovery of damages paid, which is usually known as contribution. **5.76**

This complex issue is addressed in most systems of national tort law.[88] For example, under the law of the UK, contribution is dealt with under the Civil Liability (Contribution) Act 1978. Pursuant to s1(1), any person liable in respect of any damage suffered by another person may recover contribution from any other person liable in respect of the same damage. Pursuant to s2(1), '*... in any proceedings for contribution ... the amount of the contribution recoverable from any person shall be such as may be found by the court to be just and equitable having regard to the extent of that person's responsibility for the damage in question*' (emphasis added).[89] **5.77**

Furthermore, the Commission's proposal provides that, as a general rule, each system of national law must institute a system of contribution. Contribution is to be determined in the light of a defendant's relative blameworthiness or responsibility for the harm caused by the infringement.[90] **5.78**

Contribution raises particular complexities in a cartel settlement context. For example, even where a defendant decides to settle an antitrust damages claim, **5.79**

---

87 Witness in this respect the recent claim brought on behalf of unnamed claimants against Shell and Exxon Mobil for their involvement in the paraffin wax price-fixing cartel, which involved several other major producers of paraffin wax (see para 4.079).

88 It is noteworthy that in the US there is no right of contribution among defendants in antitrust proceedings. See *Texas Industries, Inc.* v *Radcliff Materials, Inc. et al.* 451 US 630 (1981) at paras 646 and 647: '*In declining to provide a right to contribution, we neither reject the validity of those arguments nor adopt the views of those opposing contribution. Rather, we recognize that, regardless of the merits of the conflicting arguments, this is a matter for Congress, not the courts, to resolve. The range of factors to be weighed in deciding whether a right to contribution should exist demonstrates the inappropriateness of judicial resolution of this complex issue. Ascertaining what is "fair" in this setting calls for inquiry into the entire spectrum of antitrust law, not simply the elements of a particular case or category of cases. Similarly, whether contribution would strengthen or weaken enforcement of the antitrust laws, or what form a right to contribution should take, cannot be resolved without going beyond the record of a single lawsuit.*'

89 See *Davies* v *Swan Motor Co* [1949] 2 KB 291 per Denning LJ, who held that '*just and equitable*' '*involves a consideration, not only of the causative potency of a particular factor, but also of its blameworthiness*'. See also *Dubai Aluminium Co Ltd* v *Salaam and others* [2002] UKHL 48, at para 164: '*But in any case the statutory jurisdiction is to order contribution in an amount which the court finds is "just and equitable". I do not read the words which follow as limiting words. Where the wrongdoing has produced not only a loss to the plaintiff but a profit to the defendants, it is obviously just and equitable to direct that any contributions required to allocate the cost of meeting the claim fairly among those responsible should be paid first out of their retained profits. It is increasingly recognised today that the ends of justice sometimes go beyond compensating a plaintiff for his loss and may extend to stripping a defendant of his profits.*'

90 Article 11(3).

and therefore attempt to bring finality to a case, it remains potentially exposed to claims for contribution from the other cartelists. While a settlement will generally as a matter of practice be concluded on a confidential basis, a non-settling cartelist may become cognisant of the fact of settlement by another defendant and seek to claim contribution from such defendant. This can have the consequence of reducing the incentive to settle in a case involving multiple defendants.

5.80 This particular conundrum is addressed in the Commission's proposal. In order to strengthen the incentives to settle, the proposal provides that, as a general rule, a national court should take into account the existence of a settlement arrangement entered into by a co-defendant.[91] As a matter of principle, a settling co-defendant should not have to contribute to non-settling co-defendants when they have already paid damages to the injured party with whom a co-defendant has settled. Recovery against a settling defendant should only be possible where non-settling co-defendants cannot meet the claim in full.[92]

5.81 The general applicability of the doctrine of joint and several liability and its application in the context of leniency, in particular, has been subject to broad debate within the context of the reform of the system of damages actions in the EU. A series of proposals has been made to exclude or limit the liability of the applicant for leniency from the general rule of joint and several liability.

5.82 Already at the time of the Green Paper, a solution was advanced whereby the liability of the leniency applicant would be limited to the share of the damage corresponding to the leniency applicant's share in the cartelised market.[93] Another solution advanced was the introduction of a so-called 'conditional rebate' on any damages claim made against a leniency applicant.[94]

5.83 The Commission's legislative proposal seeks to ensure that the principle of joint and several liability becomes a fundament of national law in relation to competition law damages actions.[95]

---

91 Article 18(2).

92 Article 18(1).

93 Green Paper, Option 30.

94 Green Paper, Option 29.

95 Article 11(1), which reads as follows: '*Member States shall ensure that undertakings which have infringed competition law through joint behaviour are jointly and severally liable for the damage caused by the infringement: each of the infringing undertakings is bound to compensate for the harm in full, and the injured party may require full compensation from any of them until he has been fully compensated.*'

Under the proposal, concrete protection from the general rules of joint and several liability is to be afforded to the *immunity* recipient under a leniency programme. In a bid to strengthen the integrity of leniency programmes, the proposal seeks to afford the immunity recipient particular protection in terms of the extent of its liability vis-à-vis damages claimants on the one hand and its co-defendants, on the other. The special treatment afforded to the immunity recipient is not extended to other leniency applicants. Given that the proposal takes the form of a Directive, Member States would, however, be able under their respective laws to go further and extend the protection afforded to an immunity recipient from the general operation of joint and several liability to other leniency applicants. **5.84**

Under the proposal, an immunity recipient is only to be liable to the extent of the harm incurred by its own direct or indirect purchasers or in the case of a buying cartel its direct or indirect providers. Claimants that do not fall into these categories would only be able to claim against the immunity recipient to the extent that their claim could not be satisfied in full by the other co-defendants, that is, an immunity recipient is treated as a debtor of last resort under the proposal.[96] **5.85**

With regard to a potential contribution claim against an immunity recipient by a co-defendant, an immunity recipient must not according to the proposal be liable to pay a sum in contribution which exceeds the amount of harm it caused to its own direct or indirect purchasers or providers.[97] Furthermore, where harm is incurred by a party other than a direct or indirect purchaser/provider of the companies held to have breached the competition rules, an immunity recipient is only liable to pay a sum in contribution that reflects its relative blameworthiness or responsibility for that harm.[98] Such share should be assessed against factors such as the turnover or market share of the immunity recipient or the role played by the immunity recipient in the cartel, for example. **5.86**

Nevertheless, until such time as EU legislation on damages actions is adopted, these proposals remain open to debate.[99] **5.87**

96 Article 11(2).
97 Article 11(3).
98 Article 11(4).
99 See, for example, the 2013 BIS response, at section 7.

6

COLLECTIVE ACTION

I INTRODUCTION 6.001
A The rationale for collective action 6.008
B Terminology 6.014
C Opt-in and opt-out collective action 6.015
D Assignment of claims 6.033

II COLLECTIVE ACTION AT EU LEVEL 6.034
A Collective action as a matter of EU law 6.034
B EU policy developments 6.041
1 The Green Paper 6.044
2 The White Paper 6.047
3 The draft Directive 6.051
4 The Commission's joint information note 6.055
5 The Commission's 2011 consultation paper 6.057
6 The Commission's proposal and 2013 collective redress initiative 6.061

III COLLECTIVE ACTION IN THE MEMBER STATES 6.072
A United Kingdom 6.073
1 Representative actions 6.076
2 GLOs 6.081
3 s47B of the Competition Act 6.084
4 Further policy developments 6.092
a 2006 DTI consultation 6.093
b 2007 OFT recommendations 6.096
c 2012 BIS consultation 6.098
d 2013 BIS response 6.106
B The Netherlands 6.110
1 Article 3:305a Burgerlijk Wetboek 6.111
2 Bundled claims 6.113
3 Wet Collectieve Afhandeling Massaschade, 2005 6.117
C Denmark 6.127
D Sweden 6.135
E France 6.142
F Italy 6.148
G Assignment of claims 6.150

IV CLASS ACTIONS IN THE UNITED STATES 6.157
A Rule 23 of the Federal Rules of Civil Procedure 6.158
B The Class Action Fairness Act of 2005 6.169

I INTRODUCTION

6.001 Over the last decade or so, the issue of collective action in a competition law context has received a considerable amount of attention amongst policymakers in the EU. Though collective action as a concept forms part of EU legal tradition and culture, its application, especially in the sphere of antitrust, remains an uncommon, and at the same time controversial, phenomenon. Antitrust enforcement in the large majority of Member States remains the quasi-exclusive preserve of the public authorities.

6.002 It has been recognised that collective action may act as an effective complement to public enforcement by '*accomplish[ing] the cessation or prevention of unlawful business practices which affect a multitude of claimants or the compensation for the* *harm caused by such practices*'.[1] Collective action may therefore, in principle, contribute directly to the overarching aims of deterrence and compensation, as well as that of encouraging the development of a competition culture.[2] This is because a collective action should allow parties that would otherwise be unlikely to bring a claim to do so.[3]

Regarded as a fundamental tenet of an effective complement to the system of public antitrust enforcement, proposals on collective action have been at the core of recent policy papers, consultations and even draft legislation (the draft Directive) that have been promulgated by the Commission. However, a concrete, legally binding measure in this context remains some way from being adopted. Testimony of this is borne by the recommendation on collective redress (discussed in more detail below), which tentatively suggests that Member States adopt common collective redress measures within two years of its publication. There is no obligation to do so. Furthermore, it is unlikely, given the controversial nature of the topic, that formal EU legislation on collective action will ever see the light of day. **6.003**

The last decade or so has witnessed the introduction of some form of collective action in nearly all Member States. Given the autonomy of the Member States in the field of procedure and remedies, the systems of collective action throughout the EU perhaps unsurprisingly display a remarkable degree of divergence. The multi-coloured collective enforcement framework in the EU manifests itself in an assorted set of procedural and institutional rules. These rules not only render intra-Member State collective action difficult, but may also pose an obstacle to inter-Member State action. **6.004**

A common thread which runs through the mechanisms for collective action in national law is that potential claimants become parties to an action pursuant to taking a decision to actually take part in such action, that is, to opt-in. An advantage of this systemic feature is that it permits a potential claimant to elect whether to take part in an action or not. Opt-out, on the other hand, and as described in further detail below, is eschewed as a mechanism in many Member States on the grounds that it is incompatible with national constitutional **6.005**

1 Commission Staff Working Document, 'Public Consultation: Towards a Coherent European Approach to Collective Redress', 4 February 2011 (SEC(2011)173), at para 7.

2 See speech by N. Kroes, *loc. cit.*

3 According to research performed by the Commission, 87 per cent of UK consumers, for example, would be more willing to defend their rights in court if they could combine their claim with others (see European Commission, Flash Barometer 299 (2010)).

principles. Another common denominator amongst the Member State mechanisms for collective action is that there are limitations on who can bring a claim.

6.006 The instruments enshrined in the legal systems of the Member States that allow for collective action are not always perceived to offer *effective* redress, however, or even any redress at all.[4] This might be because procedural obstacles render the system for collective action excessively difficult to use. In this respect, barriers that discourage claimants from initiating proceedings in meritorious cases may run counter to the EU law principle of effectiveness.[5] In terms of practical impact, the inability to bring a collective claim can leave victims of illegal conduct out of pocket with no avenue of recourse to obtain effective redress.

6.007 The situation in the EU stands in marked contrast to that in the US, where class actions are a common feature of the antitrust enforcement landscape. Depending on the benchmarks used to assess effectiveness, however, it remains very much a subject of debate, especially in the EU, whether the US system has achieved the optimal use of this legal mechanism. In general, EU policymakers have been careful to avoid transposing elements of the US system into their proposals for fear of opening the floodgates to what they perceive as the worst excesses of that system.[6]

A The rationale for collective action

6.008 Despite current reticence to adopt a more formal, legally binding measure, it is clearly recognised that there is a direct correlation between the absence of collective action and sub-optimal enforcement of the EU antitrust rules.

6.009 A system of collective action can have a positive impact on the litigation process by consolidating a potentially large number of different actions into a single action. This can save time, cost and valuable resources,[7] thus potentially

---

4 See the final report submitted to the Directorate-General for Health and Consumers of the European Commission (DG Sanco) by Civil Consulting/Oxford Economics, 'Evaluation of the Effectiveness and Efficiency of Collective Redress Mechanisms in the European Union' (2008), available at: http://ec.europa.eu/consumers/redress_cons/finalreportevaluationstudypart1-final2008-11-26.pdf.

5 Renato Nazzini, 'The Objective of Private Remedies in EU Competition Law' (2011) 4(4) GCLR 131.

6 See Hovenkamp, who writes, against the availability of treble damages and lawyers' success fees in the United States, that '… *many marginal and frivolous antitrust cases are filed every year, and litigation is often used as a bargaining chip to strengthen the hands of plaintiffs who really have other complaints*' (Herbert Hovenkamp, *The Antitrust Enterprise: Principle and Execution* (Harvard University Press, Cambridge, Massachusetts, 2005), at 59).

7 See Jürgen Basedow, *Private Enforcement of EC Competition Law* (Kluwer Law International, Alphen aan den Rijn, 2007), at para 193.

overcoming what is termed as the 'rational apathy problem', that is, a situation where potential claimants are not individually motivated to claim for small monetary amounts or 'individually non-recoverable claims' in view of the cost of doing so.[8] This applies particularly to end-consumers, who, unlike other groups of potential claimants, are potentially the most vulnerable to antitrust harm.[9] Perhaps a trite observation, but a logical corollary of this is that a system of collective action, where the interests of individual claimants are consolidated into one claim, can therefore improve access to justice.

Organised collective action can therefore be important in balancing the resources and bargaining position of otherwise diffuse and individually resource-austere claimants against well-organised and potentially resource-rich defendants. This can be particularly true in the context of a large-scale antitrust infringement where the defendants can be very large organisations and where antitrust injury is scattered along the supply chain down to and amongst end-consumers. It is often the latter who bear the full impact of anti-competitive conduct and who, by their nature, do not have the ability to pass on an overcharge.[10] In the absence of a system of collective action addressing the welfare loss incurred by a large number of individual consumers and businesses, large corporations can often have little to fear from actions against them. This can undermine the policy objective of deterrence.[11] **6.010**

Of course, striking a balance between the interests of claimants and those of defendants is important. In this respect, a system of collective action avoids the risk of what can be termed tactical litigation, that is, where one group of claimants waits to see how a prior case goes before they themselves bring an action.[12] It reduces costs for defendants and allows common issues to be **6.011**

8 Tiana L. Russell, 'Exporting Class Actions to the European Union' (2010) 28 Boston University International Law Journal 141.

9 That being said, small to medium-sized enterprises (SMEs) are also reticent to bring an individual claim in the face of complex economic damage analysis and protracted and expensive legal proceedings. Furthermore, SMEs have to factor in that on-going commercial relationships may be put under pressure. Representation can act as a screen between the defendant and the claimant, thus allowing an SME to invoke its right to damages whilst preserving the contractual relationship.

10 According to the Impact Assessment, the lack of effective instruments for obtaining compensation may well cost European consumers and businesses more than €20 billion per year.

11 A study analysing the deterrent effect of 40 successful private antitrust class actions in the US found that class actions have significant deterrent power: see Robert H. Lande and Joshua P. Davis, 'Benefits from Private Antitrust Enforcement: An Analysis of Forty Cases' (2008) 42 University of San Francisco Law Review 879.

12 Basedow, *loc. cit.*, at para 193.

decided '*once and for all rather than litigating the same issues repeatedly*'.[13] This is advantageous to the defendant since such actions could potentially be very numerous.

6.012 From an administrative point of view, collective action can be useful in situations where an antitrust infringement gives rise to multiple claims. The procedural laws and case management tools of many Member States leave the courts badly equipped to process large caseloads in an efficient manner and within a reasonable timeframe. Furthermore, the risk of contradictory outcomes is lessened.

6.013 In theory, therefore, a system of collective action can be utilised to attain the objectives of compensation and deterrence.[14] In practice, however, there are a number of factors that must be considered to ensure that those objectives can be attained, and which also go beyond the mere availability of some form of collective action *per se*. Some of these factors, such as funding, are touched upon in the discussion below pertaining to the recommendation on collective redress.

B Terminology

6.014 As a preliminary issue, it is of help to identify certain categories of collective action. This categorisation underpins the analysis which follows. Firstly, the term '*collective action*' refers generally to the consolidation of individual, separate claims into one claim brought on behalf of more than one person.[15] A '*class action*' is an action brought on behalf of either an unidentified or identified class of claimants, the former being the model used in the US. A '*representative action*' refers to an action brought by a representative association, such as a consumer association, on behalf of its members. '*Group actions*' refer broadly to those actions which are less than a class action but more than joinder, and are not representative actions. '*Group action*' therefore implies some sort of collective management of a number of separate claims, that is, a case management tool.

---

13 Edward H. Cooper, 'Class Action Advice in the Form of Questions' (2001) 11 Duke Journal of Comparative & International Law 215.

14 It should be noted, however, that the deterrence objective has become of secondary importance in the eyes of EU policymakers. For example, para 3.1 of the communication on collective redress states that punishment and deterrence should fall within the remit of the public enforcer. This perhaps explains why, in the view of the Commission, exemplary damages should not be awarded in collective redress proceedings (see para 31 of the recommendation on collective redress). In terms of the views put forward in the Commission's legislative proposal, deterrence as a policy aim has dropped out completely, being replaced by '*optimising*' the relationship between public and private enforcement.

15 In this sense, it is used co-terminously with '*collective redress*', which has become the more common term in policy documents.

C Opt-in and opt-out collective action

At the heart of the debate on the identification of common principles for collective action in the EU lies the controversial issue of opt-in as opposed to opt-out collective action. Standing or identification of who is to be included in an action is crucial to the ability to bring a claim before a judicial body. **6.015**

In an opt-in collective action, claimants become party to an action only *if* they take a step to include themselves in the proceedings. In an opt-out collective action, on the other hand, individuals become party to litigation *unless* they take a step to 'opt out' of it. The distinction between the two is not always that clear, however, given that at one moment or another a party must step forward to make a claim.[16] **6.016**

At EU level, as a matter of policy, a distinct preference has been shown for the opt-in option. This reflects the fact that in the majority of the Member States in which a collective action mechanism is in place, an opt-in mechanism is preponderant, with opt-out being the exception and available in Portugal,[17] Spain[18] and the Netherlands. Denmark has adopted a 'hybrid' system displaying characteristics of the two. **6.017**

Under the opt-in model, claimants are required to expressly indicate their intention to be part of an action, consent to being represented in the relevant litigation proceedings and subsequently be bound by the final judgment. As a result, the judgment only has the force of *res judicata* as against those who opted in to the proceedings. **6.018**

The opt-in model has both advantages and disadvantages.[19] The advantages of an opt-in system are manifold. Principally, however, and as is universally recognised among legal commentators, the main advantage of the opt-in system is that individuals can choose whether or not they wish to take part in an action.[20] By identifying claimants, such a form of action can avert potentially excessive and vexatious litigation, and ensure that a collective action is more readily and practically implemented. **6.019**

---

16 2012 BIS consultation, para 5.16.

17 Article 26A of the *Código do processo civil* (Code of civil procedure). The procedure is known as the *acção popular*.

18 See Articles 11.2 and 11.3 of the *Ley de enjuiciamiento civil*.

19 For a good discussion of the advantages and disadvantages of the opt-in model, see Charlotte Leskinen, 'Collective Antitrust Damages Actions in the EU: the Opt-in v. the Opt-out model', Working Paper, IE Law School, WPLS10–03, 26 April 2010, available at: http://papers.ssrn.com/sol3/papers.cfm?abstract_id=1612731.

20 Rachael Mulheron, 'Some Difficulties with Group Litigation Orders – and Why a Class Action is Superior' (2005) 24 CJQ 40.

6.020 Another advantage of the opt-in system is that all parties involved know how many persons are in the group. This can allow for a more realistic, efficient and fair conduct of the litigation, also perhaps with regard to negotiations for settlements, as the defendant then knows how many potential claimants would be bound by it. In the US by contrast, where an opt-out mechanism is in place, the defendant is not in a position to know how big the group will be that is bound by a judgment or settlement.

6.021 A further advantage of the opt-in model is that those members who have opted-in might follow the proceedings in a more active manner. That does not mean that they will actually take part, but as they have undertaken to subscribe to the group it is not unlikely that they have a keener interest in seeing the results. It can be assumed, therefore, that the take-up of awards and settlements in the opt-in model will be higher than in an opt-out system. This alleviates problems as to how and to whom (unclaimed) damages awards should be allocated. Furthermore, it is a welcome move towards connecting the citizen more closely to the law.

6.022 The opt-in system does suffer from some drawbacks. For example, it can translate into a lower participation rate, since claimants need to take affirmative action and invest time and money.[21] Especially when the individual value at stake is low, the potential gains from the action may not cover the costs for claimants of taking part.

6.023 In an opt-in system there is, therefore, an inherent difficulty in engaging potential participants. Thus, where the individual claim is low the sum that needs to be invested may outweigh any gains, thus acting as a significant disincentive to claiming. An apposite example of the practical weakness of the opt-in system is represented by the UK cartel case 'Price fixing in Toys',[22] where despite the fact that *total* monetary damage to consumers is likely to have been very high, the monetary value of each individual claim by contrast is likely to have been very low. The upshot of this is that claims could only effectively be brought under an opt-out, as opposed to an opt-in, system.[23] This is *inter alia* because of the 'hassle factor' of, or 'rational apathy' towards, opting in.

---

21 See also BEUC, 'European Group Action – Ten Golden Rules', April 2008, stating that '*[r]ecent experience in Europe of the opt-in procedure in consumer claims showed that the rate of participation is very low (less than 1%). On the contrary, under opt-out regimes, rates are typically very high (97% in the Netherlands and almost 100% in Portugal).*' The report is available at: http://www.groupaction4consumers.eu/docs/European%20Group%20Action_Ten%20Golden%20Rules.pdf.

22 See the decision of the Office of Fair Trading, CA98/8/2003, 21 November 2003.

23 2012 BIS consultation, para 5.20, accompanying Box 4.

Another disadvantage that obtains with respect to the opt-in system is that defendants may be faced with open-ended claims against them, that is, there is 'insufficient finality' once each set of proceedings has come to a conclusion. If only a minority of the class opts in, it may be possible for another action to be brought on behalf of those who did not opt in.[24] **6.024**

By contrast, under the opt-out model, all affected parties become party to the litigation, unless they take a step not to be. Indeed, individuals need not actually know about the litigation in order to be party to it. As a result, unless a victim opts out, he or she will be bound by any judgment issued by the court, or by any potential settlement reached between the claimants and the defendant.[25] **6.025**

In an opt-out case, an action is brought on the basis of a broad estimation of the size of the group, with claimants coming forward following the quantification of damages to claim their share.[26] This has a number of advantages. Most persons who have incurred harm are likely to have a remedy: claimants only have to step forward after the judgment and amount of award are decided, and the publicity of the award on the merits is likely to raise awareness among potential claimants. Research conducted for the Civil Justice Council made the observation that median participation rates in opt-out cases are typically very high, and can be up to 99 per cent.[27] However, a key issue in this regard relates to the manner in which claimants can be made aware of the proceedings in practice, on which only little guidance at EU level has been given.[28] **6.026**

The disadvantages of the opt-out system compared to the opt-in system were extensively discussed in the 2007 report for the Commission which formed the background to its Impact Assessment. Essentially, the report cited the following main arguments against an opt-out system: (i) an opt-out system is more expensive; (ii) opt-outs pose constitutional problems regarding the 'day in court' ('*rechtliches Gehör*' in Germany); (iii) the person who lodges a claim, that is, the **6.027**

24 Samuel Issacharoff and Geoffrey P. Miller, 'Will Aggregate Litigation Come to Europe?' (2009) 62(1) Vanderbilt Law Review 179.

25 *Collective Redress in Antitrust* (IP/A/ECON/ST/2011–19), June 2012, at 65.

26 2012 BIS consultation, para 5.26.

27 Rachael Mulheron, 'Reform of Collective Redress in England and Wales: a Perspective of Need', research paper for the Civil Justice Council of England and Wales, 2008, available at: http://www.judiciary.gov.uk/JCO%2FDocuments%2FCJC%2FPublications%2FOther+papers%2Freform-of-collective-redress.pdf.

28 See paras 10 and 11 of the recommendation on collective redress, discussed further below. See also in this respect the decision of the French *Conseil constitutionnel* of 25 July 1989 (Decision No 89–257) at paras 25 and 26, which took a rather old-fashioned approach to notification in the context of a collective action mechanism in the realm of labour law. Notice had to be sent via registered mail with confirmation of delivery.

class representative, would be over-compensated if not all class members claim damages; and (iv) opt-outs create principal/agent problems.[29]

6.028 Concerns have also been raised as to the perceived risk that an opt-out system may lead to claims which lack merit and are used to force settlement against a fear on the part of the defendant of protracted proceedings involving a large number of claimants.[30] Furthermore, concerns abound that under an opt-out mechanism individuals may find themselves bound by a judgment – such as a negative costs order – that they had no cognisance of.[31]

6.029 Indeed, the constitutions of several Member States, such as Germany, prohibit opt-out actions where a claim is brought on behalf of unknown claimants, on the grounds that those claimants would not be free to decide that they do not want to bring, or be involved in, an action (*Dispositionsfreiheit*, or the 'disposition principle').[32]

6.030 This ties in with the concern that an opt-out model may clash with fundamental rights enshrined in the ECHR, Article 6 of which guarantees a right of access to justice. Such concerns relate to the legal autonomy of the individual.

6.031 In addition, opt-out systems carry with them the risk of 'internal class conflict', as claimants might incur different losses and, as a result, have different motivations in pursuing litigation – particularly in antitrust cases where there could be very large and very small claimants.[33] Conflict may also arise between counsel and the class, with the former being incentivised to go for what critics

---

29 The report is, however, conspicuous for its cursory and perfunctory treatment of, and explanation for, the criticisms of the opt-out system. See Robert Gaudet, 'Turning a Blind Eye: the Commission's Rejection of Opt-out Class Actions Overlooks Swedish, Norwegian, Danish and Dutch Experience' (2009) 30(3) ECLR 107.

30 See, for an example from the US, *In re Rhone-Poulenc Rorer Inc.* 51 F. 3d 1293 (7th Cir 1995), at 1298 (quoting Judge Henry Friendly).

31 See S. Stuart Clark and Christina Harris, 'Multi-Plaintiff Litigation in Australia: a Comparative Perspective' (2001) 11 Duke Journal of Comparative & International Law 289, at 300: '*there remains a real possibility that a person who is deemed to be a class member by virtue of the class description may never actually become aware that proceedings have commenced and will nevertheless become bound by the result of those proceedings by default*'.

32 R. Deutlmoser and M. Weston, 'Status of Collective Redress in Germany – Expansion Uncalled For', International Comparative Legal Guide to Class and Group Actions 2010, Global Legal Group, 14, at 17: '*[f]rom a German perspective no individual person may lose his right under a class action ruling or settlement if he did not actively choose to participate in the proceeding. This argument alone makes clear that the German legal system is incompatible with an opt-out system of collective redress.*' The paper is available at: http://m.cbmlaw.com/Templates/media/files/articles/ca-10-chapter-4.pdf.

33 John H. Beisner, '"Opt-in" vs. "Opt-out" Procedures in Collective and Representative Litigation', US Chamber Institute for Legal Reform, available at: http://www.instituteforlegalreform.com/sites/default/files/images2/stories/documents/pdf/international/optoutpaper.pdf. Beisner is a critic of the opt-out system. For further discussion of the opt-out class action mechanism, see Jocelyn G. Delatre, 'Beyond the White Paper: Rethinking the Commission's Proposal on Private Antitrust Litigation' (2011) 8(1) Competition Law Review 29.

call 'sweetheart settlements', that is, the representative lawyer who has invested significant resources in the case as opposed to the claimants negotiates with the defendant to obtain the most advantageous deal for himself. In doing so risk is averted as far as possible and fees are maximised.[34] However, one commentator has observed that there is no evidence of principal-agent problems in those EU jurisdictions which operate an opt-out system. According to this commentator, '*all of these nations treat lawyers and class representatives with the same watchful eye, regardless of whether the case is opt-out or opt-in*'.[35]

Furthermore, as mentioned above, striking a balance between the rights of both the defendant and the claimant is important. In this respect it is observed that opt-out class actions could increase the costs of a Type I error for the defendant because of the magnified effects on the defendant of a false condemnation.[36] **6.032**

D Assignment of claims

The assignment of claims represents an alternative method of collective action. Such a method can be used to circumvent the often restrictive procedural requirements inherent in the systems of collective action in the Member States. Broadly speaking, assignment is where a claimant assigns his claim to a body which brings and pursues the claim on behalf of the assignors. An instructive example of this kind of enforcement constellation is CDC, which has initiated damages proceedings in some of the largest EU cartel cases by bundling the claims of multiple assignors. The terms of the assignment will determine the nature of the action (that is, as to costs, distribution of damages awarded, and so on). Such a mechanism can clearly only work, however, in respect of claimants that have already been identified who have made the assignment, and crucially where such bundling of claims is permitted under the relevant national law. **6.033**

---

34 Beisner, *ibid.*

35 Gaudet, *loc. cit.*

36 Type I errors are cases in which a court condemns conduct that was not anti-competitive, or mandates compensation of harm for which there was no causation.

II COLLECTIVE ACTION AT EU LEVEL

A Collective action as a matter of EU law

6.034 Despite the recent focus on the role of collective action in the system of antitrust litigation, collective action as a concept is not new to EU law. As noted by Advocate-General Jacobs in his Opinion in *Österreichischer Gewerkschaftsbund*[37]:

> Collective rights of action are an equally common feature of modern judicial systems. They are mostly encountered in areas such as consumer protection, labour law, unfair competition law or protection of the environment. The law grants *associations or other representative bodies* the right to bring cases either in the interest of persons which they represent or in the public interest. This furthers *private enforcement of rules adopted in the public interest* and supports individual complainants who are often badly equipped to face well organised and financially stronger opponents. The danger of abuse of such collective rights of action is again normally tackled by national procedural rules. Consequently, the Court has never objected to national rules providing for such collective rights of action and in practice often deals with questions referred in proceedings brought by interested associations (emphasis added).

6.035 Extending the Advocate-General's reasoning, the ECJ in *Eschig* held as follows[38]:

> ... even supposing that new situations, at Member State level, were to lead to an increase in the number of actions seeking to protect the collective interests of members of a group of persons, such situations cannot, as Community law currently stands, restrict the freedom of persons with legal expenses insurance to either participate or not in such an action and to choose, where appropriate, a legal representative.

6.036 Collective action as a concept can therefore be said to be firmly embedded in European legal culture.[39] It also pervades several pieces of existing EU legislation.

---

37 Case C-195/98 *Österreichischer Gewerkschaftsbund* v *Austria* [2000] ECR I-10497, at para 47.

38 Case C-199/08 *Erhard Eschig* v *Uniqa Sachversicherung AG* [2009] ECR I-8295, at para 64.

39 See the judgment of the European Court of Human Rights of 27 April 2004 in *Gorraiz Lizarraga and others* v *Spain* (62543/00), at para 38, where the Court held as follows with respect to representative actions: '*in modern-day societies, when citizens are confronted with particularly complex administrative decisions, recourse to collective bodies such as associations is one of the accessible means, sometimes the only means, available to them whereby they can defend their particular interests effectively*'. See further the judgment of the ECtHR of 8 July 1986 in *Lithgow and others* v *United Kingdom* (9006/80, 9262/81, 9263/81, 9265/81 9266/81, 9313/81, 9405/81).

For example, Article 7 of Directive 93/13 on unfair terms in consumer contracts provides as follows[40]: **6.037**

> Member States shall ensure that, in the interests of consumers and of competitors, adequate and effective means exist to prevent the continued use of unfair terms in contracts concluded with consumers by sellers or suppliers.
>
> The means referred to in paragraph 1 shall include provisions whereby persons or *organizations, having a legitimate interest under national law in protecting consumers*, may take action according to the national law concerned before the courts or before competent administrative bodies for a decision as to whether contractual terms drawn up for general use are unfair, so that they can apply appropriate and effective means to prevent the continued use of such terms (emphasis added).

Directive 98/27 on consumer injunctions (the 'consumer injunctions Directive')[41] established a right for '*qualified entities*' (organisations representing the collective interests of consumers or independent public bodies responsible for protecting the collective interests of consumers) in one Member State to seek an injunction with respect to infringements of national law provisions implementing certain EU consumer protection directives in another Member State.[42] **6.038**

Article 4(1)(c) and (d) of the IPRs protection Directive[43] provide respectively for actions by representative groups ('*intellectual property collective rights management bodies*' and '*professional defence bodies*' which represent IPR holders) to bring actions, both injunctive and for damages, in relation to breach of EU intellectual property law. The original proposal had stated that this provision was '*without prejudice to the applicable rules on the representation of parties in court* **6.039**

40 Council Directive 93/13/EEC of 5 April 1993 on unfair terms in consumer contracts (OJ L 95, 21.4.1993, p 29).

41 Directive 98/27/EC of the European Parliament and of the Council of 19 May 1998 on injunctions for the protection of consumers' interests (OJ L 166, 11.6.1998, p 51), as amended and codified by Directive 2009/22/EC of the European Parliament and of the Council of 23 April 2009 on injunctions for the protection of consumers' interests (OJ L 110, 1.5.2009, p 30).

42 For a discussion on the functioning of this Directive since 2008, see the Commission's report of 6 November 2012 concerning the application of Directive 2009/22/EC (COM(2012)635). According to section 2.4 of this report, '*[t]he latest list of qualified entities includes a total of 313 qualified entities. The number and characteristics of these entities vary widely from one Member State to another. While several Member States have designated just one qualified entity (Ireland, Latvia, Lithuania, The Netherlands, Romania and Sweden), others have designated more than 70 (Germany and Greece). Spain, Italy and France are in an intermediate position, with more than 15 and less than 30 designated qualified entities. In general terms, when Member States have designated a single qualified entity, it is typically a public authority in charge of consumer protection, although there are exceptions, such as the Netherlands.*'

43 Directive 2004/48/EC of the European Parliament and of the Council on the enforcement of intellectual property rights (OJ L 157, 30.4.2004, p 45).

proceedings',[44] while the final text suggests that such representative actions should take place '*in so far as permitted by and in accordance with the applicable law*'.[45]

6.040 More recently, the Commission considered the introduction of a collective action mechanism in the context of the data protection rules. The Commission recognises that many cases where an individual is affected by an infringement of data protection rules also affect a considerable number of other individuals in a similar situation. The Commission therefore stated that it will '*consider the possibility of extending the power to bring an action before the national courts to data protection authorities and to civil society associations, as well as to other associations representing data subjects' interests*'.[46]

B EU policy developments

6.041 It is only of late that there has been substantive debate at EU level on how best to ensure that a system of collective action can operate effectively throughout the EU so as to facilitate the ability of citizens to enforce their rights under EU law. Against the backdrop that the enforcement of the right to damages at national level is governed by the institutional and procedural rules of the Member States – which requires that the EU tread carefully when intervening in this area – a series of proposals have been made by the Commission to introduce minimal harmonised requirements at Member State level both to give impetus to collective actions as a complement to public enforcement and to facilitate the bringing of claims in a cross-border context.

6.042 At the same time, however, discussions on how best to kick-start a real competition culture in the EU, with collective action as one of its cornerstones, has also focussed on whether any measure should in fact be specific to antitrust, for example, or encompass a wider range of policy domains.

6.043 Current thinking on the matter displays a preference for a horizontal approach. Though not of a legally binding nature, the Commission's recommendation on collective redress makes it clear that there should be minimum requirements in the Member States with respect to collective actions (whether of an injunctive or compensatory nature) in particularly, but not only, the fields of consumer protection, competition, environmental protection and financial services. At

44 COM(2003)46, Article 5(2), third subparagraph.

45 Recital 18.

46 Communication on a comprehensive approach on personal data protection in the European Union (COM(2012)609).

the same time unilateral reform initiatives are taking place at national level. Such initiatives are specifically tailored to the idiosyncrasies of the system for antitrust damages actions within the Member State undergoing reform. The UK represents an apposite example here with its recent consultation on the reform of the system for bringing private actions (discussed in further detail below).

1 The Green Paper

Serious, yet rudimentary, discussion of the introduction of collective action in an EU antitrust context came with the adoption by the Commission of its Green Paper in 2005. Referring to collective action under the rubric of what was then termed a '*special*' procedure, the Green Paper sought opinion on whether there should be an instrument for bringing collective action, and specifically on whether firstly a cause of action for consumer associations could be established, with individual consumers still being permitted to bring an action, and secondly whether provision should be made for collective action by groups of purchasers who are not end-consumers.[47] **6.044**

With regard to the first option, the Commission requested that consideration be given to standing (whether there should be a registration or authorisation system), and distribution (whether damages should be awarded to an association or to its members), as well as quantification of damages ('*damages awarded to an association could be calculated on the basis of the illegal gain of the defendant, whereas damages awarded to the members are calculated on the basis of the individual damage suffered*'). **6.045**

The Green Paper was conspicuous for the absence of a third option, collective action by end-consumers. As noted by some commentators, the likely reason for this was that the idea of US-style class actions would not be palatable in the EU, where collective action by consumer associations was, at that time, still a nascent and evolving concept in a number of Member States, and unknown in many others.[48] **6.046**

2 The White Paper

Identifying a '*clear need for mechanisms allowing aggregation of the individual claims of victims of antitrust infringements*',[49] the White Paper represented the next step in the delineation of the contours of a system of collective action in the **6.047**

47 Options 25 and 26.

48 See, for example, Donald I. Baker, 'The EU Green Paper on Private Damage Actions – an Ambitious Response to a Very Difficult Set of Practical and Philosophic Issues' (2005) 4(4) Comp L J 239.

49 White Paper, Section 2.1.

sphere of antitrust in the EU. In its Section 2.1, it considered and put forward proposals regarding policy choices and specific measures seeking to ensure that all victims of infringements of EU competition law (including businesses) had access to effective redress mechanisms so that they could be fully compensated for any harm suffered. No doubt with the perceived excesses of the US class action system in mind, the White Paper was, however, careful to stress that a '*genuinely European approach*' be taken, and that the treatment of damages actions be '*rooted in European legal culture and traditions*'.[50]

6.048 The Commission advocated a combination of two complementary mechanisms both for follow-on and stand-alone actions to address a perceived lack of effective redress faced by individual consumers and SMEs. In addition, the White Paper specifically proposed the possibility of representative actions brought by qualified entities. Such qualified entities might encompass consumer associations, state bodies or trade associations who bring the action on behalf of identified or, *in rather restricted cases*, identifiable victims. These entities would either be officially designated beforehand, or certified on an *ad hoc* basis by a Member State for the purposes of bringing an action for relief following a *particular* antitrust infringement on behalf of some or all of their members. It also proposed opt-in collective actions, whereby those who have incurred damage expressly decide to agglomerate their individual claims for harm suffered into one single action.

6.049 The White Paper went on to state that it was important that victims of an antitrust infringement must still be permitted to bring an individual action for damages. However, it quite rightly noted that safeguards should be put in place to avoid the same harm being compensated more than once. The White Paper omitted, however, to provide a suitable proposal to ensure that double (or greater) compensation did not occur. Furthermore, the White Paper did not address the important issue of mutual recognition of a representative entity among the Member States, an issue dealt with in the consumer injunctions Directive, for example, and proposed in the draft Directive (see further below).[51] In addition, there was no concrete proposal on the important practical issue of how damages should be distributed among claimants.[52] Of note, however, is that the White Paper arguably seemed to tacitly endorse an opt-out

---

50 Section 1.2.

51 For a good commentary on the White Paper, see Russell, *loc. cit.*

52 See, however, the Staff Working Paper, at para 47, which saw distribution as a '*key issue*'. The Staff Working Paper noted that '*[d]istribution of the award itself may be direct (e.g. by the defendant or by an independent fund, with various possible degrees of action requested from the victims) and may exceptionally be more indirect (e.g. cy-pres distribution, distribution to a public interest foundation)*'.

model, given that it did not propose that either written authorisation or approval would be needed on the part of the persons harmed.[53]

The European Parliament's resolution on the White Paper recognised that an integrated or horizontal approach to collective redress might not necessarily require the adoption of a single instrument, and must not delay or avoid the development of proposals and measures identified as necessary for the full enforcement of EU competition law.[54] Four years later, during which time the Commission's work on competition law damages actions was caught up in the net of its horizontal work on collective redress, this is exactly the solution which has been chosen. **6.050**

3 *The draft Directive*

Two complementary mechanisms of collective action were proposed in the draft Directive, so-called '*group actions*' and '*representative actions*'. **6.051**

Under Article 4, two or more injured parties who had incurred harm caused by the same infringement of Article 101 or 102 TFEU could jointly bring a single action for damages (a '*group action*'). It was further proposed that other parties who had suffered damage as a result of the same violation could join the group after the court had been seized of the action. **6.052**

With respect to representative actions under Article 5 of the draft Directive, such actions could only be brought by so-called '*qualified entities*'.[55] According to the proposal, such a qualified entity was not required to identify all injured parties belonging to the group on an individual basis. It only needed to specify a '*defined*' class of parties represented in the proceedings. Furthermore, such entity must ensure that the action is made known to all of those who may have claims for damages. Furthermore, any injured party must be able to exercise the right not to be represented by the qualified entity, and any decision on the merits of the action would be binding on all individuals who had not taken steps to remove themselves from it. It was also proposed that qualified entities **6.053**

53 Dimitrios-Panagiotis L. Tzakas, 'Effective Collective Redress in Antitrust and Consumer Protection Matters: a Panacea or a Chimera?' (2011) 48 CMLR 1125.

54 Resolution of 26 March 2009, P6_TA(2009)187, at paras 5 and 6.

55 Article 6(1) of the draft Directive provided that such an entity could be either (i) a body which '*[represents] legitimate interests and is designated by a Member State as an entity generally entitled to bring representative actions on behalf of injured parties who have suffered harm caused by infringements of [Article 101 or 102 TFEU]*', or (ii) a body '*representing legitimate interests of its members [which] is authorised by a Member State, in relation to a <u>specific</u> infringement of [Article 101 or 102 TFEU], to bring a representative action on behalf of all or some of its members who have suffered harm caused by such infringement*' (emphasis added).

designated in one Member State should have the right to bring representative actions in all other Member States.

6.054 Despite an almost unanimous rejection by stakeholders of an opt-out model during the consultation process, the proposal for representative actions under the draft Directive bore the hallmarks of an opt-out class action. For example, a representative action can be initiated on behalf of each party without specifically identifying the parties represented. Furthermore, in a similar fashion to an opt-out system, the draft Directive proposed a court-approved notice and opt-out procedure to determine who would be in the final class.[56] The main difference between an opt-out class action and the representative action as proposed in the draft Directive was that under an opt-out system, any class member can initiate the proceeding. Under the draft Directive, on the other hand, only a qualified entity can bring a representative action.[57]

4 The Commission's joint information note

6.055 In the wake of the shelving of the draft Directive, on 5 October 2010 the Commissioners for Justice, Competition and Consumer Policy issued a note identifying a set of core principles which could form part of a European framework for collective redress.[58]

6.056 The note stated that any EU action on collective redress should primarily ensure that any right of a party to compensation can be effectively and efficiently obtained. Parties must be able to avail themselves of the possibility to resort to a collective consensual resolution of their dispute. This may be achieved either via settlement or via an alternative dispute resolution mechanism. Furthermore, it was stated that judgments should be enforceable throughout the EU and adequate means of funding should be available so that citizens and businesses can obtain access to justice. In order to avert risks of abusive litigation the Commissioners strongly opposed the introduction of class actions along the lines of the US model into the EU legal order.

5 The Commission's 2011 consultation paper

6.057 In a continued attempt to grapple with the issue of how collective action was to be addressed, in February 2011 the Commission issued its consultation paper on collective redress. Against the backdrop of the patchwork of existing

---

56 US Chamber Institute for Legal Reform, 'Response to the Proposed DG Competition Directive on Rules Governing Damages Actions for Antitrust Infringements', available at: http://www.instituteforlegalreform.com/sites/default/files/images2/stories/documents/pdf/legislation/responsetodgcompproposal093 009.pdf.

57 *Ibid.*

58 '*Renforcer la cohérence de l'approche européenne en matière de recours collectif: prochaines étapes*', information note by Mme Reding, M. Almunia and M. Dalli (SEC(2010)1192).

national systems and their different levels of effectiveness, the consultation was opened within the framework of the Europe 2020 strategy and the Stockholm Programme, which emphasised a need for consumers and SMEs to be able to enforce their rights under EU law.

Unlike prior Commission initiatives, however, the consultation on collective redress adopted an approach that was not limited to competition law infringements, but also covered other areas of EU law, such as the environment and financial services. The consultation invited comment on ten aspects of a potential regime for collective action. For example, a question arose as to whether an EU collective redress initiative is in fact necessary given the remedies available at the Member State level. Another question arose as to how to deter potentially abusive collective litigation, including the controversial issue of whether a system should be opt-in or opt-out. **6.058**

Of note in the responses is that most national governments, consumer organisations and academics were in favour of the Commission's objective of introducing a mechanism of collective redress, whilst private practitioners were generally against it.[59] The general concern of the latter was that there is no evidence of an 'enforcement deficit', meaning that the Commission's initiative is therefore untimely.[60] The issue of whether action does need to be taken ultimately depends, however, on the extent to which national systems of collective action do provide effective redress in furtherance of the twin objectives of compensation and deterrence. **6.059**

In its response,[61] the European Parliament called for a horizontal instrument on collective redress at EU level, covering different sectors, but with additional sectoral rules where necessary.[62] Despite its apparently positive tone, the resolution can be interpreted as an attempt to block any real moves towards a measure at EU level by conflating the different interests involved.[63] **6.060**

---

59 For a synthesis of the responses, see *Evaluation of Contributions to the Public Consultation and Hearing: Towards a Coherent European Approach to Collective Redress* (Study JUST/2010/JCIV/CT/0027/A4), University of Heidelberg, 2011. See also the detailed minutes of the public hearing on collective redress of 5 April 2011, available at: http://ec.europa.eu/competition/consultations/2011_collective_redress/index_en.html.

60 See the synthesis of responses, *ibid.*

61 Resolution of 2 February 2012 on 'Towards a coherent European approach to collective redress' (P7_TA(2012)21).

62 *Ibid.*, at paras 15 and 17.

63 See in particular para 15, where the resolution calls for a horizontal instrument '*in the event that it is decided after detailed consideration that a Union scheme of collective redress is needed and desirable*', which rather begs the underlying policy question.

6 The Commission's proposal and 2013 collective redress initiative

6.061 As a result of the 2011 consultation, and as part of its further attempt to legislate on damages actions, the Commission adopted a recommendation and accompanying communication on collective redress in June 2013. The Commission made it clear that it sees these two documents, as well as the legislative proposal, as a package, in terms of competition law enforcement at least.[64]

6.062 On the one hand, the communication sets out the Commission's views on certain central tenets of a system of collective redress. On the other, the recommendation *suggests* that all Member States have a system of collective redress in place which adheres to a core set of non-binding principles applicable in all areas where collective claims for an injunction or damages would be relevant in order to enforce a right protected by EU law. Not only do the principles seek to facilitate the bringing of collective actions, but strong procedural safeguards are recommended to prevent abusive litigation.

6.063 As far as standing is concerned, the recommendation provides that entities that represent claimants must be subject to clearly defined conditions of eligibility. For example, such entities are required to be of a non-profit making nature,[65] and to have adequate resources to represent a group of claimants.[66] Public authorities must also be permitted to bring representative actions.[67] Courts must screen whether the conditions for eligibility are met.[68]

6.064 As regards cross-border collective redress, the recommendation suggests that single collective actions for the protection of interests located in more than one Member State should be possible.[69] Furthermore, a representative entity that has already been officially designated in one Member State should be permitted to seize a court in another Member State.[70]

6.065 Member States must ensure that a representative entity or group of claimants are able to inform potential claimants about a breach of the law and the intention to seek redress. Methods used to inform potential claimants must be such as to effectively safeguard the interests of these claimants involved whilst

64 See footnote 10 in the communication. Bizarrely, the Commission states in the main text that the legislative proposal '*leaves it to Member States whether or not to introduce collective redress actions in the context of the private enforcement of competition law*'. In fact, the proposal is simply silent on the matter.

65 Para 4(a).

66 Para 4(c).

67 Para 7.

68 Paras 8 and 9.

69 Para 17.

70 Para 18.

not unduly encroaching on the rights of the defendant, such as not to have its reputation sullied before a finding of guilt has been made.[71]

The 'loser pays' and 'opt-in' principles should be applicable in the Member States.[72] Any exception to the 'opt-in' principle '*by law or by court order, should be duly justified by reasons of sound administration of justice*'.[73] **6.066**

Contingency fees should, as a general rule, be prohibited.[74] Where a type of contingency fee system is available, however, it should be appropriately regulated.[75] In relation to funding more generally, a court is required to stay proceedings where third-party funding may cause a conflict of interest between that party and the claimant party, for example.[76] Furthermore, in line with the goal of compensation, exemplary damages should not be permitted.[77] **6.067**

Collective actions should not undermine public enforcement proceedings. Therefore, collective actions should only start once the proceedings of a public authority (such as a competition authority) have been brought to a close.[78] Given that the recommendation is but soft law, it remains to be seen whether the Member States will adopt the measures proposed. One can at least say that the Commission has taken the least controversial approach possible, in terms of instrument and its content, to ensure that collective action becomes a cornerstone of antitrust enforcement throughout the EU. Arguably, therefore, we are likely to see the Commission's suggestions implemented in one form or another in most, if not all, Member States. In the absence of such action, the current patchwork of national systems for collective action in the field of antitrust, discussed in further detail below, will persist. **6.068**

In terms of the interrelationship between the Commission's legislative proposal and the issue of collective action, the Commission has, as expected, removed the latter from the former, it being widespread knowledge that the presence of provisions on collective action was one of the principal reasons for the strong political resistance in certain quarters to the draft Directive in 2009.[79] As a consequence, Article 12(2) of the proposal contains a rule whereby, when it is **6.069**

71 Paras 10 and 11.
72 Paras 13 and 21.
73 Para 21.
74 Para 30.
75 *Ibid.*
76 Para 15(a).
77 Para 31.
78 Para 33.
79 On this, see Chapter 1.

'*legally impossible*' for the class of purchaser to whom on overcharge has been passed on to claim compensation, the passing-on defence shall not be available.[80]

6.070 It seems fairly clear that this rule is designed to compensate for the lack, within the proposal, of a provision on collective action. However, it is unclear, to say the least, how such a provision would work in practice. Recital 30 to the proposal, as well as the explanatory memorandum,[81] speaks of redress being unavailable to certain classes of purchaser as a result of national rules on matters such as causation and remoteness. This may well be the case, but the introduction of a rule of the nature proposed in Article 12(2) does not remedy the underlying problem, that is, the lack of a provision on collective action.

6.071 The idea of a national court assessing whether a class of purchasers is '*legally able*' to claim compensation seems tautologous. What is the court to do if it finds that this is not the case? And what yardstick is it to use in making this assessment? If it is its own law, as surely it would be,[82] how could it come to a negative conclusion?

III COLLECTIVE ACTION IN THE MEMBER STATES

6.072 Most Member States allow for one or other type of collective action. Of the 27 Member States, there are eight that currently have no collective action scheme in place: Belgium,[83] Cyprus, the Czech Republic, Estonia, Latvia, Luxembourg, Slovakia and Slovenia. Where a system for collective action is available, however, action in the sphere of antitrust remains rare.

---

80 For further analysis of Article 12, see Chapter 3.

81 Section 4.4.

82 Subject, albeit, to EU law, such as the principles of effectiveness and equivalence, as suggested by the Commission in recital 30.

83 It is however of note that, under Article 30 of the Belgian *Code judicaire* (Judicial Code), claimants can in certain situations join their individual claims into one action. The claims must be so closely connected that it is appropriate to try them together in order to avoid possible incompatible decisions ('*[d]es demandes en justice peuvent être traitées comme connexes lorsqu'elles sont liées entre elles par un rapport si étroit qu'il y a intérêt à les instruire et juger en même temps afin d'éviter des solutions qui seraient susceptibles d'être inconciliables si les causes étaient jugées séparément*'). In these circumstances, the claims will be heard and tried together. Each claimant must, however, be identified and have an immediate, personal and actual interest in the claim. The provision recalls Article 6(1) of Regulation 44/2001 (on which see Chapter 7).

A United Kingdom

Of those Member States that have introduced a collective action mechanism, only the United Kingdom has incorporated a statutory provision that is specific to competition law. This provision allows for claims to be brought by a '*specified body*' for and on behalf of consumers in follow-on claims for damages for breach of EU or UK competition law before the CAT (see further below). **6.073**

Beyond the statutory provisions which apply to the United Kingdom as a whole, collective action in England and Wales has long been integral to the legal system. In view of perceived deficiencies in the system, procedural reform is currently being debated with respect to collective action as a whole, and specifically in the competition law arena.[84] The salient elements of the relevant reform proposals in the antitrust sphere are discussed further below. **6.074**

Currently, three key mechanisms for collective action exist under the procedural law of England and Wales, namely representative actions, Group Litigation Orders (GLOs), and competition-specific consumer actions. A common thread runs through all mechanisms in that they are opt-in. **6.075**

1 Representative actions[85]

Representative actions are governed by Part 19-II of the CPR. Pursuant to Rule 19.6(1), representative actions may be brought '*by or against one or more persons who have the same interest*'. Usually representative actions bind all persons represented, but can only be enforced by or against a person who is not a party with the permission of the court (Rule 19.6(4)). **6.076**

With respect to competition-based actions, the test relating to the '*same interest*' renders it difficult to bring a collective action via the representative action route, and has been used sparingly. Testimony of this is borne by the *Emerald Supplies* proceedings, a claim brought by Emerald Suppliers Limited (ESL), an importer of flowers into the United Kingdom, against British Airways (BA) in relation to price-fixing agreements entered into by BA for the supply of air freight services. **6.077**

BA sought an order to strike out the representative elements of the claim on the ground that ESL and the other claimants it sought to represent did not have the **6.078**

84 Gerald Barling, 'Collective Redress for Breach of Competition Law – a Case for Reform?' (2011) 10(1) Comp LJ 5.

85 Not to be confused with the usual sense of this term in a competition law context, i.e. an action brought by a representative body, such as a consumer organisation, in respect of a competition law violation.

same interest and thus that the representative element of the claim fell outside the scope of Rule 19.6(1).

6.079 The High Court granted the application in favour of BA and struck out the representative part of the action.[86] The Court of Appeal also found in favour of the defendant, holding that ESL failed to satisfy the conditions of Rule 19.6.[87]

6.080 The *Emerald Supplies* proceedings highlight two important aspects of collective action in England and Wales, namely the inherent difficulty in bringing a representative action under Rule 19.6, and the fact that claimants seeking to group claims likely have a better chance of doing so by availing themselves of the GLO instrument or the mechanism in place for representative action under s47B of the Competition Act 1998.[88]

2 GLOs

6.081 The restrictive interpretation of representative actions led directly to the invention of the GLO. In England and Wales, the GLO provides for the common management of similar claims (Part 19-III CPR).[89] Introduced in 1999 as part of the Woolf reforms, the GLO '*provides more structured case management than was practicable under the pre-existing mechanisms*'.[90] A register of claims in the group is maintained, and any judgment entered against any claim on the register is binding as against all claims entered on the register. New claims can be entered on the register once proceedings have already started, in which case any judgment already entered is binding against them, subject to a right of appeal.

6.082 The GLO is distinguishable from a class action in that all parties to a GLO have to have a pre-existing and identified cause of action. A court can make a GLO when there are a number of similar claims that '*give rise to common or related issues of fact or law*', also known as GLO issues (Rule 19.10). In competition law cases, an application for a GLO can only be brought before the High Court. An application should include (i) a summary of the nature of the

86 *Emerald Supplies Limited* v *British Airways plc* [2009] EWHC 741 (Ch). The finding of the High Court was based on analysis of the three conditions for a representative claim set out by Lloyd LJ in *Pan Atlantic Insurance Company Limited and another* v *Pine Top Insurance Company Limited* [1989] 1 Lloyd's Law Reports 568 at 571, namely that the parties must have the same interest in the proceedings and that they must have a common grievance, and that the relief sought must be beneficial to all.

87 [2010] EWCA Civ 1284, in particular at para 69.

88 For an extended analysis and critique of the reasoning in *Emerald Supplies*, see Rachael Mulheron, 'A Missed Gem of an Opportunity for the Representative Rule' (2012) 23(1) European Business Law Review 49.

89 A list of GLOs is published on the English courts' website at http://www.hmcourts-service.gov.uk/cms/150.htm. The number of GLOs to date has been limited, on account of what many commentators attribute to the lack of an opt-out system.

90 Barling, *loc. cit.*, at 11.

litigation, (ii) the number and nature of claims already issued, (iii) the number of parties likely to be involved, (iv) the common issues of fact or law that are likely to arise in the litigation, and (v) whether there are any matters that distinguish smaller groups of claims within the wider group.

To date, there has been only been one competition law case in which a GLO has been made.[91] It should be noted that this case preceded the introduction of a competition-specific collective action mechanism by the Enterprise Act 2002. **6.083**

3 s47B of the Competition Act

Inserted by s19 of the Enterprise Act 2002, s47B of the Competition Act allows a '*specified body*' to bring a damages action for breach of UK or EU competition law on behalf of named consumers before the CAT. A specified body must meet certain criteria designed to ensure its independence, impartiality, integrity and ability to represent the interests of consumers. To date, Which? (officially known as the Consumers' Association) is the sole body '*specified*' for the purposes of s47B.[92] **6.084**

In March 2007, the first collective action for damages under s47B was brought by Which? on behalf of some 130 individual consumers against JJB Sports.[93] The claim arose from an OFT decision of August 2003 that JJB Sports and others had participated in practices contrary to the Chapter I prohibition contained in s2(1) of the Competition Act 1998 (the UK law equivalent of Article 101(1) TFEU) by fixing the price of certain England and Manchester United football shirts.[94] **6.085**

The OFT had found that JJB Sports was a party to the following four agreements or concerted practices: one relating to the retail price of official England replica kit at the time of the European Championships in 2000 (the 'England Agreement'); another, made in June 2000, relating to the retail price of official Manchester United replica kit shortly before the launch of Manchester United's new strip at the beginning of August 2000 (the 'MU Agreement'); a third, called the 'Continuation Agreement', said to have lasted from mid-2000 until August 2001, relating to England and Manchester United replica kit, and including the launch of the Manchester United centenary shirt in July 2001; **6.086**

91 2001 Folio 398 *Prentice Ltd* v *DaimlerChrysler UK*. The case was settled before trial. For a discussion of the proceedings, see Marjorie Holmes, 'The Commercial Court of the Queen's Bench Division of the High Court of England and Wales Makes a Group Litigation Order in a Competition Case in the Automobile Sector (Prentice/DaimlerChrysler UK)', e-Competitions, No 36124, available at: http://www.concurrences.com.

92 See the Specified Body (Consumer Claims) Order 2005 (SI No 2365 of 2005).

93 *Consumers Association* v *JJB Sports plc*, registered on 5 March 2007. The 130 claimants represented only around 0.1 per cent of those thought to have been affected by the illegal practice in question.

94 OFT Decision No CA98/6/2003, 1 August 2003.

and a fourth, called the 'England Direct Agreement', relating to the price at which England replica kit was sold online on behalf of the Football Association (FA).

6.087 The CAT, in its judgment on liability,[95] found that JJB was not a party to the England Direct agreement, and that although it was a party to an agreement relating to the Manchester United Centenary shirt, it was not a party to the Continuation Agreement as such. Accordingly, the CAT established JJB's participation in the England Agreement, the MU Agreement and a further agreement, known as the 'Manchester United Centenary Shirt Agreement'. All of these were found to be trilateral agreements. Only in relation to the England Agreement did JJB Sports appeal, and the terms of its appellant's notice did not challenge the finding of a bilateral vertical agreement between itself and Umbro in relation to the England shirt for the Euro 2000 competition.[96]

6.088 However, no judgment in relation to the damages claims was ultimately delivered in the case: on 9 January 2008, JJB announced that it had agreed to settle, with £20 being paid to registered claimants and £5 to £10 being awarded to 'unregistered claimants'. The CAT subsequently issued an order on 14 January 2008 that the claim be withdrawn. JJB Sports was ordered to pay Which?'s costs.

6.089 A number of comments on Which?'s collective action against JJB Sports is warranted. In particular, concerns were raised regarding the effectiveness of the measure provided for under s47B of the Competition Act 1998. Which?, in preparing the case against JJB, encountered a number of practical yet fundamental problems. Which? had to find and recruit claimants (which was recognised as being difficult with the passage of time and the low value of the claims), and had to consider evidence of eligibility (the issue being whether customer receipts were sufficient) and which method to use in calculating the overcharge or loss. Which? also had problems in obtaining disclosure and in having enough information to assess a fair settlement.[97]

6.090 The above issues are important. They show the defects of the system under s47B, and perhaps allay any fears that opt-out collective action will open the floodgates to a large number of unmanageable or unmeritorious cases. This is a fear recently raised by *inter alia* the Confederation of British Industry, which

95 *JJB Sports plc and Allsports Limited* v *Office of Fair Trading* [2004] CAT 17.

96 *Umbro Holdings Ltd, Manchester United plc, Allsports Limited, JJB Sports plc* v *Office of Fair Trading* [2005] CAT 22, further appealed to the Court of Appeal, *JJB Sports plc* v *Office of Fair Trading* [2006] EWCA Civ 1318.

97 See Which? Press Release of July 2011, 'Collective Redress – JJB Sports: a Case Study in Collective Action'.

strongly prefers the use of swifter alternative dispute resolution mechanisms as opposed to litigation as a means of bringing finality to a claim.[98] In particular, a behavioural remedy such as the one imposed in the 'independent schools' cartel case is seen as a viable alternative.[99]

Following its experience with the claim against JJB Sports, Which? concluded, contrary to the warnings of bodies that oppose opt-out actions for fear of instilling abusive US litigation practices in to the UK system, that '*had the collective redress system been based on "opt out" and "cy pres", the case would have made a greater financial impact thereby ensuring that affected consumers were properly compensated, either directly or indirectly, and tangentially this would have had the effect of acting as a stronger deterrent to companies from engaging in activities that cause consumer detriment*'.[100] Moreover, according to Which?, '*the single biggest hurdle to the effectiveness of the current statutory representation procedure is the requirement to name claimants on the claim form*'.[101] **6.091**

4 *Further policy developments*

As a result of the perceived inadequacies of the system of collective actions in the UK as highlighted *inter alia* by the Which? case, there have been a series of reform initiatives in the field of collective action in antitrust, most notably the OFT's November 2007 recommendations to the UK Government,[102] and the 2012 consultation by BIS, which is itself a continuation of earlier reform efforts undertaken by the UK Government. **6.092**

a *2006 DTI consultation*

Recent efforts on the part of the UK Government to reform consumer redress in fact go back to 2005, when the then Department of Trade and Industry **6.093**

98 See 'Private Actions in Competition Cases – Delivering Effective Redress to Consumers', the CBI's response to the BIS consultation, 24 July 2012. It should be noted that alternative dispute resolution mechanisms are also used in the US. The Gulf Coast Claims Facility made awards of $6.2 billion to over 220,000 individual and business claimants during the course of its 18 months of operations (see Department of Justice Press Release of 19 April 2012, 'Audit of Gulf coast Claims Facility Results in $64 Million in Additional Payments'). It is also of note that, in November 2011, the Commission adopted a communication on improving alternative dispute resolution (ADR) in relation to consumer-to-business disputes in the EU (COM(2011)791). This did not cover competition cases, however.

99 OFT Decision Number CA98/5/2006, 20 November 2006. The OFT fined the independent schools just under £500,000, and ordered them to make payments totalling £3 million into an educational charitable trust designed to benefit the pupils who had attended the schools during the relevant period.

100 See Which? press release, *loc. cit.* 'Cy pres' or 'fluid recovery' means that any money left over from damages paid out to eligible consumers can be used in a way specifically related to the claim, for example to fund a relevant consumer-based project, rather than returned to the defendant. This is similar to a behavioural remedy, as imposed in the 'independent schools' case (see above).

101 *Ibid.*

102 OFT, 'Private Actions in Competition Law: Effective Redress for Consumers and Business', Recommendations, November 2007.

(DTI) issued a consultation on representative actions for breach of consumer protection legislation as part of the Government's consumer strategy.[103] This was followed by a further consultation in July 2006,[104] in relation to which responses were published by the then Department for Business, Enterprise and Regulatory Reform (BERR) in March 2008.[105] It should be noted that at this point the reform proposals being floated related to consumer redress in general, and were not competition-specific.

6.094 The OFT and consumer groups voiced their support for the proposals as a whole, but were of the view that any mechanism introduced should cover both named consumers and consumers at large. They suggested that covering the whole class would be economically the most efficient approach.[106]

6.095 Generally, business groups were not in favour of the proposals. In their view there was a lack of evidential support for the introduction of representative actions. They were concerned that if introduced, such actions would signal the first step in a move towards US-style class actions and a culture of increased litigation.[107] They also expressed a preference, if representative actions were to be introduced, for their restriction to named consumers, instead of being brought for the benefit of consumers at large, on the basis that this would make the quantification of potential damages more straightforward.[108] The trading standards authorities that responded were also in favour of limiting representative actions to named consumers, and suggested that permission should be sought from a court as a prelude to the commencement of litigation.[109]

b 2007 OFT recommendations

6.096 In its 2007 recommendations, the OFT suggested that representative bodies have the capacity to bring both stand-alone and follow-on actions on behalf of both consumers and businesses. According to the OFT, this could have been achieved by expanding the scope of either s47B of the Competition Act 1998, which applies only to follow-on actions, or the GLO mechanism.[110]

---

103 DTI, 'A Fair Deal for All – Extending Competitive Markets: Empowered Consumers, Successful Business' (2005).

104 DTI, 'Representative Actions in Consumer Protection Legislation: Consultation', 12 July 2006.

105 BERR, 'Representative Actions in Consumer Protection Legislation: Responses to the Government consultation', March 2008.

106 *Ibid.*, at 5.

107 *Ibid.*, at 4.

108 *Ibid.*, at 5.

109 *Ibid.*, at 4.

110 Para 5.9.

The OFT also proposed that an opt-out mechanism should be available, and that a judge could have discretion to decide, based on defined criteria, if a given claim should be brought on an opt-in, opt-out or individual basis.[111] **6.097**

c 2012 BIS consultation

Since then, the focus of the reform efforts undertaken by BIS shifted to the field of competition. As noted above, in April 2012, BIS examined collective action within a wider framework of reforms of private competition law enforcement, and published its consultation on options for reform, supported by an impact assessment. **6.098**

The UK Government saw two principal ways in which the current collective action regime could be extended, quite apart from the question of opt-out or opt-in collective action. The Government considered, firstly, whether to allow collective actions to be brought on behalf of both businesses and consumers, and, secondly, whether to allow collective actions to be brought in both stand-alone and follow-on cases. **6.099**

With regard to the first option, the Government considered that businesses which have suffered loss as a result of an infringement of competition law should not be deprived of the right to bring a collective action to recover that loss. Collective action must, however, be the most appropriate means of pursuing the case.[112] With regard to the second option, the Government noted that one of the principal ways in which private action reforms could help to reduce anti-competitive behaviour would be by addressing cases where the competition authority had not brought a case.[113] The Government recognised that there is general scepticism towards stand-alone actions being brought in practice, but in support of its proposal cited a study on collective actions in Canada showing that between 1997 and 2008 approximately 25 per cent of competition proceedings were stand-alone actions.[114] **6.100**

As regards the issue of opt-in and opt-out collective action, interestingly, in considering options for reform, the Government included a third model, known as 'pre-damages opt-in', which is a hybrid model containing elements of both opt-in and opt-out.[115] **6.101**

---

111 Para 7.28.

112 Para 5.10.

113 Para 5.13.

114 *Ibid.*, referring to Rachael Mulheron, 'Competition Law Cases under the Opt-out Regimes of Australia, Canada and Portugal', research paper for BERR, 10 October 2008, available at: http://www.berr.gov.uk/files/file49008.pdf.

115 Paras 5.24 and 5.25.

6.102 Pre-damages opt-in describes a situation where parties must choose to join the action as members of the represented group. They can do so at any point up until damages have been quantified, even once liability has been determined. Any individual who does not affirmatively opt-out is bound by the outcome of the case.

6.103 According to the UK Government, pre-damages opt-in offers crucial advantages over the opt-in model. For example, it does not require the representative claimant to identify a sufficiently large proportion of parties that have been affected by an antitrust infringement before legal proceedings become viable. However, it is recognised that pre-damages opt-in remains an opt-in system and would be likely to lead to a lower level of redress (and indeed deterrence) than an opt-out regime. As with a pure opt-in system, there will be those cases, especially those where the level of individual damages is very low, which are fundamentally unlikely ever to be brought. Furthermore, '*securing funding for such a claim could be more difficult than in an opt-out regime, as uncertainty would remain until the very end as to the number of claimants and the overall size of the claim*'.[116]

6.104 The Government also consulted on who should be allowed to bring collective actions. The Government considered whether or not to allow actions to be brought by private bodies, such as representative bodies, third-party funders, or law firms. The Government also considered the adoption of a Nordic model, in which only a public body is allowed to bring an opt-out action (see the discussion on Denmark below). The OFT was proposed by the Government as the most natural body to bring such actions.[117]

6.105 It was recognised by the UK Government that any opt-out system would require strong safeguards to prevent speculative litigation and to provide defendants with a fair hearing.[118] In its response, the OFT strongly supported the possibility of opt-out collective actions for businesses and consumers in both follow-on and stand-alone cases. With respect to relevant safeguards, the OFT considered *inter alia* that there should be a rigorous certification procedure so that unmeritorious claims cannot be taken forward; no treble damages; and that the 'loser pays' principle be maintained.[119]

---

116 Para 5.25.

117 Para 5.42.

118 Para 5.53.

119 'Private Actions in Competition Law: a Consultation on Options for Reform – the OFT's Response to the Government's Consultation', July 2012.

d 2013 BIS response

In January 2013, the UK Government published its long-awaited response to its 2012 consultation. Pointing to the weaknesses of the current opt-in system, and clearly having considered alternative systems in other Member State jurisdictions, the UK Government decided to introduce a limited opt-out system of collective action, with attendant safeguards. Given the novelty of such a system, it is applicable to competition law cases only. Furthermore, cases are to be heard before the CAT, whether on a stand-alone or a follow-on basis. **6.106**

According to the UK Government, the CAT will be required to certify in a robust and meticulous manner whether a collective action should proceed on an opt-in or opt out basis.[120] Such an assessment would include a preliminary merits test, an evaluation as to whether the representative is suitable or not and a requirement that an additional assessment be made as to whether there is no more appropriate method of bringing the case. Furthermore, claims would be capable of being brought either by claimants themselves, or by 'genuine' representatives of claimants only. Such a representative might be a consumer association, for example. Law firms, third-party funders or special purpose litigation vehicles would not be able to bring claims. **6.107**

As far as relevant safeguards are concerned, in addition to a robust process of judicial certification before the CAT, the opt-out aspect of a claim will apply to claimants domiciled in the UK only (although there is no bar to non-UK claimants being able to opt-in if they so request), there would be no treble or exemplary damages, the loser pays principle would apply, there would be no contingency fees, and unclaimed fees would be transferred to the Access to Justice Foundation. **6.108**

Interestingly, the Government has also decided to introduce a new opt-out collective settlement regime for competition law in the CAT. This system would be similar to that under the Dutch *Wet Collectieve Afhandeling Massaschade*, discussed below. The test that will be applied by the CAT would be first to consider whether the case was suitable for settlement, before proceeding to assess the substantive merits of the settlement to ensure it is '*fair, just and reasonable*'. Following approval of a settlement, the CAT would then issue directions to set the procedural parameters of the settlement specifying, for example, the time limits for those wishing to opt-out, and any requirements pertaining to publicity. **6.109**

120 Interestingly, the UK Government proposes to abolish the requirement for the list of suitable bodies specified by the Specified Body (Consumer Claims) Order 2005.

B The Netherlands[121]

6.110 In the Netherlands, there are currently three mechanisms in place for collective action, namely collective action under Article 3:305a of the *Burgerlijk Wetboek*, bundled claims and collective settlements under the *Wet Collectieve Afhandeling Massaschade* (Act on Collective Settlement of Mass Claims, WCAM) of 2005. Each of these mechanisms will be discussed in turn.

1 Article 3:305a Burgerlijk Wetboek

6.111 Under Article 3:305a of the *Burgerlijk Wetboek*, a foundation (*stichting*)[122] or association (*vereniging*)[123] may, subject to a number of requirements, act in order to protect the common interests of third parties. The foundation or association is required to have articles of association that clearly state that it has as its aim the protection of the interest that is the subject of the collective action. In addition, it must possess the requisite legal capacity to bring the collective action.[124]

6.112 It is important to note that under the current provisions of Article 3:305a, while the clamant party may seek general remedies such as an injunction, damages cannot be sought. Nevertheless, once liability has been established pursuant to Article 3:305a and a declaratory judgment has been obtained, that judgment can be relied upon in a bundled claim or a collective settlement under WCAM.

2 Bundled claims

6.113 Developed through customary legal practice and subject to the general rules governing Dutch civil procedure, bundled claims are common in the Netherlands.[125] Notwithstanding the lack of express provision contained in the *Burgerlijk Wetboek*, claims bundling is on the rise in the Netherlands. It allows individuals seeking a judicial remedy to allocate their rights to a third party for the purpose of bringing court proceedings.

6.114 These actions are commonly brought through a foundation (*stichting*) that acquires the rights to bring claims on behalf of numerous individuals by either authorisation or assignment. In the former case, the foundation seeks the

---

121 For a discussion of the mechanisms for collective action in the Netherlands, see Jeroen Kortmann and Marieke Bredenoord-Spoek, 'The Netherlands: a "Hotspot for Class Actions"?' (2011) 4(1) GCLR 13.

122 As defined by Article 2:285 *Burgerlijk Wetboek*.

123 As defined by Article 2:26 *Burgerlijk Wetboek*.

124 See Kortmann and Bredenoord-Spoek, *loc. cit.*, at 14 for the argument that the underlying intention of the Dutch Parliament in putting in place this requirement was to prevent the proliferation of entities set up solely as litigation vehicles.

125 This practice is similar to the more general device of assignment. For further details of the bringing of collective claims by means of assignment, see below.

authorisation of the claimants to act on their behalf by obtaining mandates or powers of attorney from each of them. In the latter case, claims are purchased from individuals and subsequently bundled together by the foundation.[126]

Irrespective of which of the two methods is used, under Dutch law the foundation seeking damages is under an obligation clearly to outline the capacity in which it is acting, and to state on whose behalf it is acting. In this respect, if called upon to do so, the foundation must provide proof of every assignment or authorisation it has obtained. **6.115**

A recent example of collective action in an antitrust context in the Netherlands is an initiative by the not-for-profit *Stichting Meldpunt Collectief Onrecht* (SMCO), which set up a website (www.liftenkartel.nl) calling on possible victims of the elevator cartel[127] to come forward in preparation for a collective damages claim against the cartel participants. The SMCO is charging €465 per claimant to cover part of the legal costs of the collective action, and 20 per cent of any damages awarded.[128] **6.116**

3 *Wet Collectieve Afhandeling Massaschade, 2005*

Adopted on 23 May 2005, WCAM was introduced to enable the extension of a settlement agreement to all claimants in a similar situation.[129] WCAM draws inspiration from the US opt-out class action model, and contains *some* similar features.[130] **6.117**

A precondition for the application of WCAM is the existence of an amicably concluded settlement agreement. Thus, a claim under WCAM can only be **6.118**

126 Kortmann and Bredenoord-Spoek, *loc. cit.*, at 14, note that these purchases are usually in the form of a percentage of any eventual damages received.

127 On 21 February 2007, the Commission imposed a total fine of €992 million on the elevator cartel (case COMP/E-1/38.823, elevators and escalators (OJ C 75, 26.3.2008, p 19)).

128 See the general conditions for the handling of the case, available at: https://www.collectiefonrecht.nl/Voorwaarden_Zaakbehandeling_Liftenkartel.pdf.

129 See LJN AZ7033, *Gerechtshof* Amsterdam, at para 10.1: '*Gewaarborgd moet zijn dat de individuele belegger, casu quo ook zijn eega, redelijkerwijs geacht kan worden op de hoogte te zijn van het bestaan en de strekking van de WCAM-overeenkomst, van de verbindendverklaring en van zijn uitstapmoge-lijkheid, en voorts dat hij voldoende tijd heeft gehad om zich te vergewis-sen van de pro's en contra's van het gebruikmaken van de uitstapmogelijk-heid en voldoende gelegenheid om daartoe deskundig advies in te winnen* … .' Essentially, '*individuals harmed by an infringement must be made reasonably aware of the existence of the WCAM agreement and its content, its binding effect and the possibility to opt-out*'. For extended analysis of WCAM, see Hélène van Lith, 'The Dutch Collective Settlements Act and Private International Law', 2010, Erasmus School of Law, available at: http://ec.europa.eu/competition/consultations/2011_collective_redress/saw_annex_en.pdf.

130 See in this respect the memorandum of the US Chamber Institute for Legal Reform, 'Collective Redress in the Netherlands', 6 February 2012, available at: http://www.instituteforlegalreform.com/sites/default/files/Collective_Redress_Netherlands.pdf.

brought once the parties have come to an agreement on the amount of compensation.

6.119 As set out in WCAM, there are a number of requirements that must be fulfilled by the settlement agreement. There must be a description of the common grounds reached by the parties; an outline of the basis for the offering of the compensatory award; a precise description of the class eligible to obtain compensation under the agreement; and a clear statement as to how members of the class may obtain their award.

6.120 For the purposes of reviewing the collective settlement agreement agreed upon by the parties and obtaining a decision declaring the binding effect of the agreement, the Amsterdam *Gerechtshof* (Court of Appeal) has exclusive jurisdiction. This means that it can develop case management expertise. The court has the discretion to set an opt-out period. This is usually for a period of not less than three months. At the end of the opt-out period, any potential claimant that has not exercised the right to opt out of the settlement agreement is bound by it.

6.121 The notification requirements under WCAM are set out in detail. All class members must be sent a copy of the binding court declaration, and a notification of the decision must be duly published in the national press.

6.122 An illustrative example of how WCAM is applied can be found in the seminal *Converium* case.[131] Converium Holding AG was a Swiss-based reinsurance company whose shares were listed on the SWX Swiss Stock Exchange, and which also listed American Depositary Receipts on the New York Stock Exchange. Following the decline of its share value due to false statements made as to the company's financial health, its shareholders brought securities class actions against the company in the United States. Whilst a settlement was reached and duly approved by the United States District Court for the Southern District of New York, that court declined jurisdiction vis-à-vis the non-US claimants, excluding them from the settlement.[132]

6.123 Represented by two Dutch interest groups, the *Stichting* Converium Securities Compensation Foundation and the *Vereniging* VEB NCVB (Association of Securities Holders), the non-US claimants, who numbered approximately

131 As discussed in some detail in Kortmann and Bredenoord-Spoek, *loc. cit.*, at 16.

132 This reasoning was confirmed by the US Supreme Court in *Morrison* v *National Australia Bank Ltd.* 130 US 2869 (2010).

12,000, were able subsequently to reach a settlement. They then sought a binding declaration before the Dutch courts pursuant to the provisions of WCAM.

By an interim decision of 12 November 2010,[133] the Amsterdam *Gerechtshof* held that it was sufficient that performance of the settlement agreement would be in the Netherlands. However, the court deferred its final decision ensuring that the right of access to court of the parties who were not present was protected in accordance with Article 17 of the Dutch *Grondwet* (Constitution) and Article 6 ECHR. The interim decision was later declared binding by the Amsterdam *Gerechtshof*, pursuant to Article 1017(3) *Wetboek van Burgerlijke Rechtsvordering* (Code of Civil Procedure), in a decision of 17 January 2012.[134] **6.124**

It is interesting to note that only 3 per cent of the non-US claimants were resident in the Netherlands.[135] The case highlights the willingness of the Amsterdam *Gerechtshof* to assume jurisdiction over claims arising in instances where the link to the Netherlands appears to be somewhat tenuous at best in order to anchor a claim. Nevertheless, it should be remembered that in *Converium* and other such cases under WCAM,[136] the Dutch courts assumed jurisdiction primarily for the ratification of a collective settlement and the granting of a declaration as to its binding nature. The reasoning of the court at no stage suggests that the litigation prior to the settlement be brought in the Netherlands, nor does it imply that in the event that such litigation is brought before the Dutch courts, that those courts would necessarily have the requisite jurisdiction.[137] **6.125**

Notwithstanding the successes of the Dutch collective settlement mechanisms, in particular WCAM, the system in relative terms remains at an embryonic stage and there are calls for the implementation of effective safeguards.[138] In addition, it should be noted that since the WCAM mechanism is based on **6.126**

---

133 LJN BO3908, Amsterdam *Gerechtshof*. An unofficial translation into English is available at: http://www.converiumsettlement.com/images/stories/documents/Judgment%2012%20November%202010.pdf.

134 LJN BV1026, Amsterdam *Gerechtshof*. An unofficial translation into English is available at: http://www.converiumsettlement.com/images/stories/documents/Decision%2017%20January%202012.pdf. In addition, an English-language version of the binding settlement agreement is available at: http://www.converiumsettlement.com/images/stories/documents/Notice%20Binding%20Declaration.pdf.

135 Out of approximately 12,000 non-US claimants, only 200 were Dutch domiciled. For the most part, the non-US claimants were domiciled in Switzerland and the United Kingdom.

136 For example, the DES settlement of 1 June 2006, the Dexia settlement of 25 January 2007, the Vie d'Or settlement of 29 April 2009, the Shell settlement of 29 May 2009, the Vedior settlement of 15 July 2009, and the Ahold settlement of 23 June 2010.

137 For a succinct comparative assessment of the WCAM, see Karen Jelsma and Manon Cordewener, 'The Settlement of Mass Claims: a Hot Topic in the Netherlands' (2011) International Law Quarterly 13.

138 See in this respect the memorandum of the US Chamber Institute for Legal Reform, *loc. cit.*

amicable settlement, it can only be applied once the wrongdoer agrees to negotiate. For this reason, consumer organisations have called for the mechanism to be strengthened, as at present they cannot use it if the companies concerned decline to amicably discuss. This also explains the relatively low number of cases brought to date under WCAM.

C Denmark

6.127 In Denmark, new rules on collective action were adopted in 2007,[139] following recommendations made in 2005 by the *retsplejerådet* (Standing Committee on Procedural Law). These rules entered into force on 1 January 2008, and took the form of amendments to Denmark's Administration of Justice Act (*retsplejeloven*[140]) and other legislation.

6.128 There are a number of general conditions that have to be fulfilled in order to bring a collective action before the Danish courts. Each of these will be discussed, before turning to a discussion of the hybrid nature of the system.

6.129 Pursuant to section 254(a) of the *retsplejeloven*, as amended, for a collective action to be brought, the claim in question has to be uniform (that is, have a common factual and legal basis) and brought on behalf of a number of persons.

6.130 Under section 254(b) of the *retsplejeloven*, the competent jurisdiction for all collective action claims is Denmark. Notwithstanding this condition, the claimants bringing the action can be from other Member States.

6.131 A collective action has to be the most suitable means of assessing the claims brought. In order to assess this condition, the court must look at the merits of proceeding with the claim in a collective manner, or whether there are other alternative routes better suited to dealing with the claims.

6.132 The rules governing the appointment of group representatives are set out in section 254(c) of the *retsplejeloven*. For an opt-in collective action, a group representative can be appointed from the members of the group, an organisation, private institution or another association if the action falls within the scope of the association's objectives, or a public authority duly authorised by law. As will be discussed below, owing to the hybrid nature of the Danish system of collective action, this is not the case, strictly speaking, for all collective actions brought.

---

139 *Lov om ændring af retsplejeloven og forskellige andre love (Gruppesøgsmål m.v.)* (law No 181 of 28 February 2007).

140 *Lov om rettens pleje (retsplejeloven)* (LBK No 1008 of 24 October 2012).

The Danish model is predominately an opt-in system. Interestingly, however, the Danish regime does provide for an opt-out system to be used in exceptional circumstances where the claim is of such a low value that it would not otherwise be expected to be pursued through individual actions,[141] and where the opt-in model is an inappropriate means of properly assessing the merits of the claim. This might be the case where, in the case of a large class, an *ex ante* identification of the members of the class would be cumbersome and difficult, and where it would be onerous in practice to distribute opt-in notices to such a large class. **6.133**

Moreover, unlike claims under the opt-in model, opt-out actions can only be instituted by a public authority. As things currently stand, that public authority is the Danish consumer ombudsman. **6.134**

D Sweden

The *Lag om grupprättegång* (Act on class actions),[142] which entered into force on 1 January 2003, provides for actions to be brought by an individual on behalf of a group. Such an action can only be brought where it is the best procedural alternative, that is, the majority of claims can only be brought on a group and not an individual basis. **6.135**

In particular, an action can only be brought where (i) the action is founded on circumstances that are common or of a similar nature for the claims of the members of the group; (ii) group proceedings are not inappropriate due to the fact that some claims of the members of the group are based on different grounds[143]; (iii) the majority of the claims to which the action relates cannot equally well be pursued by individual actions by members of the group; (iv) the group, taking into consideration its size, ambit and otherwise, is appropriately defined; and (v) the claimant, taking into account its interest in the substantive matter, its financial capacity to bring a group action and the circumstances generally, is appropriate to represent the members of the group.[144] **6.136**

---

141 According to the explanatory notes that accompanied the draft legislation, this would normally be the case where the amount of the individual claim is not in excess of approximately DKK 2000.

142 *Lag* 2002:599. For an excellent discussion of the Swedish system, see Hans-W Micklitz and Astrid Stadler, 'Gruppenklagen in den Mitgliedstaaten der Europäischen Gemeinschaft und den Vereinigten Staaten von Amerika', Gutachten im Auftrag des Vereins für Konsumenteninformation Wien, 21 August 2005, at 20 *et seq*.

143 According to the explanatory memorandum accompanying the draft legislation, the driving motivation was to ensure efficiency of proceedings. Therefore, this requirement should probably be interpreted broadly, that is, so as to cover the factual as well as the legal grounds for the different claims (*Regeringens proposition* 2001/02:107, at section 5.2.2).

144 §8.

6.137 Importantly, the *Lag om grupprättegång* is based on the opt-in solution.[145] Only such members who have given a written notice to the court to opt-in can participate in the proceedings as passive members, and are then bound by a final decision of the court. Failure to provide written notice to the court within the time period set by the court results in the individual's withdrawal from the group. The passive class members have as a general rule no obligation to pay any legal costs to a successful defendant, while for the representative claimant the normal rule under Swedish procedural law applies that the loser has to pay the winning party's costs.

6.138 Three forms of action are available under the *Lag om grupprättegång*. Public class actions are brought by authorities designated by the Government to bring an action to court. This form of action is intended to allow governmental authorities to pursue claims where the public interest demands that action be taken.

6.139 As regards antitrust proceedings, Swedish Government policy is that the system of fines sufficiently serves the public interest, so that publicly run class actions would be overly resource-intensive and not make a significant contribution to competition law enforcement. On this basis, the national competition authority has not been designated as a body competent to bring this sort of action.[146]

6.140 The second form of action is a representative action brought by organisations which do not have a claim of their own, but which represent a group, for instance consumers or employees. Actions of this type brought by consumer organisations must concern cases between consumers and suppliers of goods and services.

6.141 The last option is a private action, which can be initiated by any individual. Prior to its amendment, the *Konkurrenslag* (competition act) restricted the right to claim damages to undertakings and parties in a contractual relationship to the infringer.[147] This restriction has since been removed.[148]

---

145 It is understood, however, that an opt-out solution was proposed and discussed during the *travaux préparatoires* of the legislation (Roberth Nordh, 'Group Actions in Sweden: Reflections on the Purpose of Civil Litigation, the Need for Reforms, and a Forthcoming Proposal' (2001) 11 Duke Journal of Comparative & International Law 381.

146 As in Denmark, the Swedish consumer ombudsman is, however, competent to bring a public class action.

147 *Lag* 2008:579.

148 See Chapter 3, §25.

E France

In France, a collective claim for competition law damages can be brought under Article L. 422–1 of the *Code de la consommation*. Such an action can be brought where several identified individuals have incurred individual harm having a common origin through the actions of the same person. Any approved association recognised as being nationally representative may, if instructed to do so by at least two of the consumers concerned, claim for damages in any court on behalf of those consumers. The association may only initiate the action once it has been instructed to do so by at least two consumers, who must give their prior authorisation to sue in their name and on their behalf.[149] **6.142**

Perhaps as a result of the very restrictive conditions of this procedure, the only collective competition law damages action to be brought to date in France is the opt-in representative action brought by the consumer association UFC Que Choisir on behalf of subscribers of mobile phone services against three mobile operators for price-fixing and market sharing practices. UFC Que Choisir set up a website enabling consumers to calculate their harm and join the action. Potentially, the number of claimants could have reached 20 million, but in the end the rate of participation was very low, at only 0.03 per cent. The processing of the case was extremely resource-intensive (20 per cent of the association's total staff spent approximately 2000 hours preparing the action), and cost over €500,000 to finance, for a total claim of approximately €750,000.[150] **6.143**

The Paris *Tribunal de commerce* and the Paris *Cour d'appel* dismissed the claim on the basis that the association had brought the action in breach of the provisions of L. 422–1 of the *Code de la consommation*. The *Cour de cassation* upheld the decision to dismiss the claim,[151] relying on the spirit of Article L. 422–1(2) to reach the conclusion that seeking a mandate to bring a claim via the internet is prohibited.[152] In practice, therefore, the procedure is expensive and restrictive, as associations must obtain and manage the mandate of each individual consumer in writing.[153] **6.144**

---

149 '*Lorsque plusieurs consommateurs, personnes physiques, identifiés ont subi des préjudices individuels qui ont été causés par le fait d'un même professionnel, et qui ont une origine commune, toute association agréée et reconnue représentative sur le plan national en application des dispositions du titre Ier peut, si elle a été mandatée par au moins deux des consommateurs concernés, agir en réparation devant toute juridiction au nom de ces consommateurs.*'

150 UFC Que Choisir, 'Trade Practices and Competition/Mobile Telephone Cartel', presentation to CLEF, 17–18 May 2007, Brussels.

151 *Première chambre civile*, judgment no 531 of 26 May 2011 (10–15.676).

152 Article L. 422–1(2) of the *Code de la consommation* provides as follows: '*Le mandat ne peut être sollicité par voie d'appel public télévisé ou radiophonique, ni par voie d'affichage, de tract ou de lettre personnalisé. Il doit être donné par écrit par chaque consommateur.*'

153 Luc Chatel, 'Le Temps est venu d'introduire l'action de groupe dans notre pays' (2008) Concurrences n° 2, 21.

6.145 The upshot of this case is that it is exceedingly difficult for French consumer organisations to bring a representative competition law action as they cannot obtain the requisite mandates.[154] Much like the Which? case in the United Kingdom, the UFC Que Choisir case highlights the inadequacies of an opt-in system in practice.

6.146 In view of the difficulties in achieving collective action in France, draft legislation permitting so-called 'class actions' in the area of consumers' rights is expected to be submitted by the Government to the French Parliament in 2013. In addition, on 28 January 2013, several senators submitted to the Senate a draft law aiming at establishing a so-called 'class action' in France.

6.147 These drafts follow a report by the *Conseil d'analyse économique* (CAE) published on 11 September 2012,[155] and an opinion of the *Conseil national de la consommation* delivered on 4 December 2012.[156] The CAE's report sets out several proposals to reinforce consumer protection. The introduction of some sort of class action in French law represents one such proposal. The report tentatively proposes that the cost of participation for claimants must be low and that the subject-matter of the claim should be as broad as possible.[157] The intricacies of the Government's draft act at this stage remain uncertain.

F Italy

6.148 Article 140-bis of the *Codice del consumo* introduced for the first time into the Italian legal system a mechanism for collective actions for damages, giving associations and committees *locus standi* in proceedings for the determination of

---

154 Christine Gateau, 'The Ultimate Rejection (for the Time Being …) of Class Actions under French Law?' (2012) 2 Paris International Litigation Bulletin 11. UFC Que Choisir recognised that this case '*perfectly demonstrates how French law is poorly adapted to class actions*', UFC Que Choisir, *loc. cit.*

155 The CAE is an independent advisory body created in July 1997 by the Prime Minister, to whom it reports directly. The role of the CAE is to shed light on issues of economic policy and bring them to the wider public attention by publishing reports. It is predominantly made up of academics, but where particular expertise or knowledge is required, there is scope for the inclusion of economists from the business sector. The report, entitled '*La protection du consommateur: rationalité limitée et régulation*', is available at: http://www.cae.gouv.fr/IMG/pdf/101.pdf.

156 Created in 1983 by decree, the *Conseil national de la consommation* is a body which advises the Minister for Consumer Affairs. Its role is to coordinate the work of representatives of the collective interests of consumers and representatives of professionals, public services and public authorities as regards consumer affairs. Moreover, it can be consulted by the public authorities regarding consumer affairs, in particular concerning draft laws and regulations likely to affect consumers.

157 See Emmanuel Combe, 'Vers une action de groupe … à la française' (2008) Concurrences n° 2, 19, for a good discussion of the introduction of collective action in France.

the right to compensation or repayment of amounts due to individual consumers or users as a result of an infringement of their rights by anti-competitive behaviour.[158]

After a number of deferrals, this mechanism effectively entered into force only in January 2010, and was renamed an '*azione di classe*'. In 2012, Article 140-bis of the *Codice del Consumo* was amended to further facilitate the bringing of such actions, which can now be brought to protect homogenous individual rights and collective interests and not just identical individual rights.[159] **6.149**

G Assignment of claims

Many Member States recognise assignment of claims under their tort laws. Assignment requires an express and verifiable decision by an individual to sell their claim to a third party. Being effectively an opt-in requirement, it is largely in line with European legal traditions. In the study carried out at the request of the European Parliament's economic and monetary affairs committee (ECON), the assignment model in an antitrust context was considered as a viable alternative to collective action.[160] **6.150**

The assignment model offers a synergistic approach to litigation. It brings about economies of scale in terms of costs and resources which benefit the claimant. The claimant can further be sure that the case is handled by an experienced litigator. It also benefits the defendant in terms of a reduced level of exposure to further litigation. In principle the streamlined nature of the assignment model addresses the difficulties associated with protracted parallel proceedings. **6.151**

A number of actions have been brought in the EU on the basis of assignment of claims. The *German Cement* case is the outstanding example. CDC brought a follow-on legal action against cartel operators bringing together the damages claims of 36 companies affected by a cartel in the German cement sector via the assignment of their claims. Following a prohibition decision by the *Bundeskartellamt*,[161] CDC agreed with the members of the 'class' of purchasers of **6.152**

158 Article 140-bis was introduced by Article 2, comma 446, of L. 244/07.

159 *Decreto legge* no 1, 24 January 2012. For a good discussion of the system in Italy, see Roald Nashi, 'Italy's Class Action Experiment' (2010) 43 Cornell Int'l LJ 147.

160 '*While it is not yet clear whether this form of funding can successfully apply to mass actions (i.e. those involving final consumers), claims transfer to a third party may help to overcome the problem of lack of participation by injured parties and represent an alternative and effective way of stimulating collective actions*' (*loc. cit.*, at 37).

161 See press release of 14 April 2003, '*Bundeskartellamt verhängt Bußgelder in Höhe von 660 Mio. Euro wegen Kartellabsprachen in der Zementindustrie.*'

cement to acquire their damages claims for a payment of €100 each and between 15 per cent and 25 per cent of damages obtained.

6.153 Before the *Oberlandesgericht* Düsseldorf,[162] the defendants argued that the claim brought by CDC was not precise enough as CDC had not specified each individualised claim and had not indicated the amount of the total damages claimed, and that CDC lacked standing to bring the claim as the assignment of the claims was void.[163] The court, however, held the action to be admissible.

6.154 In 2009, the *Bundesgerichtshof* confirmed the lower court's judgment by summarily holding the action to be admissible.[164] The judgment of the *Bundesgerichtshof* is based on two main grounds. Firstly, that the potential size of the number of claims does not, in itself, preclude admissibility.[165] Secondly, that the judge is able, in such an action, to estimate the damage suffered by the claimants on the basis of §287 *Zivilprozessordnung*.[166] This means that each and every claim does not need to be specified to the last detail.

6.155 The substantive action still appears to be pending before the *Landgericht* Düsseldorf.

6.156 Admissibility of the assignment model remains very much a live issue in the EU. This is particularly the case in the Netherlands, to which the authors refer the reader to the discussion on the Dutch system above. Following the Commission's decision to impose fines on 11 airline companies for a cartel on particular surcharges imposed on their respective customers,[167] Equilib, a French company, commenced a damages action in the Netherlands against members of the cartel on behalf of claimants that had assigned their rights to bring a claim, pursuant to an agreement governed by Dutch law. Within this framework, members of the Air France group argued for the invalidity of the

---

162 *Oberlandesgericht* Düsseldorf, VI-U (Kart) 14/07, 14 May 2008 (WuW 2008, 845), confirming the admissibility of the action and upholding the judgment of the *Landgericht* Düsseldorf, 34-O (Kart) 147/05, 21 February 2007 (WuW 2007, 519).

163 Paras 28–31.

164 *Bundesgerichtshof*, CDC/Dyckerhoff AG, KZR 42/08, 7 April 2009. Procedurally, an appeal to the *Bundesgerichtshof* is only admissible if there is an unsolved legal question that is of fundamental importance, or if the coherent application of a legal provision is threatened. Concerning the arguments brought forth against the judgment of the *Oberlandesgericht* Düsseldorf, the *Bundesgerichtshof* found these conditions not to have been met.

165 '*Allein die Fülle des Prozessstoffs führt nicht zur Unzulässigkeit der Klage.*'

166 '*In Fällen, in denen die Schadenshöhe von einer richterlichen Schätzung nach § 287 ZPO abhängt, kann ein unbezifferter Zahlungsantrag nach § 253 Abs. 2 Nr. 2 ZPO zulässig sein*'. On §287 *Zivilprozessordnung*, see the discussion of the 2004 decision of the *Landgericht* Dortmund in the vitamins case, Chapter 4. §253 sets out the requirements for the statement of claim in civil litigation before the German courts.

167 Commission Decision of 9 November 2010, case COMP/39258, airfreight (not yet published).

action on the grounds *inter alia* that Equilib was a front company, and thus that the proceedings were contrary to public policy. The Paris *Tribunal de commerce* declared the summons against Equilib inadmissible and dismissed the action.[168] The action is still pending in the Netherlands before the Amsterdam *Gerechtshof*.

IV CLASS ACTIONS IN THE UNITED STATES

The first recorded antitrust class action in the US was in the 1960s, and evolved from actions that were taken in respect of anti-competitive price-fixing on the market for electrical equipment.[169] Indeed, the historical rise of antitrust class actions has largely coincided with procedural developments that made class actions a means of providing redress for a large number of claimants. While an extended analysis of the US class action regime is outside the scope of the present work, the salient elements of the US system will be discussed. To that end, it is necessary first to outline the provisions of Rule 23 FRCP, before going on to highlight the underlying shift in policy following the most recent procedural reforms of 2005. **6.157**

A Rule 23 of the Federal Rules of Civil Procedure

Class actions in the US are governed by Rule 23 FRCP. The four prerequisites for a class action set out in Rule 23(a) are commonly referred to respectively as numerosity, commonality, typicality and adequacy. In addition to these four cumulative preconditions, the class has to meet one of the three conditions set out in Rule 23(b). **6.158**

By numerosity is meant that the class is so numerous that joinder is impracticable as a means of dealing with the class. Commonality refers to the need for common questions of law or fact which pertain to the class. Typicality means that the claims being advanced by the representatives of the class are typical of the class. Adequacy means that the representatives will adequately represent the class. **6.159**

The first means of certifying a class action under Rule 23(b), that is, Rule 23(b)(1), is where separate actions would create a risk of '*inconsistent or varying* **6.160**

168 Paris *Tribunal de commerce*, *1ère chambre*, RG 2011030421, judgment of 31 January 2012.

169 *Atlantic City Electric Company* v *General Electric Company* 226 F. Supp. 59 (SDNY 1964).

adjudications',[170] or adjudications which would prejudice claims brought by third parties who were not party to the proceedings in question.

6.161 Rule 23(b)(2), in turn, provides for certification where the defendant has refused to act in a way that responds to the class as a whole, meaning that, for example, injunctive or declaratory relief is necessary for the class.

6.162 Finally, Rule 23(b)(3) provides for certification where the court finds that the questions common to the class '*predominate*' over individual questions, and that '*a class action is superior to other available methods for fairly and efficiently adjudicating the controversy*'.

6.163 In the case of a class action certified under Rule 23(b)(1), members of the class may not opt out of the action. However, if an action is certified under Rule 23(b)(3), the members of the class who are absent have an opportunity to opt out once they receive notice.

6.164 Once a claim has been certified as representative, there are no limitations on who can bring a class action. In essence, they may be initiated by individuals, businesses, groups or even representative bodies.

6.165 Of the three provisions of Rule 23(b), the most rarely used provision is Rule 23(b)(1). This is due to the fact that while certification under this provision is mandatory in nature, it applies to classes where the fund is ultimately limited. Put otherwise, it applies '*when claims are made by numerous persons against a fund insufficient to satisfy all claims*'.[171] Similarly, Rule 23(b)(2) is not of an opt-out nature and certification is also mandatory. In addition, there is no requirement to provide notice. Rule 23(b)(2) allows for the granting of injunctive or declaratory relief.

6.166 The majority of class actions in the field of antitrust are brought under Rule 23(b)(3). In the case of class actions certified under this provision, which are often referred to as '*common-question actions*',[172] the absent members of the class have to be accorded the opportunity to opt out. Thus upon receipt of a notice any member of a class who so wishes may decide to opt out of the class.[173]

---

170 Rule 23(b)(1)(a).

171 *County of Suffolk* v *Long Island Lighting Co.* 907 F. 2d 1295 (2nd Cir 1990), at 1303.

172 Thomas D. Rowe Jr, 'State and Foreign Class-actions Rules and Statutes: Differences from – and Lessons for? – Federal Rule 23' (2007) 35(1) Western State University Law Review 101, at 110.

173 Michael P. Murtagh, 'The Rule 23(b)(3) Superiority Requirement and Transnational Class Actions: Excluding Foreign Class Members in Favor of European Remedies' (2011) 34 Hastings International and Comparative Law Review 1, at 6–7.

Moreover, pursuant to this provision, plaintiffs are required to establish that '*class action is superior to other available methods for fairly and efficiently adjudicating the controversy*'. Factored into this consideration is an assessment of the '*likely difficulties in managing a class*'. In practice, this requirement of predominance has proved to be somewhat of a major hurdle.

Incidentally, the theory underpinning Rule 23(b)(3) is that of constructive notice, whereas in other jurisdictions, as is the case in the majority of Member States with a collective action system, the mechanism '*start[s] from the principle that absent class members who have not had actual notice of the litigation, and who did not participate in that litigation, cannot be bound by its outcome*'.[174] **6.167**

It is trite when discussing US class actions to refer to them as being opt-out in nature. The accompanying analysis, often unduly, is of a negative complexion. However, as things currently stand, reforms enacted in 2005 to deal with some of the criticisms levelled at the US class action system have resulted in a number of changes to the procedural landscape of US class actions. Thus, the traditional view held abroad of class actions in the US may not have entirely kept up-to-date with more recent developments, such as the Class Action Fairness Act of 2005 (CAFA).[175] **6.168**

B The Class Action Fairness Act of 2005

Signed into law during the second term of President George W. Bush, CAFA sought to reform the class action system by recalibrating the Rule 23 provisions in order to address a number of issues. Its aims were threefold: firstly, to '*assure fair and prompt recoveries for class members with legitimate claims*'; secondly, to '*restore the intent of the framers of the United States Constitution by providing for Federal court consideration of interstate cases of national importance under diversity jurisdiction*'; and, thirdly, to '*benefit society by encouraging innovation and lowering consumer prices*'.[176] **6.169**

Put otherwise, the underpinning aim of CAFA was to deter the bringing of unmeritorious cases that ultimately inflated settlement and civil awards as well as legal bills in the US. It was hoped that this endeavour would be achieved by fine-tuning the procedural mechanisms in place. In fact, as envisaged, through the tightening of the requisite conditions for class actions, CAFA shifted cases **6.170**

174 Hannah Buxbaum, 'Multinational Class Actions under Federal Securities Law: Managing Jurisdictional Conflict' (2007) 46 Columbia Journal of Transnational Law 14, at 32.

175 Stephen B. Burbank, 'International Civil Litigation in U.S. Courts: Becoming a Paper Tiger?' (2012) 33(3) U. Pa. J. Int'l L. 663, at 669.

176 Public Law 109–2, §2(b)(1)-(3).

which might ordinarily have been dealt with at state level to the federal level. As one commentator has noted, '*CAFA has taken care of most of the mischief, real or imagined, perpetrated by state courts in large class actions*'.[177]

6.171 CAFA also made it far more likely that claims brought under State antitrust laws (typically by indirect purchasers) would be litigated alongside direct purchaser claims. This is because CAFA effectively relaxed the jurisdictional rules that had precluded claimants from bringing State law claims in federal court. Thus one additional consequence of CAFA is the proliferation of complex cases in federal court involving both direct and indirect claimants.

6.172 Whilst CAFA has reduced the inconsistency between class actions at state and federal level by redirecting national and multistate actions to federal court, this new-found consistency is threatened *inter alia* by recent splits between different circuits on the issue of class certification under Rule 23 and the use of aggregate proof in the class action certification process.[178] CAFA has not therefore been an unqualified success.

6.173 As a matter of policy, therefore, the measures implemented in the US through CAFA to curb the gratuitous use of class actions have in fact coincided with the attempts described above in the EU to expand the use of collective actions.

177 Burbank, *loc cit*.

178 See J. Britton Whitbeck, 'Identity Crisis: Class Certification, Aggregate Proof, and How Rule 23 May Be Self-defeating the Policy for Which It Was Established' (2012) 32(2) Pace Law Review 488, at 490.

7

PRIVATE INTERNATIONAL LAW ASPECTS*

I CHOICE OF COURT 7.005
- A The governing law: Regulation 44/2001 7.006
- B Variety of choices of court 7.010
- C The application of Regulation 44/2001 to parties domiciled outside the EU 7.013
- D General jurisdiction: Article 2(1) 7.016
- E Special jurisdiction: Article 5(3) and Article 6(1) 7.018
- F Founding jurisdiction in tortious actions: Article 5(3) 7.023
  - 1 The application of the *Bier/Shevill* jurisprudence to competition-based litigation 7.026
  - 2 Article 5(3) as a basis for torpedo litigation 7.037
- G Consolidation of claims: Article 6(1) 7.042
  - 1 The English authorities on Article 6(1) 7.043
    - a Interpretation of the EU law concept of 'undertaking' 7.045
    - b Causation 7.050
  - 2 The application of Article 6(1) by the Dutch courts 7.052
- H *Lis pendens* 7.053
  - 1 *Lis pendens* I: Article 27 7.055
  - 2 *Lis pendens* II: Article 28 7.063
    - a Irreconcilability for the purposes of Article 28(3) 7.066
    - b Connected but not identical actions 7.068
    - c The English authorities on Article 28 7.072
    - d Article 28 and the Commission proposal 7.077
  - 3 The application of *lis pendens* to parties domiciled outside the EU 7.081
- I The review of Regulation 44/2001 7.083
  - 1 *Lis pendens* 7.083
  - 2 Litigation involving parties domiciled outside the EU 7.086

II APPLICABLE LAW 7.092
- A The Rome II Regulation and the *lex fori* approach 7.094
  - 1 The general rule: Article 4 7.097
  - 2 Competition-based litigation: Article 6(3) 7.099
    - a Functioning of Article 6(3)(b) 7.102
    - b US law 7.112
  - 3 The desirability of the *lex fori* approach 7.114
- B Alternative solutions: the effects-based approach 7.119
  - 1 Article 6(3)(a) of the Rome II Regulation 7.122
  - 2 Problems with the effects-based approach: *Mosaikbetrachtung* 7.124
  - 3 *Mosaikbetrachtung* as a concurrent matter of jurisdiction and applicable law 7.128

This chapter deals with the questions of jurisdiction and applicable law in claims based on an infringement of EU competition law. Competition-based litigation will often feature a single infringement whose effects cut across national boundaries. The international nature of the underlying infringement of substantive law is at odds with the national remedial and procedural rules for the enforcement of obligations arising out of that substantive law. For this reason, rules on jurisdiction and applicable law are important for such litigation. **7.001**

* This chapter is based on Ashton, David and Vollrath, Christian, 'Choice of court and applicable law in tortious actions for breach of Community competition law' (2006) 1 ZWeR 1.

Jurisdiction will determine which court will hear the case. As courts in principle will always apply their own procedural law, rules on jurisdiction will determine the procedural conditions under which a claim for damages based on an infringement of EU competition law will be brought. Rules on applicable law will determine the substantive civil law which will provide the conditions for the claim.

7.002 In the current state of EU law, there exists a set of harmonised rules concerning jurisdiction in civil litigation.[1] There is also a harmonised set of rules on applicable law in non-contractual disputes,[2] adopted on 11 July 2007, and which has applied since 11 January 2009.[3] This chapter will examine how these rules apply to damages claims based on an infringement of EU competition law.

7.003 It should be borne in mind that in the *Empagran* proceedings,[4] the US Supreme Court ruled that the Foreign Trade Antitrust Improvements Act precluded foreign purchasers from bringing damages actions in the US, where injury is independent of any adverse domestic effect. This means that the US courts are not available to hear damages actions in relation to anti-competitive behaviour where the harm being pleaded is suffered outside the US.

7.004 Finally, for the reasons set out in Chapter 2, it should be borne in mind that actions for breach of EU competition law are generally classified as tortious. For these reasons, in this chapter, only certain provisions of Regulation 44/2001 are relevant, and the Rome II Regulation is treated to the exclusion of the Rome I Regulation.[5]

---

1 Council Regulation (EC) No 44/2001 of 22 December 2000 on jurisdiction and the recognition and enforcement of judgments in civil and commercial matters (OJ L 12, 16.1.2001, p 1). This has been repealed by Regulation (EU) No 1215/2012 of the European Parliament and of the Council of 12 December 2012 on jurisdiction and the recognition and enforcement of judgments in civil and commercial matters (recast) (OJ L 351, 20.12.2012, p 1), which, according to its Article 81, applies from 10 January 2015. For ease of reference, we have chosen to keep the references to the provisions of Regulation 44/2001 apart from the section dealing with its review, where references to the numbering of Regulation 1215/2012 are, by necessity, used.

2 Regulation (EC) No 864/2007 of the European Parliament and of the Council of 11 July 2007 on the law applicable to non-contractual obligations (Rome II) (OJ L 199, 31.7.2007, p 40).

3 Article 32. Pursuant to the judgment of the ECJ in Case C-412/10 *Homawoo* v *GMF Assurances* (not yet reported) at para 30, the Regulation entered into force on the 20th day after that of its publication, that is 20 August 2007.

4 See the decision of the US Supreme Court, and the decision of the US Court of Appeals for the District of Columbia in *Empagran S.A.* v *F. Hoffmann-LaRoche Ltd.* 417 F. 3d 1267 (DC Cir 2005).

5 Regulation (EC) No 593/2008 of the European Parliament and of the Council of 17 June 2008 on the law applicable to contractual obligations (Rome I) (OJ L 177, 4.7.2008, p 6).

I CHOICE OF COURT

Since competition-based litigation will often feature a single infringement whose effects cut across national boundaries, the parties in litigation based on such an infringement will often have a wide variety of courts in which they can, as they choose, bring the action, as will be shown below. **7.005**

A The governing law: Regulation 44/2001

The governing instrument as a matter of EU law for jurisdiction and choice of court is Regulation 44/2001. This Regulation, which entered into force on 1 March 2002, replaced and modified the 1968 Brussels Convention on jurisdiction and the enforcement of judgments in civil and commercial matters[6] with respect to determination of jurisdiction as between the courts of the Member States. **7.006**

Regulation 44/2001 lays down uniform rules of jurisdiction for all defendants domiciled in a Member State.[7] It applies to all Member States with the exception of Denmark.[8] A defendant domiciled in Denmark remains subject to the Brussels Convention. **7.007**

Regulation 44/2001 applies to civil and commercial matters whatever the nature of the tribunal.[9] Antitrust claims are not included in the list of exceptions at Article 1(2) (though arbitration proceedings are). The Commission's notice on cooperation with the national courts recalls that Regulation 44/2001 '*is applicable to all competition cases of a civil or commercial nature*'.[10] Competition-based damages claims must be seen as being of such a nature. The Regulation is **7.008**

6 Consolidated version, OJ L 299, 31.12.1972, p 32. The Brussels Convention was an international treaty concluded on the basis of Article 220 of the EEC Treaty (Article 293 EC, repealed by the Lisbon Treaty). Recital 19 to Regulation 44/2001 calls for continuity between the case law interpreting the Brussels Convention and the Regulation. The Lugano Convention on jurisdiction and the enforcement of judgments in civil and commercial matters of 16 September 1988 (OJ L 319, 25.11.1988, p 9) was a parallel international treaty between the Member States of the (then) European Community and the European Free Trade Association. It was replaced by the new Lugano Convention of 30 October 2007 (OJ L 339, 21.12.2007, p 3), which originated from the same considerations as had led the Brussels Convention to be adapted into Regulation 44/2001. Pursuant to its Article 69(4), the new Lugano Convention entered into force for the EU and Norway on 1 January 2010. Pursuant to Article 69(5), it entered into force for Denmark also on 1 January 2010, for Switzerland on 1 January 2011, and for Iceland on 1 May 2011.

7 Article 2. The special jurisdiction rules in Article 5(3) and Article 6(1) also apply to '*persons domiciled in a Member State*' (for the meaning of the term 'Member State', see below).

8 Article 1(3) defines the term 'Member State' as meaning '*Member States with the exception of Denmark*'.

9 Article 1(1).

10 *Loc. cit.*, at footnote 4. Cf. the previous notice on cooperation between national courts and the Commission in applying Articles 85 and 86 of the Treaty (OJ C 39, 13.2.1993, p 6), at point 44 (in relation to the Brussels Convention), taking broadly the same position.

a maximum harmonisation instrument which leaves no room for higher standards, such as for example a rule of *forum non conveniens* whereby a court that has jurisdiction under Regulation 44/2001 could seek to decline to exercise it on the ground that it is not an appropriate forum in the case in hand.[11]

7.009 The effect of the judgment of the ECJ in *Owusu* concerning the doctrine of *forum non conveniens* will be that in proceedings brought, for example, by a US-domiciled company against a company domiciled in England, the English court could not decline jurisdiction on the basis that the US was the more suitable forum (a result which might be reached on the basis of consideration of factors such as the location of evidence and witnesses). It can be said that *Owusu* enlarges EU jurisdiction against the jurisdiction of non-EU courts, though its effect can perhaps be seen as being at the margins.

B Variety of choices of court

7.010 In the vast majority of cases of infringement of EU competition law, parties to the dispute will have a choice of more than one court in which to litigate the action. The exact nature of this choice is explored below. It suffices for the time being to explain that in cartel cases and other types of conduct based on multilateral behaviour, there will almost always be more than one court available for the action. This is because, in order for there to be the requisite effect on cross-border trade for Article 101 TFEU to come into play at all, there will normally be parties to the infringing agreement based in more than one Member State. The only exception is where parties based in a single Member State conclude an infringing agreement which has effects beyond the borders of that Member State, and even in these circumstances there will only be one court available in the unlikely event that the prospective claimant itself has suffered damage in the same Member State again. This becomes almost impossible if the *Provimi* test of causation is applied (see further below), such that a potential claimant can be said to have suffered damage as the result of an agreement which infringes Article 101 TFEU even where that claimant has not made a purchase from the infringing parties.

7.011 As for actions based on Article 102 TFEU, again in the majority of cases there will be a choice of court open to the claimant, though perhaps less systematically so than in the case of an infringement of Article 101 TFEU. Again, no choice will be open to the claimant only, as a rule, in the situation where it and the defendant are from the same Member State, and the cross-border effects of the abuse in question are not being litigated.

---

11 See Case C-281/02 *Owusu* v *Jackson and others* [2005] ECR I-1383, at paras 37–46.

The two most attractive solutions to the problem of parallel proceedings under the law as it currently stands are consolidation under Article 6(1) of Regulation 44/2001, and the operation of *lis pendens*, primarily under Article 28. However, neither are panaceas. Article 28 offers momentary relief to the defendant while certain issues are tried in the main proceedings, before the case returns to the second court, if that court has ordered a stay. Article 6(1) may allow for consolidation of claims relating to the same substantive infringement, depending on exactly how that provision is applied by the national courts, but it offers the choice of such consolidation only to the claimant and not the defendant. The defendant faced with multiple litigation in different jurisdictions cannot make use of Article 6(1) but only hope that the national court applies Article 28, and, if applicable, Article 27. Most importantly, forum shopping in all scenarios is an issue because the procedural rules of the different jurisdictions are not the same. Consolidation before one jurisdiction may be desirable, but if one jurisdiction is more attractive than others then the vast majority of consolidated actions can be expected to take place there. **7.012**

C The application of Regulation 44/2001 to parties domiciled outside the EU

A defendant not domiciled in a Member State is in general subject to the national rules of jurisdiction applicable in the territory of the Member State seized.[12] The only exceptions to the rule that Regulation 44/2001 applies only when the defendant is domiciled in a Member State are the rules on exclusive jurisdiction (Article 22, applying to certain specific claims such as *in rem* claims), and Article 23 on jurisdiction agreements, which requires that only one of the parties, regardless of identity, be domiciled in a Member State. **7.013**

Therefore an action against a company domiciled outside the EU would not be governed by the provisions of Regulation 44/2001. This does not cover the case where the defendant is a subsidiary domiciled in a Member State of a parent company domiciled outside the EU. Under Article 60(1) of Regulation 44/2001 (see further below), a firm domiciled outside the EU would not be considered to be domiciled in a Member State for the purposes of Regulation 44/2001 on the strength of the fact that it was only doing business in Europe. **7.014**

On the other hand, it is settled law that an action brought by a company domiciled outside the EU against a company domiciled within the EU is covered by the scope of Regulation 44/2001, the place of domicile of the claimant being generally irrelevant (at least for the application of the general **7.015**

12 Article 4(1).

rule of jurisdiction on the basis of the place of the defendant's domicile under Article 2).[13]

D General jurisdiction: Article 2(1)

7.016 The basic principle under Regulation 44/2001 is that persons domiciled in a Member State may be sued in that State, irrespective of their nationality.[14] The domicile of the claimant, by contrast, is generally irrelevant for the purposes of Regulation 44/2001 (the most relevant exception being the additional protection provided to consumers). Domicile is determined in accordance with the internal law of the Member State where the court has been seized.[15]

7.017 A company or other legal person or association of natural or legal persons is domiciled at the place where it has its (i) statutory seat, (ii) central administration, or (iii) principal place of business.[16]

E Special jurisdiction: Article 5(3) and Article 6(1)

7.018 There are also special jurisdiction rules, which constitute alternative options for the claimant to the basic principle of suing the defendant in his Member State of domicile.[17]

7.019 In matters relating to tort, delict or quasi-delict (for example, unjust enrichment) a person domiciled in a Member State may be sued in the court of another Member State in the place where the harmful event occurred or may occur.[18] As regards a civil claim for damages or restitution which is based on an act giving rise to criminal proceedings, a person domiciled in a Member State may be sued in the courts of another Member State where such court is seized of the proceedings, to the extent that that court has jurisdiction under its own law to entertain civil proceedings.[19] As regards a dispute arising out of the operations of a branch, agency or other establishment, a person domiciled in a

---

13 See the judgment of the ECJ in Case C-412/98 *UGIC* v *Group Josi* [2000] ECR I-5925.

14 Article 2(1).

15 Article 59(1).

16 Article 60(1).

17 That Article 5(3) and Article 6(1) provide bases for founding jurisdiction which are alternative to one another is apparent from the scheme of Regulation 44/2001, Article 6 of which provides that the claimant may '*also*' seek to found jurisdiction on the basis of that Article.

18 Article 5(3).

19 Article 5(4). The *partie civile* proceedings known to France and other Member States in the same legal family are relevant in this regard.

Member State may be sued in the courts for the place in which the branch, agency or other establishment is situated.[20]

Founding jurisdiction on the basis of Article 2 leads to a single jurisdiction for the action, though it may *a priori* be desirable for the claimant to seek to found jurisdiction away from the place of domicile of the defendant. **7.020**

The general jurisdiction rule of Article 2 is the basic rule. It is at the option of the claimant to seek to found jurisdiction in the alternative on the basis of one of the heads of special jurisdiction. None of the heads of special jurisdiction imposes an obligation or even a discretion on the court, for example a court seized on the basis of Article 2, to decline jurisdiction where the conditions of one or other of those articles respectively are met. Neither does Article 2 contain any provision to this effect. If the claimant chooses to found jurisdiction on the basis of Article 2 when, for example, Article 6(1) would have been available to him had he so chosen, then the choice on the basis of Article 2 is final. **7.021**

It follows that it is not open to the defendant to challenge the claimant's choice of jurisdiction merely on the basis that one of the special bases of jurisdiction provided for in the Regulation was available. **7.022**

F Founding jurisdiction in tortious actions: Article 5(3)

The ECJ has held that for the purposes of Article 5(3) the place where the harmful event occurred can be either (a) the place where the event giving rise to the damage occurred or (b) the place where the damage itself occurred (at the option of the claimant).[21] **7.023**

In *Shevill*, the ECJ held, in relation to a defamation claim, that the place where the event giving rise to the damage occurred (limb (a)) was the place of establishment of the publisher,[22] and that the place where the damage occurred (limb (b)) was the place(s) where the offending publication was distributed and where consequently the claimant suffered damage to his reputation (being the foundation of a defamation claim).[23] Thus it can be seen that limb (a) refers to **7.024**

---

20 Article 5(5).

21 Case 21/76 *Bier* v *Mines de Potasse d'Alsace* [1976] ECR 1735, at paras 24–25; Case C-68/93 *Fiona Shevill and others* v *Press Alliance SA* [1995] ECR I-415, at para 20.

22 As observed by the Court, this will '*generally*' give the same jurisdictional result as Article 2, namely the place of domicile of the defendant.

23 *Shevill*, at paras 19–33. The Court has held that limb (b) does not allow for a claim of jurisdiction by the claimant in his place of domicile on the grounds that the place where the damage was sustained is the place of

the place of acting, so to speak, while limb (b) refers to the place where the resulting loss is actually suffered.

7.025 Furthermore, the Court held that were the claimant to choose to found jurisdiction in the place where the event giving rise to the damage occurred (that is, the place of establishment of the publisher), that court, being the only court seized of the matter, would have jurisdiction to award damages for all of the loss suffered by the claimant in all places where the offending publication had been distributed, but that were the claimant to choose to found jurisdiction on the basis of the place where the damage occurred (that is, the different places where the publication had been distributed), then in that case the various courts seized would have jurisdiction only to award damages for the injury suffered on their respective territories, on the grounds that each individual court would be better placed to assess and award damages in respect of its own territory.[24]

1 *The application of the* Bier/Shevill *jurisprudence to competition-based litigation*

7.026 In competition-based litigation, different and legitimate applications of Article 5(3) will lead to different results. Under limb (a) of the *Bier/Shevill* jurisprudence, the place where the event giving rise to the damage occurred could be that where the agreement, in the case of actions for breach of Article 101 TFEU, was concluded. Alternatively, it could be that where the agreement was put into operation,[25] analogously to the place where the abuse took place in an action for breach of Article 102 TFEU.

7.027 It has been argued that the place of operation of the agreement, rather than the place of its conclusion, is the better test for foundation of jurisdiction, as this would result in a closer nexus between the court having jurisdiction and the affected market.[26] Against this view, in *Bord Na Mona*, the English High Court appears to assume that the place where the event giving rise to the damage

---

business (that is, the bank account/financial nerve centre) of the claimant. See for example the Opinion of AG Warner in Case 814/79 *Netherlands* v *Ruffer* [1980] ECR 3807; Case C-220/88 *Dumez France* v *Hessische Landesbank* [1990] ECR I-49; and Case C-364/93 *Marinari* v *Lloyds Bank* [1995] ECR I-2719. It should be noted that in *Marinari*, this was held to be the case where the damage both arose and was suffered by the same claimant in another Member State (para 14). This appears to have been implicitly accepted in an antitrust context by the decision of the English High Court in *Bord Na Mona* (see para 87).

24 *Shevill*, para 25 and paras 31–32.

25 See Joined Cases C-89/85, C-104/85, C-114/85, C-116/85, C-117/85 and C-125–129/85 *A Ahlström Osakeyhtiö and others* v *Commission* (*Wood Pulp I*) [1988] ECR 5193 for the significance of the place of implementation of an agreement to the evaluation of the substantive reach of EU competition law.

26 C. Withers, 'Jurisdiction and Applicable Law in Antitrust Tort Claims' [2002] JBL 250.

occurred was the place where the infringement was concluded.[27] On this basis, the judge dismisses limb (a) of *Bier/Shevill* as a valid grounds for founding jurisdiction, preferring instead to examine limb (b), since limb (a) would lead to an excessive number of potential places with jurisdiction. This part of the judgment is, it should be recalled, *obiter*, as founding of jurisdiction on the specific facts of that case pursuant to Article 6(1) was possible.

Alternatively, under limb (b), jurisdiction can be claimed in the Member State where the claimant suffered loss. This could be, depending on the nature of the infringement, the market from which it was excluded, or the place where it paid the higher price. **7.028**

The solution of the place where the higher price was paid appears to have been applied by the English High Court in *Bord Na Mona*, where the judge accepted that the place where the higher price was paid (the UK, or specifically Scotland) was the correct place to found jurisdiction under Article 5(3).[28] This conclusion was, again, *obiter*. **7.029**

Furthermore, the situation in relation to limb (b) becomes extremely flexible if one accepts the *Provimi* ruling on causation[29] in the case of cartel/excessive pricing cases where there was no purchase by the claimant, where jurisdiction could be founded in a Member State on the basis that loss occurred there since the claimant could have paid a lower price there. In the case of a pan-European cartel, this could conceivably be in any Member State, which leads to relatively unrestrained freedom to forum shop in proceedings relating to pan-European cartels or other abuses with effects felt throughout Europe. **7.030**

The jurisdictional result under limb (b) and under the implementation interpretation of limb (a) of *Bier/Shevill* might in certain circumstances be the same. The same goes for exclusionary abuses. **7.031**

Were the claimant to choose to found jurisdiction under limb (b) of *Bier/Shevill*, then as the law stands at present, under *Shevill* the court seized would only be able to award damages for the loss suffered in its territory.[30] In the case of an infringement with pan-European effects this would require the claimant **7.032**

---

27 Para 86.

28 Paras 87 and 90.

29 See further below.

30 This was considered *obiter* by the judge in *Cooper Tire & Rubber Company and others* v *Shell Chemicals UK Limited and others* [2009] EWHC 2609 (Comm), at para 65: '… *it is also common ground that if jurisdiction is established on that basis [Article 5(3)] it is only established in respect of the damage which occurred in England. That is, I understand, a very small part of the whole.*'

to launch parallel actions in all the Member States in which he suffered loss. The rules on *lis pendens* may help, though in these circumstances it may be the case that the stay of proceedings is as to liability, while quantification of the award remains within the competence of the court which has made the stay.

7.033 In addition and concurrently, applying the implementation interpretation of limb (a) of *Bier/Shevill* to competition-related litigation, the claimant would also presumably be faced with a multitude of jurisdictions in which to bring actions as there would in most cases be no single Member State in which the abuse in question was implemented.[31] Differently from the tort in question in *Shevill*, it would be impossible in a competition context to find a single jurisdiction in which the harmful event occurred as the multiplicity of actors involved, as well as the substantive scope of EU competition law, would normally exclude such a result.

7.034 Founding jurisdiction in the court of the place where the infringement was concluded under limb (a) could, applying *Shevill*, lead to a single jurisdiction in relation to all the damage suffered by the claimant, though the place of conclusion, as noted above, may be arbitrary and there is no reason why on a systematic basis there should be a connection between that place and the place of domicile of either of the parties or of the place where the damage was actually suffered. The advantage of a single jurisdiction may be offset in the individual case by the actual court available, and on a systematic basis the same advantage is offset in the same way by the arbitrary nature of the choice.

7.035 Moreover, there is no reason why there should be a single place of agreement in the case of, for example, a cartel operated over a significant period of time and with several meetings taking place in a variety of locations.[32] In this case, in order to found jurisdiction under this interpretation of limb (a) of *Shevill*, the claimant would additionally need to show that the damage he suffered arose as a result of the specific meeting which took place in the forum whose courts he is seeking to use. It would seem furthermore that, in such a situation, the jurisdictional limit applied by the court to limb (b) in *Shevill* would have also to apply to limb (a).

7.036 It is therefore submitted that the application of the *Bier/Shevill* jurisprudence of the ECJ to competition-based litigation leads to the conclusion that the claimant will be forced to launch parallel actions in a number of Member States

---

31 See also Basedow, Jürgen, 'International Cartels and the Place of Acting under Article 5(3) of the Brussels I Regulation', in Basedow, Francq and Idot, *loc. cit.*, 31, at 34.

32 For such a factual scenario, see again the judgment of the English High Court in *Cooper Tire*, at para 65.

in relation to the same underlying infringement. This is the case under limb (b) of *Bier/Shevill* as the law currently stands, that is, if the claimant chooses to found jurisdiction in the place where the loss is suffered, but it is submitted that in a competition context, limb (a) of *Bier/Shevill* will in most cases, and perhaps even preferably from a policy perspective, be emasculated to the point where the unifying effect of *Shevill* disappears. If the place where the event giving rise to the damage is considered to be where the anti-competitive behaviour is implemented, this will be the case. If it is considered to be the place where the anti-competitive behaviour was concluded, which is often perceived as the worse view, only in certain limited scenarios can a single place of jurisdiction be founded on the basis of Article 5(3).

2 *Article 5(3) as a basis for torpedo litigation*

The ECJ recently gave judgment in proceedings which had raised the question of whether Article 5(3) could be used to found jurisdiction in an action for a declaration that certain behaviour is not unlawful.[33] **7.037**

The proceedings concerned an alleged violation of competition law in relation to the defendant's distribution policy, as well as its refusal to grant patents. The claimants sought damages before the Italian courts in relation to the former issue. The action for a negative declaration was brought first, and the action seeking damages and a grant of patents was then stayed pursuant to Article 27, the parties to the two sets of proceedings being identical. **7.038**

The question considered by the ECJ was the narrow point as to whether jurisdiction to hear an action for a negative declaration could be founded on Article 5(3). The defendants had brought that action before the German courts on the basis, apparently, that the affected market was the German market.[34] Neither the defendants nor the claimants were domiciled in Germany. **7.039**

33 Case C-133/11 *Folien Fischer AG and Fofitec AG* v *Ritrama SpA*, judgment of 25 October 2012 (not yet reported). See also the *Cooper Tire* proceedings, where the question considered by the English court was that of whether proceedings should be stayed under Article 28 (*lis pendens*) after some of the cartelists had commenced proceedings before the Italian courts for declarations, *inter alia*, that they were not liable in damages to the claimants.

34 It is therefore possible to see, in this case, an implicit application of an effects-based approach to jurisdiction (see, for example, para 52 of the Court's judgment). As is argued below, the same approach should be applied to the law applicable to the claim in a competition-law context. This would then lead to the determination of both jurisdiction and applicable law on such a basis, the former being determined by Article 5(3) of Regulation 44/2001, and the latter by Article 6(3)(a) of the Rome II Regulation.

7.040 Despite the fact that the Advocate-General had argued for the opposite outcome,[35] the Court held that the action was well-founded. The Court held that it was immaterial that the usual roles in the proceedings were reversed (that is, in an action for a negative declaration, the party that would normally be the claimant was the defendant, and *vice versa*),[36] particularly given the fact that the type of action in question did not have any specific consumer protection aspect.[37] Furthermore, the Court based its decision on the premise that the '*same matters of law and fact*' were being applied in the action for a negative declaration as would be applied in the normal action for damages or other form of relief sought.[38]

7.041 By analogy, as recalled by the Court at paragraph 49 of its judgment in *Folien Fischer*, it should also be remembered that, in the context of *lis pendens* (see further below), Article 27 had been held by the Court to apply to an action for a negative declaration in *The Tatry*.[39]

G Consolidation of claims: Article 6(1)

7.042 Furthermore, a person domiciled in a Member State may also be sued, where he is one of a number of co-defendants, in the courts for the place where any one of them is domiciled, provided the claims are '*so closely connected that it is expedient to hear and determine them together to avoid the risk of irreconcilable judgments resulting from separate proceedings*'.[40] Alternatively, such a person may be sued on a counter-claim arising from the same contract or facts on which the original claim was based in the court in which the original claim is pending.[41]

1 The English authorities on Article 6(1)

7.043 In the *Provimi* proceedings, the English High Court held that a series of different claims resulting from the same cartel (the vitamins cartel) were

---

35 The Advocate-General's point of view was based *inter alia* on the argument that jurisdiction could not be founded on Article 5(3) in relation to an action alleging the absence of liability (see for example para 50 of the Opinion, within the section entitled '*Literal interpretation of Article 5(3) of Regulation (EC) 44/2001*'). The ECJ dealt with this point specifically at para 55 of its judgment.

36 Para 44.

37 Para 46.

38 Para 48.

39 Case C-406/92 *The Tatry* [1994] ECR I-5439.

40 Article 6(1). This condition is a codification of Case 189/87 *Athanasios Kalfelis* v *Bankhaus Schröder, Münchmeyer, Hengst and Co and others* [1988] ECR 5565, para 12, interpreting Article 6(1) of the Brussels Convention. The *Kalfelis* judgment took its language from Article 22 of the Convention, that is, Article 28(3) of the Regulation, as it did not appear in Article 6(1) of the Convention.

41 Article 6(3). The damages claim in the *Crehan* proceedings was in the form of a counter-claim (the main claim being for non-payment of monies due under the beer tie contract).

sufficiently closely connected for Article 6(1) to apply. Furthermore, the court held that, in the absence of any evidence as to the case law on the conditions for damages claims in the other relevant Member States (Germany and France) and as to the interpretation of substantive concepts such as the level of knowledge required on the part of the infringer in the law of those Member States, there was sufficient risk of irreconcilable judgments for Article 6(1) to apply. Finally, the court held that it was '*expedient*' to hear the different claims together to avoid the risk of irreconcilable judgments from different national courts.[42] The view of the English court in short was that claims made by different parties in different Member States but resulting from the same pan-European cartel could be heard by one court in one Member State under Article 6(1).

The conclusions of the judge in *Provimi* on the application of Article 6(1) should, however, be treated with caution, for two reasons. **7.044**

a Interpretation of the EU law concept of 'undertaking'

Firstly, in order to find an infringement of Article 101 TFEU, the judge applied an interpretation of the term 'undertaking' based on EU competition law, making no distinction between parent and subsidiary.[43] This leads to the result, in terms of founding jurisdiction, that almost any Member State becomes a possible venue for an action brought against a large multinational with a pan-European presence and renders the idea of founding jurisdiction in the Member State of domicile under Article 2 of Regulation 44/2001 almost meaningless.[44] **7.045**

In the judgment of the English High Court in *Cooper Tire*, the judge followed the conclusions of *Provimi* as to the use of the notion of 'undertaking' to found jurisdiction pursuant to Article 6(1). **7.046**

The broad notion of 'undertaking' used in substantive EU competition law has its uses insofar as it allows the Commission to impose fines on the entity within a corporate structure which is most likely to be able to pay, and prevents **7.047**

42 See paras 47–49 of the judgment.

43 See para 31 of the judgment.

44 It is worth noting that strike-out actions were not brought against the English defendants where the claimant had purchased from the defendant in question, despite the fact that those defendants were equally subsidiaries of the parent company which was implementing the cartel, meaning that in those cases, the defendants appear to have accepted that the subsidiary could be liable for damages resulting from the infringement even when it had not been shown that that subsidiary was aware of the infringement (see Wilderspin, Michael, 'Jurisdiction Issues: Brussels I Regulation Articles 6(1), 23, 27 and 28 in Antitrust Litigation', in Basedow, Francq and Idot, *loc. cit.*, 41 at 46).

companies from escaping liability by creating subsidiaries to which the infringing activities are assigned.[45] The Commission justifies this approach on the basis that parent companies exercise actual decisive influence over their subsidiaries, such that the latter do not act as independent entities.[46]

7.048 However, this approach is of more dubious validity when applied to private law claims. In the context of the fine, it is often, if not always, the behaviour of the subsidiary which is attributed to the parent, which is usually the object of the fine. In the context of the private law claim, this operation will often take place the other way round, for example, in the factual scenario of *Provimi*, the behaviour of the parent is attributed to the subsidiary which is the subject of the litigation. Assuming influence on the part of the parent over the subsidiary is a very different matter from assuming influence on the part of the subsidiary over the parent.[47]

7.049 In fact, the English courts appear to be moving towards this sort of conclusion. In both the judgment of the Court of Appeal in the *Cooper Tire* proceedings and its recent *Toshiba* judgment, the view has been expressed firstly that knowledge on the part of the defendant is required to found a damages claim, and secondly that knowledge of the conduct of the parent cannot automatically be imputed to a subsidiary.[48]

b Causation

7.050 Secondly, the judge in *Provimi* applied a very generous interpretation of the notion of causation in order to preserve the central claim (and thereby allow for the consolidation in the English courts sought by the claimants on the basis of Article 2).[49] In the claim brought by the German claimant against the English subsidiary, there had not actually been any purchase from that subsidiary by the

45 As noted by the English Court of Appeal in *Cooper Tire & Rubber Company and others* v *Dow Deutschland and others* [2010] EWCA Civ 864, at para 34.

46 Case C-107/82 *AEG Telefunken AG* v *Commission* [1983] ECR 3151, in which it was held that, in order to be able to impute the conduct of a subsidiary to a parent company, the Commission cannot merely find that the parent company is in a position to exercise decisive influence over the conduct of its subsidiary, but must also check whether that influence was *actually* exercised (para 50).

47 See Bulst, Wenzel, 'The Provimi Decision of the High Court: Beginnings of Antitrust Litigation in Europe' 4 EBOLR (2003) 623, 638.

48 *Cooper Tire*, at paras 45–47; *Toshiba Carrier UK Ltd and others* v *KME Yorkshire Limited and others* [2012] EWCA Civ 1190, at para 37. In both cases, the Court of Appeal considers the second point *obiter*, holding that the first point is satisfied insofar as the claim alleges that the relevant defendant had knowledge of the infringement. Since the proceedings in both cases are preliminary hearings on jurisdiction, it is not necessary for the Court to go further into the issue than this. In *Cooper Tire*, the Court of Appeal adds that a reference to the ECJ would have been necessary had it had to decide on the issue.

49 It is interesting that the judge does not rely on the same notion of 'undertaking' at this stage of his reasoning in the judgment.

claimant in question. Nevertheless, the judge found that that claimant could be held to have suffered a loss at the hands of that subsidiary since if that subsidiary had not charged at the cartel price, the claimant would have bought from it at a reduced price. This stretches the notion of causation to its logical limit and again allows very wide freedom to forum shop.[50]

The problematic point on causation from *Provimi* did not apply in the *Cooper Tire* case as sales had been made by the English-domiciled defendants, though the judge at first instance did remark that these were '*small*'.[51] He apparently saw no difficulty in the use of the claim against the three English-domiciled defendants as a '*tactic*' to found jurisdiction against the remaining defendants pursuant to Article 6(1).[52] **7.051**

2 *The application of Article 6(1) by the Dutch courts*

A result similar to those reached by the English courts in *Provimi* and *Cooper Tire* has also been seen in the Dutch courts. In its judgment of 1 May 2013, the *Rechtbank* of The Hague, in deciding to apply Article 6(1), held that it had to be taken into account whether the defendants had acted independently of one another when they caused the damage. The court found that the claims against all defendants arose from a single EU law infringement, since cartels are always the result of common action and a common understanding, liability being founded on a direct infringement or actions of the parent company. Furthermore, the court held that the positions of all the defendant addressees of the Commission Decision in this case were comparable with one another, and not sufficiently different to justify that Article 6(1) not be applied. **7.052**

H *Lis pendens*

The rules on *lis pendens* do not solve the problem of forum shopping in competition-based litigation under the law at present. What they can do however is offer some relief for the defendant who is exposed to litigation from more than one party based in more than one Member State by ensuring that that defendant is not the subject of multiple litigation in more than one **7.053**

---

50 This same causation point was answered in the opposite way by the US Court of Appeals on remand from the Supreme Court in the *Empagran* litigation, applying a more stringent test than a simple but-for test of causation.

51 *Cooper Tire* at para 38.

52 *Cooper Tire* at para 35: '*Counsel for the Dow Defendants said that it was plain that the three Defendants domiciled in England ... had been selected as a tactical device ... to establish jurisdiction against the other Defendants pursuant to Article 6(1) of the Judgments Regulation. This does appear to be likely ... However, the question for the Court is whether it is a tactic which has succeeded in establishing jurisdiction over the Dow Defendants.*'

Member State in relation to the same infringement. Whether or not this will be the case, and the extent to which it shall be, depends on the interpretation of the relevant provisions of Regulation 44/2001 by the courts. It should be remembered that the rules on *lis pendens* are not themselves grounds for founding jurisdiction, but exceptions to the usual rules on the founding of jurisdiction. They can only lead to consolidation through the operation of the law of the first court seized under Article 28 of Regulation 44/2001 (see further below).

7.054 *Lis pendens* is governed within the scheme of Regulation 44/2001 by Articles 27 and 28.[53] Under Article 27 of Regulation 44/2001, if proceedings concerning the same cause of action and between the same parties are brought in the courts of different Member States, any court other than the court first seized must of its own motion stay its proceedings until the jurisdiction of the court first seized is determined.[54] If the jurisdiction of the court first seized is established, any other court must decline jurisdiction in favour of that court.[55] Under Article 28, where '*related actions*' are pending in the courts of more than one Member State, the court second seized may stay proceedings and may, on the application of one of the parties, decline jurisdiction if the court first seized has jurisdiction and is able under its own law to consolidate the claims. Actions are deemed to be related where they are '*so closely connected that it is expedient to hear and determine them together to avoid the risk of irreconcilable judgments resulting from separate proceedings*'.[56] Where actions come within the exclusive jurisdiction of several courts, any court other than the court first seized must decline jurisdiction in favour of that court.[57]

1 Lis pendens *I: Article 27*

7.055 In relation to the provision of Article 27 as to '*same cause of action*', the ECJ has held that this is satisfied when the different actions have the same facts and rule of law relied on as the basis for the action.[58] The French language version of

---

53 The equivalent provisions in the Brussels Convention, Articles 21 and 22 respectively, are for all practical purposes, and such purposes as are relevant to this analysis, identical in wording to Articles 27 and 28 of Regulation 44/2001. There is as yet no case law of the EU courts on the interpretation of Articles 27 and 28 of Regulation 44/2001. The case law of the ECJ on Articles 21 and 22 of the Brussels Convention, which does exist, can be applied to the interpretation of Articles 27 and 28 of Regulation 44/2001, as called for by recital 19 to the Regulation (above).

54 Article 27(1). In this juncture, it is worth noting that the Commission's Green Paper of 21 April 2009 on the review of Regulation 44/2001 put forward as an option in its section 3 on choice of court (at page 5) that, in order to give contractual choice of court agreements the fullest effect possible, the mandatory stay provision of Article 27(1) could be waived in respect of a court designated by such an agreement.

55 Article 27(2).

56 Article 28(3). This wording is the same as that of Article 6(1).

57 Article 29.

58 *The Tatry*, para 38.

Article 27 refers to '*objet*' and '*cause*', and the ECJ has held that the former condition is fulfilled (in relation to the English language text) when the ends of the action are the same.[59]

In relation to the requirement of Article 27 that the actions be between the '*same parties*', the Court has held that the parties in the two sets of proceedings under consideration must be '*identical*': it is not enough that some of the defendants or claimants are parties to the other proceedings. In the words of the Court: **7.056**

> Consequently, where some of the parties are the same as the parties to an action which has already been started, Article [27] requires the second court seised to decline jurisdiction only to the extent to which the parties to the proceedings pending before it are also parties to the action previously started before the court of another Contracting State; it does not prevent the proceedings from continuing between the other parties.[60]

The parties can have different procedural positions in the two actions: the defendant in the first can be the claimant in the second.[61] However, the Court has held that actions brought by insurer and insured may be considered to be between the same parties when the interests of the two are '*identical … and indissociable*',[62] thus broadening the *prima facie* condition of Article 27 as to the identity of the parties. **7.057**

At first sight, it might appear that this condition constitutes a considerable obstacle to effective consolidation of disputes arising out of the same substantive infringement across the courts of the Member States. In relation to cartel-based litigation, it would appear extremely unlikely that the different direct purchasers could be considered to be the '*same parties*' for the purposes of Article 27. The same logic must extend to an indirect purchaser class, which would be even more diverse, and *a priori* to mixed direct and indirect purchasers, not to mention consumer litigants or consumer associations, which would evidently be more diverse again. **7.058**

---

59 *Ibid.*, para 40. The broad interpretation by the ECJ of the part of Article 27 relating to cause of action might explain in part the relative lack of case law on the interpretation of Article 28, since a systematically wide application of Article 27, as and when possible, precludes the application of Article 28. Article 28 is not required where Article 27 applies and to this extent the two provisions are mutually exclusive.

60 *The Tatry*, para 33.

61 *Ibid.*, para 30.

62 Case C-351/96 *Drouot Assurances SA* v *Consolidated Metallurgical Industries* [1998] ECR I-3075 at para 25.

7.059 However, this requirement has been interpreted more broadly than might at first sight appear warranted by the national courts of England and Wales. In *Cooper Tire*,[63] Teare J, referring to the judgment of Lawrence Collins LJ in *Kolden Holdings Limited* v *Rodette Commerce Limited*,[64] which in turn purported to be based on the judgments of the ECJ in *The Tatry* and *Drouot*, held that the requirement that the parties in the different proceedings be '*identical*' was not '*destroyed by the mere fact of there being separate legal entities involved*', and could be satisfied if (i) judgment entered against one of the parties would have the force of *res iudicata* against the other; and (ii) the interests of the parties are '*identical and indissociable*'.[65]

7.060 It is submitted that the application of the law by the English High Court in *Cooper Tire*, and also, by implication, in *Kolden*, is wider than the ECJ authorities allow. In *Drouot*, the condition as to '*identical and indissociable*' was added because the parties were not strictly identical, but were insurer and insured, as noted above. The further test appears to have been added to widen Article 27 in certain very specific circumstances. The point on *res iudicata* was used by the Court in *Drouot* as an indicative illustration,[66] rather than decisive, and not as a condition, necessary or otherwise, as the English authorities imply.

7.061 The diversity of the parties in the factual situation of *Cooper Tire* is much wider than in the more prosaic factual situations of *The Tatry* and *Drouot*. It is submitted that this is always likely to be the case in antitrust litigation. As Teare J acknowledges, there may well be differences of degree of involvement in a given antitrust infringement such that the quantum of damages sought and payable by the different defendants might vary.[67] It is submitted that he could have arrived at this conclusion more quickly by applying the ECJ authorities more at face value, and that the long discussion in this judgment as to *res iudicata* is unhelpful.[68] The test as to '*identical and indissociable*' interests

63 Paras 66ff.

64 [2008] EWCA Civ 10.

65 It should be noted in this regard that Teare J, purporting to follow Lawrence Collins LJ in *Kolden*, treats the condition relating to *res iudicata* as indicative, and that relating to identical and indissociable interests as necessary (*Cooper Tire*, at para 74).

66 See para 19: a sufficient degree of identity between the parties in question '*may*' exist when a judgment given against one would have the force of *res iudicata* as against the other, as for example when the insured subrogates its right of action to the insurer. This however is only given as an example.

67 See paras 86 and 88 of *Cooper Tire*, where the judge notes that the infringer in the Italian proceedings may feel more exposed than the infringers in the English proceedings as it was perceived to have had a more prominent role in the infringement, which would have an impact on contribution between the infringers.

68 Teare J comes to the conclusion that, as a matter of English law, whether or not the fact that the defendants are joint tortfeasors will mean that judgment against one will have the force of *res iudicata* as against another will depend on the facts of the case (para 80), and that in the case in hand this is not the case (paras 84–86, via a further test of '*sufficient degree of identification*').

should be applied narrowly,[69] and the issue of *res iudicata* should not be treated as a test at all.

If Article 27 does not apply, the national court would be required to look to Article 28 to deal with simultaneous litigation arising out of a common infringement of EU competition law. **7.062**

2 Lis pendens *II: Article 28*

It would appear as a matter of logic that the concept of '*related actions*' in Article 28 requires a looser connection than Article 27. Consequently, on the face of the text the rules as to stay and declining of jurisdiction are weaker than in Article 27 (a discretion for the second court to stay and/or decline jurisdiction, rather than an obligation, as under Article 27). **7.063**

The point that Article 28 is intended to be of use where the parties are not identical and so the conditions of Article 27 are not satisfied can be derived from the case law of the Court. The Court assumes this in its judgment in *The Tatry* as follows[70]: **7.064**

> Admittedly, that interpretation of Article [27] [ascertaining whether the parties to the different proceedings are identical] involves fragmenting the proceedings. However, Article [28] mitigates that disadvantage. That article allows the second court seised to stay proceedings or to decline jurisdiction on the ground that the actions are related, if the conditions there set out are satisfied.

As to the condition that the national law in question be capable of consolidating proceedings contained in Article 28(2), in this regard it should be borne in mind that such consolidation may often be possible under Article 6(1) of Regulation 44/2001, which as a provision of a regulation is directly effective in the national court. **7.065**

a Irreconcilability for the purposes of Article 28(3)

The ECJ has held that the term '*irreconcilable*' in Article 28(3) requires that the two sets of proceedings would involve the risk of '*conflicting decisions*', rather than the stricter requirement of '*mutually exclusive legal consequences*', as is **7.066**

---

69 As Teare J observes, as a general rule, joint and several liability is probably not enough to allow for the conclusion that the interests of the parties are '*identical and indissociable*' for the purposes of *Drouot* (para 90). The relationship between the partiers is not as close as in the case of a subrogated claim, as was the factual scenario in *Drouot*, or as in the case of an assigned claim, as was the factual scenario in *Kolden*. Only in such very specific circumstances should the test set out in *Drouot* be considered to be satisfied.

70 Para 34.

arguably the case in relation to the application of Article 34(3) (governing the recognition of conflicting judgments in different Member States).[71]

7.067 It would appear that damages actions launched in different Member States in relation to the same underlying behaviour would be likely to lead to a risk of '*conflicting decisions*' and thus qualify as '*related*' for the purposes of Article 28(1). Were the courts of two Member States to reach differing conclusions on liability this would clearly be the case, as it would be were those courts to reach differing conclusions on certain aspects of the procedural/remedial points in the action (such as causation, which can be contentious (see for example the *Provimi* case in England and Wales), or quantification of damages).

b Connected but not identical actions

7.068 Actions with differing formal aims launched in the courts of different Member States in relation to the same infringement (that is, not just for simultaneous *damages* actions) would also be considered to be '*related*' for the purposes of Article 28(1). For example, were one undertaking to launch an action for a declaration that certain conduct was legal before the courts of one Member State, and then another party were to launch a damages action before the courts of another Member State, such actions (supposing the parties were not identical[72]) would appear to be capable of being treated as '*related*' for the purposes of Article 28(1) and thus of entitling the court seized second to stay proceedings.

7.069 This derives from the fact that such judgments could create the risk of '*conflicting decisions*', for the reasons given above, on the basis of the existing case law on Article 28 (*The Tatry*, above).

7.070 Furthermore, this conclusion derives from analogous case law on the interpretation of Article 27. The ECJ has held that a court is required to decline jurisdiction under Article 27 where a prior application for enforcement of a contract had been brought in the courts of one Member State and the second court, on which the obligation to decline jurisdiction lay, was subsequently seized with an application relating to annulment of the same contract.[73] The parties were identical (save their roles in the litigation – *qua* claimant and defendant – were reversed: the two actions were simply the mirror image of each other).

---

71 For the interpretation of Article 28(3), see *The Tatry*, at para 57. For the stricter test, interpreting Article 34(3), see Case 145/86 *Hoffmann* v *Krieg* [1987] ECR 645 at para 22. The issue of which test should be applied in relation to Article 6(1) is unresolved.

72 In this situation, the case law (as discussed below) would require the second court to decline jurisdiction under Article 27 in any case.

73 Case 144/86 *Gubisch Maschinenfabrik* v *Palumbo* [1987] ECR 4861.

The same has been held under Article 27 in relation to a prior application for a declaration of legality (in relation to a contractual dispute) and a later claim for damages, the reasoning of the Court being that the prior application presupposes in that application a disputing of any obligation to pay damages, such that the ends of the two actions (for the purposes of Article 27) are the same.[74] This case law is by analogy applicable to Article 28 stays, especially in view of the fact that the requirements for stay under Article 28 are looser as a matter of logic than the requirements for mandatory declining of jurisdiction under Article 27.[75] **7.071**

c *The English authorities on Article 28*

By way of analogy, the English High Court in *Provimi* held that different actions (it appears all damages actions in form) in relation to the same substantive infringement (in this case a horizontal price-fixing cartel) were liable to result in '*irreconcilable judgments*'. The English court decided this point in the context of the founding of jurisdiction on the basis of Article 6(1) of Regulation 44/2001 (see above), but given that the wordings of Article 6(1) and Article 28(3) are identical, the point holds by analogy for Article 28(3). **7.072**

Thus the view of the English court in this case supports the view put forward above that simultaneous proceedings arising out of the same substantive infringement of EU competition law would be likely to lead to '*irreconcilable judgments*', or '*conflicting decisions*', for the purposes of Article 28(3) of Regulation 44/2001, which applies even where such proceedings are not brought between identical parties, and hence entitle the second court seized, in these circumstances, to stay proceedings or, on application of one of the parties and at first instance, decline jurisdiction. **7.073**

In *Cooper Tire*, Teare J at first instance accepted in essence the ratio of *Provimi* as to the connectedness of the actions in question and the possibility of conflicting decisions.[76] However, he declined to order a stay pursuant to Article 28 for essentially formal reasons relating to the stage which the various actions **7.074**

---

74 *The Tatry*, para 43.

75 The reasoning of AG Mancini in *The Tatry* was very different. The Advocate-General argued that the second court should decline jurisdiction as to those aspects covered by the prior application (that is, the question of liability) with a stay of the aspects not strictly covered by that application (that is, the damages claim) (para 18). The result under this analysis would be that had the first court found favourably for the party seeking damages, the second court would then have gone on to assess liability on the basis of the finding of the first court as to liability (jurisdiction over which the second court would have declined).

76 See para 106: '*a clear risk of conflicting decisions*', apparently (and correctly) applying the wider test from *The Tatry*, rather than the narrower test from *Hoffmann*, referred to at para 105 of the judgment.

had reached in the two jurisdictions in question, England and Wales and Italy.[77] It so happened in the factual scenario of *Cooper Tire* that the Italian judge at first instance had declined to hear the sole point in the Italian proceedings that had a substantive impact on the civil law issue of damages claims. Her findings had been appealed and, in the opinion of the Italian law experts heard by the English court, that point of appeal was likely to succeed. Teare J found that there was a reduced risk of conflicting decisions insofar as the Italian appeal might not succeed,[78] and, even if it did, the Italian court would then have the benefit of the English decision, the Italian appeal not being likely to be decided until after the English proceedings were brought to a close.[79] In addition, he declined to order a stay on the grounds that some of the defendants in the English proceedings had not sought such a stay. The Court of Appeal declined to reverse his judgment, holding that it was not convinced either that the judge at first instance had erred in law, or that his decision on the point was outside the range of options reasonably available to him.[80]

7.075 It is submitted that the reasoning of the High Court is misleading. The fact that certain of the English defendants had not sought a stay argues in the opposite direction, that is, that a stay was desirable in order to avoid the parallel proceedings which otherwise would have been inevitable. As regards the point on the timing of the proceedings, it should be noted that the Italian appeal court postponed its hearing in the proceedings to January 2014 after the judgment of the English High Court was given.[81] It must be the case that certain issues of substance would be similar, if not the same, in proceedings relating to the same cartel. It may have been better to stay the English proceedings pending the resolution of the relevant substantive issues in the Italian court, and then to have resolved the outstanding issues in the English court.

7.076 Introducing tests additional to those already set out in Article 28 and the relevant case law of the ECJ relating to the procedural conditions of the different proceedings is, it is submitted, unfortunate. In this regard, it should be

77 In his analysis (para 105), Teare J followed the three-fold schema proposed by Advocate-General Lenz in his Opinion in Case C-129/92 *Owens Bank* v *Bracco* [1994] ECR I-117, at para 76, namely that when deciding whether or not to exercise its discretion under Article 28 (or, as was the case in those proceedings, Article 22 of the Brussels Convention), the national court '*could*' look at the following: (a) the degree of relatedness of the proceedings in question; (b) the stage reached in each of them; and (c) the closeness of the courts to the subject-matter of the action.

78 Para 109 of the judgment.

79 This was the only substantive point addressed by the Court of Appeal (paras 54–56), holding that it was legitimate for the court to take account of the time when a decision was likely to be reached in the other jurisdiction when making its assessment under limb (b) of the test set out by Advocate-General Lenz in *Owens Bank* (see para 78 of that Opinion).

80 Paras 48–53 of the judgment of the Court of Appeal.

81 See para 25 of the judgment of the Court of Appeal.

emphasised that in *Owens Bank*, Advocate-General Lenz presented these arguments briefly and '*in the alternative*' to the first question in the proceedings in hand. His list is explicitly non-exhaustive.[82] In any case, his Opinion was not followed by the Court as it dismissed the issue on other grounds, so that this question did not arise for consideration.

d Article 28 and the Commission proposal

One of the genuinely novel aspects of the Commission proposal on damages actions is the rule, contained in its Article 15(1), that, in assessing whether an indirect purchaser has shown that an overcharge has been passed on to it,[83] the court shall take account of other actions relating to the same infringement, but at different levels of the supply chain. Such actions might have been brought in the courts of other Member States, and could be either pending, or brought to judgment. **7.077**

The aim behind this provision is to consolidate actions in different Member State jurisdictions which relate to the same underlying infringement.[84] In the Commission's view, such actions could be considered as '*related*' within the meaning of Article 28. As both a policy aim and an interpretation of Article 28, this is to be welcomed. **7.078**

Given that the tests in Article 6(1) and Article 28 of '*related*' actions are the same, one might have wondered why the Commission does not say anything about the former provision in the proposal. The answer would appear to be that the Commission is envisaging specifically the consolidation of litigation brought at different levels in the supply chain.[85] This would go beyond the scope of Article 6(1), which, as can be seen from the case law discussed above, is used rather in order to consolidate litigation involving different parties, primarily defendants, at the same level in the supply chain. **7.079**

Indeed, the Commission goes so far as to state in the explanatory memorandum that the proposed directive has a '*wider scope*' than Regulation 44/2001.[86] This would appear rather circular, given that the Commission refers to Article 28 as a basis for the consolidation of litigation at different levels in the supply chain. However, the Commission is correct to state that the scope of the proposal is wider than that of Regulation 44/2001 insofar as it deals with litigation brought **7.080**

82 The three factors identified '*may be relevant*', and '. . . *other considerations may*. . . *be important*'.

83 Article 13(2) establishes a rebuttable presumption of overcharge in the case of an action for damages brought by an indirect purchaser. On this provision, see further Chapter 3.

84 See the Commission's explanatory memorandum, at section 4.4.

85 See the wording of Article 15(1)(a) of the proposal, and the explanatory memorandum, *ibid.*

86 Explanatory memorandum, *ibid.*

not only in the courts of different Member States, but also before different courts in the same Member State, or even in the same court *tout court*.

3 *The application of* lis pendens *to parties domiciled outside the EU*

7.081 It is not necessary that either one or the other of the parties to the dispute in question be domiciled in a Member State for the purposes of Articles 27 and 28. It is only necessary that proceedings have been instituted, or been sought to be instituted, in the courts of two or more Member States. This applies in the case where proceedings are brought against a defendant who is not domiciled in a Member State or against whom jurisdiction is not founded otherwise pursuant to any provision of Regulation 44/2001, such that jurisdiction will have been founded against that defendant under the applicable national law pursuant to Article 4(1).[87]

7.082 Therefore, where proceedings between the same parties and involving the same cause of action for the purposes of Article 27 are instituted, for example, by a US-domiciled company in France and that same claimant seeks to institute proceedings in England, the English court must stay/decline jurisdiction. If however, prior to the review of Regulation 44/2001 (see below), the same US-domiciled company was to have instituted proceedings first in the US and then sought to institute proceedings against the same defendant(s) in a Member State, the *lis pendens* provisions of Regulation 44/2001 would not apply and it would be a question of national law as to whether or not the courts of the Member State so seized would stay or decline jurisdiction.

I The review of Regulation 44/2001

1 Lis pendens

7.083 The Commission's Green Paper on the review of Regulation 44/2001 suggested that, in order to address '*current problems*', the *lis pendens* rules could be excluded in the case of parallel proceedings brought for negative declaratory relief.[88] The Green Paper also asked whether consolidation of proceedings by and/or against several parties should be provided for at EU level.[89]

---

87 Case C-351/89 *Overseas Union Insurance Ltd* v *New Hampshire Insurance Co* [1991] ECR I-3317 at para 14. *Overseas Union Insurance* was decided in relation to Article 27, but could by analogy be extended to Article 28 of Regulation 44/2001. There is some support for this proposition in para 16 of the judgment, which refers to both provisions.

88 Sections 3 and 5.

89 Section 5.

The point relating to negative declaratory actions would catch exactly the type of factual scenario at issue in the *Cooper Tire* proceedings. It is submitted however that the approach suggested by the Commission is mistaken in that the exclusion of the *lis pendens* rules in such cases would create the risk of conflicting decisions in relation to the same substantive infringement, and would not be in the interests of economy of decision-making and the proper administration of justice. It would facilitate the sort of forum-shopping which can be seen in the *Cooper Tire* proceedings. It is submitted that an approach seeking to consolidate related proceedings to the greatest extent possible is instead, in the context of competition-related litigation, the better approach. **7.084**

In the event, the Commission's proposal contained no such rules.[90] The principal rule which might have streamlined competition litigation was that, in the case of a mandatory stay in the sense of Article 27 of the current legislation, the court first seized was obliged, as a rule, to decide on its own jurisdiction within a period of six months.[91] This was intended to dispense with the sort of 'torpedo' applications for a negative declaration as seen in the *Cooper Tire* proceedings, although it would have been of doubtful use, as in the *Cooper Tire* proceedings, for example, the parties were not the same, meaning that Article 27 did not apply. In any case, this rule disappeared from the final text, being replaced by a more limited obligation on any court seized to inform any other court seized of the date on which it had been seized.[92] **7.085**

2 *Litigation involving parties domiciled outside the EU*

The Commission also sought to expand the principle established by *Overseas Union Insurance* by introducing a rule whereby, when the courts of a third State are first seized, the courts of a Member State, when seized in proceedings relating to the '*same cause of action and between the same parties*', could, if it wished, decline jurisdiction.[93] This would be subject to certain conditions clearly in the interests of the parties to the litigation undertaken in the Member State, such as there being a reasonable prospect of judgment being reached in the third State, and this judgment then being capable of recognition and enforcement by the courts of the Member State in question. **7.086**

---

90 Proposal for a regulation of the European Parliament and of the Council on jurisdiction and the recognition and enforcement of judgments in civil and commercial matters (recast) (COM(2010)748).

91 Article 29(2) of the proposal.

92 *Ibid.*

93 Article 34 of the proposal. This provision would therefore have had the same scope as Article 27 of Regulation 44/2001, and been less wide than Article 28.

7.087 In the final act, the European Parliament and the Council kept the Commission's proposed rule, though they split it into one rule corresponding to the scope of Article 27 of Regulation 44/2001, and one corresponding to the scope of its Article 28.

7.088 Article 33 of Regulation 1215/2012 corresponds to Article 27 of Regulation 44/2001, which, after the revision, has become Article 29 of Regulation 1215/2012. It introduces a rule whereby the court of the Member State has discretion to stay the action where litigation '*involving the same cause of action and between the same parties*' is pending before the courts of a third state, subject, as mentioned above, to the caveats designed to protect the litigants before the Member State court. This test repeats Article 29 of Regulation 1215/2012. The only difference, which is significant, is that the court of a Member State has discretion to make the stay in these circumstances, whereas a stay under Article 29 is mandatory.

7.089 It could be expected that, in the case of litigation pending also before a court in the US, which satisfies the conditions of Article 33 of Regulation 1215/2012 as to the identity of the parties and the nature of the cause of action, the court of the Member State will exercise the discretion provided for.

7.090 Article 34 of Regulation 1215/2012 replicates, in the same way, the discretionary stay of Article 28 of Regulation 44/2001, now Article 30 of Regulation 1215/2012, and correspondingly introduces a test, additional to those set out in Article 33 of Regulation 1215/2012, of irreconcilable judgments, using the same language as Article 30 of Regulation 1215/2012.[94]

7.091 Thus, unlike in the case of the Commission's attempts to expand the scope of application of the Regulation as a whole, there has been a perceptible change on the issue of the application of the rule on *lis pendens* to litigation involving a party domiciled outside the EU as compared to Regulation 44/2001.

II APPLICABLE LAW

7.092 A court having jurisdiction to rule on the case will have to determine which substantive law to apply. Insofar as the anti-competitive practice in question

94 Article 34(1)(a). The only remaining difference in the schema of Articles 29, 30, 33 and 34 of Regulation 1215/2012 is that, where a judgment capable of recognition and enforcement in the Member State in question has been delivered by the court of the third state, under Article 34(3) the court of the Member State is still not bound to dismiss the action, but has discretion as to whether or not to do so, whereas in the corresponding circumstances, Article 33(3) obliges the court of the Member State to dismiss the action.

may affect trade between Member States, EU competition law will be applicable. The remaining question in this situation is therefore the determination of the law governing the civil remedies for the infringement, and possible stricter national rules on unilateral behaviour pursuant to Article 3(2) of Regulation 1/2003.[95]

As has been seen above, the choice of applicable law is significant insofar as it governs the substantive aspects of the civil law governing the proceedings in question.[96] The detailed conditions for civil redress for an infringement of competition law contain important policy choices which are specific to competition law issues. **7.093**

A The Rome II Regulation and the *lex fori* approach

In 2003, the Commission put forward a proposal for the harmonisation of the rules on the law applicable to non-contractual obligations.[97] The proposal was part of a larger scheme of harmonisation of instruments of private international law which the Community had been pursuing since the introduction of the former Articles 61 and 65 EC. At the same time as the so-called 'Rome II' proposal, the Commission was pursuing the transformation of the 1980 Rome Convention on the law applicable to contractual obligations into a Regulation ('Rome I').[98] **7.094**

The Commission's proposal did not contain a specific rule for damage claims based on an infringement of competition law. In the Green Paper, the Commission had discussed whether it would be advisable to amend the Rome II proposal with a specific rule for damage claims based on an infringement of competition law.[99] **7.095**

As noted above, the so-called 'Rome II' Regulation was finally adopted as legislation on 11 July 2007, and has applied since 11 January 2009. **7.096**

95 For the jurisprudence of the ECJ on the applicability of EU competition law to practices which have an effect within the European Union, see *Wood Pulp I*.

96 See Chapter 1 for the distinction between the procedural and substantive aspects of the rules governing a civil law claim.

97 Proposal for a regulation of the European Parliament and the Council on the law applicable to non-contractual obligations ('Rome II') (COM(2003)427, 22 July 2003).

98 Proposal for a regulation of the European Parliament and the Council on the law applicable to contractual obligations (Rome I) (COM(2005)650, 15 December 2005).

99 Green Paper, question K, options 32–34. See also the Staff Working Paper at paras 242ff.

1 *The general rule: Article 4*

7.097 Articles 5 to 9 of the Rome II Regulation foresee rules for specific tort claims, such as product liability claims, claims of unfair competition, environmental damage or infringement of intellectual property rights. Insofar as a claim is not covered by one of these more specific rules, it falls under the general rule of Article 4.

7.098 Article 4 contains three different approaches to the determination of the applicable law for tort claims governed by that article. According to Article 4(1), tort claims shall be governed by the law of the country in which the damage arises irrespective of the country in which the event giving rise to the damage occurred, and irrespective of the country or countries in which the indirect consequences of that event arise. According to Article 4(2), where the person claimed to be liable and the person sustaining damage both have their habitual residence in the same country when the damage occurs, the law of that country shall govern the claim brought by the one against the other. Finally, under Article 4(3), where it is clear from all circumstances of the case that the claim is manifestly more closely connected with another country, the law of that other country shall apply.

2 *Competition-based litigation: Article 6(3)*

7.099 Article 6(3) of the Rome II Regulation provides as follows:

> (a) The law applicable to a non-contractual obligation arising out of a restriction of competition shall be the law of the country where the market is, or is likely to be, affected.
> (b) When the market is, or is likely to be, affected in more than one country, the person seeking compensation for damage who sues in the court of the domicile of the defendant, may instead choose to base his or her claim on the law of the court seised, provided that the market in that Member State is amongst those *directly and substantially affected* by the restriction of competition out of which the non-contractual obligation on which the claim is based arises; where the claimant sues, in accordance with the applicable rules on jurisdiction, more than one defendant in that court, he or she can only choose to base his or her claim on the law of that court if the restriction of competition on which the claim against each of these defendants relies *directly and substantially affects* also the market in the Member State of that court (emphasis added).

7.100 The *lex fori* had been proposed as one of the Commission's options in the Green Paper for a specific rule on the law applicable to antitrust damage claims.[100]

100 Green Paper, question K, option 33.

During the course of negotiations on the Rome II regulation, this solution eventually found its way into the final act.[101]

Under Article 6(4) of the Rome II Regulation, this provision may not be derogated from by a contractual choice of law clause.[102] **7.101**

a Functioning of Article 6(3)(b)

Article 6(3) has not yet been the subject of interpretation by the ECJ. Nevertheless, some comments can be made as to how it is likely to function, as follows. **7.102**

It should be noted that there are limitations on the application of the *lex fori* solution contained in Article 6(3)(b). As an initial remark, Article 6(3)(b) only applies to litigation connected to an infringement with effects in more than one Member State. However, as seen below, in most cases of litigation for breach of EU competition law, this will be the case, as an effect on trade between Member States is a condition for the substantive applicability of EU competition law. This means that this threshold condition is not a barrier to the application of this provision in relation to this branch of the law. **7.103**

Secondly, Article 6(3)(b) applies firstly where the claimant has elected to found jurisdiction on the basis of Article 2 of Regulation 44/2001, that is, where he or she sues in the courts of the place of domicile of the defendant. This can either be in such a situation *tout court* or, as per the second sentence of the same provision, where the claimant then sues additional defendants pursuant to Article 6(1) of Regulation 44/2001. In the current state of litigation in the national courts in relation to breach of EU competition law, that seems to be the most significant pattern. Article 6(1) operates, as noted above, only where Article 2 operates in the first place, and so is additional to it. The important point to note here is that the rule contained in Article 6(3) of the Rome II **7.104**

---

101 The Commission's original proposal did not contain a provision relating to breaches of Articles 101 and 102 TFEU. In its explanatory memorandum to its amended proposal (COM(2006)83, 21 February 2006), which likewise did not feature a rule relating to those provisions, the Commission explicitly reserved its position on the issue in the light of the debate to be provoked by the Green Paper (page 6, in relation to amendment 29 of Parliament's first reading position). What was to become Article 6(3)(a) in the final act entered the text first as Article 6(3) of the Council's common position of 25 September 2006. Recital 20 to that Common Position furthermore contained the restriction that the effect on the market in question should be '*direct and substantial*'. This restriction does not appear in the final act in relation to that provision. Article 6(3)(b) was introduced only at the end of the legislative procedure during the conciliation in the joint text approved by the Conciliation Committee on 25 June 2007 without any explanation.

102 This provision may have been unnecessary if one takes the view, as argued in Chapter 2, that competition-based litigation is always tortious in nature.

Regulation does not apply where the claimant elects to found jurisdiction on the basis of Article 5(3) of Regulation 44/2001.

7.105 The significant limitation on the operation of Article 6(3)(b) is the condition that the market of the forum must be either '*directly and substantially affected*' by the infringement when there is only one claim, as per the first sentence of Article 6(3)(b). Where, as per the second sentence of that provision, there is more than one claim, the market of the forum must be affected by the same infringement on which each of those claims is based. Given that, in the case of litigation for breach of EU competition law, in a given set of claims the underlying infringement will be the same, which in turn allows the condition of '*irreconcilable judgments*', or '*conflicting decisions*', for the purposes of Article 28(3) or Article 6(1) of Regulation 44/2001 to be satisfied (see above), the second sentence does little more than repeat what is set out in the first in such a way as to clarify its operation where Article 6(1) of Regulation 44/2001 is relied upon to found jurisdiction.

7.106 There is no judicial guidance as yet as to what constitutes a '*direct and substantial effect*' for the purposes of Article 6(3)(b), and the academic literature is in general unhelpful.[103] The practical effect of the condition may be to counteract forum shopping.[104] The language echoes that of the criteria developed by the General Court for the jurisdictional reach of the Merger Control Regulation[105] in the *Gencor* judgment.[106] At paragraph 90 of that judgment, the Court held as follows:

> Application of the Regulation is justified under public international law when it is *foreseeable* that a proposed concentration will have an *immediate and substantial effect* in the Community (emphasis added).[107]

---

103 See Francq, Stéphanie and Wurmnest, Wolfgang, 'International Antitrust Claims under the Rome II Regulation', in Basedow, Francq and Idot, *loc. cit.*, 91, at 124–125: '*[i]t is not entirely settled under what conditions a certain market must be regarded as "directly and substantially" affected by the anti-competitive conduct. As a starting-point, commentators seem to argue that this prerequisite demands a more intensive link between the anti-competitive conduct and the market of the forum than required under Article 6(3)(a) Rome II. But the difficulty is how such a link may be demonstrated in practice.*' It would appear, for example, that in the factual scenario of the *Cooper Tire* proceedings, where it was agreed by the parties that the sales made by the anchor defendants in England were '*small*' (see para 38 of the judgment of the High Court), this test would not be satisfied.

104 See the explanatory statement to the report of the Legal Affairs Committee of the European Parliament on the joint text approved by the Conciliation Committee (A6–257/2007), where it is stated (page 7) that the rule on '*unfair competition*' '*limit[s] to a large extent the danger of "forum shopping"*'.

105 Council Regulation (EEC) No 4064/89 of 21 December 1989 on the control of concentrations between undertakings (OJ L 395, 30.12.1989, p 1).

106 Case T-102/96 *Gencor Ltd* v *Commission* [1999] ECR II-753.

107 Therefore, like the Sherman Act in the US (see further below), the case law on the substantive reach of the Merger Control Regulation also has a foreseeability test.

The elaboration of the '*substantial*' limb of the test, that which could be conceived of as being relevant for the purposes of Article 6(3)(b) of the Rome II Regulation, might offer some guidance for the interpretation of that provision.[108] At paragraph 97, the Court indicates that sales levels and market share are relevant factors in determining whether the effect of the proposed operation is '*substantial*'. A total market share of around 65 per cent is quoted.[109] Furthermore, the Court holds that the fact that the proposed operation is of concern to other geographical areas is not decisive as to the competent authority.[110] **7.107**

Other authors have argued, in relation to the '*substantial*' limb of the test set out in Article 6(3)(b), that the substantive *de minimis* test of EU competition law should be applied, as well as a substantive rule taken from public international law, which sets a liminal condition for the application of one law or another. In addition, in relation to the '*direct*' requirement, it has been argued that an effect on competition and an effect on trade flow should be distinguished, with the Article 6(3)(b) rule being directed at the former and not the latter.[111] This equates to a traditional effects-based approach. **7.108**

Although helpful, this jurisprudence is concerned with the reach of a different area of substantive law.[112] There is no equivalent qualification as regards the scope of Articles 101 and 102 TFEU.[113] It could be seen as unfortunate to import a test from a different area of law. If the test could have been brought in **7.109**

---

108 Paras 96–99 of the *Gencor* judgment.

109 The figures given in the judgment are incomplete as sensitive information has been withheld.

110 '*The fact that, in a world market, other parts of the world are affected by the concentration cannot prevent the Community from exercising its control over a concentration which substantially affects competition within the common market by creating a dominant position*', at para 98.

111 See Hellner, Michael, 'Unfair Competition and Acts Restricting Free Competition', Yearbook of Private International Law, Volume 9 (2007) 49, at 61–64.

112 See Whish, Richard and Bailey, David, *Competition Law* (7th edition, Oxford University Press, 2012), at 500, for the view that the *Gencor* judgment does not establish an effects-based test as a matter of EU law, but rather locates that test within public international law.

113 See the judgment of the ECJ in *Wood Pulp I* at paras 11ff for the reach of Article 101 TFEU. This judgment does not contain a legal test such as that set out in *Gencor*, but treats as a question of fact the issue of whether the conduct in question was '*implemented*' in the EU. Sales within the EU can constitute one such means of implementation (see *Gencor* at para 87). See the Opinion of Advocate-General Darmon in *Wood Pulp I* for the discussion and development of principles delimiting the jurisdiction of substantive EU competition law. Essentially, the Advocate-General, basing his arguments on the public international law doctrine of prescriptive jurisdiction, suggests a test of '*direct, substantial and foreseeable effect*', which was itself rooted in similar solutions proposed in US law, in doctrine, and, in particular, in the Joined Opinion of Advocate-General Mayras in the *Dyestuffs* cases (Cases 48, 49 and 50–57/69 *ICI and others* v *Commission* [1972] ECR 619) (see paras 47–59 of the Opinion of AG Darmon). See Plender, Richard and Wilderspin, Michael, *The European Private International Law of Obligations* (3rd edition, London: Sweet & Maxwell, 2009), at para 20–058, footnote 125, for further discussion of the difference in approach of the ECJ between the *Wood Pulp I* and *Gencor* judgments.

from the substantive law in the same field, there would have been a uniform condition across both the substantive and the remedial aspects. This is the case in US law. However, given the lack of an equivalent test in the case law of the ECJ regarding the reach of Articles 101 and 102 TFEU, it may be that the *Gencor* test was the best language available to the drafters of Article 6(3)(b) of the Rome II Regulation.

7.110 Furthermore, a test such as that of direct and substantial effect is a generally accepted principle of public international law,[114] and as such necessary, or at least usual, in this context. A test of this nature, in this context as in the substantive law context of *Gencor*, helps to preserve a link between at least one relevant market and the law applying to the claim. In this sense, it accords with the conception of competition law as a branch of the law concerned with public policy.[115] Without the *lex fori* approach adopted by Article 6(3)(b), such a limitation would not have been necessary, but at least a test of this nature improves what otherwise would have been a very rough rule.

7.111 Given all of the above, it may be helpful to turn to the laws of some third states for guidance as to the possible interpretation of the condition set out in Article 6(3)(b) of the Rome II Regulation.

b US law

7.112 The language of Article 6(3)(b) is also a direct echo of §7(1) of the Sherman Act, inserted by §6a of the Foreign Trade Antitrust Improvements Act of 1982. §7 of the Sherman Act reads as follows:

> Sections 1 to 7 of this title [the Sherman Act] shall not apply to conduct involving trade or commerce (other than import trade or import commerce) with foreign nations unless
>
> (1) such conduct has a direct, substantial and reasonably foreseeable effect
>
> (A) on trade or commerce which is not trade or commerce with foreign nations, or on import trade or import commerce with foreign nations; or
>
> (B) on export trade or export commerce with foreign nations, of a person engaged in such trade or commerce in the United States; and
>
> (2) such effect gives rise to a claim under the provisions of sections 1 to 7 of this title, other than this section.

114 As observed by the Court in the *Gencor* judgment.

115 See, on this very point, the Opinion of Advocate-General Darmon in *Wood Pulp I*, at para 50.

The test of '*direct, substantial and reasonably foreseeable effect*' in §7(1) derives from the judgment of the US Court of Appeal in the *Alcoa* case.[116] In the recent *Empagran* litigation, the primary focus was on whether conduct with effects in the US '*gave rise to*' the foreign claim for the purposes of §7(2).[117] The first Court of Appeals decision[118] did address the '*direct, substantial and reasonably foreseeable effect*' issue, but only as a preliminary issue, since it was conceded by the appellees (the cartelists) that the test was satisfied.[119] It should be borne in mind in any case that, in the US context, the conditions set out in §7 of the Sherman Act are substantive in that they determine the scope of application of substantive US federal competition law, and are not limited to determining the civil law conditions relating to such claims. **7.113**

3 *The desirability of the* lex fori *approach*

The application of the substantive law of the forum in those cases in which damages are sought for the infringement of EU competition law would doubtlessly facilitate such actions. The judge hearing the case will be far more familiar with the substantive civil law of his own jurisdiction than with the rules of other jurisdictions, which might be called upon to govern the dispute if an effects-based rule was adopted. Given the considerable technical difficulties associated in most cases with competition-related civil litigation (such as the consideration of complex economic data, especially in the quantification of damages), such a facilitation must be seriously considered. **7.114**

There are, however, serious reservations against such a rule. Firstly, while it is true that choices about competition policy are established at Union level, Member States are free to adopt stricter rules for unilateral behaviour (Article 3(2) of Regulation 1/2003). As described in Chapter 1, in the absence of EU legislation, civil remedies for infringement of EU antitrust law are governed **7.115**

116 *United States* v *Aluminium Co of America* 148 F. 2d 416 (2nd Cir 1945). See Plender and Wilderspin, *loc. cit.*, at para 20–058, footnote 123 for a discussion of the US jurisprudence.

117 The issue was addressed primarily by the second Court of Appeals decision, where it became a causation issue: given that the domestic and foreign injuries were held to be independent, the infringement could only be said to have given rise to the foreign claim on the grounds that the claimants would have purchased in the US but for the infringement.

118 Decision of the US Court of Appeals for the District of Columbia in *Empagran S.A.* v *F. Hoffmann-LaRoche Ltd.* 315 F. 3d 338 (DC Cir 2003).

119 See the following passage from the first decision of the Court of Appeals: '*The complaint in this case alleges an international price-fixing conspiracy among the vitamin companies, and appellees "do not contest that the vitamin cartel produced substantial effects in the United States" for the purpose of this appeal… In light of this concession by the appellees, it is unnecessary for us to explore further the precise parameters of the definition of "conduct", since there is no real dispute that the vitamin companies' conduct had "a direct, substantial and reasonably foreseeable effect" on U.S. commerce. We therefore accept that the "direct, substantial and reasonably foreseeable effect" requirement under § 6a(1) of FTAIA is met.*'

by national civil law. The way in which civil redress is structured by national law and the rules adopted by the Member States in the field of unilateral conduct cannot be regarded as being of lesser importance. While considerations about the practical workability of rules on choice of laws are important, such consideration needs to be weighed carefully with regard to the substantive appropriateness of the rule adopted.

7.116 The application of the law of the forum also contravenes the policy of the Union in the field of judicial cooperation. The general philosophy behind the legislation in this field is that the free movement of judgments within the Union is enhanced if, irrespective of the forum, rules on choice of law designate the same applicable substantive law to govern the dispute. The heightened predictability which such a system of harmonised rules on applicable law would bring to litigation is regarded as an essential building block for judicial cooperation between the Member States. Indeed, recital 6 to the Rome II Regulation reads as follows:

> The proper functioning of the internal market creates a need, in order to improve the predictability of the outcome of litigation, certainty as to the law applicable and the free movement of judgments, for the conflict-of-law rules in the Member States to designate *the same national law irrespective of the country of the court in which an action is brought* (emphasis added).

7.117 The Commission's avowed aim in the field of its policy in the area of judicial cooperation between the Member States is to facilitate the enforcement of judgments rendered in other Member States. It was ostensibly for this reason that the EU adopted rules which harmonise the determination of jurisdiction and why it aimed at harmonising rules on applicable law. It is believed that a uniform set of rules on applicable law which will lead to the application of the same substantive law to a claim, irrespective of where that claim is brought, would better enhance trust between the judicial systems of the Member States and thus contribute to making cooperation between those judicial systems more effective.[120] A specific rule for damages actions for breach of EU competition law, designating that the substantive law of the forum shall always be applicable, departs from these principles. It is difficult to see why this departure is justified.

7.118 Also, it could be argued that the application of the law of the forum substantially increases the uncertainty associated with litigating damages claims for the

120 The above-mentioned policy is reaffirmed in several documents pertaining to the judicial cooperation of the Member States (see, for example, the Commission's Green Paper on the conversion of the Rome Convention of 1980 on the law applicable to contractual obligations into a Community instrument and its modernisation (COM(2002)654), at p 9).

infringement of EU competition law. As has been shown above, under the current system a number of courts from different Member States might have jurisdiction in any one case. As the claimant would then have a choice between those different courts, it would be essentially up to it to designate not only the procedural rules which would govern the action, but also the substantive rules governing the claim.

Furthermore, it is by no means certain that the claimant has to be in all cases the person which has suffered from the infringement. It is easily imaginable that the infringer could find ways to pre-empt any action from the victim by suing the victim first and asking for a declaratory judgement that there is no liability. Such 'policy shopping' by either the potential infringer or the potential victim would essentially render litigation far more uncertain.

B Alternative solutions: the effects-based approach

When Article 6(3)(b) does not apply, that is, when the condition as to '*direct and substantial effect*' is not satisfied, or when the claimant founds jurisdiction under Article 5(3) of the Brussels Regulation, then Article 6(3)(a) will apply. Article 6(3)(a) uses an effects-based approach.[121] **7.119**

Prior to the adoption of the Rome II Regulation, an effects-based approach was most commonly adopted for the determination of the applicable law in actions for breach of competition law. The effects-based approach is still relevant under certain national laws, such as Swiss law.[122] **7.120**

The effects-based approach starts from the assumption that competition law serves a special function by regulating conduct on a certain market. Competition law is not purely about private interests but embodies ultimately choices about economic policy. EU competition law, for example, is concerned with competition on the common market and is applicable therefore where behaviour may affect trade between Member States. Competition law is therefore necessarily linked to a certain territorial market and the effects-based approach proposes that the rules of a certain competition law shall be applicable to behaviour where such behaviour has effects on the territory for which that **7.121**

121 It should be noted that it is at the discretion of the claimant to apply the *lex fori* to the action pursuant to Article 6(3)(b): from the wording of Article 6(3)(b), the claimant has the choice between this and the law determined by the effects-based approach under Article 6(3)(a). It should further be noted, as remarked by Plender and Wilderspin, *loc. cit.*, at para 20–068, that even where jurisdiction is founded on Article 2 of Regulation 44/2001, if there is not a '*direct and substantial effect*' within that jurisdiction, then Article 6(3)(b) of the Rome II Regulation cannot be relied upon.

122 See further Ashton and Vollrath, *loc. cit.*, 16–19.

competition law has been enacted. In terms of civil disputes, the use of an effects-based approach to determining the law applicable to a certain claim links the civil redress for a certain behaviour to the consequences of that behaviour. This nexus between the rules on civil redress and competition law choices justifies that the law applicable to the civil redress should be determined by reference to the effects of the anti-competitive behaviour on which the claim is based.

1 *Article 6(3)(a) of the Rome II Regulation*

7.122 Article 6(3)(a) clearly applies an effects-based approach to the determination of the law applicable to a civil claim for breach of EU competition law as an alternative to the rule set out in Article 6(3)(b), that is, the law applicable to that claim is the law of the market in which the anti-competitive behaviour is felt. If, for instance, a number of companies who act as suppliers on a market in country A enter into an anti-competitive agreement which has an effect on that market, and a company located in country B purchases on the market in country A from one of the cartel members, the claim of that purchaser against the cartel members for recovery of the damage (namely, the overcharge paid by him because of the anti-competitive agreement) would be governed by the laws of country A, because the damage to competition as the protected interest occurred in country A.[123]

7.123 It appears that this would also be the correct interpretation of the general rule set out in Article 4 in terms of the location of the place where the damage occurs (as opposed to the law of the place where the financial loss is sustained, for example).[124]

2 *Problems with the effects-based approach:* Mosaikbetrachtung

7.124 As shown above, it can be argued that an effects-based approach is the most appropriate way for the determination of the applicable law for claims based on an infringement of competition law. Some difficulties associated with this approach should nonetheless be confronted. An effects-based approach will have to tackle the difficulties associated with localising the damage. These

---

123 Contra is the rather meandering discussion in Plender and Wilderspin, *loc. cit.*, at paras 20–064–20–067, which, after considering both the strict effects-based solution and a solution applying the applicable law of the place where the indirect purchaser suffered damage, assuming the latter to be different from the former, comes to the conclusion that the point '*cannot … be regarded as settled*'.

124 On this, see Ashton and Vollrath, loc. cit., 19–22, discussing Article 3 of the Commission's original proposal for the Rome II Regulation, the wording of which is not significantly different from that of Article 4 of the adopted act. Article 5 of the original proposal, which dealt only with unfair competition law and which formed the basis for Article 6 of the adopted act, contained an effects-based rule for claims based on unfair competition law. Recital 21 to the final act states that '*[t]he special rule in Article 6 is not an exception to the general rule … but a clarification of it*'. This is obviously not true of Article 6(3)(b) (see Hellner, *loc. cit.*, 55).

difficulties, however, will not be present if the affected market is a national market. Due to the wide interpretation given to the notion of effect on trade between Member States by the ECJ, it is entirely possible that an anti-competitive practice is governed as a matter of substantive competition law by Articles 101 and 102 TFEU, while the actual effects of that conduct are felt purely on one single national market. In such a case, the effects-based approach would quite easily determine the applicable law.[125]

If, however, the affected market is a supra-national one, specific difficulties arise concerning the localisation of the effects. It is submitted that an effects-based approach means in civil litigation that the court applies the law of the state on whose territory the distortion of competition by the illicit behaviour in question is felt by the victim. In short, in such circumstances an effects-based approach for the purpose of determining applicable law refers to the subjective effects of an anti-competitive behaviour felt by the victim. It will be necessary to link a certain damage – such as an overcharge paid by a purchaser – to a certain territory of a certain state so that the laws of that state can be called upon to govern the claim for the recovery of that loss. Often, the place where the subjective effects will be felt is the domicile of the claimant (*qua* victim). **7.125**

Beyond the difficulty of finding a determining criterion for localising the damage, it has to be seriously considered whether the application of different laws in the course of one single set of actions will not render such litigation inordinately complicated. The application of an effects-based approach in the case of an international cartel will quite possibly lead to the application of the laws of several states within the framework of a single litigation. The court would have to determine for each of the different claims the national law applicable to it and would have to find out what that law is. Such an exercise in *Mosaikbetrachtung* could be very burdensome for litigation.[126] **7.126**

At the same time, the application of several different laws within a single litigation is not unusual in international civil procedure. It is also questionable whether there will be indeed that many cases in which several different national laws will be applicable. Such a case would only arise if not only the infringing action had effects in several different states, but the losses for which a recovery is sought before the court have also been suffered in different states. In the case of **7.127**

---

125 In a similar fashion, several distinct markets which are all in the territory of one single state will yield the same result.

126 In the Green Paper, the Commission had put forward for debate an option designed to remedy this situation by giving the claimant in those cases in which the application of the effects-based approach would lead to the application of several different national laws the choice to determine which law would be applicable for the entirety of his loss (see question K, option 34).

a single purchaser, it is on the contrary quite likely that, while the infringing action may well be international, its purchase would have taken place in one single state. In such a case, no *Mosaikbetrachtung* would have to take place.

3 Mosaikbetrachtung *as a concurrent matter of jurisdiction and applicable law*

7.128 As has been explained above, a *Mosaikbetrachtung* exists as a matter of jurisdiction under the *Shevill* decision of the ECJ. Were a claimant to seek to found jurisdiction pursuant to Article 5(3) of Regulation 44/2001, under Article 6(3)(a) of the Rome II Regulation it would appear that this would lead to an exactly corresponding *Mosaikbetrachtung* as regards the applicable law.

7.129 It has been argued that the jurisdictional result under limb (b) of *Bier/Shevill* and the law applicable under Article 6(3) of the Rome II Regulation might not always coincide.[127] This assumes that limb (b) of *Bier/Shevill* is given a limited geographic interpretation. However, as stated above, a market-based interpretation can also be taken to limb (b) of *Bier/Shevill*, and more geographically limited interpretations, such as the place of financial loss, are in fact excluded under the case law of the ECJ.[128] A market-based interpretation would accord with the effects-based approach which can be taken to Article 6(3)(a) of the Rome II Regulation, and is in any case probably the most persuasive view to be taken of Article 5(3). It should nevertheless be remembered that, even if a market-orientated approach to limb (b) of *Bier/Shevill* is taken, the court seized only has power to award damages for loss suffered on its territory.

7.130 There is some support for the view that the application of the *Shevill* theory of jurisdiction renders consolidation of claims pursuant to Article 6(1) of Regulation 44/2001 irrelevant.[129] In any case, the claimant has to choose to found jurisdiction on the basis of one of the provisions of Regulation 44/2001, and Articles 5(3) and 6(1) are mutually exclusive. As noted above, the trend at the moment seems to be to seek to found jurisdiction on the basis of Article 6(1) in an attempt to bring as many claims as possible before the court of choice of the claimant. It may also be the case that, where the defendants are sued on a joint and several basis, this would exclude founding jurisdiction on the basis of

---

127 Dickinson, Andrew A, *The Rome II Regulation: the Law Applicable to Non-contractual Obligations* (Oxford: Oxford University Press, 2008), at para 6.14.

128 See the *Marinari* ruling and the other case law of the ECJ referred to above.

129 See Hess, Burkhard, Pfeiffer, Thomas, and Schlosser, Peter, Report on the application of Regulation Brussels I in the Member States (study JLS/C4/2005/03), at para 213: '*some Dutch lawyers even go as far as to argue that the Shevill-decision has to its effect that Article 6(1) JR can be deleted*'.

Article 5(3) as it may simply be too difficult to reconcile the *Shevill* doctrine with joint and several liability.[130]

130 See Chapter 5 for discussion of joint and several liability. The issue was raised at para 63 of the judgment of the High Court in *Cooper Tire*, though the judge did not come to any conclusion.

8

QUANTIFICATION OF ANTITRUST DAMAGES*

Frank Maier-Rigaud and Ulrich Schwalbe*****

I INTRODUCTION 8.001

II DAMAGE CAUSED BY CARTELS AND ABUSIVE CONDUCT 8.005
- A Damage caused by cartels 8.010
  - 1 Types of damage caused by cartels 8.010
  - 2 Economic actors damaged by cartels 8.020
    - a Upstream effects 8.024
    - b Downstream effects 8.029
    - c Effects on producers of complements 8.032
    - d Summary of effects analysis 8.033
  - 3 Illustration 8.036
- B Damage caused by abusive conduct 8.044
  - 1 Types of damage caused by exploitative and exclusionary conduct 8.045
  - 2 Economic actors damaged by exploitative and exclusionary conduct 8.049

III QUANTIFICATION OF DAMAGES 8.052
- A Quantification of damages in cartel cases 8.053
  - 1 Time series analysis 8.055
  - 2 Cross-sectional analysis 8.061
  - 3 Difference-in-differences method 8.065
  - 4 Simulated comparator markets 8.067
  - 5 Cost-based and profitability-based approaches 8.069
- B Damage quantification in abusive conduct cases 8.074
  - 1 Damage caused by abusive behaviour and the counterfactual scenario 8.074
    - a Exploitative abuse 8.075
    - b Exclusionary abuse 8.078
  - 2 Illustration: quantification of damages in case of an exclusionary abuse 8.084
    - a Phase one 8.086
    - b Phase two 8.088
    - c Phase three 8.090
- C Further aspects of damages quantification 8.095
  - 1 Compounding and discounting damages 8.095
  - 2 Estimation of after-effects 8.099
  - 3 Accuracy of statistical methods 8.101
  - 4 Remoteness and causality 8.104

IV CONCLUSIONS 8.109

BIBLIOGRAPHY 259

* We thank Roman Inderst, Makis Komninos, Andreas Reindl, Daniel Sokol and Wouter Wils for comments on an earlier version. Disclaimer: Frank Maier-Rigaud was involved in the damages actions project of the European Commission in its early stages. He was responsible for the Ashurst study and the economic parts of the Green Paper. The views expressed are his own and not necessarily those of the European Commission.

** Department of Economics & Quantitative Methods, IÉSEG School of Management (LEM-CNRS), Paris, and NERA Economic Consulting, Brussels and Berlin, email: maier-rigaud@microeconomics.de.

*** Department of Economics, University of Hohenheim, Stuttgart, Germany, email: ulrich.schwalbe@uni-hohenheim.de.

I INTRODUCTION

An economically founded quantification of the damage caused by competition law infringements has increased in importance in particular through the advancement of competition law damages actions in the EU. Damages claims are increasingly brought, in particular as follow-on claims, and it is very likely that this trend will continue in the future.[1] If a damages claim is presented in court and compensation of the harm suffered is sought, quantifying the level of the damage suffered becomes necessary. On the basis of these developments several theoretical and applied studies investigating the fundamental economic principles and empirical-econometric methods to determine damage have been presented in the last few years with the aim to provide guidance to the courts on how the quantification of damage should be approached and what aspects have to be taken into consideration.[2] **8.001**

Estimates of the magnitude of damage caused by competition law violations show that they are quite substantial. The empirical literature concerned with estimating aggregate damages has so far, however, exclusively focussed on cartel cases. Empirically estimating the total damage caused by all cartels is, however, conceptually very difficult, as the total number of cartels is unknown and only discovered cartels can be analysed. The damage caused by European and national cartels have therefore been estimated using simplifying assumptions.[3] Presuming a certain detection rate, it is possible to estimate the number of existing cartels.[4] By further assuming a relationship between fines and damage caused, the harm inflicted by cartels in Europe was estimated.[5] The estimation led to a lower bound of the yearly damage of approximately €16.8 billion. Measured as a percentage of European gross domestic product (GDP), total cartel damage is 0.15 per cent. An upper bound for the yearly cartel-induced damage lies at €261.22 billion. This corresponds to 2.3 per cent of EU GDP. These numbers show that cartel-induced damage is quite substantial. **8.002**

1 See Chapter 1.

2 See in particular European Commission (2011) and, for example, Bishop and Walker (2010) or Niels et al. (2011). For a German text see Inderst et al. (2013a).

3 European Commission (2007).

4 The underlying assumption being that undetected cartels are as damaging as detected cartels. The majority of EU cartel cases since the introduction of the first leniency programme in 1996 are due to leniency applications. Excluding other reasons for triggering leniency applications such as due diligence in a merger for example, a data set based mainly on leniency applications may bias the results downward as the most profitable cartels will not find it attractive to go for leniency whereas leniency applications – if economically motivated – must be based on a change in the cartel incentive constraints, that is, a leniency application will become attractive if cartel profitability decreases either due to a higher detection probability coupled with damages claims and fines or due to the fact that the cartel is inherently becoming less profitable. See Friederiszick and Maier-Rigaud (2007, 2008) for a discussion of the EU leniency programme and the need for *ex officio* cartel detection.

5 European Commission (2007: 96).

8.003 In this chapter, the main conceptual and methodological aspects that are of relevance for an economically sound quantification of damage in the context of competition law infringements are presented. The chapter is structured as follows. Section two discusses the conceptual foundations for the quantification of damage. Firstly, the types of damage caused by cartels and the economic actors affected by cartel activities are characterised in detail. A distinction is made between damage to the overall economy in the form of inefficiencies or welfare losses and individual damage, which also includes redistribution from the consumers to the cartel, for instance due to abnormally high prices, and that are therefore typically larger than the economic welfare losses. Secondly, the repercussions of cartel-induced price increases on the value chain as well as on neighbouring markets are spelled out. Thirdly, damage caused by abusive behaviour of dominant firms and the affected actors is described.

8.004 Section 3 deals with the methods employed in the quantification of damage in cartels as well as abuse of dominance cases. To estimate the damage, it is necessary to compare the factual situation with a hypothetical counterfactual scenario. The problem of choosing the appropriate counterfactual scenario is discussed as this has a crucial impact on the damages to be calculated. Also, the available economic and econometric methods for the calculation of damages, giving prominence in particular to comparator-based methods and approaches (yardstick or benchmarking) either relying on actual or on simulated, artificial markets are introduced. The quantification of damages in cases of abusive behaviour is illustrated by an example of an exclusionary abuse. In addition, further aspects in the quantification of damages such as, for example, compounding and discounting damages and the consideration of after-effects are discussed. Also, the precision of the available statistical methods and problems of causality and the remoteness of damage with respect to the infringement are discussed. The final section concludes with a summary of the main results and an outlook.

II DAMAGE CAUSED BY CARTELS AND ABUSIVE CONDUCT

8.005 The restriction of competition by a cartel or abusive conduct by a dominant firm leads to economic welfare losses and also harms the purchasers and ultimately the consumers of the products or services through increased prices, lower quality and reduced variety.[6] If the functioning of competition between firms is impaired or eliminated by illegal cartel agreements or by abuse of a

6 This chapter focusses on cartel and abuse of dominance cases. Of course, vertical agreements also can cause damages and trigger damages claims.

dominant position, the competitive mechanism will no longer fulfil its allocative function and market outcomes will become unsatisfactory from an economic point of view because they will generate welfare losses due to inefficiencies. In addition to these inefficiencies, competition law infringements lead to a redistribution of wealth from direct and indirect purchasers to the cartel, and also affect economic actors that are neither part of the supply chain nor purchasers of the goods or services provided by a cartel or directly affected by an abusive conduct.

The primary goal of cartels and abusive practices is to increase profits by **8.006** softening competition. By cartel agreements, the intensity of competition between rival firms is either substantially reduced or fully eliminated. Such agreements can be based on different strategic parameters. In price-fixing cartels competitors collectively decide on the prices of their products, whereas in quota cartels a collective agreement is reached concerning the quantities to be produced and marketed by the cartel participants. Other forms of cartel agreements include market sharing arrangements, where firms geographically divide the market, for instance by determining regions that are served, or, in particular in the case of public procurement auctions, agreements are reached concerning price and conditions of the bids to be submitted (bid-rigging cartel).

In all of these instances, cartels generally result in higher prices and lower **8.007** quantities than would have been observed in the absence of the cartel. In price-fixing or bid-rigging cartels the competitors explicitly agree on a price that generally is substantially above the price that would have been obtained under competitive conditions. Quota cartels reduce the quantity supplied strategically in order to obtain a price increase indirectly. Market sharing agreements allocate geographic markets to individual competitors, allowing the firm to act as monopolist, charging the monopoly price, in the respective region.

Abusive conduct by dominant firms can be either exploitative or exclusionary. **8.008** Exploitative abuses work similarly to cartels by increasing prices directly, while exclusionary abuses aim mainly at eliminating competitors by foreclosing the market or limiting competitors in their expansion. In addition, a dominant firm may aim to discourage the entry of potential competitors or limit the scale of market entry, that is, it may try to quell the beginning of competitive pressure or at least any increase in the intensity of competition. It may also attempt to leverage its market power into neighbouring markets.

From a conceptual point of view, damage is quantified by a comparison of the **8.009** factual situation, that is, the situation of the competition law infringement with a hypothetical situation, the so-called counterfactual or but-for scenario, a situation that would have obtained in the absence of an infringement.[7] Firstly, the types of damage that is caused by cartels or abusive behaviour have to be specified and secondly, the victims, that is, the economic actors that were negatively affected by the illegal conduct have to be identified. In the following subsections, the types of damages and the affected economic agents are specified for cartels and for abusive conduct respectively.

A Damage caused by cartels

1 *Types of damage caused by cartels*

8.010 From an economic point of view, the cartelisation of a market leads to two types of effects: a transfer of wealth and inefficiencies, both of which have to be considered as damage from the point of view of the affected economic actors. To illustrate the two types of damage using a simple example, a cartel in a final products market, selling goods directly to final consumers, is considered.[8] Concerning the allocation of resources, the cartel leads to a welfare loss due to non-exhausted gains from trade in the form of lost utility for final consumers. This is called the dead weight loss (DWL) and represents an economic or allocative inefficiency. Due to the higher price induced by the cartel there is also a transfer of economic rent from consumers to producers. These two effects are shown in Figure 8.1, which depicts consumer demand for a cartelised product, the pre-cartel price of p_c and the cartel price of p_k, where c stands for competition and k for cartel. The quantities sold in the competitive and in the cartelised market are denoted by q_c and q_k.

8.011 Based on a price p_c that would prevail under effective competition, that is, the counterfactual or but-for price (here assumed to be the perfectly competitive price[9]), the cartel increases the price to p_k. This increase in price results in a DWL of welfare depicted as a black triangle and a redistribution of wealth in the form of a transfer of T (depicted as the grey area). The welfare loss that is caused by the cartel which induced a price increase from p_c to p_k, results from the fact that for prices between p_c and p_k gains from trade are not exhausted. Consumers exist who would have been willing to pay a price p, $p_c < p < p_k$ for additional units of the product and there are firms that could produce those

7 More details on how to establish the appropriate counterfactual are provided in sections III.A and III.C.

8 Furthermore, it is assumed here that all inputs of the cartel are produced in perfectly competitive markets so that no damage occurs upstream of the cartel. It is also assumed that there are no effects outside the value chain, for example for producers of complements or buyers of substitutes. These assumptions are relaxed in section II.B.

9 The price under effective competition is not necessarily the price that would prevail under perfect competition. In particular, in oligopolistic markets, the price under effective competition may be substantially above the perfectly competitive price.

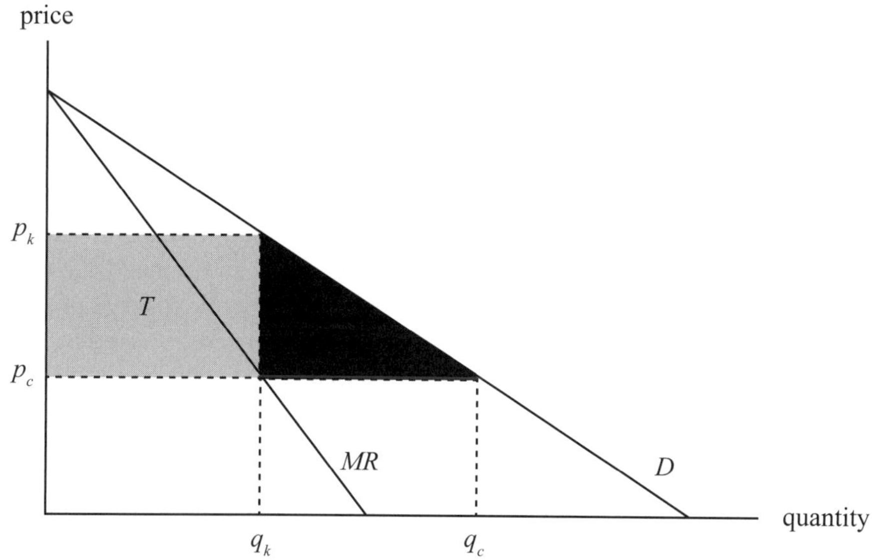

Figure 8.1 Transfers and (dead weight) welfare losses caused by cartelisation

units and still cover their costs. Due to the cartel, these transactions do, however, not occur. Consumers are thus damaged by a loss of utility as at the higher cartel price, a smaller quantity of the good is bought. This is the quantity effect, which is the main economic rationale for the prohibition of cartels under competition law.

The transfer, *T*, however, does not represent a welfare or efficiency loss as it is a pure redistribution of wealth and has no impact on efficiency. As the additional expenditure for the quantity bought at the cartel-induced higher price is, however, a loss to consumers, it has to be counted as damage.[10] This damage is known as the overcharge, or more generally, the price effect of a cartel. The total damage inflicted on consumers is thus composed of the transfer *T*, that is, the price effect (grey rectangle), and the welfare loss, that is, the quantity effect, depicted as black triangle, and is therefore higher than the economic efficiency losses and also higher than the profits generated by the cartel that correspond to the transfer. A cartel typically causes both types of harm and there are no convincing economic arguments that would suggest giving preference to either type of harm in estimating total damage. In practice, it may, however, be more difficult to estimate quantity effects with a high degree of accuracy. This is due to the fact that it is usually easier to demonstrate that a higher price has been paid on units of the good bought in contrast to demonstrating that a certain **8.012**

10 In this particular setting, where only final consumers are purchasing from the cartel, the price effect is also called overcharge, which in turn is simply the illegal gain.

number of goods were not bought but would have been had the price not increased. This holds in particular for those consumers who did not buy the product at the high cartel price but would have bought at the lower price under effective competition.

8.013 The magnitude of cartel-induced damage depends on a range of factors such as the duration and the market coverage of the cartel, as well as the magnitude of the price increase or the reduction in quantity. Obviously, the damage due to a cartel will be higher the longer the cartel is in place. Economic theory has also shown that the size of the cartel, that is the share of the market covered by the cartel, has a substantial impact on the welfare effects. Generally speaking the negative welfare effects, and therefore also the damage, increase with market coverage.[11]

8.014 A further essential determinant of the damage is the extent of the price increase or the quantity reduction. This in turn depends on several factors, for instance the intensity of competition that would have prevailed but for the cartel. Some markets are characterised by a relatively low intensity of competition even in the absence of a cartel, whereas other markets may be subject to fierce competition.[12] In the first scenario, the damage created by the cartel would be relatively low as prices would have been comparatively high even in the absence of the cartel. In the second scenario, the damage is more significant because, without the cartel, prices would have been substantially lower due to the intense competition. An additional factor impacting the extent of the price increase is the degree of coordination in the cartel. Cartels will not always be able to achieve perfect coordination, implying that they will not be able to fix the price or quantities at the level that maximises total cartel profits. Under certain circumstances, perfect coordination cannot be achieved and only a partial coordination will be feasible, so that prices will remain below the cartel profit-maximising price.[13] Damage therefore increases with the degree of

---

11 On welfare effects of cartels with partial market coverage see Schwalbe (2011). In this context, so-called 'umbrella effects' are relevant, that is, price increases of firms active in the same relevant market but not participating in the cartel, which can also increase their prices under the umbrella of the higher cartel prices. See Inderst et al. (2013b).

12 On this see also section III.A.

13 The factors that may contribute to a cartel being able to set the profit-maximising cartel price are the same as the factors that have been identified as facilitating non-coordinated effects in a merger context. See the judgment of the then CFI of 6 June 2002 in Case T-342/99 *Airtours plc* v *Commission* [2002] ECR II-2585 and the judgment of the ECJ of 10 July 2008 in Case C-413/06P *Bertelsmann AG and Sony Corporation of America* v *Independent Music Publishers and Labels Association (Impala)* [2008] ECR I-4951. Intuitively, it is clear that firms with different variable costs will find it difficult to agree on the quantity that will equate marginal revenue with their respective marginal cost as those will differ between firms.

coordination.[14] Finally, the slope of the demand curve has a substantial impact on the magnitude of the price increase and the welfare losses. This can be illustrated with an example where it is assumed that in the absence of the cartel, the market is perfectly competitive and firms produce with equal marginal and average cost. In this case, the competitive price is determined by the marginal cost and thus independent of the demand function. *Ceteris paribus,* a price inelastic demand will lead to a larger price increase than a price elastic demand. If demand is inelastic with respect to price, consumers have only a few options to substitute and can therefore not switch to alternative products once the price increases, implying that a cartel can charge substantially higher prices before reductions in quantity demanded become important. If consumers, however, have many possible substitutes at their disposal, demand is price elastic and a cartel will not increase the price substantially as it would otherwise only sell a much reduced quantity. This implies that under perfect competition the damage caused by a cartel is higher the lower the price elasticity of demand is. This is demonstrated in Figure 8.2.[15]

Again, a scenario is considered where price in the absence of the cartel is given by p_c and the quantity demanded is q_c. With a price inelastic demand (D^{in} and a corresponding marginal revenue curve MR^{in}), the cartel will increase the price to p_k^{in}, where *in* stands for *in*elastic, and the corresponding damages will be given by areas shaded in dark and light grey. If demand is price elastic (D^e and a corresponding marginal revenue curve MR^e), the cartel will increase the price only to p_k^e, where *e* stands for *e*lastic, and the damage for the consumer is thus given by the area shaded in dark grey, that is, substantially lower than the damage incurred with a less price elastic demand. In contrast to the damage suffered by the consumer, the magnitude of the efficiency loss is not directly related to the price elasticity of demand. While the price increase given a price elastic demand function is relatively small, the quantity demanded is reduced substantially. If the demand function is price inelastic, the quantity effect is limited, but the price increases substantially. As a result, the welfare loss may increase or decrease with the price elasticity of demand. Whether the quantity or the price effect prevails is an empirical question and depends on the specifics of the demand function. **8.015**

In addition to the allocative inefficiencies captured by the DWL depicted in Figures 8.1 and 8.2, cartels may also give rise to productive and dynamic **8.016**

14 Note, however, that the same factors that will enable a higher degree of coordination are also factors that would tend to soften competition in the market naturally, implying that cartel coordination may be high but the cartel mark-up over the competitive price is correspondingly low.

15 For a more detailed discussion of elasticities, emphasising in particular that the concept is in itself not a suitable indicator for damages, see Inderst et al. (2013a).

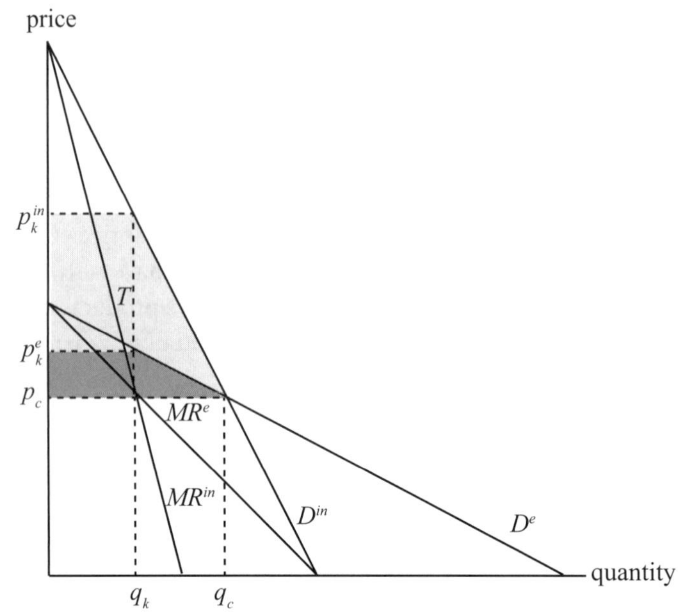

Figure 8.2 Damages and welfare effects with demand functions of differing price elasticity

inefficiencies. Productive inefficiencies may arise because cartelists, due to the softening of competition, face reduced incentives to produce efficiently or search for the most cost-efficient production technology.[16] As a result, a cartel can create a situation where inefficient firms producing with higher costs remain in the market although they would have been forced to exit under effective competition.[17] If a cartel leads to higher cost, this should be taken into account when quantifying cartel damages. In particular, when cost-based methods (see section III.A) are employed, higher costs induced by cartelisation should be accounted for. Such inefficiencies could also give rise to after-effects that extend beyond the cartel period.

8.017 Cartels might also change market characteristics such as concentration or production capacities and could also have a negative impact on innovation. Usually, a cartel will try to foreclose the market to avoid market entry, to stabilise the cartel and to prevent an erosion of profitability. The softening of competition due to a cartel could also reduce the incentives for firms to innovate on both products and services but also regarding the production process and the

16 This type of inefficiency is known as X-inefficiency (Leibenstein 1996) often associated with the 'quiet life' of a monopolist (Hicks 1938: 8).

17 In turn, a perfectly efficient cartel will imply that less efficient firms no longer produce and only receive transfers.

technology employed. This can lead to substantial dynamic inefficiencies in the long run, that is, reduced research and development (R&D), and a lower rate of technological progress leading to substantial additional welfare losses. Theoretical results with respect to the impact of cartels on innovation are, however, ambiguous; on the one hand higher cartel profits allow for investments in R&D but on the other hand there are increased incentives for 'business stealing'.[18] In addition, cartels may reduce product variety as it is in general easier to stabilise a cartel in a homogeneous product market. Also, all expenditures related to organising the cartel and to protecting the cartelists from detection by the competition authority have to be considered welfare losses.

Existing empirical studies on cartel damage have concentrated on mark-up and overcharge calculations. Quantity effects have often been neglected.[19] The results of these studies show some variance. In the study by Posner (2001) that considers 12 cartel cases, the median amount by which the price increased is estimated at 28 per cent,[20] whereas the OECD analysis of 2002, based on cases between 1996 and 2000, estimates a median increase in price of 16–18 per cent. In a meta study by Werden (2003), where 13 studies are analysed, a median increase of 15 per cent is found. The most comprehensive study on cartel-induced price increases is by Connor and Lande (2008), who analysed more than 670 cases taken from approximately 200 studies. They conclude that the median price increase is about 20 per cent of the cartel price and the average at about 23 per cent. Based on this study, the distribution of cartel-induced price increases was calculated; however, only those cartel cases were considered that were established after 1960 and that fulfilled several other selection criteria, so 114 cartel cases were eventually considered.[21] For this sample, the median of the price increase was approximately 18 per cent and the average was about 20 per cent of the cartel price. The distribution of cartel-induced price increases of this sample is depicted in Figure 8.3. **8.018**

Figure 8.3 reveals the substantial variance of cartel-induced price increases. Whereas in 7 per cent of the cartel cases analysed no increase could be estimated, the increases can in certain cases exceed 50 per cent, implying a cartel price more than twice as high as the competitive price.[22] **8.019**

18 See Schumpeter (1950) and Arrow (1962). There is as yet no conclusive empirical evidence.

19 The neglect of quantity effects is a general problem of the mostly US-influenced literature on damages. In addition, the focus on the overcharge instead of the quantity effect is due to the fact that US damages actions at the federal level are brought by direct purchasers in the absence of the passing-on defence, rendering the overcharge the only relevant damages category.

20 The cartel-induced price increase or mark-up is normally expressed as a percentage of the cartel price.

21 European Commission (2009: 91).

22 Other studies include Levenstein and Suslow (2006); Connor (2006); Connor (2006); Connor and Bolotova (2005); Bolotova et al. (2009); Griffin (1989); OECD (2003); and Combe and Monnier (2007).

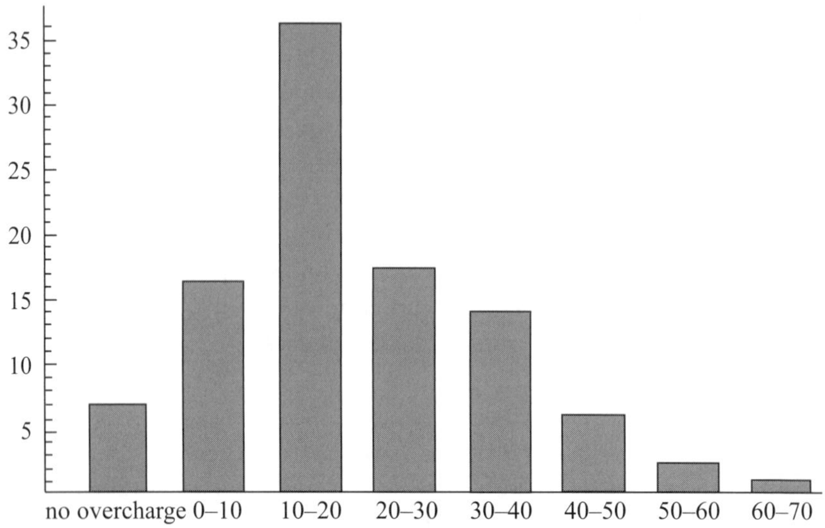

Source: The analysis is based on the underlying data in Connor and Lande (2008), described previously, and selection criteria described in European Commission (2009).

Figure 8.3 Distribution of cartel-induced price increases in per cent

2 Economic actors damaged by cartels

8.020 Section II.A.1 discussed the two basic effects through which firms or consumers can be harmed by anti-competitive conduct, namely price and quantity effects. This section will provide a more systematic analysis of the vertical, horizontal and other (non-vertical and non-horizontal) cartel effects in order to give a better understanding of how cartel damage percolates through the economy.

8.021 Horizontal effects are generated on the same antitrust market and therefore concern all producers of cartelised goods or services irrespective of whether they take an active part in the cartel or not. Also, producers of products that only become substitutes at the cartel price are affected.[23] Vertical effects are effects along the different levels of the production chain and concern firms providing direct and indirect inputs to the cartelised firms as well as firms and consumers that act as direct or indirect purchasers. Non-horizontal and non-vertical effects accrue, for example, to firms that provide complements or firms and consumers purchasing from firms providing complements. Such effects also accrue to firms that purchase from some of the direct or indirect cartel input providers or some of the firms purchasing from firms offering substitutes to direct or indirect cartel inputs or firms offering substitutes to the products offered in the value chain of the cartelists.

23 In that sense, horizontal effects may also arise outside the relevant market as is intuitively clear if one considers the cellophane fallacy.

Figures 8.4a and 8.4b set out five levels of a value chain, locating the cartel at level three in the chain. Correspondingly, there are also five separate horizontal markets of cartel-affected inputs and cartel-affected outputs as well as their substitutes. In addition, the figures also capture three neither horizontal nor vertical effects, that is, a producer of complements to the cartel product, a purchaser of substitutes to a direct cartel input and a direct and indirect purchaser of a cartel substitute. Furthermore, the figures show some typical outcomes in terms of positive damage (dark grey) and negative 'damage' or profit increases (light grey). **8.022**

In principle, a whole range of economic actors can be affected by anti-competitive conduct. General equilibrium theory shows that all actors in an economy can potentially be positively or negatively affected by a cartel. By increasing the price of the cartelised product, the cartel changes the relative prices and thus causes substitution and income effects that can affect the whole economy, similar to how a stone that is thrown into a small pond will generate waves that will spread across the whole pond.[24] To realise that effects accrue not only downstream in the supply chain is important in an EU context as the US literature that focuses on direct and indirect purchaser standing may have obfuscated this point.[25] We first consider the effects of a cartel on the upstream levels of the supply chain and then discuss the effects on the downstream levels. Finally, we consider cartel effects on economic agents outside the supply chain. **8.023**

a Upstream effects

Figure 4a depicts some possible upstream effects that could be generated by a cartel, that is, level 1 of indirect input suppliers and level 2 of direct input suppliers as well as producers of substitutes for direct (firm A) and indirect (firm B and firm C) inputs. **8.024**

The cartel-induced price increase leads to a reduction in the demand of the cartelised product and therefore also diminishes the demand of the cartelised firms for direct inputs required to produce this good. It should be noted that the decrease in input prices due to the reduction in input demand is an aggregate effect and that indeed firms not participating in the cartel but producing the same products (firm E) or producers of substitutes to the cartel product (firm F) **8.025**

---

24 From a practical point of view damages claims will, however, realistically only be brought by a small subset of those actors affected. Similar to the small pond metaphor, however, where the height of the wave is normally greatest near the point where the stone sank into the water but also depending on the depth topology of the pond, the economic effects or damage are not necessarily greater for direct as opposed to indirect purchasers or those that are even further removed from the actual economic dealings of the cartel. Indeed there are – empirically probably rare – constellations where direct purchasers may even benefit from the cartel to the further detriment of indirect purchasers.

25 See Chapter 3 for a discussion of standing in antitrust litigation in the EU and the US.

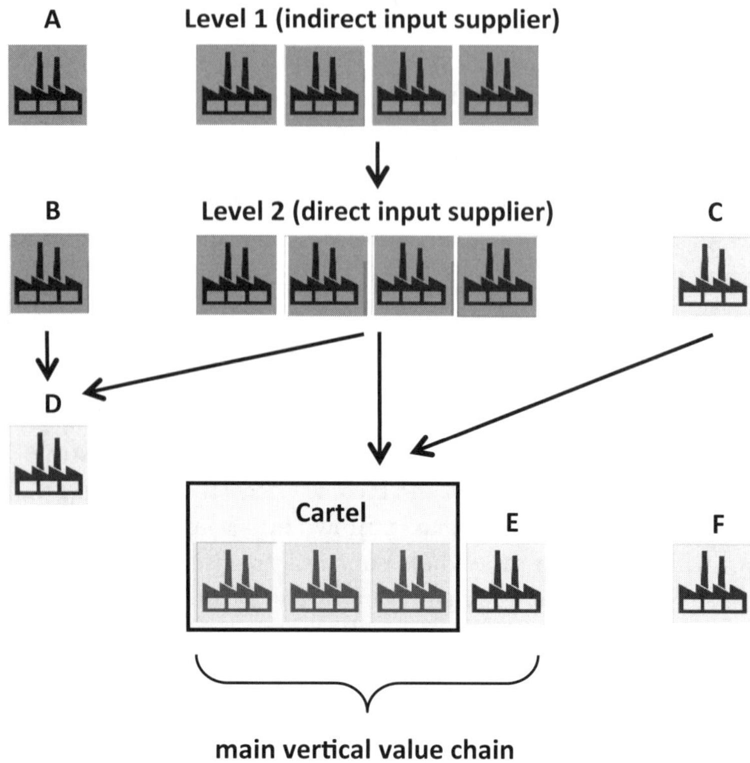

Figure 8.4a *Stylised vertical, horizontal and other cartel effects upstream of the cartel*

– to the extent that F requires the same inputs – may actually increase their production (for example, in case of a market characterised by Cournot competition). This increase will, however, not compensate for the reduction in input quantities demanded by the cartelists.[26]

8.026 As a result of the reduced demand for the direct input[27] produced, level 2 firms' profits are reduced despite the fact that their profit-maximising response results

26 Firms E and F are drawn with a light grey background as they benefit from so-called umbrella effects. The quantity reductions or price increases of the cartel allow both firms to increase prices or increase quantity depending on whether the market is characterised by Bertrand or Cournot competition. Indeed firm E and, depending on the degree of substitutability, also firm F benefit most from the cartel as their profits increase more than the profits of the cartelists. Under quantity competition these firms do not follow the cartel in restricting their output at the cartel price but expand production thereby mitigating cartel effects both up and downstream, but also increasing their own profits. A similar free-rider effect exists under price competition, where firms E and F follow the cartel in increasing prices but do not increase prices as much as the cartelists, again resulting in a quantity increase. See Inderst et al. (2013b).

in a reduction of their own prices, thereby mitigating the negative effect of the cartel. The lower prices charged by the level 2 firms benefit firms such as D (and of course any firm that may have been buying from level 2 producers but is not depicted in the figure) for whom the input provided by level 2 direct input providers now becomes an attractive substitute. This has a negative impact on firm B, a producer of substitutes to level 2 direct input suppliers' product as B finds it profitable to adjust its price downward in a reaction to the price decrease of level 2 direct input suppliers. This in turn benefits firm D.[28] Level 2 firms are, however, not only negatively affected by the drop in demand induced by the cartel but may be further harmed if for instance this industry was experiencing economies of scale prior to the drop in demand. This may lead to firms such as C, that use a different production technology and that were not competitive at the pre-cartel production levels, becoming attractive suppliers of substitutes. Indeed, the reduction in demand by the cartelists and the undercompensating demand increase by firms E and F may lead to a partial shift of the remaining demand away from level 2 suppliers to firm C.

So far, level 2 firms have been considered to have been equally impacted by the different effects discussed. This need not be the case. While market conditions for these firms change as described and lead to a decrease of prices for level 2 supplier products, some firms may in fact be more affected than others. **8.027**

Similar arguments apply for the indirect input suppliers (level 1). Indeed, these indirect input suppliers face a reduced demand from level 2 firms and, as a result of their own profit-maximising response to this drop in demand, reduce prices to mitigate these effects. Overall prices and quantities decrease, resulting in lower profits also for producers of substitutes such as firm A. Again, the aggregate quantity and price effects are independent of whether only one or all four of the firms depicted are selling inputs to level 2 firms, although the resulting damage may of course not be equally distributed and depend on the respective market shares. **8.028**

b Downstream effects

Figure 8.4b depicts the effects downstream of the cartelised market. Clearly, the direct purchasers (level 4) as well as the indirect buyers (level 5) are negatively affected by the increase in price of the cartelists. The cartel, however, also has an **8.029**

27 Note that the figure assumes that this input is solely used for producing the cartelised product and possibly also for the production of substitutes to the cartelised product. This does not need to be the case and depending on what fraction of total sales on level 2 go to other industries, or are diverted into other industries as exemplified by firm D subsequent to the decrease in price that level 2 firms implement, the effect on the direct input suppliers relative to their total profits are mitigated.

28 Firm D may therefore benefit from the cartel even if it does not substitute to products from level 2 firms.

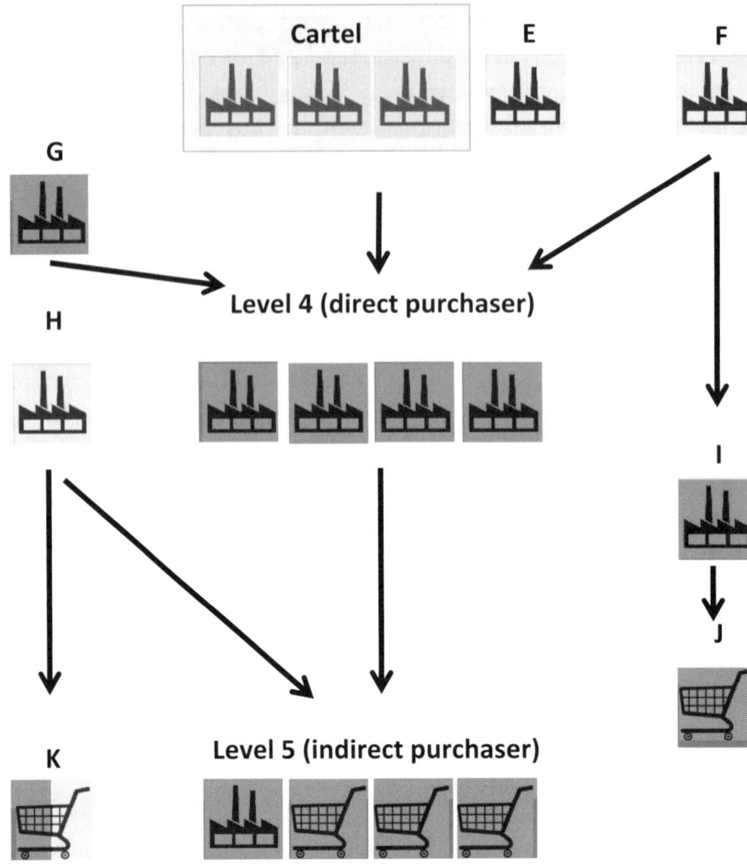

Figure 8.4b Stylised vertical, horizontal and other cartel effects downstream of the cartel

effect on firms like E, producing the same product as the cartel, and F, producing substitutes to the cartel product. These firms do not participate in the cartel but profit from so-called 'umbrella effects'.[29] The cartel-induced price increase leads to a diversion of demand to non-cartelised firms producing the same good as the cartel and to firms producing substitutes of the cartelised product. The increase in demand causes these firms to raise the prices of their products and to increase their supply. This increase in supply is, however, insufficient to compensate for the reduction in supply by the cartel, as otherwise the cartel would not be formed.[30] In the case of a homogeneous product, the

29 For a detailed discussion of umbrella effects see Inderst et al. (2013b).

30 The assumption has to be that a sufficient amount of firms (or firms covering a sufficient share of the market) in a market are cartelised. If entry is easy or firms are not at capacity or otherwise constrained it is not possible to form a profitable cartel.

umbrella effect induced by the cartel leads to a price increase by the same amount as the cartel price, that is, the damage that accrues to customers of non-cartelised firms is the same as for the customers of the cartel as both pay the same price. If products are differentiated, the increases in price and supply under the umbrella of the higher cartel price depend on the amount of demand diverted from the cartel to non-cartelised producers of substitutes. The higher the degree of differentiation, the less pronounced the reaction of the non-cartelised competitors will be. In addition, the relative magnitude of that effect crucially depends on the reaction of the indirect purchasers (level 5) as will be seen in the discussion below. In anticipation of that reaction, level 4 firms unintentionally mitigate the negative effects of the cartel by not increasing prices as much as the increase in input cost would seemingly warrant, simply in order to maximise profits. Nevertheless, there is an increase in price compared to the counterfactual price that prevailed absent the cartel and therefore the indirect purchasers and consumers (level 5) pay a higher price and buy a reduced quantity of the product.

While the existence of the cartel results in positive effects for firm F, as set out above, its direct and indirect customers I and J are harmed (see Figure 8.4b). The reason for this is that as the demand that firm F faces increases (due to substitution and the possibility to act as a price follower to the cartel), its profit-maximising prices increase as well. This is a notable result as it indeed shows that consumers in otherwise completely unrelated markets may suffer damage from the cartel. A further concern may be that the only, albeit indirect, link with the cartel is through firm F, which actually benefits from the cartel and would therefore not have any incentive to disclose information on a possible cartelisation to its own customers. **8.030**

Similar to the effects on firm F already discussed, the substitute producer H is positively affected as indirect purchasers partially substitute consumption away from the level 4 direct purchasers to firm H, which in turn sells a higher quantity at a higher price. The consumers K that were buying from H before are harmed in this case as the price is higher than in the absence of the cartel due to the fact that H is now also facing demand from level 5 consumers. Alternatively, one may envision that this increased demand allows the firm to produce at lower cost due to some increasing returns to scale technology. If that is the case, the price may go down so that consumers K are benefitting from the cartel. **8.031**

c *Effects on producers of complements*

Further effects of the cartel accrue for firm G, a producer of complements to the cartel products. With a reduced demand for cartel products, the demand for complements also decreases. As a result, the profits of firm G decrease despite a **8.032** profit-maximising reaction, consisting of lowering price to partially offset the quantity effect.[31] What is notable is that this firm is negatively affected by the cartel although its input prices are completely independent of the cartel and, in that sense, no damage has been 'passed-on'.[32] Nevertheless, G clearly is harmed by the cartel and may even stand a good chance of demonstrating this harm if, for example, its complementary products are sold in a fixed proportion to the cartelised product.

d Summary of effects analysis

8.033 This discussion has shown that while the total net effects of a cartel are necessarily negative due to the resulting welfare losses, the cartelisation of an industry can have positive effects for some consumers and firms and negative effects for others.[33] It should also be clear that the notion of 'passing-on' of damages is misguided as the cartel does not produce a certain fixed 'quantity of damage' that is then passed up and down the different levels of the value chain. Rather, by changing relative prices, the cartel actually triggers responses up and down the value chain and also outside (outside vertical or horizontal relationships) that, while solely induced by profit-maximising behaviour, mitigate cartel damages.

8.034 In US cartel damages cases, the focus is mainly on price effects and on the value chain downstream of the cartel. In addition, damages claims at the federal level are restricted to direct purchasers who consequently are allowed to claim the total downstream damages based on price effects. As price effects are pure transfers, the sum of all price effects is equal to the overcharge, which is the illegal gain. Using US terminology, the passing-on-adjusted overcharges of all downstream levels sum to the entire overcharge. As in some US states, indirect purchasers are also allowed to claim damages; the concept of passing-on is introduced in addition to the concept of overcharges. This allows the retrospective calculation of price effects at different levels of the value chain starting from the overcharge, but makes it difficult for courts to apportion damages across several claims pertaining to one infringement. These concepts are ill-suited for calculating damages when full compensation is the goal as quantity effects need to be taken into account and total damages are therefore not equal to the overcharge. From an economic point of view, the concepts of overcharge and

31 Note that price reductions will be more significant if the complement is not sold in fixed proportion to the cartelised product. If it is, the price reduction will be more mitigated as quantity reactions will only depend on the price of both, the complement and the cartelised product.

32 This is another incidence demonstrating the problematic nature of the notion of 'passing-on' for calculating damages in an EU context.

33 This is actually inherent in the notion of transfer, although the figures show that such transfers not only accrue to the cartelists but that there are transfers that benefit consumers or firms that are not in the cartel (firm E, for example, will benefit more than the cartelists relative to its size) and may not even be active in the same industry.

passing-on are therefore at best complicated methods of deriving price effects as they neither provide a basis for calculating total damages nor capture effects upstream of the cartel or outside the vertical value chain.[34]

The discussion of Figures 8.4a and 8.4b assumed certain typical industry responses and did not explicitly consider the reactions of firms to changes in demand and input prices. In the following, a graphical analysis analogous to the one in section II.A.1 is used to describe some of the reactions that were summarised in the discussion above. The presentation focuses on the special case where the direct purchasers are not harmed by the cartel, that is, the case where all 'damage' is 'passed-on' so that only indirect purchasers and final consumers are affected. Modifying this case and assuming that there is only a monopoly direct purchaser serving final consumers leads to another special case where almost no 'damage' is 'passed-on'.[35] With one possible exception all relevant cases lie in-between these two special cases.[36] **8.035**

3 *Illustration*

The previous subsection discussed the effects that a cartel can have throughout the economy and the economic actors likely to be affected by a cartel. This subsection focuses on the price and quantity effects as they accrue in a vertical value chain in more detail. In explaining these, the sometimes inconsistently used concept of overcharge will also be discussed.[37] More specifically, as set out **8.036**

34 Doubts are in order as to whether these concepts are compatible with European law as they are derived from a legal context that does not allow all victims standing and that is not geared towards full compensation of harm suffered. This of course does not imply that these terms are absent in the EU debate and have not created confusion. For example the problem of unjust enrichment is solely a relic of the overcharge approach. Also the controversially debated US question on whether the passing-on defence should be allowed is no longer of relevance in Europe where all victims have standing. The proposal of the European Commission concerning a directive on the rules governing actions for damages (see European Commission (2013); and Maier-Rigaud (2013)) has not succeeded in overcoming these difficulties.

35 Of course there exist very realistic cases where no passing-on occurs. This is, for example, the case if the cartelised product is part of the fixed cost of the downstream purchaser, as would be plausible for instance in an elevator cartel.

36 The exception is a scenario in which direct purchasers actually benefit from the cartel. See Hellwig (2007). An alternative scenario in which the direct purchasers benefit is due to side payments and is discussed in Schinkel et al. (2008).

37 Here, the term cartel-induced price increase or mark-up is consistently used to describe the effect the infringement has on price, that is, if the infringement results in a price of €15 when the but-for price would have been €10, the mark-up is €5. The term overcharge is consistently used to denote the monetary amount obtained by multiplying the mark-up with the quantity bought by the purchaser under the infringement. This overcharge is identical to the price effect if no passing-on occurs, for example, if final consumers are considered. The term overcharge is, however, sometimes also used in the literature to denote the mark-up. Some authors also use the term interchangeably, contributing further to the confusion between price effects and overcharge as defined here. See, for example, European Commission (2009), which first defines overcharge as defined here, then later on uses the term as a synonym for mark-up. This approach is repeated in European Commission (2011), which also adopts the US terminology of overcharge and passing-on that is of limited use in an EU context. See also European Commission (2013).

in Figure 8.5, a cartelised market for an intermediary product is considered. This intermediary product is an input for the production of a further intermediate good that is produced on a perfectly competitive market. The intermediate product on that market is finally sold to a monopolist who produces a final product sold to consumers. In order to simplify the exposition, it is assumed that no other inputs are required to produce the intermediate as well as the final product than the one impacted by the cartel. Furthermore, marginal costs for each firm in the value chain are assumed to be equal to c so that total production costs for the downstream monopolist are $3c$ under perfect competition and $2c + p_k$ in case there is a cartel on the first intermediate product market. It is further assumed that one unit of input is used to produce one unit of output throughout the value chain.

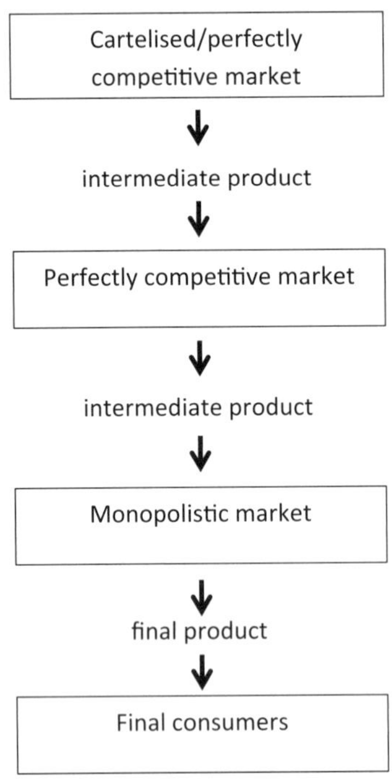

Figure 8.5 Possible effects of a cartel on a downstream value chain

8.037 Consider first what happens in the absence of a cartel. If there is no cartel and given the demand function D_M, consumers are charged the price p_M^*, corresponding to a quantity q_M^* depicted in Figure 8.6. This price is higher than the marginal cost curve of $3c$ because the indirect purchaser (monopolist) has market power and charges a price higher than marginal cost. The monopolist pays $2c$ for its input as the first intermediate supplier market is competitive, charging a price $p_1 = c$, and the second one is competitive as well, charging a price of $p_2 = c_2 = 2c$, so that total marginal costs are $3c$. As the production of the final product is assumed to occur in a monopolistic market, final consumers will be confronted with a price that corresponds to the quantity q_M^*, where marginal revenue (depicted as MR_M equals marginal cost ($3c$).

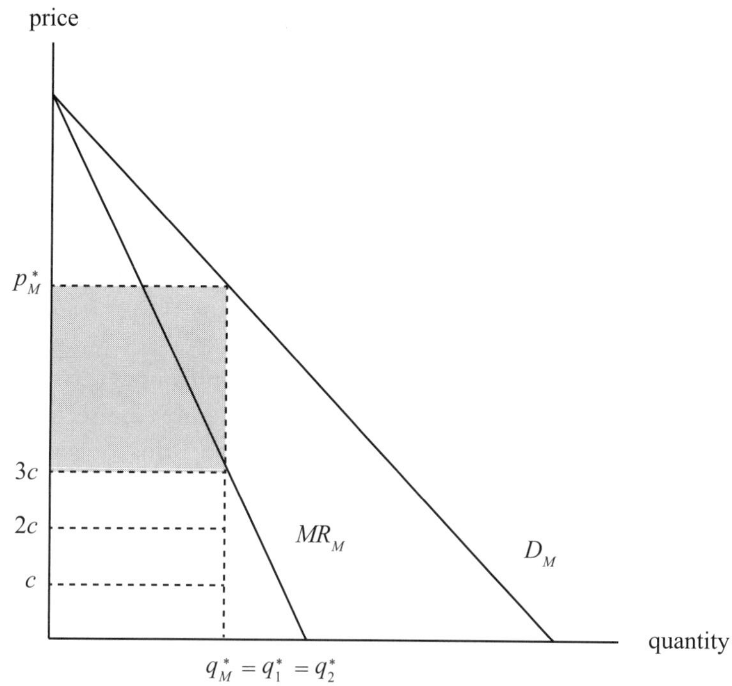

Figure 8.6 Situation in the absence of a cartel

The monopoly profits of the indirect purchaser are depicted in Figure 8.6 as the area shaded in light grey. As all other markets are assumed to be perfectly competitive, other firms make zero profits, that is, they only earn a normal rate of return.[38] **8.038**

Consider now the situation with which the upstream producers are confronted if they want to form a cartel. Originally, that industry was perfectly competitive, charging a price equal to marginal cost. Now the market is assumed to be perfectly cartelised and the cartelists produce a quantity where marginal cost equals marginal revenue and the resulting price is the monopoly price on that market. Clearly, marginal revenues depend on the demand that the cartel faces downstream in the competitive market, which in turn depends on the demand of the monopolistic market, which in turn depends on final demand. In order to **8.039**

38 The zero profit result under perfect competition does not imply zero profits in an accounting sense, but only implies that the firms do not earn more than a normal rate of return, that is, they earn zero profits defined as any amount exceeding a normal return.

be able to find the profit-maximising price, the cartel has to take into account all reactions throughout the value chain.

8.040 As discussed in section II.A.1, the calculation of damage resulting from the cartel for final consumers is conceptually easy. Consumers are hurt as they no longer purchase a quantity q_M^* but reduce consumption to q_{Mk}^* at the corresponding prices p_M^* and p_{Mk}^*, where k denotes the fact that this is the price-quantity combination chosen by the monopolist under the cartel (see Figure 8.7). The DWL (the black triangle) is the damage due to the reduction in quantity and the price effect is given by the transfer indicated by the area shaded in medium grey above the price p_M^*, that is, the increase in price for all units that continue to be bought.[39]

8.041 The cartelised industry benefits from the cartel as it no longer earns the normal rate of return at $p_1 = c$, but realises a profit indicated by the rectangular area shaded in dark grey below p_{1k}^* in Figure 8.7. The firms operating on the perfectly competitive intermediary product market continue to earn only a normal rate of return and are therefore not affected, although they sell a lower quantity, that is, $p_{2k} = p_{1k}^* + c > p_2 = 2c$. As marginal cost has increased, prices have increased as well and a lower quantity is being sold.

8.042 The downstream monopolist is negatively affected by the cartel as its profits decrease. Instead of the rectangular area shaded in light grey depicted in Figure 8.6 and again in Figure 8.7, the monopolist now only earns the profits in the amount of the area shaded in medium grey above the price p_M^*.

8.043 Several aspects are noteworthy with respect to this stylised example. Firstly, net cartel profits are given by the price increase multiplied by the quantity that continues to be sold at that price.[40] The benchmark conveniently assumed is a perfectly competitive industry, so that there are no negative quantity effects of the price increase to be taken into account.[41] Secondly, total damage far exceeds the cartel profits as the area shaded in dark grey in Figure 8.7 is smaller than the difference between the areas shaded in light grey and in medium grey above the price p_M^* (damage accruing to the monopolist) plus the area shaded in medium grey above the price p_M^* and the black triangle (damage accruing to final consumers). This also implies that the overcharge which is identical to the illegal gain substantially underestimates total damage. Thirdly, while the

39 With final consumers, and only with final consumers, this price effect is equal to the overcharge of the firm(s) selling to the final consumers.

40 This illegal gain is of course identical to the overcharge faced by the direct purchaser.

41 There are quantity effects but they do not result in harm as there is no profit loss.

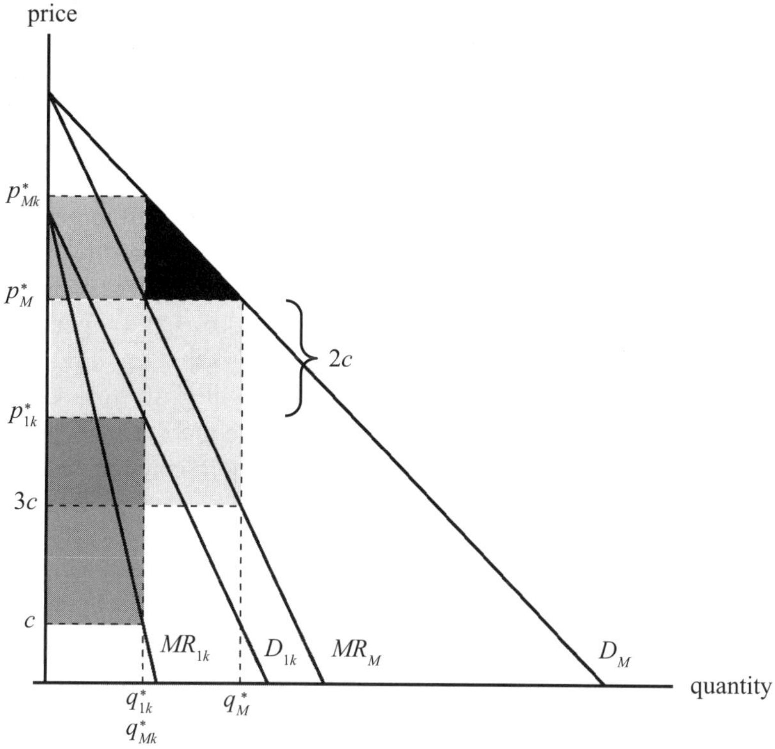

Figure 8.7 Situation with a cartel

damages to final consumers can conceptually be easily calculated by multiplying the price increase of the indirect purchaser (here the monopolist) with the quantity that consumers continue to buy and adding the quantity effect, this is not possible for the monopolist. The monopolist loses the profits on the quantity he no longer sells, but generally also on the quantity he continues to sell as his own cost mark-up changes, because he is pushed into a more elastic section of the demand function. This happens as soon as an imperfectly competitive market is considered and would therefore also have to be expected in oligopolistic markets.[42] It is thus incorrect to calculate the damage accruing to the monopolist by adding to the lost profits due to the quantity reduction an amount equal to the overcharge, that is, the mark-up over the but-for price multiplied by the quantity it continues to sell, as this would be a substantial

42 The most important factors determining the reduction in mark-up are generally the degree of competition downstream, whether all downstream firms are equally affected by the price increase, the shape of the demand function and the type and nature of the cost function. In addition, if the monopolist (in that instance it would be more appropriate to call it a single seller) or the oligopolists are constrained, for instance by foreign importers that are not affected by the cartel, it becomes more difficult to maintain a higher mark-up as the cost increase may have to be fully absorbed.

overcompensation.[43] Fourthly, the scenario demonstrates that damage may not accrue to direct purchasers but may concentrate at lower levels of the value chain. Although jurisdictions that only give standing to direct purchasers allow these firms to claim total damages, including those occurring further downstream, some scepticism may arise as to the potentially substantial informational problems that a direct purchaser would have to overcome to elicit the required information from indirect purchasers or, for that matter, from producers of complementary products. The scenario also shows that quantity effects can only be ignored if – as assumed here for the direct purchaser – the market is perfectly competitive or the cartel only affects fixed costs.[44] In perfectly competitive markets, however, there is also no damage, so that in all relevant cases where variable costs are affected, quantity effects will play a role. Given these conditions, quantity effects are more important the more market power the concerned firms have, that is, approximately, the more concentrated the industry is.

B Damage caused by abusive conduct

8.044 Abuse of a dominant position can take the form of exclusionary or exploitative conduct. Whereas an exploitative abuse directly increases the profits of a dominant firm through price increases,[45] exclusionary abuses increase profits indirectly. Through the abusive practice the competitive pressure emanating from actual or potential competitors is reduced. Practices such as predatory prices, retroactive rebates, margin squeeze, refusal to deal or exclusive dealing aim at reducing the competitiveness of rivals in order to strengthen the market position of the dominant firm. While a particular practice is only considered abusive if anti-competitive effects can be demonstrated, implying that consumers are made worse off, the increase in market share of the dominant

43 Of course, it is possible to decompose the damage suffered by a purchaser into an overcharge, a passing-on and a quantity effect, as is done for example by van Dijk and Verboven (2008, 2009) or Kosicki and Cahill (2006). Although artificial, such a decomposition may be justified in a jurisdiction where quantity effects are considered irrelevant. If in addition only direct purchasers have standing and the passing-on defence is not allowed, it is sufficient to calculate the overcharge, that is, the illegal gain, and disregard both the quantity effect and the price effect which would require adjusting the overcharge by subtracting passing-on. For an economically appropriate calculation of damages this is, however, not required.

44 In economics, a distinction between fixed and variable costs is made. Fixed costs do not vary with changes in output, whereas variable costs do. In a short-term analysis, changes in fixed costs would not result in any quantity effect. From a business perspective it is crucial to determine how fixed costs are allocated to outputs.

45 See OECD (2012a) for a detailed discussion of excessive prices. Just as for cartels, exclusionary conduct has as its primary goal increasing profits by softening or eliminating competition. Whereas a cartel reduces or eliminates the competition between firms, abusive conduct aims at foreclosing the market for actual or potential competitors or at least to limit their growth and development.

undertaking at the expense of its competitors amounts to a transfer of profits from competitors to the dominant undertaking.[46]

1 Types of damage caused by exploitative and exclusionary conduct

In the case of an exploitative conduct, similar welfare implications result as in a cartel context. The prices are higher and the quantities are lower than under functioning competition so that the resulting allocative inefficiencies take the form of profit or utility losses. Just as in a cartel context, there is also a transfer from purchasers to the dominant firm. **8.045**

Whereas cartels generally entail higher prices,[47] reduced quantities and lower quality for customers and ultimately final consumers, abusive practices may – at least in the short term and to the extent that they entail profit sacrifices – also entail positive effects for the purchasers. With predatory prices, for example, purchasers are better off in the first implementation phase of the predation strategy as prices decrease. Only once competitors have exited the market and the dominant firm can recoup its profit sacrifice will prices increase beyond the price that prevailed prior to the implementation of the predation strategy and the harm for purchasers and final consumers will become apparent. The repercussions of the abusive practice may therefore vary across phases, increasing the difficulties of estimating both the welfare consequences of the practice and also the individual damage. **8.046**

Many of the business practices of dominant companies that can be classified as abusive, however, also entail positive effects on competition. For instance, tying can be used to leverage market power from one market to another but might also entail substantial reductions in transaction costs for consumers.[48] The harm generated by abusive practices is therefore often much more difficult to pin down than in cartel cases. In contrast to the latter, they do not exclusively exhibit anti-competitive effects but also entail efficiency enhancing effects that are procompetitive. In addition, different types of purchasers may be affected **8.047**

---

46 It is important to bear in mind that a calculation of individual damage is distinct from an effects analysis that would be conducted to establish whether an infringement took place. An effects analysis aimed at establishing an infringement will focus on anti-competitive effects and in particular on consumer harm. It will not consider the loss of market shares of competitors as such as a problem. Once the infringement is established, however, the loss of market share, if it can be attributed to the abusive conduct, presents a clear individual damage. In other words, and drawing on the welfare discussions above, the efficiency justifications for competition law lead to a focus on the overall welfare effects of a particular practice and therefore disregard pure transfers of wealth. From an individual damage perspective, however, these transfers are typically the most important part of the damage suffered even if they are not welfare losses.

47 A caveat is of course indicated with respect to episodes of price wars in cartelised industries. During these price wars, prices are likely to be below cost and would therefore also fulfil a predation standard. See the model by Green and Porter (1984) and its empirical application in Porter (1983).

48 Of course such efficiencies may be reached without anti-competitive effects by bundling instead of tying.

differently. Under price discrimination, for example, purchasers with a price elastic demand generally stand to gain as they are paying a lower price than under uniform pricing, but purchasers with a less elastic demand are faced with a higher price. The total effect of the price discrimination on welfare may even be positive.

8.048 Under exclusionary abuse, the behaviour of a dominant firm usually changes over time. In the first phase of such an abuse, for example in the case of predatory pricing, competition may be very intense up until the point where competitors leave the market and where competition will subsequently be substantially weakened. Some abusive practices may also lead to a permanent change of the market structure so that the negative consequences on the market structure become quasi-permanent and possibly irreparable, something that is more difficult to imagine in the context of cartelised markets. It may, however, also be possible to imagine a situation where remedies of the competition authority, in particular if structural remedies are considered, lead to a much more competition prone environment than prior to the abuse. This is discussed in more detail in section III.B.1.

2 Economic actors damaged by exploitative and exclusionary conduct

8.049 If the abusive practice is exploitative, the harmed parties are, using the analogy of a cartel situation, the direct and indirect purchasers as well as the direct and indirect suppliers, but also the producers of complementary products and the purchasers of substitutes. Under price discrimination, different consumer types are affected differently. If there are two groups of customers, some with an elastic and others with a less elastic demand for the product, those with an elastic demand will stand to benefit and those with an inelastic demand will stand to lose if prices are compared to a uniform price. This represents a substantial difference to cartel-induced price increases that typically affect all purchasers uniformly.[49]

8.050 If the abusive practice is exclusionary, the bulk of the damage is borne by competitors of the dominant undertaking. Due to the exclusionary practice, competitors lose market share and may eventually even have to exit the market. This could for instance be the case under a retroactive rebate scheme or under predatory pricing, which have a direct bearing on the revenues of competitors.

49 While a cartel-induced price increase may be identical for all purchasers, the consequences of such a price increase for individual purchasers and therefore also the damage suffered can be quite distinct. Consider for example a situation where due to the cartel-induced input price increase a firm's product is now priced substantially higher than before, resulting in alternative products becoming viable substitutes for its purchasers. In an extreme case, this firm may have to exit the market in the long term whereas other purchasers of the cartel may only face reductions in profit due to much more mitigated price and quantity effects on their products.

This could in turn result in damage for the suppliers of these firms as they can only sell a reduced quantity. If the abusive conduct stems from a vertically integrated undertaking, similar effects can be obtained through a margin squeeze or a refusal to deal strategy that successfully raises rivals' costs. In addition, potential competitors also may be among the victims if the abuse is instrumental in erecting entry barriers that keep other, potentially even more efficient, rivals out of the market.

While the bulk of the damage accrues to competitors, purchasers of the dominant firm are, in particular once the infringement takes effect, also harmed by higher prices, reduced quantities, lower quality and less innovation. If the abusive conduct is terminated prior to competitors losing substantial market share, the damage to purchasers is limited and they may even have benefited from the increased competition.[50] In practice it seems therefore reasonable to expect competitors to be the key victims in such cases. **8.051**

III QUANTIFICATION OF DAMAGES

Once the type of competition law violation is established in the context of a specific damages claim, the affected economic agents can be determined and the damage caused by the infringement can be assessed at least conceptually. In order to fully compensate victims, the specific level of damages for each victim has to be calculated. As discussed previously, the approach for determining the damage is based on a comparison of the actual wealth position as impacted by the competition law infringement with a wealth position in a hypothetical counterfactual situation that would have prevailed in the absence of the infringement.[51] In principle, the market outcome of a comparable factual or hypothetical market is the basis for estimating the damage that is caused by the competition law infringement. In that sense all methods employed for estimating damages are comparator-based and the main distinguishing feature is simply whether the comparator is theoretically constructed or taken from an **8.052**

50 Note that this crucially depends on whether the abusive practice involves a profit sacrifice or not. This is the case with predation but may very well not be the case under retroactive rebate schemes or other abusive practices such as refusal to deal. For a discussion of whether rebate schemes involve a sacrifice, see Maier-Rigaud and Schwalbe (2013).

51 Wealth position is a more general term than profit, which could wrongfully be construed as implying that losses in utility are not considered relevant. The term wealth position is, therefore, not used coincidentally as quantity effects for consumers are typically not expressed as profit losses but as utility losses, but, nevertheless, can be expressed in monetary terms and should be counted as damages.

existing market.[52] In the following subsections the different approaches for assessing the counterfactual scenario for the two basic competition law infringements of cartel agreements and abusive conduct are presented.

A Quantification of damages in cartel cases

8.053 In the context of a cartel, the counterfactual scenario is given by the price, quantity and quality that would have prevailed if there had not been any cartelisation in the industry and firms had competed within the structural conditions prevalent in the market.[53]

8.054 In order to construct a counterfactual scenario, an actual market that is similar or comparable to the cartelised market in terms of time, geographic location or in terms of products could be used. An alternative to a factual comparator market is the design of an artificial market based on models from industrial organisation theory and empirical analysis that could be used to establish the but-for price, the corresponding quantity and finally the cartel-induced damage. A further possibility to estimate the counterfactual price consists in using the production cost and a 'normal' mark-up, that is, a mark-up that could have been realised on a market under competitive conditions. Alternatively, other factors, such as, for example, the profitability of a firm, could be used to assess the counterfactual scenario. The following sections discuss the different methods that have been proposed to estimate damages in the context of cartel cases. While most of these methods can also be employed in cases of abusive conduct, the specificities of estimating damages in these cases are relegated to section III.B.

1 Time series analysis

8.055 In many cases it will be appropriate to use a comparison in time to estimate the cartel-induced damage. This method typically involves using the same market before and/or after the cartel period and is conducted with the help of regression analysis or other methods of time series analysis.[54] Such an approach has the advantage that the companies in the factual and counterfactual scenario are mostly the same, so that the counterfactual is a good comparator at least in

---

52 This distinction seems more intuitive than the structure proposed by the European Commission (2009: 43) that distinguishes between comparator-based, financial analysis-based and market structure-based. See also European Commission (2011) distinguishing between comparator-based and simulation, model and cost-based analysis.

53 A cartel may also cause additional damage if for example the incentives to innovate are reduced or if firms explicitly agree on a reduction of product quality or product variety. In practice, however, quantification of these damages will usually be difficult as it is necessary to prove a causal relationship with the cartel infringement.

54 On the empirical and econometric methods for calculating damages see for example Davis and Garcés (2010: 347–381).

that respect. It should be noted, however, that with the use of a before-and-after method a number of problems can also arise. In some cartel cases, when the cartel actually started is unknown, which creates difficulties in determining the period of time when the market was not cartelised.[55] The reason for the existence of a cartel may also be due to a period of fierce and ruinous competition, so that the prices prior to the cartel do not reflect normal competition. In other instances the time period after the end of the cartel may be too short to allow a reliable estimation of competitive prices. In addition, it may well be the case that the end of the cartel is followed by a phase of fierce competition and price wars so that again the prices observed in that phase are not a good indicator of competitive prices.[56] Furthermore, it cannot be omitted that the preceding cartel agreements created a focal point allowing the former cartelists to continue to charge prices that are very close to those agreed upon during the cartel phase and that are therefore not a good benchmark for prices under normal competition.

The main approach that has been proposed to estimate the counterfactual using a factual comparator market is the before-and-after method,[57] that is, prices before and after the end of the cartel period are used to establish the appropriate benchmark prices within the cartel period had the infringement not taken place. The method is based on the simple idea that to the extent that cartel prices differ in a statistically significant way from the prices prior to the implementation of the cartel agreement and the prices once the cartel ceased to operate, the difference could be attributed to the cartel. The before-and-after approach is usually implemented within a multiple regression framework that is used to estimate the price over the entire period covering both non-cartel periods prior to the start of the cartel and after the cartel ceases to exist and includes a dummy variable, that is, a binary indicator taking the values of 0 and 1 depending on whether the time window falls into the cartel period or not. Estimating the coefficient of this dummy variable then measures the amount of the cartel-induced price increase. For this to be a valid inference, control variables accounting for other factors that may have impacted prices, for example increases in input prices, must be included.[58] Failure to include such controls may result in significant distortions in the calculation of damages as **8.056**

55 As long as required data is available, an econometric analysis may be able to pin down the starting date of the cartel based on structural breaks, but these methods are not error free, for instance in cases where the cartel increased prices slowly.

56 This type of price war probably occurred after the breakdown of the German cement cartel, meaning that the prices of this phase were weighted down in the estimation of damages. See Friederiszick and Röller (2010).

57 Also called before, during and after method, see OECD (2011: 14).

58 This is particularly important if these factors are correlated with the cartel period.

price effects are causally attributed to the cartel when they are in fact due to circumstances that are independent of the cartel.

8.057 Consider for example a situation where the before-and-after method is used to estimate the price effects of the cartel and that entry occurred at about the same time as the cartel ended.[59] Clearly, additional entry will tend to decrease prices in the market and if this aspect is not controlled for in the regression the observed price reduction after the cartel ended will be taken as caused by the breakdown of the cartel agreement, resulting in damage caused by the cartel being overestimated. As a result, it is crucial to include all factors that have an impact on price and that changed during the relevant time period in the estimation. This would call, for instance, for an inclusion of demand factors such as the price of substitutes and complements but also cost factors such as capacity utilisation and input prices.

8.058 An empirical example of this type of before-and-after estimation was performed in the context of the vitamin cartel in the 1990s. In his expert report for the Vitamin Antitrust Litigation, Bernheim (2002) estimated the prices that would have prevailed absent the conspiracy using reduced form regressions. This is depicted in Figure 8.8.

8.059 In contrast to an analysis where the structural breaks, that is, the beginning and ending phase of the cartel period, are exogenously determined, endogenous structural break models allow for a statistical determination of the start and ending periods of a cartel, possibly also including gradual price changes at the beginning and end in a dynamic analysis.[60]

8.060 In general, caution may be required in focussing on prices after the cartel ended. There are essentially three reasons for this. Firstly, former cartelists expecting damages claims in the aftermath of the cartel episode will find it in their interest to maintain higher prices than would otherwise be warranted, to the extent that the profit loss associated with such higher prices is overcompensated for by lower damages claims if post-cartel prices are used in the estimation of damages; for example, in the context of a before-and-after methodology. Secondly, the breakdown of a cartel could result in a price war and the exceptionally low prices during this period do not reflect prices that would prevail under normal competitive conditions.[61] Thirdly, some cartel cases exist where the

59 It may even be that entry is in fact the very reason that the cartel broke down.

60 On this topic see for example Harrington (2008).

61 This was presumably the case in the German cement cartel, see for example Friederiszick and Röller (2010).

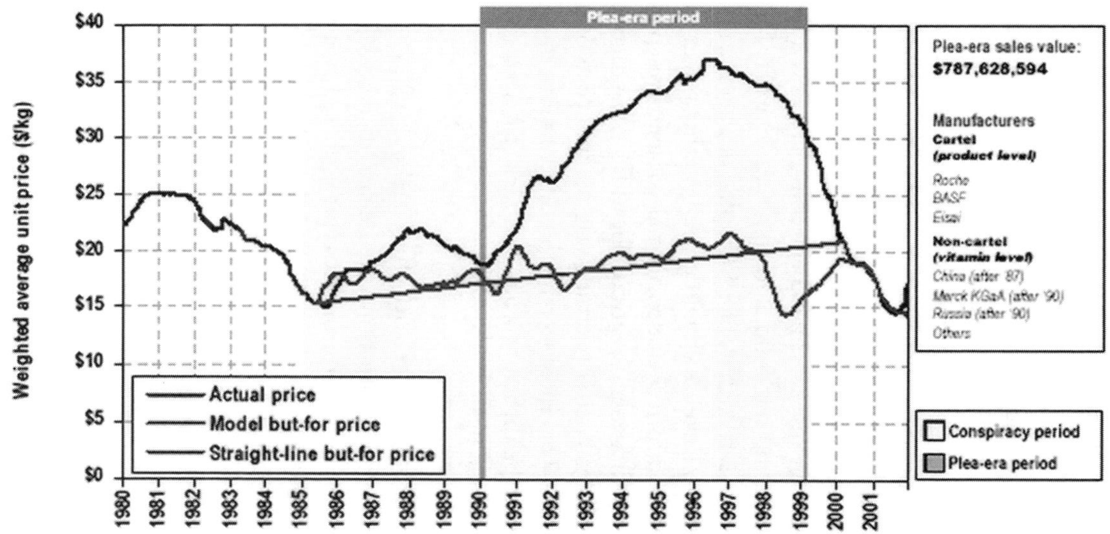

Source: Seven-month centred moving average for US 'tel quel' food, pharma and cosmetic price from Roche ROVIS data.

Figure 8.8 Vitamin E Acetate Oil USP price and counterfactual price

competition authority was not satisfied with fining the cartelists and implementing a cease and desist decision but also tried to reduce the future possibility of tacit collusion.[62] As a result, prices observed after the cartel ended may remain supra-competitive and it may be prudent to give such prices a lower weight than pre-cartel prices in estimating the counterfactual price.

2 Cross-sectional analysis

8.061 Alternatively to the before-and-after method, geographic comparator markets can be used to estimate the prices and quantities under normal competitive conditions. This type of cross-sectional analysis assumes that the market structure in another geographic market, for instance in another country or region, is sufficiently comparable, that is exhibiting a similar concentration, similar technologies and cost structures as well as similar demand conditions. In addition, such a geographic market can only be considered a valid benchmark if it can be ascertained that no restrictions to competition exist. This could be a problem insofar as to the extent that the geographic market is a good empirical fit, the same incentives to cartelise should prevail, so that prices in this market may similarly deviate from prices under normal competitive conditions. As a matter of fact, there will generally always be differences between the two geographic markets, for instance concerning wages, input costs or demand, that could subsequently be taken into account by adjustments in the prices. In practice it will, however, be difficult to pin down exactly what the appropriate corrections in prices should be.

8.062 Cross-sectional models estimate the price effect of the cartel by comparing data in the relevant market with comparable unaffected markets. Cross-sectional models do not have a time dimension and are typically based on a comparison of data taken from the same time period. The underlying assumption in a cross-sectional analysis is that the comparator geographic or product market has been chosen in such a way that all differences identified in a comparison will be due to the cartel. Any remaining differences between the markets would need to be identified and controlled in a similar fashion as discussed above in

62 These instances are, however, rare. See for example US Detroit Automobile Dealers Association (DADA). In 1984, the FTC alleged that the automobile dealers violated federal antitrust laws through a conspiracy to limit competition in the sale of new cars in the Detroit area by closing dealerships on Saturdays and most week nights. In addition to a cease and desist order concerning the fixing of opening hours, the FTC also imposed a behavioural remedy requiring the dealers to be open a minimum amount of hours during the week in order to avoid dealers simply sticking to the previously agreed upon opening schedules that at this stage were a natural focal point. In general the use of behavioural or structural remedies is rare in cartel cases despite the fact that tacit collusion may become much more practicable in the aftermath of a cartel phase as argued by Connor (2004). This is essentially the argument that a cartel agreement may reinforce or create focal points although one could legitimately inquire about the need to form a cartel structure based on regular meetings if indeed one initial meeting may have been enough to make a particular focal point salient.

the context of time series analysis. While such comparisons could be made between geographic markets or even distinct but comparable product markets, comparisons could also be made between individual firms.

Deriving the counterfactual price based on cross-sectional comparisons can take the form of simple comparisons of averages[63] or regression techniques. These regression models would proceed similarly to the regressions discussed in the context of time series analysis with the exception that the binary dummy variable would now identify the two comparator markets. The advantage of a regression approach is that it will allow for controlling identified differences between the comparators. **8.063**

One of the problems with this method, already touched upon previously, is that if another geographic or product market is truly comparable to the cartelised one, there are good reasons to believe that the incentives to cartelise are also similar, so that it cannot be avoided that one cartelised market is compared to another, thereby substantially underestimating damage. An advantage of this method compared to the simplest time series analysis that allows for structural breaks is that the beginning and end phases of the cartel are determined endogenously. **8.064**

3 *Difference-in-differences method*

A superior alternative is the so-called panel data analysis that combines the before-and-after and the geographic comparator method for estimating the counterfactual price. This method is based on a simultaneous observation of price developments through time on the cartelised market and on one or several comparable but geographically separated markets. This method, which is also known as the difference-in-differences method, allows a more precise estimation of the cartel-induced price increase. It analyses and compares the differences in the price developments in the cartelised and the benchmark markets allowing a more precise estimation of the cartel-induced price effect as changes in price that are, for example, identified in a time series analysis, may now no longer be attributed solely to the cartel but could for instance also be traced back to an increase in cost that affects all companies irrespective of the geographic market they operate in. Also, constant differences between the two geographic markets can be accounted for, as in the case of different production technologies. **8.065**

63 The average or arithmetic mean is the sum of all observations divided by the total number of observations. Possible alternatives are comparisons based on median or mode prices, that is, the price of the firm in the middle of a price ranked distribution or the price observed with the highest frequency respectively.

8.066 As the difference-in-differences method can be considered a combination of time series analysis and cross-sectional analysis, either the average prices in the two markets can be compared or additional factors can be considered by using a regression analysis. Two dummy variables, one for the cartelised market and one for the cartel period are introduced, as well as an interaction term that is defined as the product of the two dummy variables. The estimated coefficient of this interaction term gives an estimate of the cartel-induced price increase. Application of the difference-in-differences method, however, often encounters data constraints, so that the basis for a time series comparison across different geographic markets is not always given. Suitable comparisons between similar product markets, that is, a comparison of markets for similar products in which the market is not distorted by cartel agreements, can generally only be found in exceptional cases as the differences in production processes, cost structures and demand as well as competitive conditions will render a meaningful comparator market extremely difficult to find. In addition, the caveats mentioned in the context of a geographic market comparison also apply here, that is, the problem that the market may also be cartelised.

4 Simulated comparator markets

8.067 As a result, there will be a number of situations where neither a convincing geographic market nor product market can be found and also the application of the before-and-after method will not be fruitful. In such cases, one could resort to a simulated, that is, an artificially constructed, counterfactual market. Similarly to simulation models used in merger control, a model from industrial organisation theory would need to be designed that reflects the competitive situation on the concerned market as precisely as possible. Depending on the cartelised goods, the central competition parameters and the allocation mechanism, one could resort to standard oligopoly models with homogenous or differentiated goods and quantity competition (Cournot models), oligopoly models with differentiated goods and price competition (Bertrand models) or auction models, that would typically need to be tailored to the specific parameters of the concerned markets, for example, concerning entry barriers, capacity constraints or demand fluctuations.

8.068 Based on demand data, information on the quantities sold and on costs and prices, an empirically based model of the market could be designed that would allow the simulation of the market outcome, that is prices and quantities, that would probably have prevailed in the absence of the cartel. In addition to the question of data availability, such an approach is confronted with two fundamental conceptual problems. The first problem concerns the degree of coordination that the firms achieved in the cartel. Under perfect coordination, the cartel would choose a price that maximises total cartel profits, that is, it would act as a monopolist on the cartelised market. For various reasons, for example a possible market entry by potential competitors or an incomplete market coverage, a cartel might be able to achieve only a partial coordination, so that the cartel price remains below the profit-maximising price a monopolist would charge.[64] As a result, it is important to explore whether, and, if so, to what extent the cartel price was below the monopoly price. The second conceptual problem lies in identifying what price would have prevailed in the market absent the cartel agreement. This in turn depends on the intensity of competition absent the cartel agreement. This intensity may have been relatively low in the first place, for instance if the market is characterised by a small amount of similar companies operating on a transparent and stable market with limited innovation and the existence of an effective punishment mechanism. In such a case, a relatively high counterfactual price would result and the cartel-induced damage would correspondingly be limited. It is not appropriate to generally presume that the counterfactual is given by the maximum degree of competition that the oligopoly model adopted to simulate the market allows. If the damage is supposed to be estimated as accurately as possible, the possibility of a lower intensity of competition in the absence of the cartel needs to be considered. This is analogous to other areas of competition law such as merger control, where coordinated conduct is taken into consideration.[65]

5 Cost-based and profitability-based approaches

An alternative comparator-based method for determining the counterfactual scenario involves using the variable cost of production and adding an appropriate mark-up in order to derive a counterfactual price in a 'bottom-up' way.[66] The mark-up could be estimated using information on margins in comparable competitive markets or theoretically determined information. Thus, these methods can also be considered as comparator-based approaches. **8.069**

The use of the variable cost raises some questions because cartelised firms may have inflated costs due to X-inefficiencies and/or may simply face higher variable costs due to the reduced cartel output and economies of scale. With multiproduct firms there is the additional problem of common cost allocation. To solve these problems, variable costs would need to be compared and adjusted based on information on the variable costs of firms in competitive markets, which can be fraught with difficulties. **8.070**

64 Due to factors such as the existence of potential mavericks or a competitive fringe, the level of coordination will often be less than perfect. Even when firms are all interested in coordination, production technologies are likely to diverge sufficiently for marginal revenues not being equal to marginal costs for all cartelists, implying that coordination is not perfect even if compensatory side-payments are envisioned.

65 See Inderst and Schwalbe (2011).

66 See Konings et al. (2001) on mark-ups.

8.071 Whereas the presented methods emphasise the estimation of prices and quantities in the counterfactual scenario, other methods focus on profitability or price-cost margins directly. For a cartel on an input market, it will generally be the case that cartel profits increase, whereas the profits of purchasers decrease.[67] As the bulk of the cartel damage is based on the transfer of wealth from the purchasers to the cartelists, increases or decreases in profits can be used as an indicator of damage.[68]

8.072 To measure profitability, two general concepts can be used. On the one hand, an accounting approach focussing on the profitability of the firm based on the return on capital employed (ROCE) can be used, or, on the other hand, a finance approach can be used that, drawing on the capital asset pricing model (CAPM), is based on net present value (NPV) and the internal rate of return (IRR).[69]

8.073 An alternative method for estimating the profitability or the change in profitability is the calculation of the price-cost margin or, stated otherwise, the percentage mark-up. In this context, the cost concept is crucial and long run average incremental costs (LRAIC) are typically considered the most suitable cost concept.[70] These costs are defined as the average of all variable and fixed cost associated with the production and supply of a particular good in relation to the total quantity produced. Stated otherwise, the LRAIC denote the costs that would be saved if in the long run the production of the good would be stopped. Due to the long-run perspective, not only the variable cost but also the fixed cost that could be saved are taken into account. A change in the profitability as indicated by this method could equally be considered an indicator for the transfer and therefore for part of the damage caused by the cartel.

B Damage quantification in abusive conduct cases

1 Damage caused by abusive behaviour and the counterfactual scenario

8.074 To estimate damages resulting from abusive conduct, the same basic conceptual framework as in the case of cartels applies. The actual situation with the infringement has to be compared to the hypothetical counterfactual situation in the absence of the abuse. The damage is then the difference in wealth of economic actors in both scenarios. A practical application, however, is often

67 As was explained in section II.A, the change in profitability of the purchasers depends on the price and quantity effect which in turn depends on downstream demand.

68 The increase in profits of the cartelists being the lower bound of total damage if no quantity effects are considered. As shown in section II.A, this lower bound may be far off.

69 See OECD (2012a: 63–66); and Gregory (2011).

70 See OECD (2012a: 66–70).

fraught with severe difficulties. In what follows, the general problem of constructing a suitable counterfactual scenario in abuse of dominance cases is discussed. As this differs in cases of exploitative and exclusionary abuse, these two cases are dealt with separately. Section III.B.2 discusses the practical problems in the quantification of damages in the case of an exclusionary abuse by means of some examples. Damage calculations in abuse of dominance cases are usually more difficult than in cartel cases and this may also be the reason that to the best of our knowledge there is no empirical study estimating the damage caused by abusive conduct.

a Exploitative abuse

If a dominant firm charges an excessive price, the comparable geographic market or the before-and-after method can be employed, for example, time series analysis or cross-sectional data, provided that the data exist and that a suitable comparator market can be identified. The former could be an appropriate approach if the dominant firm is offering the product in question in another geographic market where it is confronted with competition at a lower price. Of course, differences in the geographic markets, for example, concerning the demand behaviour or supply cost, would need to be considered. Alternatively, cost-based methods could be used in order to determine the counterfactual price.[71] **8.075**

From an economic point of view, to what extent the behaviour in a different market or, more generally, the terms for other buyers or suppliers can be considered a suitable counterfactual scenario is important. This can be illustrated using an example of retailers with different degrees of market power vis-à-vis producers. If retailers have different degrees of market power, they can negotiate different contract terms with the producer. This buying power may have been achieved by establishing strong customer loyalty or by serving certain regions. In these cases, a producer would be willing to accept inferior conditions as the retailer has a special position and cannot be substituted easily by a different retailer. Also, a retailer with buyer power could negotiate different contract terms for different suppliers or in different regions. If this depends on different substitution options, the different contract terms only reflect market forces. In this context the question arises as to whether the retailers were able to achieve a position of market power by competition on the merits or by abusive **8.076**

71 Under an excessive price abuse, the finding of an excessive price implies the definition of an appropriate counterfactual price, at least implicitly. While competition authorities will try to avoid indicating the threshold price at which the price would no longer be considered excessive, the decision of the authority in case of a follow-on claim for damages will contain more clues as to the counterfactual price than for example a cartel decision. On excessive price abuses and the available methods to determine whether a price is excessive see again OECD (2012a).

practices. Only in the former case, can such a market be considered a suitable comparator market.

8.077 In case of an exploitative abuse in the form of price discrimination, leading to price increases for purchasers with a less elastic demand, the question arises as to whether the higher price level or the price discrimination is considered a breach of competition law.[72] With respect to the damage quantification, this could make a substantial difference. While in the first case the higher price may have to be reduced to the level of the lower price, the second case requires determining the uniform price the firm would have charged in all markets and for all consumer groups. Furthermore, it has to be considered that under a uniform price the firm might not have served all markets given the uniform price constraint. A reasonable approach to quantifying the damage could involve deriving the appropriate counterfactual by using an empirically calibrated industrial organisation model, for instance a model with a dominant firm and a competitive fringe, to determine the counterfactual price absent the discrimination. Also, the market prior to the introduction of differentiated prices or another geographic market where a single price prevails could be considered. It has to be examined, however, whether different market conditions could be the reason why the firm has chosen a different pricing scheme.

b Exclusionary abuse

8.078 To calculate the damage caused by an exclusionary abuse, the situation that would have occurred in the market absent the exclusionary abuse will have to be assessed in order to address the question of what profits competitors would have been able to obtain in the counterfactual scenario and what prices the purchasers would have had to pay.

8.079 In terms of comparator-based methods, the primary candidate generally is the before-and-after method, that is, a consideration of the market prior to the initiation of the exclusionary strategy.[73] As an exclusionary abuse typically unfolds in time and in different phases, a comparison with a unique moment in time only provides an incomplete picture of the effects. Normally, the question would need to be answered about how the market would have developed had the anti-competitive conduct not taken place. This could for instance be highly relevant in a market with network effects. In the case of a dominant firm preventing another company from winning a critical mass of consumers and

72 Buccirossi (2010) emphasises that it is crucial to determine what anti-competitive practice generated the damage so that it becomes central to develop a full theory of harm in the context of damages claims if they are not follow-on actions.

73 Focusing on the market prior to the introduction of the exclusionary strategy may turn out to be problematic as the market structure may have completely changed as a result of the abuse.

taking over the market, considering the situation prior to the abuse may not be a particularly meaningful counterfactual scenario as the other company would have earned substantial profits in the absence of the abuse in the meantime.

In all likelihood there will also be no comparable geographic or product markets that come close to the market at hand. In order to guarantee a minimum degree of comparability, the market would need to exhibit a similar concentration, comparable cost structures as well as similar demand conditions, something that will be rather rare. Therefore, many of the empirical methods discussed in the context of cartels cannot be applied because the necessary data are not available. **8.080**

A further conceptual problem exists in establishing what is implied by 'in the absence of the exclusionary abuse'. This is unclear as there are a multitude of possible scenarios that a dominant firm could have followed in order to achieve competition law compliance and these different scenarios are likely to have entailed very different market outcomes. For instance, in case of exclusion through a retroactive rebate, several possibilities ranging from a linear price to a two-part tariff or an incremental quantity discount could be appropriate counterfactual pricing schemes, all entailing potentially different market outcomes. In principle, the counterfactual scenario would have to be characterised by an oligopolistic equilibrium in which the dominant firm maximises profits under the constraint of complying with competition law.[74] In some cases the possibility may exist to develop such a counterfactual scenario, for example, in the case of tying. In such instances the question concerning what profits the competitors of the dominant firm would have made absent the tying, that is, in case the products had also been sold independently, would need to be answered. In other cases of exclusionary abuses, however, as for instance in the case of entry barriers, the construction of an economically well-founded counterfactual is likely to be difficult. A possible solution in these cases could be a simulation-based approach. Here, a simulation model of the market would have to be developed that might give an indication of the possible development of the market absent the abusive behaviour. To apply simulation techniques, the relevant data have to be available to calibrate the model. If these data are lacking, they have to be substituted by reasonable assumptions. **8.081**

For these reasons, estimating damages in exclusionary abuse cases often has to rely on a more or less rough estimation of the lost profits of competitors and the **8.082**

74 It should, however, be noted that the doubts voiced earlier with respect to the likelihood of a profit-maximising equilibrium being reached in a cartel context, equally apply here. In particular, if the firm reaches a high level of independence, one will not be able to rely on (evolutionary) market forces 'pushing' the firm to such a profit-maximising equilibrium.

damage that accrued to the purchasers as opposed to a comparison between the actual and a fully developed hypothetical counterfactual. When using such a rough estimate, the conditions of the relevant market should be taken into account such as the size and geographic extent of the market, the importance of entry barriers, the type of products traded (homogenous, differentiated, intermediate or final goods), the market development, the degree of innovation, etc.

8.083 All things considered, it becomes clear that the type of abuse plays a central role in the derivation of the counterfactual and therefore also in the precision with which damages can be estimated. Whereas it is relatively clear what scenario would have obtained but for the infringement in cartel and exploitative abuse cases, the determination of the appropriate counterfactual scenario may be much more difficult in exclusionary abuse cases.[75] Firstly, it will be difficult to find suitable comparator markets, and secondly, a multitude of alternative business strategies conforming to competition law conduct exist. Thirdly, the market may have developed very differently in the absence of the abuse.

2 *Illustration: quantification of damages in case of an exclusionary abuse*

8.084 As demonstrated in section III.B.1, the damage estimation in an exclusionary abuse context is generally much more complex than in cartel cases or cases of exploitative abuse.[76] On the one hand, exclusionary abuses typically unfold in different phases, some of which will potentially affect economic actors positively and others negatively. This considerably increases the complexity of the analysis. In addition, it has to be considered that usually different exclusionary practices will have different competitive effects. A predatory strategy for example may result in the exit of a competitor, whereas other practices may result in entry being barred. In what follows, the complexity of the quantification of damages is illustrated using an example of an exclusionary abuse that aims at the market exit, or at least the marginalisation, of an actual competitor.

8.085 The actors affected by an exclusionary abuse are primarily the direct competitors and the purchasers of the products of the dominant company. In addition, suppliers of firms that were forced to exit the market are affected. In the following, the quantification of damages is analysed in the context of an exclusionary abuse aiming at the foreclosure, or at restricting the expansion of, a competitor. An exclusionary abuse typically proceeds in several phases. In phase one a competitor is forced to exit the market. The increase in market power is

75 This difficulty is exacerbated by the fact that competition authorities will only indirectly have investigated the relevant aspects in bringing their infringement case, something that is typically done in exploitative cases.

76 This may be one of the reasons that there is almost no literature focusing on the calculation of damages in exclusionary abuse cases. A notable exception is the contribution by Fumagalli et al. (2010) that introduces the notion of different damages at relevant phases that we will partially follow here.

then exploited by the dominant firm in phase two by higher prices and increased profits. In the following phase (phase three), after the abusive behaviour has ceased, new (or re-)entry may occur. This phase is therefore characterised by a restoration of competitive conditions. An important aspect of phase three also concerns the remedies that the competition authority may impose. In contrast to cartel cases that typically end with a cease and desist order and the imposition of fines, abusive practices trigger behavioural or structural remedies. As a result, assessing harm in the context of such cases may involve taking into account potential benefits that are due to remedies imposed by the competition authority.

a Phase one

In the first phase of an exclusionary abuse, the profits of competitors and their market shares would decline. This phase would continue until the competitor(s) leave(s) the market or, if there is no exit, until the market shares stabilise at a comparatively low level, implying the marginalisation of the competitor(s). The dominant firm can, depending on the strategy adapted, continue to earn profits, as is for instance the case in retroactive rebates. It is, however, also possible that the dominant firm is realising losses in the first phase, as would be the case under a predatory strategy.[77] **8.086**

The repercussions for purchasers of the firms depend in this phase on the type of abuse. In case of a predatory strategy, the repercussions on purchasers are in all likelihood positive. They pay lower prices for the products than they would have paid in the absence of the predatory strategy. Similar arguments apply in case of a margin squeeze where low prices will also be observed. These effects can propagate and also reach indirect purchasers that would equally benefit from the predatory prices. Different repercussions on purchasers arise if the abuse is focussing on an increase in input prices (raising rivals' costs) or refusal to deal. In such instances the costs of competitors increase so that the price level on the downstream market tends to increase and purchasers pay higher prices than in the absence of the infringement. Repercussions for indirect purchasers are also likely in this case. **8.087**

b Phase two

In a case where the abuse leads to exit, the competitor is unable to realise any profits in the second phase and may under certain circumstances even have to **8.088**

77 The question is not necessarily whether overall profits are positive or negative but rather whether there is a profit sacrifice that would require at least probabilistic future recoupment to make the strategy profitable, or whether exclusion may be compatible with profit maximisation considering only the first phase. Both scenarios are possible and depend on the abuse.

bear sunk costs.[78] The bulk of the damage to the firm therefore comes from lost profits. In a case where the competitor remains in the market, albeit with lower market shares, it would be able to realise profits in the second phase but the profits are substantially lower than in the absence of the abuse. Also, in this case the damage is in the form of lost profits. The dominant firm in contrast has reached its goals in the second phase and is able to reap the benefits of increased market power by setting higher prices and earning higher profits.

8.089 Concerning the repercussions of the abuse on the purchasers, they are analogous to those of a cartel or an exploitative abuse. Direct and indirect purchasers pay higher prices. In addition to this, there is also damage in the form of reduced choice. In particular, in markets with differentiated products the elimination of competitors reduces the product variety and thereby reduces consumer welfare.[79] Proving and quantifying such damages is, however, difficult. Suppliers of the dominant company face a lower demand due to the reduced quantities supplied by the dominant firm. This results in damage in the form of lost profits.

c *Phase three*

8.090 The third phase starts with the end of the abusive practice, typically, at least in follow-on suits, roughly before the decision to cease the abuse by the competition authority. The third phase is in some sense the reversal of the first phase, although the damages calculation in this phase is likely to be extremely difficult already due to the added complications in the form of very likely behavioural or structural remedies imposed by the competition authority. Generally speaking, the third phase will see a return to competitive conditions, implying the entry of new competitors or the re-entry of the firms that exited, or corresponding increases in market shares of the firms that were marginalised. As a result of these developments the profits of the dominant firm decrease irrespective of any potential fine imposed by the competition authority, and the profits of competitors would increase. The third phase can be considered to be terminated once a situation takes place that approximates the situation that would have existed in the absence of the infringement. Once an approximation of the situation occurs some competition authorities, notably the European Commission, are obliged to effectively end the infringement, which also implies removing the possibility of any future recurrence of abuse which may preclude the return to a situation as it existed prior to the abuse.[80]

---

78 Of course it would be incorrect to add the sunk costs to a calculation of damages based on lost profits. A firm can either claim the sunk costs or the lost profits, but not both.

79 Fumagalli et al. (2010: 209).

80 The obligation of the European Commission to effectively end an infringement implies that any future recurrence needs to be prevented. While it is not possible to develop the details concerning behavioural and

In particular, outside the context of follow-on claims, the abusive practice may have resulted in permanent changes to the market structure that are not impacted by compensatory payments so that the third phase does not lead to an approximation of the situation prior to the infringement. Even if a decision by a competition authority exists, a dominant firm may have been able to build up a reputation of fighting market entry with predatory prices.[81] In such a case, entry would not be observed immediately and may eventually occur only after a long time has passed. **8.091**

A similar problem exists in cases of an exclusionary abuse that does not aim at the foreclosure of a competitor already active in the market but which targets potential competitors that are kept from considering entry. In such a case, potential competitors are harmed in the form of the lost profits that they may have been able to realise after entry. Possibly this has led to entry in another, less lucrative, market, where a lower profit was realised. In this context it is also important to consider the technology a potential competitor would have used upon entry, that is, whether it would have deployed a superior, inferior or identical technology. Without additional information or proof that the company could have produced more efficiently, it may be useful to assume that such a competitor would have entered using the same technology, exhibiting a similar efficiency as the dominant undertaking. **8.092**

In order to estimate the damage that accrued to the different actors in the different phases, a comparison with the counterfactual is necessary. As already discussed in section II.B, this is considerably more complicated in exclusionary abuse cases than in cartel or exploitative abuse cases. In order to fully utilise all available information, it seems appropriate to consider several realistic counterfactual scenarios that are compatible with the underlying characteristics of the markets in question. Different scenarios could be generated by utilising different approaches from the tool kit of factual and hypothetical comparator methods. They could also be generated by varying some of the crucial determinants of the outcome in a simulation model used in the hypothetical comparator approach, which would further increase the robustness of results derived with these methods. In order to explain the quantification of damages in this context, a particular counterfactual scenario is considered. For the **8.093**

structural remedies as well as the Commission's mandate here, it is clear that the European Commission has imposed structural remedies so far only in cases where behavioural remedies were unlikely to be effective in terminating the abuse *and preventing any future recurrence of the abuse*. As the situation prior to phase one clearly was not a situation that prevented the future abuse, the Commission will be bound to choose remedies that exclude the possibility that the end of phase three results in the same situation as existed prior to phase one. Any remedy falling short of this could actually not be considered a suitable remedy. On the issue of remedies see Maier-Rigaud (2012).

81 See the classic paper by Selten (1978).

competitors, the profits obtained during the different phases would need to be compared with the profits obtained in the counterfactual scenario. As an exclusionary abuse can target the revenues or costs of competitors, it may be useful to estimate the change in profits of the competitors through a separate analysis of the development of revenues and costs. Such an approach could facilitate the distinction between changes in profit that are not due to the abusive conduct and those that are due to the abusive conduct. Generally speaking, reduced sales result in cost changes so that changes in profit can be derived from the difference between revenues and changes in cost.

8.094 As discussed in section III.A, when quantifying damages, all those factors have to be controlled that bear no causal relationship with the incriminated behaviour. The extent to which the factors have an impact on the profits follows from the respective multivariate regressions. The quantification of damages is thus corrected for the effects of these factors. An important factor in this context could be the business model used by the firm, which may differ in situations with and without abusive conduct. In principle, the econometric methods allow for an estimation of the impact of these factors on cost, revenues and profits and the determination of the extent to which the changes in profits can be explained by these factors. Depending on the case at hand, however, this may be difficult. For an estimation of the damages that is as precise as possible, it is, however, of central importance to identify all these factors and to control them in an econometric analysis. Otherwise, it is possible that changes in profits will be attributed to the abusive conduct even though the changes will have had – at least in part – different causes.

C Further aspects of damages quantification

1 Compounding and discounting damages

8.095 In general, the harm caused by a competition law infringement usually occurs at a different point in time to the payment of compensation to the injured party. In order to also compensate the injured party for their financial loss, knowledge of that loss needs to be available, otherwise it is necessary to calculate the present value of the damages at the time of compensation. From an economic point of view, the choice of the rate of interest used for compounding is non-trivial. The choice depends on whether an *ex ante* or an *ex post* consideration is used.

8.096 Consider for example the case of a firm that has been forced to exit a market. To simplify the analysis we assume that the infringement occurred at a single point in time. The damages in the form of lost profits, however, accrued until the time of compensation. *Ex ante*, that is, at the time of the infringement, the profit that the injured party might have realised if it had not been forced to exit the market was uncertain as, for example, business fluctuations or the market entry of other firms could not be predicted with certainty. According to an *ex ante* analysis, the damages should not be computed retrospectively, but from the point of time of the infringement as the expected lost profit. This ensures that the injured party is in the same position as it would have been in the absence of the infringement. The expected profits that may have been realised without the infringement have to be discounted to the point of time of the infringement using a risk-adjusted rate of interest. This rate of interest is based on the cost of capital of the injured party. Finally, this amount is then compounded to the point in time when the compensation is paid. As this amount is no longer subject to any uncertainty, the risk-free interest rate is proposed for the compounding.

An *ex post* assessment, however, considers only the realised damages, that is, the profit that the firm would have realised given the factual situation without the infringement. In the case of an on-going infringement, as for example in the case of a price cartel, the differences between the two approaches disappear. The computed damages for the respective period are compounded to the point in time of the compensation. In this case, the use of the risk-free rate of interest is again recommended. **8.097**

Under an *ex post* approach it might be necessary to take that damage into consideration that might be caused by after-effects as in the case of cartels. Also, abusive practices can exhibit considerable after-effects that may lead to future damages that have to be discounted to their present value. These damages should be considered using the *ex ante* approach by discounting the expected damages with the cost of capital of the damaged firm.[82] **8.098**

2 *Estimation of after-effects*

In the context of damage caused by cartels or abusive behaviour, it has been pointed out that after-effects caused by a competition law infringement may extend beyond the period when the infringement occurred. In some cases the after-effects might even extend beyond the point in time of the compensation. As this damage bears a causal relationship with the infringement they should be included in the calculation of damages. As it can be assumed that the injuring party at the time of compensation and further on will refrain from the incriminated behaviour, these after-effects are not equally relevant for all types of anti-competitive behaviour. As an example, the after-effects of a price cartel are considered.[83] Here, prices could be above the competitive level even after **8.099**

82 Note, however, that eventual remedies imposed by the competition authority may mitigate or fully reverse these after-effects.

83 The discussion is based on Inderst and Jakubovic (2013).

the cartel has been abandoned as the explicit collusion during the cartel period could help to establish an implicit collusion, or the higher prices might continue because of long-term contracts. Also, the former cartel members could have an incentive to charge higher prices than under competitive conditions to artificially increase the estimation of the counterfactual price and to thereby reduce the damages claims.[84]

8.100 If these after-effects are not taken into account, the damage that occurs after the cartel period will be disregarded, and there is also the danger of underestimating the damage during the cartel period. This happens if the time after the cartel has been detected is considered to be part of the comparator market. As the prices are above the competitive level due to the after-effects during this time period, the counterfactual price is too high and thus the damage during the cartel period is underestimated. There are, however, methods available that avoid this problem. For example, when using the 'dummy approach' the cartel dummy gets a weight of 1 during the cartel period, but is not immediately set to 0 after this period, but instead only gradually reduced.[85] If there are after-effects because of long-term contracts and lagged price adjustments, these can be estimated using price data from periods before the cartel ended. This includes the cartel period if it is assumed that prices are adjusted with a comparable lag if for example costs have changed. This lagged price adjustment is taken into account in a regression by letting the current price level depend to a greater or lesser extent on the past price level.[86]

3 Accuracy of statistical methods

8.101 Of central importance when considering the different econometric methods discussed above are the properties or the theoretical accuracy of the respective models or estimators used to calculate for example the counterfactual price. Statistical theory is concerned with the properties of different estimators or models and their robustness. An important empirical trade-off exists, for instance between using an unbiased estimator with a low precision versus a biased estimator with a high precision. In order to understand what is meant by biased (or unbiased) and by the precision of the estimate, consider the estimate derived from an unbiased estimator. This estimate may have a very low precision, that is, be far away from the true value despite the fact that the

84 See Harrington (2004).

85 See for example Hüschelrath et al. (2012) for an application. The functional form this reduction takes has to be assumed according to the facts of the individual case.

86 This can be estimated by first considering a model for the profit-maximising price which is then combined with a model that describes the price adjustment process. This price adjustment model can be interpreted in a way that only some firms adjust their prices and all other firms keep their prices unchanged. For details see Gujarati (2002: 673).

method, that is, the estimator, was unbiased. The reason for this is that an unbiased estimator leads to unbiased estimates *on average*. This can be visualised by considering a normal distribution with a high variance around the true mean. If the distribution has a high variance but the mean is the true mean, the estimator is unbiased. This unbiased average could, however, be obtained solely by estimates that over and underestimate the true value substantially, so that (and here we leave the example of a normal distribution) no estimate actually reflects the true value and the estimator is only unbiased because the deviations from the true value cancel each other out. As a result, it may be preferable to take recourse to biased estimators such as structural empirical models with a high precision, that is, a low error margin in individual estimates although the estimator is biased, than to resort to an unbiased estimator that generates estimates with large errors, that is, is less precise.[87] In the context of the discussion of methods above, the more the economic model is enriched with assumptions that are imposed on the estimation, the more precise the estimates are likely to be, although results may be biased if not all relevant effects are taken into account or some assumptions are incorrect.

An additional consideration in the empirical analysis of damages is the concept of practicality as for instance developed in OECD (2011: 22). A methodology is practical when it yields a verifiable and transparent estimate within a reasonable timeframe and the proportional use of resources. Verifiability and transparency depend largely on data submission and presentational format, that is, the submission of raw data together with any documentation of adjustments and the statistical procedure used that would allow a replication of the results presented. **8.102**

Regarding the significance of statistical results, higher than usual p-values could be considered as the *a priori* probability of the but-for price in the context of a condemned cartel being significantly lower than the cartel price, for example, is not 50 per cent but substantially higher, as has been pointed out by Fumagalli et al. (2010).[88] It may therefore make perfect sense to take the fact that an infringement was established into account in follow-on damages claims. **8.103**

87 This trade-off is considered using the weighted square error criterion.

88 The statistical bases for hypothesis testing using the usual significance levels rest on a high data quality and the additional assumption of an *a priori* equal probability of rejecting or not rejecting the null hypothesis, for instance to find a statistically significant difference between actual and counterfactual prices. As both these assumptions are typically not fulfilled in follow-on damages claims, lower significance levels could be considered.

4 *Remoteness and causality*

8.104 In addition to the effects that a cartel or abusive behaviour causes, the aspects of remoteness and causality have to be considered. Remoteness often refers to the 'distance' between the harmed party and the infringement, for example in a value chain, where an indirect purchaser or indirect supplier of a cartel would be considered more 'remote' or 'distant' than a direct purchaser or supplier, but it may also relate to the types of effects constituting the harm suffered.

8.105 Regarding the former, it has already been noted in section II.A.2 that the quantification of damages may not necessarily be easier for those occurring, for example, in a direct interaction with cartelised firms as opposed to firms that are more remote. Nevertheless, the more remote the damage caused by the infringement either within or outside the value chain, the more difficult it is usually to demonstrate causality.[89] While damages do not necessarily decrease with distance from the cartel or the abusive behaviour (the example, section II.A.3 demonstrated that damages may substantially increase), proving causality may also not necessarily become more difficult, as demonstrated, for instance, in the case of products that are complementary to the cartel product. In any case, remoteness is certainly not a criterion that would allow discrediting damages claims of more remote firms *a priori*. So while remoteness understood in this way may be one of the indicators that could be used to predict the chances of winning a damages claim, economic causality will be fulfilled irrespective of whether claimants are direct or indirect purchasers, suppliers or competitors, or may be harmed by the cartel or the abusive behaviour in an even more indirect way.

8.106 Remoteness and the idea that a causal relation may be less likely to be satisfied for different types of harm usually refers to the damage attributed to price and quantity effects. As the US courts do not award damages for quantity effects, or opportunity costs in terms of lost profits, except under specific circumstances, one may develop the idea that price effects are less 'remote' than quantity effects, not least as price effects are normally evidenced by transactions of a certain volume at the higher prices caused by the infringement, whereas quantity effects can typically not directly be evidenced. As the presentation in section II demonstrated, this is economically unfounded. In all but special circumstances will a firm that has been harmed by a price effect also have been

89 Generally speaking, causality refers to the requirement that all estimated damages have to be linked to the infringement in the sense that they would not have occurred in the absence of the infringement (the so-called 'but-for' test). If, for instance, important inputs to the dominant firm increase in price during the excessive price period, these input price increases would have resulted in increased prices even in the absence of an excessive price abuse. As a result these effects need to be separated from the pure excessive price effects for which causality can be demonstrated. See Chapter 5 for a discussion of the legal notion of causation.

affected by a quantity effect. Indeed, the harm from the quantity effect may be more substantial than the harm from the price effect.[90] From that point of view, it is hardly tenable to award damages based on price effects and deny damages for quantity effects on the basis that these are supposedly more remote.

In practice, price effects can be calculated based on the quantity purchased and the difference between the factual and counterfactual price. If this is done at every level of the value chain, one gets the respective price effects. To calculate quantity effects one requires, in addition, information on the counterfactual quantity. At least theoretically, the calculation of the counterfactual price implies knowledge of the corresponding quantity so that the informational requirements are similar.[91] *A priori* it is therefore unclear why it should be considered much more difficult to estimate damages based on quantity effects as opposed to price effects.[92] **8.107**

From an economic point of view, one should therefore exert a certain level of caution regarding the idea that distance or remoteness, irrespective of whether it is understood as distance of the victim to the cartelised market or referring to price and quantity effects, will have a bearing on causality. While there may be practical and empirical considerations that will render 'remote' damages claims statistically less likely to be successful *ex post*, there is no economic basis for discarding such 'remote' claims *ex ante*. **8.108**

IV CONCLUSIONS

The estimation of damages for individual consumers or firms is a difficult task, fundamentally requiring a comparison between the wealth position of a firm or consumer in the presence and absence of an infringement. The preceding sections analysed damages in terms of price and quantity effects, rejecting the division of price effects into an overcharge and a passing-on calculation. Clearly, it is possible to reconcile an estimation of damages based on an overcharge calculation that would only subsequently net out what has been 'passed-on' with a price effect analysis, but in the absence of a legal regime making such distinctions there is no convincing argument why such an approach would be superior to a direct calculation of price effects. As a matter of **8.109**

90 See Maier-Rigaud (2013).

91 The calculation of quantity effects for final purchasers (firms or consumers) requires additional information concerning the shape of the demand function and the cost curve between the relevant price/quantity combinations.

92 Even if one is willing to accept concepts as crude as the illegal gain as an approximation for reasons of simplicity or procedural efficiency, for example, it is not clear why quantity effects could not similarly be approximated.

fact, any argument advanced in favour of such a subdivision of price effects could only take recourse to the argument that such an approach may empirically be easier to follow. The information requirements for calculating overcharge and passing-on are, however, identical to those for calculating price effects.[93] In addition, the focalisation on price effects divided into overcharge and passing-on has led to an asymmetric treatment and ultimately a neglect of quantity effects in the analysis.[94] The justification advanced for such a step-motherly treatment of quantity effects has been that the estimation of quantity effects is more difficult than the calculation of price effects. As has been shown, calculating quantity effects requires only insignificantly more information than calculating price effects but assures that all damage is taken into account in the calculation. The calculation of both price and quantity effects should therefore also be used if a rebuttable presumption is introduced, as was recently suggested by the European Commission.[95] A further benefit of such an assessment of damages is that it automatically dispenses with the debates surrounding passing-on and standing that have unnecessarily muddied the waters of the literature on damages claims in EU competition law.[96]

8.110 While estimating damages in cartel and exploitative abuse cases is, at least on a conceptual level, relatively straightforward, it is much more complicated to quantify individual harm in exclusionary abuse cases. In particular the construction of one (or several) realistic counterfactual(s) in exclusionary abuse cases will require further economic research.

8.111 Questions with respect to the appropriate counterfactual also arise with respect to market developments when the infringement has been terminated. It is not clear how to incorporate any future reduction in competition due, for example, to focal points in cartel cases. Similar difficulties exist with assessing damages in abusive conduct cases as effects may continue to play a role even if the conduct

93 Calculating price effects is more difficult than estimating the overcharge, but calculating the overcharge is meaningless unless the cartel only sells directly to final consumers, allowing the passing-on problem to be ignored. In addition, if claims are brought by indirect purchasers or firms outside the value chain, establishing the overcharge is likely to be more difficult than calculating price effects directly.

94 See European Commission (2013).

95 See European Commission (2011) and (2013). A rebuttable presumption focusing on the overcharge endangers the Commission's accomplishment of treating price and quantity effects equally. Should a rebuttable presumption solely focusing on price effects or overcharge be introduced this would likely result in quantity effects vanishing in actual damages cases. The normative power of a rebuttable presumption focusing exclusively on price effects, together with the US approach influencing the EU debate, may be sufficient to assure that quantity effects will play no role also in the EU, thereby undermining the goal of compensation.

96 It is, for instance, not clear at all why the European Commission devotes a whole chapter to passing-on of overcharges (see European Commission (2013), Chapter IV of the proposal for a directive) in light of the compensatory goal of damages that by definition excludes an award of the overcharge and thereby naturally requires a focus on price effects, irrespective of whether these are calculated by adjusting an overcharge by passing-on or not. See Maier-Rigaud (2013).

has ceased. An analysis of effects in such cases is further complicated by the effect of remedies imposed by competition authorities. Generally speaking, competition law infringements that entail both positive and negative effects, such as tying that also reduces transaction costs, generate the need to net the harm and the gains that typically emerge across time in abusive conduct cases.

All these considerations imply that damages cannot be estimated precisely. It is for this reason that it would be sensible to move away from point predictions generating a particular number that is supposed to characterise the total damage to the individual consumer or firm.[97] The alternative is to state damages in intervals using upper and lower bounds that may naturally emerge from different estimating methods or underlying assumptions. The robustness of the estimation can be further increased by methodological pluralism and a variation of key factors in hypothetical comparator markets in the context of simulation methods.[98] It may even be possible to state the damage intervals in terms of confidence intervals,[99] indicating a certain probability for damages to lie within a certain range. **8.112**

BIBLIOGRAPHY

Arrow, Kenneth J. (1962), 'Economic welfare and the allocation of resources for invention', in R.R. Nelson (Hrsg.), *The Rate and Direction of Inventive Activity*, Princeton, NJ: Princeton University Press, pp. 609–625.

Bernheim, B. Douglas (2002), 'Expert Report in RE: Vitamins Antitrust Litigation, M.D.L. No. 1285', United States District Court for the District of Columbia, May 24, 2002.

Bishop, Simon and Mike Walker (2010), *Economics of EC Competition Law: Concepts, Application and Measurement*, London: Sweet and Maxwell.

Bolotova, Yuliya, John Connor and Douglas Miller (2009), 'Factors influencing the magnitude of cartel overcharges: an empirical analysis of the US market', *Journal of Competition Law and Economics*, **5**, 361–381.

Buccirossi, Paolo (2010), 'Quantification of damages in exclusionary practice cases', *Journal of European Competition Law & Practice*, **1** (3), 252–256.

97 Point predictions unjustifiedly imply precision and are very likely to be incorrect. They are very likely to be incorrect as the probability that a particular point estimate of damages corresponds to the actual damages is very close to zero.

98 This would include a careful consideration of whether slight changes, for example in the underlying model or other assumptions, will entail substantial changes in the estimates.

99 Confidence intervals in the context of damages claims would consist of a range or interval of damages estimates that act as good estimates of the unknown damages. The level of confidence of the confidence interval, expressed as a percentage, indicates the probability that the range or interval of damages estimates capture the true damages suffered by the victim. By definition, 100 per cent minus the level of confidence would indicate the probability that the true damages lie outside the interval, that is, are either larger or smaller than the damages indicated in the interval. In the context of a corresponding hypothesis test, this value is called the significance level.

Combe, Emmanuel and Constance Monnier (2007), 'Cartel profiles in the European Union', *Concurrences*, **3**, 181.

Combe, Emmanuel and Constance Monnier (2011), 'Fines against hard core cartels in Europe: the myth of overenforcement', *The Antitrust Bulletin*, **56** (2), 235–275.

Competition Commission (2009), 'Suggested best practice for submissions of technical economic analysis for parties to the Competition Commission', London.

Connor, John M. (2004), 'Global cartels redux: the Amino Acid Lysine Antitrust Litigation (1996)', in E. Kwoka and Lawrence J. White (eds), *The Antitrust Revolution*, 4th ed., pp. 252–276.

Connor, John M. (2006), 'Optimal deterrence and private international cartels', working paper.

Connor, John M. and Yuliya Bolotova (2005), 'Cartel overcharges: survey and meta-analysis', working paper.

Connor, John M. and Robert H. Lande (2006), 'The size of cartel overcharges: implications for US and EU fining policies, *The Antitrust Bulletin*, **51**, 983–1022.

Connor, John M. and Robert H. Lande (2008), 'Cartel overcharges and optimal cartel fines', in S.W. Waller (ed.), *Issues in Competition Law and Policy*, vol. 3, ABA Section of Antitrust Law, Chapter 88, pp. 2203–2218.

Davis, Peter and Eliana Garcés (2009), *Quantitative Techniques for Competition and Antitrust Analysis*, Princeton, NJ: Princeton University Press.

European Commission (2004), 'Study on the conditions of claims for damages in case of infringement of EC Competition Rules, part II, analysis of economic models for the calculation of damages', study prepared by Ashurst.

European Commission (2005a), 'Green Paper – Damages Actions for Breach of EC Antitrust Rules', COM(2005) 672 final.

European Commission (2005b), 'Commission Staff Working Paper: Annex to the Green Paper on Damages Actions for Breach of EC Antitrust Rules', SEC(2005) 1732.

European Commission (2007), 'Making antitrust damages actions more effective in the EU: welfare impact and potential scenarios', final report prepared by the Center for European Policy Studies, the University of Rotterdam, and the Luiss Guido Carli.

European Commission (2008a), 'White Paper on Damages Actions for Breach of the EC Antitrust Rules', COM(2008) 165 final.

European Commission (2008b), 'Commission Staff Working Paper Accompanying the White Paper on Damages Actions for Breach of the EC Antitrust Rules', SEC(2008) 404.

European Commission (2009), 'Quantifying antitrust damages. Towards non-binding guidance for courts', study prepared by Oxera.

European Commission (2011), 'Draft guidance paper on quantifying harm in actions for damages based on breaches of Article 101 or 102 of the Treaty on the Functioning of the European Union', June.

European Commission (2013), 'Proposal for a Directive of the European Parliament and of the Council on certain rules governing actions for damages under national law for infringements of the competition law provisions of the Member States and the European Union', COM(2013) 404final.

Friederiszick, Hans W. and Frank P. Maier-Rigaud (2007), 'The role of economics in cartel detection in Europe', in D. Schmidtchen, M. Albert and S. Voigt (eds), *The More Economic Approach in European Competition Law*, Mohr Siebeck, pp. 179–196.

Friederiszick, Hans W. and Frank P. Maier-Rigaud (2008), 'Triggering inspections ex officio: moving beyond a passive EU cartel policy, *Journal of Competition Law and Economics*, **4** (1), 89–113.

Friederiszick, Hans W. and Lars-Hendrik Röller (2010), 'Quantification of harm in damages actions for antitrust infringements: insights from German cartel cases', *Journal of Competition Law & Economics*, **6** (3), 595–618.

Fumagalli, Chiara, Jorge Padilla and Michele Polo (2010), 'Damages for exclusionary practices: a primer', in I. Kokkoris and F. Etro (eds), *Competition Law and the Enforcement of Art. 102*, Oxford: Oxford University Press, pp. 203–220.

Green, Edward J. and Robert H. Porter (1984), 'Noncooperative collusion under imperfect price information', *Econometrica*, **52** (1), 87–100.

Gregory, Alan (2011), 'Excessive prices and the role of profitability analysis', paper submitted for the OECD Roundtable on Excessive Prices.

Griffin, James (1989), 'Previous cartel experience: any lessons for OPEC?', in L.R. Klein and Jaime Marquez (eds), *Economics in Theory and Practice: An Eclectic Approach*, Kluwer, pp. 179–206.

Gujarati, Damodar (2002), *Basic Econometrics*, 4th ed., McGraw-Hill Higher Education.

Harrington, Joe E. (2008), 'Detecting cartels', in P. Buccirossi (ed.), *Handbook of Antitrust Economics*, Boston, MA: MIT Press, pp. 213–258.

Hellwig, Martin (2007), 'Private damage claims and the passing-on defense in horizontal price-fixing cases: an economist's perspective', in J. Basedow (ed.), *Private Enforcement of EC Competition Law*, Kluwer Law International, pp. 121–159.

Hicks, Joe R. (1935), 'Annual survey of economic theory: the theory of monopoly', *Econometrica*, **3** (1), 1–20.

Hovenkamp, Herbert (2011), 'Quantification of harm in private antitrust actions in the United States', paper submitted for the OECD Roundtable on the Quantification of Harm to Competition by National Courts and Competition Agencies.

Hüschelrath, Kai, Katrin Müller and Tobias Veith (2012), 'Concrete shoes for competition: the effect of the German cement cartel on market price', *Journal of Competition Law and Economics* (forthcoming).

Inderst, Roman and Zlata Jakubovic (2012), 'Nachwirkungen von Kartellen', *Journal of German and European Competition Law (Wirtschaft und Wettbewerb, WuW)*, **1**, 5–16.

Inderst, Roman, Frank Maier-Rigaud and Ulrich Schwalbe (2013a), 'Quantifizierung von Schäden durch Wettbewerbsverstöße', in Andreas Fuchs und Andreas Weitbrecht (ed.), *Handbuch der Privaten Kartellrechtsdurchsetzung*, München: C.H. Beck, forthcoming.

Inderst, Roman, Frank Maier-Rigaud and Ulrich Schwalbe (2014), 'Umbrella effects', *Journal of Competition Law and Economics*, forthcoming.

Konings, Jozef, Patrick van Cayseele and Frederic Warzynski (2001), 'The dynamics of industrial mark-ups in two small open economies: does national competition policy matter?', *International Journal of Industrial Organisation*, **19**, 841–859.

Korenblit, Claire M. (2012), 'Quantifying antitrust damages – convergence of methods recognized by U.S. courts and the European Commission', *CPI Antitrust Chronicle*.

Lapuerta, Carlos, Richard Caldwell and Dan Harris (2010), 'Towards non-binding guidance for courts: The Oxera Report and the quantification of antitrust damages', *Journal of European Competition Law & Practice*, **1** (5), 438–443.

Leibenstein, Harvey (1966), 'Allocative efficiency and x-efficiency', *American Economic Review*, **56**, 392–415.

Levenstein, Margaret C. and Valerie Y. Suslow (2006), 'What determines cartel success?', *Journal of Economic Literature*, **44**, 43–95.

Levenstein, Margaret C. and Valerie Y. Suslow (2011), 'Breaking up is hard to do: determinants of cartel duration', *Journal of Law and Economics*, **54** (2), 455–492.

Lopatka, John E. (2006), 'Overcharge damages for monopolization of new economy markets', *Antitrust Bulletin*, **51**, 453–505.

Maier-Rigaud, Frank (2012), 'Zur Idee der Subsidiarität struktureller Maßnahmen im europäischen Wettebwerbsrecht', *Journal of German and European Competition Law (Wirtschaft und Wettbewerb, WuW)*, **5**, 487–500.

Maier-Rigaud, Frank (2013), 'Towards a European Directive on Damages Actions', *Journal of Competition Law and Economics*, forthcoming.

Maier-Rigaud, Frank (2013b), 'The irrelevance of pass-on considerations for the quantification of antitrust damages in the EU', IESEG/LEM-CNRS Working Paper.

Maier-Rigaud, Frank and Ulrich Schwalbe (2013), 'Do retroactive rebates imply lower prices for consumers?', IESEG/LEM-CNRS Working Paper, accessed at http://ssrn.com/abstract=2276396.

Niels, Gunnar, Helen Jenkins and James Kavanagh (2011), *Economics for Competition Lawyers*, Oxford: Oxford University Press.

OECD (2002a), *Annual Report 2002*, OECD Publications.

OECD (2002b), 'Report on the nature and impact of hard core cartels and sanctions against cartels under national competition laws', DAFFE/COMP (2002), 7.

OECD (2003), *Annual Report 2003*, OECD Publications.

OECD (2011), 'Quantification of harm to competition by national courts and competition agencies', OECD Best Practice Roundtables in Competition Policy, written for the OECD Secretariat by Hans W. Friederiszick and Elisabeth Fugger, February 2011.

OECD (2012a), 'Excessive prices', OECD Best Practice Roundtables in Competition Policy, written for the OECD Secretariat by Frank Maier-Rigaud, October 2011.

OECD (2012b), 'Market definition', OECD Best Practice Roundtables in Competition Policy, written for the OECD Secretariat by Ulrich Schwalbe and Frank Maier-Rigaud, June 2012.

Porter, Robert H. (1983), 'A study of cartel stability: the Joint Executive Committee, 1880–1886', *The Bell Journal of Economics*, **14** (2), 301–314.

Posner, Richard (2001), *Antitrust Law*, 2nd ed. Chicago, IL: Chicago University Press.

Schinkel, Maarten P., Jan Tuinstra and Jakob Rüggeberg (2008), 'Illinois walls: how barring indirect purchaser suits facilitates collusion', *The Rand Journal of Economics*, **3** (39), 683–698.

Schumpeter, Joseph A. (1950), *Capitalism Socialism and Democracy*, Harper and Row.

Schwalbe, Ulrich (2011), 'The welfare effects of partial cartels. Some results from the theoretical literature', paper prepared for the Workshop on the Quantification of Antitrust Harm in Actions for Damages, EU Commission, DG Competition.

Selten, Reinhard (1978), 'The chain store paradox', *Theory and Decision*, **9**, 127–159.

van Dijk, Theon and Frank Verboven (2008), 'Quantification of damages', in S.W. Waller (ed.), *Issues in Competition Law and Policy*, vol. 3, ABA Section of Antitrust Law, pp. 2331–2348.

van Dijk, Theon and Frank Verboven (2009), 'Cartel damage claims and the passing-on defense', *Journal of Industrial Economics*, **57** (3), 457–491.

Werden, Greg J. (2004), 'The effect of antitrust policy on consumer welfare: what Crandall and Winston overlook', AEI-Brookings Joint Center for Regulatory Studies, Related Publication 04–09.

INDEX

abusive conduct 8.005–8.009, 8.044–8.051
damage caused by abusive behaviour/counterfactual scenario 8.074–8.083
exclusionary abuse 8.078–8.083
exploitative abuse 8.075–8.077
economic actors damaged by exploitative/exclusionary conduct 8.049–8.051
competitors as key victims 8.051
exclusionary abusive practice, parties harmed by 8.050
exploitative abusive practice, parties harmed by 8.049
purchasers of dominant firm harmed 8.051
exclusionary abuse, types of damage caused by 8.048
exploitative conduct, types of damage caused by 8.045–8.051
positive effects on competition 8.047
positive effects for purchasers through profit sacrifice 8.046
price discrimination effect on welfare 8.047
tying, effects of 8.047
welfare implications 8.045
exploitative or exclusionary conduct 8.008
abuse of a dominant position 8.044
increases in prices 8.044
illustration: quantification of damages in exclusionary abuse case 8.084–8.094
actors affected by exclusionary abuse 8.085
damage estimation in exclusionary abuse complex 8.084
phase one 8.086–8.087
phase two 8.088–8.089
phase three 8.090–8.094
primary goal to increase profits by softening competition 8.006, 8.008
quantifying damages in abusive conduct cascs 8.074 8.094
damage caused by abusive behaviour/counterfactual scenario 8.074–8.083
illustration: quantification of damages in exclusionary abuse case 8.084–8.094
quantifying damages by counterfactual/but-for scenario 8.009
restricted competition leading to welfare losses 8.005
applicable law 7.092–7.130
competition-based litigation/Art 6(3) 7.099–7.101
no derogation 7.101
desirability of *lex fori* approach 7.114
reservations against 7.114–7.118
effects-based approach/Art 6(3)(a) 7.119–7.123
basis of 7.121
effects-based approach, problems with 7.124–7.127
functioning of Art 6(3)(b) 7.102–7.111, 7.119
application 7.104
'direct and substantial effect', meaning of 7.106–7.110
limitations on application of *lex fori* 7.103–7.105
US law, compared 7.112–7.113
general rule/Art 4 7.097–7.098, 7.123
tort claims, approaches to 7.098
Mosaikbetrachtung
concurrent matter of jurisdiction/applicable law, as 7.128–7.130
effects-based approach, problems with: 7.124–7.127

Rome II Regulation and *lex fori* approach 7.094–7.096
Commission proposal for harmonisation 7.094–7.095
see also private international law aspects
Ashurst study 0.09, 0.10
assignment of claims 6.033, 6.150–6.156
assignment model as synergistic approach to litigation 6.151
Austria
courts as 'specialist authorities' 5.64
documentary evidence, access to 4.028–4.030, 4,032
autonomy *see under* Member States

Belgium
basis of damages actions for breach of EU competition law 2.47–2.49
collective action scheme absent 6.072
NCA, consultation of 5.72
Bernheim, B. Douglas 8.058
Brussels Convention (1968) 7.006, 7.007
burden of proof
infringement, proving 4.002
see also proving the infringement
passing-on in EU law 3.053–3.060
burden on defendant 3.053–3.055, 3.058–3.059
question of fact, as 3.056–3.058
shifting 3.056
presumption of harm 5.13–5.14
see also under individual countries

cartels
Commission settling 4.003
contribution 5.79–5.80
damage caused by cartels 8.005–8.043
economic actors damaged by cartels 8.020–8.035
harm inflicted by cartels, estimation of 8.002
higher prices and lower quantities resulting 8.007
illustration 8.036–8.043
price/quantity effects accruing in vertical value chain 8.036–8.043
restricted competition leading to welfare losses 8.005
types of damage caused by cartels 8.010–8.019
economic actors damaged by cartels 8.020–8.035
downstream effects 8.029–8.031
effects on producers of complements 8.032
horizontal effects 8.021
non-horizontal and non-vertical effects 8.021
range of economic actors affected by anti-competitive conduct 8.023
summary of effects analysis 8.033–8.035
upstream effects 8.024–8.028
vertical effects 8.021
estimating number of cartels 8.002
primary goal to increase profits by softening competition 8.006–8.007
private litigants *see* private litigants' access to documents in EU cartel actions
quantification of damages in cartel cases 8.053–8.073
constructing counterfactual scenario 8.054
cost-based approach *see* cost-based approach
cross-sectional analysis *see* cross-sectional analysis
difference-in differences method *see* difference-in differences method
nature of counterfactual scenario 8.053
profitability-based approach *see* profitability-based approach
quantifying damages by counterfactual/but-for scenario 8.009
simulated comparator markets *see* simulated comparator markets
time series analysis *see* time series analysis
types of damage caused by cartels 8.010–8.019
cartel-induced price increases, substantial variance in 8.019
cartelisation leading to transfer of wealth/inefficiencies 8.010–8.012
extent of price increase or quantity reduction 8.014–8.015

magnitude of damage dependent on range of factors 8.013
market characteristics, cartels changing 8.017
mark-ups/overcharge calculations, empirical studies on 8.018
productive and dynamic inefficiencies 8.016, 8.017
quantity effects neglected 8.018
causation 5.03–5.06
but-for test 5.03
choice of court 7.050–7.051
complexity of issue 5.06
choice of court *see under* private international law aspects
Civil Justice Council 6.026
civil law damages actions for breach of EU competition law 2.24–2.61
Germanic systems of law 2.24–2.46
Denmark 2.24–2.25
Germany 2.26–2.32
Greece 2.33–2.35
Latvia 2.36–2.38
Lithuania 2.39–2.43
Netherlands 2.44–2.46
Romanistic systems of law 2.47–2.61
Belgium 2.47–2.49
France 2.50–2.54
Italy 2.55–2.59
Spain 2.60–2.61
collective action/redress 6.001–6.173
assignment of claims 6.033, 6.150–6.156
collective action at EU level 6.034–6.071
collective action as a matter of EU law 6.034–6.040
EU policy developments 6.041–6.071
collective action as matter of EU law 6.034–6.040
consumer injunctions 6.038
data protection rules 6.040
IPRs protection Directive 6.039
unfair terms in consumer contracts 6.037
effective complement to public enforcement, as 6.002, 6.003
EU policy developments 6.041–6.071
Commission's consultation paper (2011) 6.057–6.060
Commission's joint information note 6.055–6.056
Commission proposal/2013 collective redress initiative 6.061–6.071
draft Directive 6.051–6.054
Green Paper 6.044–6.046
preference for horizontal approach 6.043
White Paper 6.047–6.050
Member States, collective action in 6.072–6.156
collective action introduced 6.004
collective action schemes, absence of 6.072
Denmark 6.127–6.134
divergent systems as obstacle to inter-Member State action 6.004
effective redress not always provided 6.006
France 6.142–6.147
Italy 6.148–6.149
limitations on who can bring claims 6.005
Netherlands *see under* Netherlands
opt-in and opt-out systems 6.005, 6.017
Sweden 6.135–6.141
UK *see under* United Kingdom
opt-in collective action 6.005, 6.015–6.024
advantages 6.019–6.021
drawbacks 6.022–6.024
EU policy preference for 6.017
nature of 6.018
standing 6.015, 6.016
opt-out collective action 6.005, 6.025–6.032
advantages 6.026
disadvantages 6.027–6.032
nature of 6.025–6.026
standing 6.015, 6.016
rationale for collective action 6.008–6.013
administrative advantages 6.012
compensation and deterrence objectives, attaining 6.013
correlation between no collective action/sub-optimal enforcement 6.008
importance in balancing resources/claimants' bargaining positions 6.010

positive impact on litigation by consolidating actions 6.009
'rational apathy problem', overcoming 6.009
tactical litigation risk, avoiding 6.011
terminology 6.014
US, class actions in *see under* United States (US)
comity principle
nature of 4.066
resisting disclosure, reliance on 4.065–4.067
Commission, EU
cartel cases
extensive resources required 4.003
settling under settlement programme 4.003
see also cartels
collective action 5.23
consultation paper (2011) 6.057–6.060
draft Directive 6.051–6.054
Green Paper 6.044–6.046
Impact Assessment 6.027
joint information note 6.055–6.056
minimal harmonised requirements, proposals for 6.041
opt-out system, main arguments against 6.027
policy initiatives 6.003
proposal/2013 collective redress initiative 0.10, 6.061–6.071
recommendation 0.10, 6.003, 6.013, 6.043, 6.061–6.068
White Paper 6.047–6.050
see also collective action/redress
consultation of 5.65
decisions of Commission/Art 9 Regulation 1/2003 4.086–4.087
commitment decisions, nature of 4.086
evidential value 4.087
not proof of infringement in follow-on actions 4.087
decisions of Commission/Art 16 Regulation 1/2003 4.072–4.081
effect of Art 16(1) 4.074
interconnection between procedural aspects/appeal on substance 4.079–4.081
judgment of English Court of Appeal in *Crehan* 4.082–4.085
negative duty of abstention 4.074
scope of rule 4.075–4.078
see also evidential value of prior administrative decisions
disclosure
Commission documents, access to *see under* documentary evidence, access to
documents held by national competition authorities 4.032–4.034
limiting discoverability in US courts *see under* United States (US)
proposals for disclosure 4.059–4.060
draft Directive
burden of proof to establish passing-on 3.054
collective action 6.003, 6.051–6.054, 6.069–6.070
indirect purchaser standing 3.033–3.034
limitation periods 5.47, 5.48
passing-on defence 3.065
withdrawal 0.09–0.10
exemplary damages 5.23
Green Paper 0.09, 5.23, 5.82
collective action 6.044–6.046
harmonisation of rules on non-contractual obligations 7.094–7.095
indirect purchaser standing 3.032–3.036
rebuttable presumption of passing-on 3.034–3.036
stand-alone and follow-on actions 3.034
leniency programmes *see* leniency/leniency programmes
national courts, cooperation with 7.008
passing-on defence 3.064–3.066
private enforcement initiative 0.08–0.14
Ashurst study 0.09, 0.10
proposal, legislative 0.10, 3.054, 3.068
burden of proof to establish passing-on 3.054
causation 5.06
contribution *see under* contribution

damages, measure of 5.07, 5.12
documents held by national competition authority, disclosure of 4.032–4.034
evidence proposals 4.059–4.060
indirect purchaser standing 3.035
limitation periods 5.49–5.53
NCA decisions, evidential value of 4.088
partial passing-on 3.063
passing-on defence 3.066
Regulation 44/2001
Art 28, Commission proposal and 7.077–7.080
Commission review of 7.083–7–7.085
White Paper 0.09, 2.63
burden of proof to establish passing-on 3.054
collective action 6.047–6.050
indirect purchaser standing 3.032, 3.033
passing-on defence 3.064
common law damages actions for breach of EU competition law 2.19–2.23
England and Wales 2.19–2.21
Ireland 2.22–2.23
compensation as policy objective
collective action 6.002, 6.013
indirect purchaser standing and passing-on 3.005, 3.008
competition culture 6.002, 6.042
competition enforcement in the EU 0.07
antitrust enforcement by public enforcement authority 0.04, 0.07, 6.001
decentralisation of enforcement of antitrust rules 0.08
private enforcement *see* private enforcement
public enforcement, meaning of 0.07
see also public authorities/public enforcement
modernisation of 0.08
compounding and discounting damages 8.095–8.098
Connor, John M. 8.018
consumers
collective action *see* collective action/redress
consumer injunctions 6.038
unfair terms in consumer contracts 6.037
contribution
Commission's proposal on contribution 5.78–5.87
cartel settlements 5.79–5.80
determining contribution 5.78
leniency, application to *see under* leniency/leniency programmes
national law system of contribution 5.78
immunity recipients, contribution claims against 5.86
joint and several liability 5.76–5.80, 5.86
UK 5.77
cost-based approach 8.069–8.071
comparator-based approaches, as 8.069
variable costs 8.069–8.070
counterfactual scenarios *see under* abusive conduct; cartels
cross-sectional analysis 8.061–8.064
advantages and disadvantages 8.064
nature of 8.062
regression techniques 8.063
Cyprus
collective action scheme absent 6.072
exemplary damages 5.24
Czech Republic
collective action scheme absent 6.072

damages, measure of 5.07–5.46
Commission proposal 5.07
exemplary damages 5.21–5.46
EU law 5.22–5.23
national law 5.24–5.46
nature of 5.21
UK *see under* United Kingdom (UK)
presumption of harm 5.13–5.20
burden of proof on defendant 5.13–5.14
EU law 5.17
impact of 5.14–5.16
national law 5.18–5.20
types of damage recoverable 5.08–5.12
'lost sales effect' 5.08–5.10
pecuniary loss 5.08
restitutio in integrum (actual loss/loss of profit) 5.11–5.12, 5.24, 5.34
damages, quantification of 8.001–8.112

abusive conduct, damages caused by *see under* abusive conduct
approach for determining damage, comparator-based 8.052
cartels, damages caused by *see under* cartels
damages caused by abusive behaviour/counterfactual scenario 8.074–8.083
exclusionary abuse 8.078–8.083
exploitative abuse 8.075–8.077
further aspects of damage quantification 8.095–8.100
accuracy of statistical methods 8.101–8.103
compounding and discounting damages 8.095–8.098
estimation of after-effects 8.099–8.100
remoteness and causality 8.104–8.108
illustration: quantification of damages in exclusionary abuse case 8.084–8.094
actors affected by exclusionary abuse 8.085
damage estimation in exclusionary abuse complex 8.084
phase one 8.086–8.087
phase two 8.088–8.089
phase three 8.090–8.094
magnitude of damage caused by competition law violations 8.002
need to calculate specific level of damages for each victim 8.052
quantification of damages in abusive conduct cases 8.074–8.094
damage caused by abusive behaviour/counterfactual scenario 8.074–8.083
illustration: quantification of damages in exclusionary abuse case 8.084–8.094
quantification of damages in cartel cases 8.053–8.073
constructing counterfactual scenario 8.054
cost-based approach *see* cost-based approach
cross-sectional analysis *see* cross-sectional analysis
difference-in differences method *see* difference-in differences method
nature of counterfactual scenario 8.053
profitability-based approach *see* profitability-based approach
quantifying damages by counterfactual/but-for scenario 8.009
simulated comparator markets *see* simulated comparator markets
time series analysis *see* time series analysis
damages, underlying right to 2.01–2.71
national law bases for damages actions for breach of EU competition law 2.18–2.71
civil law 2.24–2.61
see also civil law damages actions for breach of EU competition law
common law 2.19–2.23
see also common law damages actions for breach of EU competition law
national law analysis: the fault requirement 2.68–2.71
tortious nature of litigation for breach of EU competition law 2.62–2.68, 7.004
right to damages as matter of EU law: *Crehan* 2.03–2.17
further developments: *Manfredi* judgment 2.16–2.17
proceedings in the English courts 2.03–2.11
UK reference to ECJ 2.12–2.15
data protection 6.040
deference
deference to Commission decisions 4.082–4.083
loyal cooperation principle 4.082
Denmark
basis of damages actions for breach of EU competition law 2.24–2.25
choice of court 7.007
collective action 6.127–6.134
hybrid collective action system 6.017
deterrence as policy objective
collective action 6.002, 6.010, 6.013
indirect purchaser standing and passing-on 3.006, 3.008, 3.009, 3.016
difference-in differences method 8.065–8.066
data constraints 8.086

disadvantages 8.066
nature of 8.065
'direct and substantial effect', meaning of 7.106–7.110
US 7.112–7.113
direct effect 1.14, 2.08, 3.029
discounting and compounding damages 8.095–8.098
documentary evidence, access to
access to documents held by Commission 4.006–4.020
cartel damages actions 4.008–4.020
access to documents held by defendants 4.036–4.056
civil law systems 4.036
common law system 4.036, 4.037–4.056
access to documents held by national competition authorities 4.021–4.035
Commission proposal on disclosure 4.032–4.033
national courts, role of 4.025, 4.029, 4.034
access to documents held by third parties 4.057–4.058
Commission's proposals on evidence 4.059–4.060
proposal to introduce common law system 4.059
role of national courts 4.060
Evidence Regulation 4.050–4.056
formal discovery system in EU law absent 4.006, 4.036
leniency programmes *see under* leniency/leniency programmes
public access to documents held by EU institutions 4.006–4.007, 4.036
exceptions to general right of access 4.007, 4.012–4.020
rules on 4.007
domicile of parties
inside the EU 7.007, 7.016–7.019, 7.042
outside the EU 7.013–7.015
application of *lis pendens* 7.081–7.082
litigation involving parties outside EU 7.086–7.091
dominant position, abuse of *see under* abusive conduct
effectiveness principle 1.01, 1.03
causation 5.06
collective action systems discouraging claims 6.006
damages, measure of 5.07, 5.12
compensatory damages 5.34
limitation periods 5.47
effet utile 2.15
equivalence principle 1.01, 1.03
causation 5.06
limitation periods 5.47
Estonia
collective action scheme absent 6.072
NCA, consultation of 5.74
European Convention of Human Rights (ECHR)
access to justice (Art 6) 6.030
European Court of Justice (ECJ)
case law on remedies 1.01–1.06
collective action 6.034–6.035
documentary evidence *see* documentary evidence, access to
establishment of right to damages as matter of EU law: *Crehan* 2.12–2.15
further developments: *Manfredi* judgment 2.16–2.17
indirect purchaser standing 3.029–3.030
exemplary damages 5.22
founding jurisdiction in tortious actions 7.023–7.025
application of *Bier/Shevill* jurisprudence 7.026–7.036
Art 5(3) as basis for torpedo litigation 7.037–7.041
negative duty of abstention, doubtful cases of 4.074
no jurisdiction in private party actions for breach of competition law 1.02
passing-on defence 3.037–3.043
partial passing-on 3.061–3.063
unjust enrichment, and 3.037, 3.044–3.052
references to ECJ by national courts 5.65
teleological style of argumentation 2.07
Evidence Regulation 4.050–4.056
evidential value of prior administrative decisions 4.071–4.109

Commission decisions/Art 9 Regulation 1/2003 4.086–4.087
commitment decisions, nature of 4.086
evidential value 4.087
not proof of infringement in follow-on actions 4.087
Commission decisions/Art 16 Regulation 1/2003 4.072–4.081
effect of Art 16(1) 4.074
interconnection between procedural aspects/appeal on substance 4.079–4.081
judgment of English Court of Appeal in *Crehan* 4.082–4.085
negative duty of abstention 4.074
scope of rule 4.075–4.078
NCA decisions 4.088–4.109
Commission proposal 4.088
Germany 4.104–4.108
no rule as to evidential value in private litigation 4.088, 4.089
Romanistic jurisdictions 4.109
UK 4.090–4.103
prior administrative infringement decision as proof of infringement 4.071
evidentiary issues *see* proving the infringement
exclusionary abuse *see under* abusive conduct
exemplary damages *see under* damages, measure of
exploitative abuse *see under* abusive conduct

Finland
NCA, consultation of 5.73
forum non conveniens doctrine 7.008, 7.009
France
basis of damages actions for breach of EU competition law 2.50–2.54
competition law damages actions as claims in tort 2.68
fault requirement for non-contractual claim satisfied by illegality 2.70
collective action 6.142–6.147
disclosure
documentary evidence, access to 4.031
French blocking statute 4.049–4.055
indirect purchaser standing and passing-on 3.081–3.083
burden of proof 3.083
admissibility of passing-on defence 3.083
NCA, consultation of 5.69–5.71
NCA decisions, evidential value of 4.109

Germany
basis of damages actions for breach of EU competition law 2.26–2.32
competition law damages actions as claims in tort 2.68
intention or negligence, proof of 2.28, 2.71
collective action
assignment of claims 6.152–6.155
opt-out actions prohibited 6.029
documentary evidence, access to 4.021–4.027
exemplary damages 5.24
indirect purchaser standing and passing-on 3.074–3.080
availability of 3.075–3.078
burden of proof 3.079–3.080
limitation periods 5.48, 5.62–5.63
suspending 5.62, 5.63
NCA, consultation of 5.68
NCA decisions, evidential value of 4.104–4.108
courts bound by decisions 4.104–4.105
presumption of harm 5.18
Schutznorm concept 2.08
Greece
basis of damages actions for breach of EU competition law 2.33–2.35

harm, presumption of *see under* damages, measure of
harmonisation of remedies 1.09, 1.15
draft proposal for harmonising regulation 1.16
Hovenkamp, Herbert 3.015
Hungary
damages/presumption of loss 5.19

indirect purchaser standing and passing-on 3.001–3.111
EU law 3.014, 3.018, 3.028–3.066, 3.068
burden of proof to establish passing-on *see under* burden of proof

Commission's position on indirect standing *see under* Commission, EU
indirect purchaser standing 3.014, 3.029–3.031
partial passing-on 3.061–3.063
passing-on defence 3.037–3.043
passing-on defence and unjust enrichment 3.037, 3.044–3.052
indirect purchaser, definition of 3.012
indirect purchaser standing 3.001, 3.011–3.021
EU approach 3.014, 3.018, 3.029–3.031, 3.068
evidentiary obstacles, overcoming 3.019–3.020
importance of 3.013
judicial and academic controversy 3.014–3.017
remoteness of claims 3.013
representative/class actions 3.018
national law 3.067–3.088
England and Wales 3.069–3.073
France 3.081–3.083
Germany 3.074–3.080
Italy 3.084–3.088
passing-on defence 3.022–3.027
consequences of invoking defence 3.024–3.027
consequences of not recognising defence 3.025
passing-on, nature of 3.023
unjust enrichment, avoiding 3.025
theoretical underpinnings 3.001–3.027
awarding damages to different levels of claimants 3.001–3.003, 3.009
clash of policy objectives 3.004, 3.008–3.010
compensation/fairness as policy objective 3.005, 3.008
deterrence as policy objective 3.006, 3.008, 3.009, 3.016
economical litigation as policy objective 3.007, 3.008
indirect purchaser standing 3.001, 3.011–3.021
passing-on defence 3.022–3.027
US *see under* United States (US)
infringement, proving *see* proving the infringement
IPRs protection Directive 6.039
Ireland
basis of damages actions for breach of EU competition law 2.22–2.23
courts as 'specialist authorities' 5.64
disclosure/discovery of documents 4.036
exemplary damages 5.24
Italy
basis of damages actions for breach of EU competition law 2.55–2.59
collective action 6.148–6.149
indirect purchaser standing and passing-on 3.084–3.088
claims by indirect purchasers in theory applicable 3.087
defence of passing-on not specifically recognised 3.085–3.086
NCA decisions, evidential value of 4.109

joint and several liability 5.75–5.87
contribution 5.76–5.80, 5.86
UK 5.77
Commission's proposal on contribution 5.78–5.87
cartel settlements 5.79–5.80
determining contribution 5.78
leniency, application to *see under* leniency/leniency programmes
national law system of contribution 5.78
meaning of 5.75

Lande, Robert H. 8.018
Landes, William M. 3.009, 3.010, 3.016
Latvia
basis of damages actions for breach of EU competition law 2.36–2.38
collective action scheme absent 6.072
legal framework 1.01–1.18
application to damages actions for breach of EU competition law 1.17–1.18
case law of ECJ on remedies 1.01–1.06
doctrines of equivalence and minimum effectiveness 1.01, 1.03
private actions for breach of EU competition law 1.05, 1.06
rights to remedies, move from1.07–1.16

direct rights 1.11–1.13, 1.17
directly effective rights 1.14
distinguishing between rights and remedies 1.09
fixing boundaries between remedial/procedural rules *sensu stricto* 1.15–1.16
procedural autonomy principle 1.07
remedies and pure rights and obligations 1.11, 1.12, 1.13
rights to enforce 1.10–1.13, 1.17
leniency/leniency programmes 4.007, 4.011, 4.023–4.024
balancing exercise to be carried out 4.029, 4.034
Commission proposal 4.032
Commission's attempts to limit discovery in US courts 4.061–4.070
importance of leniency programmes recognised 4.067–4.069
reliance on comity 4.065–4.067, 4.070
joint and several liability 5.81–5.87
conditional rebate 5.82
contribution claims against immunity recipients 5.86
immunity recipients, liability of 5.85
immunity recipients, protection afforded to 5,84
leniency documents not held by third parties 4.057
national leniency programmes 4.042–4.048
policy considerations behind leniency 5.32
safeguarding effectiveness of 4.024–4.027, 4.030
lex fori
desirability of *lex fori* approach 7.114
reservations against 7.114–7.118
limitations on application of *lex fori* 7.103–7.105
Rome II Regulation, and 7.094–7.096
Commission proposal for harmonisation 7.094–7.095
liability
immunity recipients, liability of 5.85
joint and several *see* joint and several liability
strict liability 2.69, 2.70
limitation periods 5.47–5.63
EU law 5.47–5.53
proposal, limitation period in 5.49–5.53
rules on limitation periods determined by national law 5.47, 5.54
national law
Germany 5.48, 5.62–5.63
UK 5.48, 5.50, 5.55–5.61
lis pendens
application to parties domiciled outside the EU 7.081–7.082
forum shopping 7.053
multiple litigation, addressing 7.053
Regulation 44/2001, Art 27 of 7.054, 7.055–7.062, 7.063, 7.064
connected but not identical actions 7.070–7.071
Regulation 44/2001, Art 28 of 7.012, 7.054, 7.063–7.065
Commission proposal, and 7.077–7.080
connected but not identical actions 7.068–7.069
English authorities on 7.072–7.076
irreconcilability for purposes of Art 28(3) 7.066–7.067
Regulation 44/2001, Commission review of 7.083–7–7.085
Lithuania
basis of damages actions for breach of EU competition law 2.39–2.43
loyal/sincere cooperation principle 2.07
deference to Commission decisions 4.082
Luxembourg
collective action scheme absent 6.072

measure of damages *see* damages, measure of
Member States
autonomy in procedure and remedies 1.01, 1,07, 1.15, 6.004
equivalence and minimum effectiveness conditions 1.01
general obligation to ensure effectiveness of EU law 1.01, 1.04
harmonisation of remedies 1.09, 1.15
collective action in Member States 6.072–6.156

collective action introduced 6.004
collective action schemes, absence of 6.072
Denmark 6.127–6.134
divergent systems as obstacle to inter-Member State action 6.004
effective redress not always provided 6.006
France 6.142–6.147
Italy 6.148–6.149
limitations on who can bring claims 6.005
Netherlands *see under* Netherlands
opt-in and opt-out systems 6.005, 6.017
Sweden 6.135–6.141
UK *see under* United Kingdom
see also collective action/redress
damages actions for breach of EU competition law *see* damages, underlying right to
EU law ensuring effective protection of individuals' rights against 1.05
indirect purchaser standing/passing-on *see* indirect purchaser standing and passing-on
national competition authorities *see* national competition authorities (NCAs)
national courts *see* national courts
national law *see* individual countries
minimum effectiveness *see* effectiveness principle

national competition authorities (NCAs) 0.08, 4.004
access to documents held by *see under* documentary evidence, access to
consultation of 5.66–5.74
France 5.69–5.71
Germany 5.68
other jurisdictions 5.72–5.74
UK 5.67
evidential value of prior administrative decisions 4.088–4.109
Commission proposal 4.088
Germany 4.104–4.108
no rule as to evidential value in private litigation 4.088, 4.089
Romanistic jurisdictions 4.109
UK 4.090–4.103
see also evidential value of prior administrative decisions
national courts 0.08
Commission decisions, and *see* evidential value of prior administrative decisions
Commission's proposals on evidence 4.059–4.060
cooperation with Commission 7.008
direct effect 1.14
disclosure applications
balancing exercise in 4.029, 4.034
wide margin of discretion in 4.025
expertise, recourse to *see* recourse to expertise of public authorities by national courts
giving effect to EU law rights and obligations 1.01
private damages claims 1.05, 1.06
references to ECJ 5.65
national law *see* individual countries
ne bis in idem principle 5.29–5.30
Netherlands
basis of damages actions for breach of EU competition law 2.44–2.46
choice of court/application of Art 6(1) 7.052
collective action 6.110–6.126
Art 3:305a Burgerlijk Wetboek 6.111–6.112
assignment of claims 6.156
bundled claims 6.113–6.116
Wet Collectieve Afhandeling Massaschade (2005) 6.117–6.126
Commission decisions/Art 16 Regulation 1/2003 4.079–4.081
opt-out collective action system 6.017

passing-on *see* indirect purchaser standing and passing-on
Portugal
opt-out collective action system 6.017
Posner, Richard A. 3.009, 3.010, 3.016, 8.018

presumption of harm *see under* damages, measure of
prices *see under* abusive conduct; cartels
prior administrative decisions *see* evidential value of prior administrative decisions
private enforcement
  Commission's private enforcement initiative *see under* Commission, EU damages
    actions for breach of EU law committed by another individual 1.05, 1.06
    measure of damages *see* damages, measure of
  EU law not providing substantive or procedural rules in private disputes 1.02, 1.04
  increased interest in 0.08
  indirect purchasers *see* indirect purchaser standing and passing-on
  individual rights
    access to court and to class of action to protect right 1.10
    direct rights 1.11–1.13, 1.17
    establishing causal relationship, difficulties of 3.030
    see also causation
    rights to enforce 1.10–1.13, 1.17
  meaning of 0.07
  obligations imposed on private undertakings 1.08, 1.18
  procedural issues in private actions 0.12, 0.13
  proliferation of competition law damages actions likely 0.13
  proving the infringement *see* proving the infringement
  settlement of actions before final decision, frequent 0.11
private international law aspects 7.001–7.130
  applicable law *see* applicable law
  choice of court 7.005–7.091
    Art 5(3) as basis for torpedo litigation 7.037–7.041
    Bier/Shevill jurisprudence and competition-based litigation 7.026–7.036
    causation 7.050–7.051
    choices of court, variety of 7.010–7.012
    Commission proposal and Art 28 7.077–7.080
    connected but not identical actions 7.068–7.071
    consolidation of claims/Art 6(1) 7.012, 7.042 , 7.065
    Dutch courts' application of Art 6(1) 7.052
    English authorities on Art 6(1) 7.043
    founding jurisdiction in tortious actions/Art 5(3) 7.023–7.025
    general jurisdiction/Art 2(1) 7.016–7.017
    governing law: Regulation 44/2001 7.006–7.009
    lis pendens see lis pendens
    litigation involving parties domiciled outside EU 7.086–7.091
    parties domiciled outside the EU and Regulation 44/2001 7.013–7.015
    Regulation 44/2001, Commission review of 7.083–7–7.085
    special jurisdiction: Art 5(3) and Art 6(1) 7.018–7.022
    'undertaking', interpretation of EU law concept of 7.045–7.049
  EU harmonised rules 7.002, 7.008
  national boundaries, litigation effects cutting across 7.001
private litigants' access to probative documents in EU cartel damages actions 4.004–4.070
  Commission documents, access to *see under* documentary evidence, access to
  claims for damages, bringing 4.004
    follow-on actions 4.004
  existence of right to inspect evidence dependent on national/EU law 4.005
procedural autonomy principle *see under* Member States
profitability-based approach 8.071–8.073
  increases/decreases in profits as indicator for damages 8.071
  measuring profitability 8.072–8.073
proving the infringement 4.001–4.109

access to evidence/documents, importance of 4.003
prior administrative decisions *see* evidential value of prior administrative decisions
private litigants *see* private litigants' access to documents in EU cartel actions
public authorities/public enforcement
antitrust enforcement preserve of 0.04, 6.001
collective action as effective complement to public enforcement 6.002, 6.003
see also collective action/redress
evidential value of decisions in actions by public authorities 4.074
expertise, recourse to *see* recourse to expertise of public authorities by national courts
public enforcement, meaning of 0.07
punitive damages *see* exemplary damages *under* damages, measure of

quantification of damages *see* damages, quantification of

'rational apathy problem' 6.009
recourse to expertise of public authorities by national courts 5.64–5.74
EU law: consultation of the Commission 5.65
national law: consultation of the NCA 5.66–5.74
France 5.69–5.71
Germany 5.68
other jurisdictions 5.72–5.74
UK 5.67
specialist authorities, meaning of 5.64
Regulation 44/2001
Art 2(1)/general jurisdiction 7.016–7.017
Art 5(3)
application of *Bier/Shevill* jurisprudence 7.026–7.036
founding jurisdiction in tortious actions 7.023–7.025
special jurisdiction 7.018–7.022
torpedo litigation, as basis for 7.037–7.041
Art 6(1)/consolidation of claims 7.012, 7.042, 7.065
Dutch courts' application of 7.052
English authorities on 7.043–7.044
special jurisdiction 7.018–7.022
Art 27/*lis pendens* 7.054, 7.055–7.062, 7.063, 7.064
connected but not identical actions 7.070–7.071
Art 28/ *lis pendens* 7.012, 7.054, 7.063–7.065
Commission proposal, and 7.077–7.080
connected but not identical actions 7.068–7.069
English authorities on 7.072–7.076
irreconcilability for purposes of Art 28(3) 7.066–7.067
Commission review of 7.083–7–7.085
parties domiciled outside the EU 7.013–7.015
replacing Brussels Convention 7.006
scope 7.008
uniform rules of jurisdiction for defendants domiciled in Member States 7.007
remoteness
damage quantification 8.104–8.108
remoteness of claims 3.013
restitutio in integrum (actual loss/loss of profit) 5.11–5.12, 5.24, 5.34
rights
individual rights *see under* private enforcement
legal framework *see under* legal framework
Rome I Regulation 7.004, 7.094
Rome II Regulation 7.004
Art 4/general rule 7.097–7.098, 7.123
Art 6(3)/competition-based litigation 7.099–7.101
Art 6(3)(a) 7.119–7.123
Art 6(3)(b), functioning of 7.102–7.111
Art 6(4) 7.101
legislation, adoption as 7.096
lex fori approach, and 7.094–7.096

Schwartz, Marius 3.010
simulated comparator markets 8.067–8.068
artificially constructed counterfactual model, as 8.067

fundamental conceptual problems 8.068
sincere cooperation principle *see* loyal/sincere cooperation principle
Slovakia
collective action scheme absent 6.072
Slovenia
collective action scheme absent 6.072
Spain
basis of damages actions for breach of EU competition law 2.60–2.61
opt-out collective action system 6.017
substantial and procedural issues
causation *see* causation
damages, measure of *see* damages, measure of
expertise, recourse to *see* recourse to expertise of public authorities by national courts
joint and several liability *see* joint and several liability
limitation periods *see* limitation periods
Sweden
collective action 6.135–6.141
courts as 'specialist authorities' 5.64

time series analysis 8.055–8.060
advantages and disadvantages 8.055
before-and-after method 8.055–8.057
caution required in focusing on prices after cartel ended 8.060
empirical example of before-and-after estimation 8.058
nature of method 8.055
tortious nature of litigation for breach of EU competition law 2.62–2.68, 7.004
actions tortious rather than contractual 2.63, 2.64, 7.004
agreements in contravention of competition law void/nullity 2.65, 2.66
tying 8.047

'undertaking' in EU law, interpretation of 7.045–7.049
United Kingdom (England and Wales)
basis of damages actions for breach of EU competition law 2.19–2.21
causation 5.03–5.06
but-for test 5.03
standard of proof 5.05
collective action 6.043, 6.073–6.109
BIS consultation (2012) 6.092, 6.098–6.105
BIS response (2013) 6.106–6.109
Competition Act (s 478) 6.084–6.091
DTI consultation (2006) 6.093–6.095
further policy developments 6.092–6.109
GLOs 6.081–6.083
integral to legal system 6.074
OFT recommendations (2007) 6.092, 6.096–6.097
representative actions 6.076–6.080
statutory provision 6.073
Commission decisions/Art16 Regulation 1/2003 4.078
Crehan judgment 4.082–4.085
deference 4.082–4.083
competition law damages claims as tort of breach of statutory duty 2.68, 2.69
strict liability 2.69, 2.70
damages, exemplary 5.24–5.46
assessing 5.40
exceptional remedy 5.2
guiding principles 5.40–5.41
intentional or reckless breaches 5.38
ne bis in idem principle 5.29–5.30
purpose/object 5.32, 5.39, 5.40
when awarded 5.25, 5.27, 5.29, 5.38, 5.43
damages/presumption of loss 5.20
disclosure of documents/*National Grid* 4.036, 4.037–4.056
balancing exercise 4.044–4.045, 4.048
disclosure and inspection of documents 4.039
documents held by third parties, access to 4.058
Evidence Regulation 4.050–4.056
French blocking statute 4.049–4.055
history of discovery 4.038
legitimate expectations 4.044
national leniency programmes 4.042–4.048
proportionality 4.045
withholding documents from inspection 4.040–4.048

establishment of right to damages as matter of EU law: *Crehan* 2.03–2.17
proceedings in the English courts 2.03–2.11
indirect purchaser standing and passing-on 3.069–3.073
burden of proof 3.070
defence of passing-on 3.069–3.073
government consultation 3.071
OFT view 3.070
joint and several liability 5.75
contribution 5.77
jurisdiction 7.027–7.029
Art 6(1) Regulation 44/2001, authorities on 7.043–7.044
Art 28 Regulation 44/2001, authorities on 7.072–7.076
knowledge
imputing knowledge of parent's conduct to subsidiary 7.049
required on part of defendant to found damages claim 7.049
limitation periods 5.48, 5.50, 5.55–5.61
harmonising limitation periods 5.60–5.61
statutory basis for limitation periods 5.55
NCA, consultation of 5.67
NCA decisions, evidential value of 4.090–4.103
CAT decisions 4.091
damages actions following public infringement decision 4.090–4.091
identity of parties on whom administrative decisions binding 4.098–4.103
OFT decisions 4.091
scope of follow-on actions under Competition Act 4.092–4.097
teleological style of argumentation 2.07
United States (US)
antitrust injury 2.08
concept of 3.090–3.091
class/collective action 6.157–6.173
Class Action Fairness Act (2005) 6.169–6.173
common feature of antitrust enforcement 3.018, 6.007
effectiveness 6.007
Federal Rules of Civil Procedure (R 23) 6.158–6.168
indirect purchaser actions 3.111
opt-out system 6.020
Commission's attempts to limit discovery in US courts 4.061–4.070
importance of leniency programmes recognised 4.067–4.069
reliance on comity 4.065–4.067, 4.070
disclosure/discovery of documents 4.036
broad extent of discovery 4.062
evidential value of decisions in actions by public authorities 4.074
foreign purchasers, damages actions in US by 7.003
indirect purchaser standing 0.04, 3.014–3.015, 3.028, 3.099–3.111
'co-conspirator' exception 3.107
'cost-plus' exception 3.107
'direct' and 'indirect' purchasers 3.036
direct purchasers, nature of 3.103–3.104
limitations in relation to indirect purchaser actions 3.099–3.102
'ownership or control' exception 3.106
rule in *Illinois Brick* 3.099–3.104
rule in *Illinois Brick*, efficiency of 3.110–3.111
rule in *Illinois Brick,* exceptions to 3.105–3.109
leniency programme 4.067
passing-on defence 0.04, 3.092–3.098
disallowed 3.092–3.096
private antitrust enforcement 0.04
Sherman Act 3.091
direct and substantial effect, conduct having 7.112–7.113
unjust enrichment
avoiding 3.025
passing-on defence, and 3.037, 3.044–3.052

Van Gerven, Walter 1.15–1.16

Werden, Gregory J. 3.010, 8,018